LAND USE AND THE STATES

LAND USE
AND THE STATES

Second Edition

ROBERT G. HEALY

JOHN S. ROSENBERG

Published for Resources for the Future Inc.
By The Johns Hopkins University Press

Copyright © 1979 by Resources for the Future, Inc.
All rights reserved
Printed in the United States of America

Published for Resources for the Future Inc., by
The Johns Hopkins University Press, Baltimore, Maryland 21218

Library of Congress Catalog Card Number 79-4864
ISBN 0–8018–2284–X
ISBN 0–8018–2285–8 paperback

Originally published in hardcover and paperback, 1976

Second edition, 1979
Second printing (paperback), March 1981

 RESOURCES FOR THE FUTURE, INC.
1755 Massachusetts Avenue, N.W., Washington, D.C. 20036

Board of Directors: Gilbert F. White, *Chairman,* Irving Bluestone, Harrison Brown, Roberto de O. Campos, Anne P. Carter, Emery N. Castle, William T. Coleman, Jr., F. Kenneth Hare, Franklin A. Lindsay, Charles F. Luce, George C. McGhee, Ian MacGregor, Vincent E. McKelvey, Laurence I. Moss, Frank Pace, Jr., Stanley H. Ruttenberg, Lauren Soth, Janez Stanovnik, Russell E. Train, M. Gordon Wolman

Honorary Directors: Horace M. Albright, Erwin D. Canham, Edward J. Cleary, Hugh L. Keenleyside, Edward S. Mason, William S. Paley, John W. Vanderwilt

President: Emery N. Castle

Secretary-Treasurer: John E. Herbert

Resources for the Future is a nonprofit organization for research and education in the development, conservation, and use of natural resources and the improvement of the quality of the environment. It was established in 1952 with the cooperation of the Ford Foundation. Grants for research are accepted from government and private sources only if they meet the conditions of a policy established by the Board of Directors of Resources for the Future. The policy states that RFF shall be solely responsible for the conduct of the research and free to make the research results available to the public. Part of the work of Resources for the Future is carried out by its resident staff; part is supported by grants to universities and other nonprofit organizations. Unless otherwise stated, interpretations and conclusions in RFF publications are those of the authors; the organization takes responsibility for the selection of significant subjects for study, the competence of the researchers, and their freedom of inquiry.

This book is a product of RFF's Renewable Resources Division, under the direction of Kenneth D. Frederick. Robert G. Healy is senior associate at the Conservation Foundation in Washington, D.C., and John S. Rosenberg is a consultant.

This book was edited by Jo Hinkel. The index was prepared by John F. Holman & Co., Inc.

RFF Editors: Joan R. Tron, Ruth B. Haas, Jo Hinkel, and Sally A. Skillings

102002

EMORY AND HENRY LIBRARY

Contents

Preface to the First Edition   xi

Preface to the Second Edition   xv

1   Introduction—Rights in Conflict   1

The Origins of Concern   4
A Role for the States   7
   Interjurisdictional Spillovers   7
   The Clash of Interests   9
   Absence of Controls   11
   State Investments and Nonland Policies   12
A Maturing Revolution   13
Notes   14

2   A Variety of Discontents   16

The Problems We See   16
   Urban Sprawl—And Urban Splatter   17
   Loss of Farmland   18
   Fiscal Effects of Land Use Changes   20
   Degradation of the Natural Environment   22
   Degradation of the Visual Environment   23
   Limitation of Housing Opportunity   24
   Gainers, Losers, and Speculators   25
   The Size of Development Projects   26
   Resistance to Change   28
Problems to Come   29
Goals for Future Planning   34
   Efficiency   34
   Equity   35
   Preserving Long-run Options   35
   Preserving a Diversity of Environments   36
Introducing the Case Studies   36
Notes   36

3   Vermont—Eight Years of Experience   40

Vermont's "Development Crisis"   41
The State Government's Response   43
Eight Years of Act 250   46
    Statistical Overview   46
    Act 250 and Second Homes   49
    Some Gaps in the Law   54
    Appraisal   56
Capability and Development Plan (1973)   59
The Vermont Land Use Plan   61
    The Fate of the Plan   64
Innovations in Tax Policy   66
    Land Policy and Tax Policy   66
    Farm and Forest Use Value Taxation   68
    Property Tax Credits   68
    Capital Gains Tax on Land Sales   69
Conclusion   72
Notes   74

4   California—"Saving the Coast"   80

"Where's the Beach?"   80
Proposition 20   85
Permit Administration—"Everything But Glaciers"   89
    The Exemption Question   90
    A Permit Overview   91
    Beach Access—In Its Broadest Sense   93
    Density and Growth   97
    The Natural Environment   100
    Energy and the Coastline   101
    Some Permit Lessons   105
The Coastal Plan   106
    A Comprehensive Plan—One Element at a Time   107
The Legislature Responds   111
After the Coastal Act   113
    Drafting the Local Coastal Programs   114
    Current Coastal Issues   116
Conclusion   119
Notes   121

5   Florida—Harnessing the Growth Explosion   126

A New Kind of Growth   127
    New Types of Development   127
    New and Growing Markets   128
A Fragile and Unique Environment   128
    Crowding the Water's Edge   129
    Building on Wetlands   130

A Place Like Everywhere   131
The Birth of Land Policy   131
Critical Areas   135
    The Big Cypress   136
    The Green Swamp   139
    The Florida Keys   139
    Evaluating the Critical Areas Program   142
Developments of Regional Impact   144
    The Number and Scale of DRIs   148
    Three Rivers—The First Appeal   150
    Doral Park—The Regional Council Takes a Chance   153
    Lake Ola—The Power of Local Government   153
    Belcher Oil—Energy as a DRI   154
    DRI Issues   155
A Question of Expectations   157
    Regional Weaknesses   158
    Local Resistance   161
    The Developers Respond   162
Toward a Comprehensive Land Use Program   165
Conclusion   169
Notes   170

6   Alternative Approaches to State Land Use Control   177
What Does the State Control?   177
    Critical Areas   177
    Open or Unzoned Lands   180
    Developments of Regional Impact   181
    Land Uses Affecting Public Investments   182
    Developments of Regional Benefit   183
    Dealing with Specific Problems   184
Who Decides?   184
    State Zoning   185
    The Double-Veto System   189
    Nonlocal Input into the Local Decision Process   190
    State Guidelines and State Plans   191
    The "Demonstration Effect"   196
    Guiding Land Use Through the State Budget   197
    Other Positive State Actions   198
    State Participation in Federal Planning Programs   201
North Carolina—Putting It Together   201
Notes   205

7   Issues in Implementing State Land Use Controls   211
Political Power   211
    "Local Control"   211
    Citizen Participation   214

What the Public Thinks   218
Land Use and Bureaucratic Power   220
Economic Issues   223
Impact on the Overall Economy   224
Impacts on Land Uses and Prices   226
Procedural Costs   229
Tax Issues   231
Social Issues   232
Limits to Regulation—Law and Fairness   232
Elitism and Discrimination   238
Notes   242

8   Toward New Policies for the States   248
Criteria for Better Land Policies   249
Elements of a State Land Use Policy   259
Pillars of the New State Policy   259
State Policies and Standards   262
A State Development Plan   265
Improving Local Regulation   267
The Question of a Federal Land Use Law   271
A Chain of Decisions   273
Notes   274

Additional Reading   277

Index   281

Preface to the First Edition

FOR FORTY YEARS OR SO, the impetus for new kinds of economic and social programs has tended to come from the federal government. Policies are formulated, often with extensive inputs from academics and other "experts," and translated into programs, which lower levels of government are induced, cajoled, or compelled into adopting. It is a system that allows for relatively quick action but one that tends to magnify any conceptual mistakes that the original policy might have contained. It has led to the rapid dissemination of some effective programs, but also to the spread of policies breathtaking in their insensitivity to local problems and conditions.

The recent movement toward greater state involvement in land use decisions is an exception. It has to a great extent been initiated in the states themselves, in response to local and statewide needs. National legislation to encourage it has been introduced in Congress each year since 1970 but has yet to become law.

In the meantime, prodded by a citizenry increasingly sensitive to environmental concerns and disturbed by the results of local land use controls, the states have been acting on their own. Each year since 1970, additional states have begun to regulate developments whose large scale, growth-inducing potential, or environmentally sensitive location makes them of more than local concern. Often they did so because of some particular crisis within their borders—a second-home boom in Vermont, a water shortage in Florida, or the possibility of new coastal oil refineries in Delaware.

The states occasionally followed national models, particularly the Model Land Development Code drawn up by the prestigious American Law Institute. Most often, however, they created their own models, adapting them to unique problems of the state and often incorporating distinctive institutions or practices already present within state governments: Florida, for example, linked its land use program to the adjudicatory function of the Florida Cabinet, while California, seeking to control development of its coastline, continued its long-established tradition of special purpose regulatory commissions.

I began to think about writing this book in late 1972. Although Hawaii had enacted comprehensive state land use controls as far back as 1961, most of the activity in the field was little more than two years old. A well-documented study of the movement (Fred Bosselman and David Callies's *The Quiet Revolution in Land Use Control*) had just appeared, but it came too early to cover more than the shakedown period of most states' implementation of their programs. I saw a need for a study that would consider these new programs as they developed, chronicling the successes and failures that resulted when they were implemented in that sweaty and contentious place that my fellow researchers like to call "the real world."

If, as then seemed likely, the federal government was going to commit major resources to encourage this new trend of state action, what, if any, was the case for it? The result, through the support of Resources for the Future, is this book.

I have attempted to provide a comprehensive and comparative look at the role of the states in controlling the uses of privately owned land. This study focuses on the problems that have caused a demand for greater state involvement, on the variety of legislative responses, and on the problems of implementation that arise. It discusses some of the political, social, and economic issues with which the movement toward more stringent and highly centralized land use controls must inevitably contend. It concludes with a proposed program of coordinated state and local controls that might go far to ease our pervasive discontent with how we manage the land around us.

It is addressed to the policymaker who wishes to know what the states have actually done in land use policy to date. At the federal level, it provides a factual basis for the debate over the merits of federal encouragement of state land use programs. In the states, it allows legislators and administrators to draw from the successful experiences of other states in order to avoid some of the same pitfalls and mistakes. For local and regional officials, it offers reassurance that greater state involvement does not automatically mean an end to their own roles.

It is also hoped that it will be useful to academic specialists, planners, and attorneys in the land use field; to students of urban planning (many of whom may eventually work for state or regional land agencies); and to citizens who are concerned over how land is used and abused.

Many people helped and encouraged me during the course of the research, particularly those who generously made their time available during my visits to a number of states that had been early pioneers in the land use field. To list them here would try the patience of the reader, but collectively they have my deepest thanks.

I am also grateful to Resources for the Future, where I spent two years on the research staff, for making this book possible. Sterling Brubaker and Marion Clawson, respectively director of policy studies and acting president at the time of writing, were most generous with their advice and support. Two of my colleagues there, Larry Libby and Boyd Gibbons, were the source of both useful insights and deserved criticism. Their enthusiasm for the land and its problems is contagious.

Gayle Underwood spent many hours typing various drafts of the study. She has my special thanks. The manuscript was skillfully edited by Jo Hinkel.

A number of reviewers provided helpful comments on various portions of the manuscript. Among them were Worth Bateman, Herb Morton, Phyllis Myers, John Rosenberg, Terry Sopher, and Ken Weiner.

A draft of the study was used as the text in a course on state land use controls that I gave in the Department of City and Regional Planning at Harvard University in 1975. My students there were often helpful in pointing out areas of interest and in bringing new materials to my attention.

Finally, I would like to express my admiration for the many people, met in the course of the research for this book, who have given their time, unpaid, to help improve the environment that we all share. They include members of state and regional land use boards, local public officials, environmentalists, and others. By their actions they have shown that the ideal of "public service" is not yet dead in America.

Washington, D.C.   R.G.H.
November 1975

Preface to the Second Edition

IT IS CHARACTERISTIC of the rapidly changing field of land use policy that a book should quickly require extensive updating and revision. In making substantial changes only four years after completing the original study, we have attempted to preserve the First Edition's emphasis on implementation experience, the interstate comparisons and evaluations, and the discussions of precipitating problems and of social and economic side effects. In addition to analyzing the developments in state programs themselves we have also incorporated discussion of recent land use literature. The years since the book's first appearance have seen a quantum increase in the number of scholarly studies of land use regulation and its impacts. In the light of the widespread adoption of the First Edition for use in planning, law, and environmental policy courses, we have tried to take full advantage of this new research, summarizing many of its results in the text, making copious footnote references, and adding an Additional Reading list of some of the most useful works. Although we hope that the result will be even more suitable for classroom and scholarly use, we have tried hard to keep the book interesting and readable for practicing planners, policymakers, and citizens concerned about the use of land.

There is no way in which a book on a fast-changing field of public policy can ever be completely current. Thus, we have tried to use our case examples to highlight problems, issues, and policy alternatives in a manageable number of places, rather than to emphasize the current— and necessarily impermanent—status of land use policy in every state. Although the details of the programs we describe are bound to change in the future, we hope that the basic concepts presented will remain useful to the reader for an extended period.

In preparing this Second Edition, we have revisited Vermont, California, Florida, and North Carolina, and have conducted telephone interviews with knowledgeable people in many other states. We have also mined the extensive land use files of the Conservation Foundation, and the files and unpublished manuscripts of several colleagues.

The updating and revision of the book were a joint effort. Rosenberg was primarily responsible for chapters 3 and 5; Healy for chapters 1, 2, 4, 7, and 8. Chapter 6 was jointly written. There was extensive review and interaction between the authors, so that the overall tone and direction of the Second Edition is very much a collaboration. The new material is current as of January 1979 or later.

The authors are deeply grateful to many persons in the case-study states, who provided data and participated in sometimes lengthy interviews; to colleagues at the Conservation Foundation and elsewhere; to a number of persons who reviewed portions of the manuscript; and to Jo Hinkel, for her capable editorial work. We would like to thank Frank G. Mittelbach, of the University of California, Los Angeles, who made it possible for Healy to spend three months in residence there while working on the manuscript. And we would especially like to acknowledge the interest of Kenneth D. Frederick and Herbert C. Morton, respectively director of the Renewable Resources Division and director of Public Affairs at Resources for the Future, who encouraged us to produce this new edition.

June 1979   Robert G. Healy
                                         Washington, D.C.

                                         John S. Rosenberg
                                         West Hartford, Connecticut

:omprehensive" in affecting all lands in the state or a wide rang
s of development. Many of the most ardent supporters of land us
the legislatures and among the public, have moved on to othe
Why, then, should we continue to study the origins and imple-
on of state land use programs?

fficient reason is that many of the previously legislated state land
grams are still strong and active. In California, Florida, Hawaii,
, Vermont, and elsewhere decisions made at the state level con-
have great influence on the form, location, and rate of develop-
Despite recession, the energy crisis, and a widening mistrust of all
f governmental control, few of the programs have been repealed
usly weakened. By the end of 1978 more than half of the fifty
ad—if only for limited areas or types of development—land use
s with real regulatory effect. More than a dozen state coastal pro-
ad been certified by the federal government as eligible to enter
plementation phase" of coastal zone management. Interest in state
or agricultural land preservation was high in several parts of the
.

nd this practical motivation, an interest in state land use policy
ed by three basic assumptions. First, we believe that the sorting
ublic and private interests in the use of privately owned land is a
continuing social issue. It existed as an issue before the "land use
fad of the early 1970s and will continue to be an issue into the
ble future.[2] Those who have turned their attention from land use
ironmental matters to more pressing questions of energy supply,
tion, housing production, and government finance will soon find
d use is intimately linked to these concerns as well.
d, we believe that state government has a necessary role in that
process. State government is the ultimate source of the police
which is the constitutional basis for land use regulations, although
st the states have delegated most land use powers to local govern-
he states set the ground rules for local planning, zoning, and sub-
controls, formulate many environmental and health standards,
ide how land may be assessed and taxed. In many cases, state
ents have at their disposal technical skills and budget resources
rior to those of local governments. Moreover, while many land
troversies cross municipal or even county boundaries, far fewer
oss state lines. Almost everywhere the state is the only strong
purpose government above the county level. The federal govern-
n the other hand, is far removed in both interest and expertis

LAND USE AND THE STATES

CHAPTER ONE

Introduction—
Rights in Conflict

FOR MANY DECADES, controls over the use
the local level—or not at all. But, beginning at
institutional arrangement began to change. By
including California, Delaware, Florida, Main
Vermont, had passed innovative legislation giv
a direct role in approving important changes i

In some cases, the state's concern was limi
as the seacoasts in California and Delaware or
New York. In others, the state reviewed all cor
a certain size and all subdivisions with more tl
lots, no matter where the project was located
mandated planning and regulatory criteria to
regional governments.

At the height of the expansion of state infl
hailed as a "quiet revolution in land use contro
lic's rising environmental concern and a genera
centralization, it was considered only a matter
of state involvement in land use regulation was
eral legislation to encourage state efforts and to
role, if any, of the national government in lan
serious consideration by Congress. In 1972 a fe
ting up such a program for the nation's ocean an
in 1974 a bill authorizing $800 million in aid t
was defeated by the narrowest of margins.

Today, near the end of the decade, this ea
lost. A federal land use bill has never passed, an
issue in Congress. State legislatures are reluctar

seem
of typ
laws,
issue
ment
A
use
Oreg
tinue
men
form
or s
state
con
grar
the
acti
cou

is j
out
ma
pol
for
an
jol
th

so
po
in
m
di
a
g
fa
u
s
g
n

from most land use controversies and is likely to shun direct involvement in all but some special cases.

Third, we believe that the best source of lessons in a complex field such as land use is the close examination of actual implementation experience. During the last decade, state land use agencies have been in the vanguard of those actually dealing with important issues directly affecting the quality of life—urban sprawl, environmental protection, farmland retention, fiscal impacts, and public participation. Several of the state programs have exercised broader, stronger powers than have historically been granted to any land use regulatory body. The resulting implementation record is rich, and increasingly well documented. It is well worth our examination.

The present study describes some of the most significant of the new state programs, identifies the problems and policy issues that they raise, and analyzes their achievements and failures to date. The study enumerates, both theoretically and in specific cases, the observable failures of the old, exclusively local, land use control system. Then it evaluates the extent to which direct state intervention has actually improved the regulatory system's performance. In examining implementation, emphasis is given not just to the aggregate regulatory record (for example, permit approval rates) but to individual illustrative cases. And careful attention is paid to the social, political, and economic environment within which agencies operate.

The remainder of this introductory chapter describes the roots of the new public interest in land use planning and outlines a rationale for state involvement. Chapter 2 examines the multitude of specific problems that have arisen as land has been converted from one use to another, speculates on the kinds of problems that may arise in the future, and sketches some general goals for land use policy. Chapters 3, 4, and 5 examine in detail the experience to date with three of the most significant state land use laws enacted thus far—Vermont's Act 250 (1970); California's Coastal Zone Conservation Act (1972) and Coastal Act (1976); and Florida's Environmental Land and Water Management Act (1972). They show how the unique land use problems of each state caused a demand for a new kind of regulation and describe how that regulation came to be adopted. After examining the institutions that have been set up, these case-study chapters review the implementation of each law—the achievements, the failures, and the unintended side effects.

Chapter 6 presents a taxonomy of the alternative approaches to state land use policy that various states have taken or are considering. Cutting across the three case studies, and introducing ideas gleaned from the land use regulatory experience of several additional states, it looks first at *what kinds* of land uses are subject to state regulation and then at *how* this state control is exercised. While it is unlikely, and probably undesirable, that any state considering new land use controls slavishly copy the programs of those states that have already acted, there is a limited number of probable patterns for state involvement.

Chapter 7 deals individually with a number of important issues that state land regulation tends to raise. There are political issues, such as the local control controversy. There are economic issues, both for the state's overall economy and for the landowners and developers who are most directly affected. There are social issues, including the fairness of regulating land without compensating its owner and the impact of land use policy on the poor. This chapter emphasizes the real-world framework within which land use laws must operate, recognizing that the regulation of land touches both powerful economic interests and strong emotions.

Chapter 8 sets out the criteria that an effective state land use program should meet and describes the elements it should contain. It moves beyond the experience of any single state to describe a set of moderate, yet effective, policies that would do much to ease our pervasive discontent over how the United States uses its land resources.

Before going into the details of problems and policies, it is appropriate to ask, Why has debate over land use controls left the specialized realm of city planners and zoning lawyers and become a significant political issue? Why did "land use" become an issue and how did state governments come to be involved?

The Origins of Concern

For one thing, as the public has become more knowledgeable about the workings of natural ecological systems, it has learned that changes in land use can have profound effects on the environment and that these effects are not limited to the parcel of private property whose use has changed. As the tributary areas of creeks and rivers become paved over for urban development, for example, the slow seepage of storm runoff through the soil becomes replaced by the rush of water off asphalt, carrying with it oil, lead, animal wastes, and other pollutants. As shopping centers, factories, and housing tracts are built on the urban fringe, the traffic they generate begins to foul the air. As prime agricultural land is converted to urban use, farmers begin to move to less fertile lands, where larger amounts of fertilizers and pesticides are needed to produce the same amount of food. In the economist's jargon, the public has become more sophisticated about the negative external effects, or "negative externalities," that land uses can create.

But there is another, larger, impetus to the public's concern. The frantic pace of land development in our growth-oriented society has caused the destruction of many amenities that people have long enjoyed and taken for granted. The Sunday drive into the countryside has become a battle to escape the ever-expanding limits of the suburbs. The character and uniqueness of neighborhoods and communities have been changed by high-density development. Rows of high-rise condominiums have sprung up along the beaches, and recreational developments dot the mountainsides. Wildlife has retreated from the advance of man and his noisy artifacts. Even the deserts and the swamps have not been spared, as they sprout the little red flags of the subdividers.

Many of the things that the public enjoyed—the scenic vista, the undeveloped roadside, the open farmland—were part of some landowner's property rights. The public's "right" to them could be revoked quite legally at the landowner's pleasure. As population expanded and the demand for homes, stores, factories, and recreation areas rose, the landowners found it profitable to exercise property rights they had long held dormant. The density that once existed on a zoning map or a developer's drafting table became asphalt and concrete. Often what was built was not in itself unattractive—suburban homes and oceanfront apartments seem to find a ready market—but to the general public there has been a very real sense of something lost.[3] It is no coincidence that the years during which state land use regulations were most eagerly adopted were years of unusually rapid development and construction nationwide.

Citizens typically rely on local government to assert the public interest in regulating changes in the use of private land. Around the nation, the public has been disappointed. Local governments have found the tax revenues from a new shopping center or a high rise too attractive to be ignored. Funds for public purchase of open space have been inadequate to protect even the areas of exceptional beauty. Zoning maps, many prepared during a period when economic development was seen as an overriding duty of local government, have often allowed development densities far in excess of current use. In many rural places, there are no land use regulations at all.

Moreover, in addition to the well-publicized cases of corruption and venality, even the most honest and well-informed local governments face situations in which the interest of the local community and the interest of the society as a whole are not the same. A shopping center or a power plant can mean a healthy addition to a community's tax rolls—the environmental costs (but not the taxes) are shared with the entire region. The increasing mobility of the population has made the use of land in one local area the concern of a wider and wider segment of the population.

Consider, for example, the California coast. Is its beauty properly the concern of seaside local governments, of the state of California, or of the nation as a whole? To what extent does this beauty belong to the public and to what extent to the individuals and corporations that own the land?

The United States is in the midst of sorting out the rights to its land. This has resulted in new assertions of what the public interest is in changes in the use of private lands and in new institutional arrangements for asserting these rights. Typically, the new institutions have involved higher levels of government in decisions that were formerly thought to be of purely local interest.

There is a pervasive feeling that local control of land use, which in practice means local zoning and subdivision regulations, has been a failure. Zoning has succeeded only in preserving existing neighborhoods from invasions of nonresidential uses. On the urban fringe, it has done little to change the land use outcomes preordained by strong market forces. Subdivision controls have done little more than to assure that new streets and utilities will be of minimum quality and will tie in with the existing networks.

It is important to separate the failure of specific local controls from the shortcomings of the concept of "local control." If local zoning has failed, the fault may lie with the tool rather than with the level of government that wields it.[4] Given new policy instruments, new property tax systems, and tough conflict-of-interest laws, and prodded by an environmentally aware citizenry, local governments can go far toward improving the quality of their land use. A record of local government failure in dealing with land use conflicts does not in itself mean that the state could do a more effective job.

Our working presumption here will be that local control of land use is, other things being equal, the most desirable arrangement. In judging the merits of most land use changes, local authorities are not only better informed about the facts of the situation, but are also (at least ideally) more responsive to the interests affected. When higher levels of government deal with such problems, they typically must create layers of bureaucracy simply to channel the appropriate information to decision makers. The decision makers, moreover, are responsible to a constituency which is probably far larger than the group of citizens affected by most land use decisions. Thus, by virtue not only of tradition, but of efficiency and political responsiveness, there is a strong case for local control of land use.[5]

A Role for the States

We will demonstrate, however, that there are a surprising number of situations in which even the most carefully designed and conscientiously administered local program will fail to take into account the interests of some portion of the public significantly affected by the outcome of a given land use change. We might separate those cases in which we suspect state intervention is warranted into the following categories: (1) problems that spill across the boundaries of legal jurisdictions; (2) problems arising when local interests diverge from the interests of a broader public; (3) problems arising on lands not subject to effective local control; and (4) problems allied with the implementation of state policies or the carrying out of state investments.

Interjurisdictional Spillovers

There are some 3,000 county governments in the United States, along with 18,500 municipalities and 17,000 townships.[6] It has been estimated that at least 14,000 of these jurisdictions exercise some form of land use control.[7] More than 10,000 have planning boards, and a slightly smaller number have a zoning ordinance or subdivision regulations. In addition to these general purpose governments, there are tens of thousands of special purpose agencies, including school districts, irrigation districts, pollution control agencies, and flood control districts, which influence land use by their siting and investment decisions and, occasionally, by direct controls.

The effects of land use changes can spill over these jurisdictional boundaries in ways as obvious as a smokestack's plume or as subtle as a flow of retail dollars.

Take, for example, the location of an oil refinery on the New England coast, a possibility that has been the source of several land use controversies and a major impetus to Maine's Site Location of Development Law (1970). If built in the small town of Machiasport, Maine, a $150 to $300 million refinery would be assessed at $113 to $225 million—75 to 150 times the town's present assessed valuation. Under present state law, the property taxes generated would not be shared with surrounding towns, even though these latter would have to house substantial numbers of new workers and would have to provide them with schools, roads, utilities, and other public services.[8]

Or consider the environmental spillovers from development along Rock Creek, which runs for 30 miles through rural Maryland and the Washington, D.C., suburbs and into the District of Columbia. The proliferation of impermeable streets and rooftops at the expense of grass and trees has combined with sewage and storm sewer discharges to make this important urban stream unfit even for body contact. The quality of the water that flows through the District of Columbia is absolutely dependent on the land use decisions made in adjoining Maryland suburbs. An assistant secretary of the interior once said of Rock Creek:

> . . . If the upper watershed is to be subjected to the type of exploitation unleashed by the outgoing [Montgomery County, Maryland] Council in its spree, no program can hope to be effective . . . a few individuals in one county, with five Council votes at their disposal for a few giddy days, may well succeed in wrecking some of our central hopes for the metropolitan region and infringing on what we must surely regard as the rights of their neighbors both in the county itself and in the less prosperous, less scenically blessed District, to say nothing of the millions of annual visitors who look upon Washington as the Nation's own special city.[9]

Jurisdictional spillovers may cause one community's land use policy to frustrate the workings of its neighbors' policies. California's state Office of Planning and Research reports that "Santa Monica has been struggling for years to maintain and rehabilitate its small 'downtown' commercial area. That effort has probably been seriously undermined by the opening of Fox Hills Mall, a major new shopping center located in Culver City, distractingly close to Santa Monica."[10]

It would be foolish to assert that localities inevitably pursue their self-interest without regard to the effects of their decisions on their geographic neighbors. Informal arrangements between localities, personal and political ties transcending local boundaries, and simple municipal self-restraint tend to prevent the worst abuses of jurisdictional fragmentations. But in the absence of some overall mechanism for allocating the costs and benefits of development geographically, the spillovers can be great.

Probably the greatest interjurisdictional spillover is growth itself. During the postwar development of California's Santa Clara Valley (in the San Jose metropolitan area) from cropland to suburbia, no single jurisdiction out of the many in the valley could have chosen not to change. Although each municipality had its own zoning power, the decision to grow was effectively made by the similar decision of all of the other jurisdictions. Economics and the political pressures it generates make any vision of an incorporated zone of farms surrounded by other urbanized municipalities a utopian prospect.

Localities which are at present pursuing policies of "controlled growth" are similarly learning that the real sources of their growth often lie outside their own boundaries.[11]

The Clash of Interests

In many cases we find citizens of one jurisdiction concerned about land use changes in other localities, even when there are no spillovers. A classic case is the preservation of wilderness and other remote natural areas. It is almost a certainty that most of those who support wilderness legislation or who work to protect wildlife from habitat destruction will never have the opportunity to personally observe all the objects of their labors. But the vicarious pleasure associated with the knowledge that such areas exist is not to be taken lightly.

If large numbers of people are concerned about the quality of the environment in remote and little-visited areas, a far greater number feel a stake in communities they visit on their vacations, places they enjoy on weekends, and the places they drive through daily as they go about their business. Although they have no standing as citizens of these various localities, members of the wider public can have a strong interest in the land use changes that occur there.

Even though a given locality may have effective land use controls, the interests of its citizenry may be different from those of the noncitizens who also feel a stake in its land. Sometimes, values differ. A beach resort's town fathers may consider Miami Beach an ideal to emulate rather than a mistake to avoid. More frequently, however, the divergence of interests occurs because the costs and benefits from development are so distributed that the local people (or at least important local subgroups) receive economic benefits from land use changes that offset the decline in the environmental quality they experience. For example, a roadside shopping strip may ruin a rural view, but it contributes sorely needed tax dollars to the county treasury. For the local citizen, the gain on one side balances out the loss on the other. The city dweller, accustomed to enjoying that view on his drive through the countryside, experiences the loss of amenity but not the offsetting financial gain.

In editorializing in favor of state review and veto power over local planning decisions, a North Carolina newspaper commented, "Anyone familiar with zoning procedures knows why it is difficult for local officials to protect broad public interests. A friend or customer comes before the local board, makes his request and explains that his livelihood depends on the approval of the request. If the board members do not comply, they have made an enemy for life—not one that lives in Raleigh, either, but one that lives close by."[12]

This divergence of local and nonlocal interests played an important part in the controversy over New York's 1973 Adirondack Park plan. Visitors to this area, a patchwork of private holdings and public parklands, feared that a second-home boom would destroy the wild forest quality they had come to enjoy. Residents of the several towns within the park's borders, however, felt that the proposed land regulations would preserve them in picturesque poverty for the benefit of high-income vacationers.

Another example occurred in Gettysburg, Pennsylvania, where a developer proposed to erect a 307-foot, triple-deck observation tower on private land adjacent to the battlefield. The head of the U.S. National Park Service called the tower "the most damaging single intrusion ever visited upon a comparable site of American history."[13] Local officials, however, saw things from a different viewpoint. The tower would generate employment, attract more tourists, and stimulate the local economy. Through a 10 percent local tax on admissions, the borough of Gettysburg would reap as much as $70,000 in the first year alone. Within a decade, the tower could be the largest single taxpayer in the township. As the developer explained, "You don't hear the businessmen complaining. The only ones you hear are the federal park people and the college people. They aren't the ones who must make their money off the land to live."[14] The tower opened in 1974.

Similar divergences of interests have occurred on North Carolina's Outer Banks, on the Florida Keys, in northern Michigan, and along California's coast. The differences are often exacerbated by sharp differences in income between local people and visitors.[15] But similar conflicts in land use preferences may occur within metropolitan areas. Often they involve local rejection of developments that impose costs locally but benefit a larger area. Sanitary landfills and public housing projects are frequently shunned by those places where they would be best sited from a regional standpoint. Often it is the city with the least affluent, least articulate electorate that winds up with the facilities rejected by the other jurisdictions in the region.

Absence of Controls

Although most urban areas have long had some form of land use regulations, large amounts of land outside of cities have been essentially unregulated. The last decade has seen a notable extension of local land use controls in rural areas, but there is still a long way to go before many areas are effectively regulated by *any* level of government.[16] For example, one nationwide survey of county governments found that 39 percent did not exercise zoning controls, and that 35 percent did not have county subdivision regulations. These land use controls were most likely to be absent in the smaller counties and in those in nonmetropolitan areas.[17] Even where controls are exercised, many small jurisdictions lack professional staff and effective means of enforcement. As a rural West Virginia real estate agent put it, "In this county, a man can do anything he wants with his land, short of starting a plague."

In many cases local opinion holds that the rate of development is low enough relative to the quantity of land available to make controls unnecessary. In the absence of demonstrable spillovers from one piece of property to another, the tradition that the landowner should have free and unrestricted use of his property remains strong. If outsiders perceive land use problems that local people choose to ignore, the case becomes yet another instance of the divergence of interests.

In other cases, however, the lack of land controls is caused by the general small size and the lack of resources and expertise on the part of local governments. In Vermont, for example, some local governments have jurisdiction over only a few hundred persons. Not only do they lack a planning staff, often there is not a single full-time town employee. It is rural areas such as these that are frequently confronted with plans for huge recreational developments, with complex environmental and social effects.

The magnitude of some of the rural developments proposed during the development industry's most expansive days earlier in the 1970s was staggering. In Florida's Flagler County (1970 population, 4,500) a subsidiary of the International Telephone & Telegraph Corporation began laying out lots for what it claimed would be a new community of 750,000 people. The proposed 100,000-acre development would have accounted for one-third of all the land in the county. Elsewhere in Florida, and in Arizona, California, and Nevada, developments covering tens of thousands of acres were not unknown. Two proposed developments in New York's Adirondacks were to consist of 18,000 and 24,000 acres, respectively. When localities are confronted with plans of this magnitude, backed up by companies with considerable financial strength and expensive hired planning talent, they find themselves unable to properly evaluate them or to exact the appropriate concessions from the developer. Lacking their own professional staff, they must rely on data generated by the developer, who is usually quick to point out the economic advantages of development, while glossing over its long-run costs.

As the Task Force on Land Use and Urban Growth put it:

> Local officials and residents of rural localities . . . are likely to recognize that new development means income, in purchases at local stores, in construction by local contractors, in mortgages by local banks and services by local lawyers and surveyors. But they may be oblivious to the later costs that experienced localities know about—the dollar costs of providing roads and sewers and other services for scattered projects, the personal costs of congestion and changed lifestyles and disruption of cherished countryside, and the social costs of a new urban and affluent population settling among small town people and farmers.[18]

Extremely large rural projects are at the moment out of fashion in the development business, victims of changing demand patterns, high interest rates, and environmental regulation.[19] But as that specter faded, rural jurisdictions began to be faced with a revival of population growth and with the cumulative impacts of many small developments. Since 1970, Census Bureau estimates have revealed, nonmetropolitan areas all over the country have reversed long-term trends and begun to grow more rapidly than metropolitan ones.[20] Moreover, an industry trade publication recently reported new developer interest in reviving dormant, often bankrupt, existing recreational developments.[21]

State Investments and Nonland Policies

Even if we assume that state government has delegated all of its police power over land use to local government, various policies and practices of the state are highly important in promoting or preventing local land use changes. Perhaps the most obvious of these is state investment in the highway network. Highway capacity and design speeds are vital determinants of the accessibility of a given parcel of land, and hence of its value and potential for conversion to other uses. In some states the availability of water or sewer facilities is important to the growth pattern, with state involvement ranging from the massive California Water Project to small matching grants for municipal sewage plants.

The location of state facilities, such as hospitals, office buildings, prisons, and, especially, universities can be important in determining local growth rates. Many states also have programs for attracting private industry through tax concessions or industrial development bonds. Although the microlocation of these industries within the state is usually not a matter of state policy, the type of industry attracted and the rate of industrial job growth can themselves have different effects on different types of localities.

State licensing of power-generating and transmission facilities and state environmental policies can influence local land use, even if the state does not now use this power as part of a conscious growth policy. Public health standards promulgated by the state determine the areas where septic tanks will be permitted and the density of building allowed there. Land sales disclosure laws can make the state attractive or unattractive to "sagebrush subdividers."

State tax policies have important indirect effects on local land use changes. The percentage contribution of the state to financing local schools and welfare determines the extent of local reliance on property taxes, and hence the degree of local fiscal interest in land use. In more than half the states, there are state programs giving special preference in assessment to particular land uses, such as agriculture and forestry.

In addition to their own activities and investments, the states have some power over the distribution of federal grants within their borders, both through individual categorical programs and through the A-95 review procedure.[22]

With this great variety of state actions impinging on the growth patterns of regional and local subareas, we can assert that local growth is neither completely the result of market forces, nor completely under the control of local government. Decisions made by the state, whether guided by deliberate land use policy or not, significantly affect local land use changes. Although local government has several tools with which to deal with the effects of these changes, here again we might find many situations in which it is easier to deal with the state-level causes of growth than to try to mitigate its local-level effects.[23]

A Maturing Revolution

Thus the potential for state involvement in land use decisions, even after local controls are strengthened and rationalized, is considerable. Many states have already taken the initiative. As their institutions have been put to work in resolving actual land use conflicts, debate has been far from quiet and progress far from uniform.

Already, in California, Hawaii, Oregon, Vermont, and elsewhere there have been notable successes in preventing development where it is most environmentally damaging and in improving its quality where it does proceed. But the outlook is for a long and sometimes stormy course, as politicians, appointed boards, the courts, and sometimes the voters themselves continue to define the public interest in land use and to create institutional arrangements that will protect it.

Notes

1. Fred Bosselman and David Callies, *The Quiet Revolution in Land Use Control* (Washington, D.C., GPO, 1972).

2. One very recent example confirms that land use issues, if not the term *land use,* are still important concerns: A *New York Times* poll of 3,500 suburban residents in the New York metropolitan area found that, "What suburbanites say they like most about their communities is not the schools and stores and other people, but rather an amalgam of 'the environment,' which includes such factors as quiet, clean air and room. But other aspects of 'the environment' also rank at the top of the list of dislikes, suggesting a concern about such factors as congestion—the growth of apartments, traffic problems and the loss of open space." *The New York Times,* Nov. 13, 1978.

3. A popular song of the late 1960s expresses this feeling well: "They paved paradise/And put up a parking lot. . . . They took all the trees/And put them in a tree museum/And they charged all the people/A dollar and a half just to see 'em." From "Big Yellow Taxi," by Joni Mitchell, © 1970 SIQUOMB PUBLISHING CORP. (Used by Permission. All Rights Reserved.).

4. For example, the Task Force on Land Use and Urban Growth argues persuasively that detailed preregulation of land use, as exemplified by local zoning, should be replaced by administrative review of development proposals by local government. Citizens' Advisory Committee on Environmental Quality, Task Force on Land Use and Urban Growth, *The Use of Land* (New York, Crowell, 1973), pp. 182–195.

5. Speaking of metropolitan or areawide, general purpose government, Ostrom, Tiebout, and Warren argue this position: "[Areawide government] with its dominant center of decision-making, is apt to become a victim of the complexity of its own hierarchical or bureaucratic structure. Its complex channels of communication may make its administration unresponsive to many of the more localized public interests in the community. The costs of maintaining control in [its] public service may be so great that its production of public goods becomes grossly inefficient." Vincent Ostrom, Charles M. Tiebout, and Robert Warren, "The Organization of Government in Metropolitan Areas: A Theoretical Inquiry," *American Political Science Review* vol. 55, no. 4 (December 1961) p. 837.

6. U.S. Bureau of the Census, *Statistical Abstract of the U.S.* (1972 data).

7. These controls include one or more of the following: a planning board, zoning ordinance, subdivision regulation, building code, housing code, or local building permit system. Omitted from the sample were all municipalities and townships of less than 1,000 population located outside of SMSAs and township governments located in states where these governments lack municipal powers. Allen D. Manvel, *Local Land and Building Regulation: How Many Agencies? What Practice? How Much Personnel?,* National Commission on Urban Problems, Research Report No. 6 (Washington, D.C., GPO, 1968), cited in Marion Clawson, *Suburban Land Conversion in the United States* (Baltimore, Md., Johns Hopkins University Press for Resources for the Future, 1972) p. 98.

8. Carl E. Veazie, "Heavy Industry on the Maine Coast," *Report of the Governor's Task Force on Energy, Heavy Industry and the Maine Coast* (Augusta, Me., September 1972) app. I, p. 45.

9. Kenneth Holum, quoted in U.S. Department of the Interior, *The Creek and the City* (Washington, D.C., GPO, 1966) p. 28.

10. State of California, Office of Planning and Research (OPR), *Urban Development Strategy for California,* review draft (Sacramento, OPR, May 1977) p. 59.

11. Note that nearly all the "controlled growth" communities (Boulder, Colo., Boca Raton, Fla., Ramapo, N.Y., Petaluma, Calif., and Fairfax County, Va.) are functional parts of a metropolitan economy. For example, "With the new road, Petaluma became what it had not been before: an accessible extension of the San Francisco metropolitan center. Now one could live in Petaluma and hold a job in San Francisco—a long but not unusual 80-mile round trip." John Hart, "The Petaluma Case," *Cry California* (Spring 1974) p. 6.

12. Raleigh (N.C.) *News–Observer,* Dec. 8, 1973.

13. Letter of George B. Hartzog, Jr., to Rogers Morton, cited in Charles E. Roe, "The Second Battle of Gettysburg: Conflict of Public and Private Interests in Land Use Policies," *Environmental Affairs* (Spring 1972) p. 23.

14. Ibid., p. 20.

15. In the Adirondacks, per capita incomes average $500 to $1,500 less than the statewide average. In North Carolina's western mountains, ski resort and second-home developments have meant prosperity and jobs for the first time in decades. On the other hand, those who wish to preserve these environments tend to be high-income urbanites. A professor of forestry at the University of Montana commented, "Try looking where cries for less industry in Montana are coming from—from the white-collar professionals with nice safe jobs like mine." *Wall Street Journal,* June 23, 1972.

16. This increase in local controls has been caused in no small part by state encouragement or by the threat of direct state controls.

17. National Association of Counties (NACO) and International City Management Association (ICMA), *The County Yearbook* (Washington, D.C., NACO/ICMA, 1977) and unpublished tables from NACO. The survey was taken in 1975.

18. Citizens' Advisory Committee on Environmental Quality, Task Force on Land Use and Urban Growth, *The Use of Land,* p. 279.

19. The relaxation of environmental regulations, including land use controls, could easily revive developer interest in such projects, particularly lot-sales projects in which little or no investment in infrastructure is required.

20. Calvin L. Beale, "A Further Look at Nonmetropolitan Population Growth Since 1970," *American Journal of Agricultural Economics* vol. 58, no. 5 (1976) pp. 953–958; Kevin F. McCarthy and Peter A. Morrison, *The Changing Demographic and Economic Structure of Nonmetropolitan Areas in the United States,* Report R-2399-EDA (Santa Monica, Calif., Rand Corporation, January 1979).

21. *Recreation Development Today* (February 28, 1978).

22. A-95 is a procedure set up in 1969 by the Federal Office of Management and Budget (OMB) to allow states and substate regions to review and comment on certain federal programs within their borders and on local government applications for federal assistance.

23. Consider the Petaluma case cited earlier. An early decision not to improve the highway net in that area would have done more to "control" growth than the city's later, strenuous efforts at building limitations.

CHAPTER TWO

A Variety of Discontents

MANY PEOPLE ARE unhappy with the way land is used in the United States, but few can really pinpoint what they dislike. Often the dissatisfactions are expressed by such concepts as "urbanization," "growth," or "density." These vague terms are not very helpful, for they do not lead us beyond vague solutions, such as "growth controls," "comprehensive planning," and "national urban growth policy."

In fact, if we look at the whole range of ills that arise from the way we use our nation's land, we find problems that are created by growth—and problems only growth can solve. We find urbanization that devastates the natural environment and reduces the quality of human life—and urbanization that is not only functional but uplifting. We find some problems that demand sweeping solutions and new institutions, others that will submit to single-purpose legislation, and still others that merely require the conscientious enforcement of laws already on the books.

For example, suburban objection to new subdivisions may be primarily fiscal in origin and easily reduced by new school-financing methods or new boundaries for taxing jurisdictions. On the other hand, the objection of some Maine and Colorado residents to industrial development stems from deeply held social values, and at times flies in the face of their own economic self-interest. Thus a careful examination of land use problems, perceived and "real," is necessary both for policy prescription and for identifying the level of government most appropriate for solving them.

This chapter examines three questions, What do we find wrong with our present uses of land? What are likely to be the land use problems of the future? What kind of landscape would we *like* to see?

The Problems We See

The story of the simultaneous metropolitanization and suburbanization of America's population in the last thirty years is a familiar one.[1]

Even as the majority of Americans were raising their incomes, dramatically improving the quality of their housing, and adopting new leisure and recreational activities, there was a recognition of what the pursuit of these good things was doing to the land—and by implication to the natural and human environments.

Urban Sprawl—And Urban Splatter

For most of our metropolitan areas, urban growth has meant urban sprawl. Encouraged by rising automobile ownership, improved highway nets, and the suburbanization of employment, sprawl is found on the edge of the new cities of the South and West and the old cities of the Northeast and Middle West. Harvey and Clark have distinguished three distinct types.[2] First is the spread of subdivisions of homes on large individual lots. A common phenomenon of the 1950s, this practice reflects the tendency for the amount of land consumed by a family to rise with income and, perhaps, a desire by urbanites for a "return to the soil." By the 1960s, the rising price of raw land and increased attention to the advantages of cluster development had made large-lot sprawl much less common within the suburbs. It began to be replaced, however, by building on 5- and 10-acre exurban parcels, too large to be called lots but too small to be farms or ranches.

A second form of sprawl involves development along transportation arteries, with the space between them left undeveloped. Not only does this involve higher costs for the extension of utilities and other public services, but it makes the extent of urbanization seem much larger to the motorist than it actually is. Often this "ribbon sprawl" consists of commercial or industrial rather than residential uses.

A final kind of sprawl is the "leapfrog development," in which tracts of land are left vacant, while subdivision continues farther out from the center.[3] At its extreme, leapfrog sprawl becomes what Pickard calls "urban splatter," as small pockets of urban use, functionally linked to the larger metropolis, begin to dot the exurban landscape.[4]

Sprawl has many critics, who often begin with its esthetics. Whyte comments that "It takes remarkably little blight to color a whole area; let the reader travel along a stretch of road he is fond of, and he will notice how a small portion of open land has given amenity to the area. But it takes only a few badly designed developments or billboards or hot-dog stands to ruin it, and though only a little bit of land is used, the place will *look* filled up."[5] Sprawl also raises public service costs, interferes with fringe-area agriculture, encourages energy-using (and pollution-generating) automobile travel, and, it is alleged, leads to a loss of a sense of community.[6]

Urban sprawl reflects the divergence of interests between individuals, who wish to maximize private space and accessibility, and society as a whole, which seeks larger, contiguous blocks of open space. Often local land controls alone cannot internalize this conflict, for growth stopped at the edge of one jurisdiction will easily leapfrog out to the next.[7] The individual jurisdiction cannot convert sprawl on its periphery to density in its center—a more likely outcome will be that the growth (and its accompanying tax base) will be lost to some other municipality.

On the other hand, local policies can do much to reduce the visual impact of strip development, to speed traffic flows, and to assess charges for public services that more accurately reflect the costs of providing them.

Loss of Farmland

Another common land use worry is over the conversion of prime agricultural land to other uses.[8] Land that is level, well drained, and accessible to transportation lends itself to efficient crop production—but these very characteristics make it equally well suited to urban development. A recent U.S. Department of Agriculture study found that of the nearly 17 million acres converted to urban and built-up areas during 1967–75, about 60 percent was in the three most fertile soil capability classes. Thus, an average of more than 1.2 million acres of potentially productive land is lost yearly. Nearly 30 percent (600,000 acres annually) had formerly been cropland.[9]

In arid parts of the West, agriculture and urbanization have become competitors for water supplies. Arizona's state water commission estimates that if rapid population and industrial growth continue, the state's current 1.3 million irrigated acres would have to fall by nearly one-half in order to eliminate groundwater overdraft. Already, municipalities and copper companies have bought cropland for its water rights, letting it revert to desert while pumps draw off the groundwater beneath.[10]

The fear that urbanization of prime agricultural lands will interfere with the country's ability to feed itself is almost certainly an exaggerated one. Even a doubling of the area in cities would cause them to occupy less than 4 percent of the country's surface area. Currently some 25 percent of U.S. land is in farms, with the potential for considerable expansion of this figure if needed. On the other hand, recent sharp jumps in world feed grain demands have underlined the possibilities for vastly increased U.S. agricultural exports. Applications of additional factors, such as fertilizers and pesticides, to the remaining land base, or the cultivation of new, less naturally productive areas could easily make up for the loss of whatever proportion of the better land is taken out of production. But both these alternatives have their problems. More intensive farming of a smaller land base requires greater use of scarce fossil fuels and would increase air and water pollution, including the dispersion of toxic chemicals. Bringing new land into production destroys wildlife habitat, increases the need for irrigation, and, in some instances, increases the year-to-year instability of crop production. Cultivating marginal land or planting fence-to-fence can also hasten damaging soil erosion.

It can be argued that the advantages of good farmland over mediocre farmland should be reflected in land prices, and that this will in turn discourage developers from using prime land.[11] But that does not seem to be happening—perhaps because the difference in value between suburban land in agriculture and the same land in residential use (often 500 percent or more[12]) simply swamps the land-quality differential. Food demands and prices would have to be far higher than any we have known if agriculture is to compete head-to-head with urban uses. One can calculate, for example, that corn would have to be $11 per bushel, rather than the current $2.25 or $2.50, before farmland in suburban Washington, D.C., could compete seriously with new housing.[13]

Framing the issue solely in terms of the relative *fertility* of the land also misses an important point. Agriculture on the urban fringe not only produces crops, but provides valuable open space. In many cases a landscape of well-tended farms is more attractive visually than even a completely natural scene. For reasons deep in the American psyche, farming, particularly farming on a small scale, is considered a virtuous kind of enterprise. Thus the loss of farmlands on the urban fringe might be considered a social loss, even aside from the loss of the fruits of the land. The vineyards outside San Jose or the orange groves near Orlando might be moved elsewhere with little aggregate loss of production. For residents of these places, however, there would be a loss of amenity.

Conserving farmland involves both interjurisdictional spillovers and divergent interests. The fast-growing suburb can hardly be expected to voluntarily forego development simply to provide pleasant vistas to the city dweller. Nor is it easy to argue before a local zoning board that the loss of 20 acres here and 50 acres there will really make a difference to the nation's or the world's supply of food. Moreover, it is extremely difficult to isolate a rural jurisdiction's land market from development occurring just across its borders. In the absence of some mechanism for allocating costs and benefits over some larger, more appropriate region, development will take place in ways that will leave important public interests—and many individuals—dissatisfied.

Fiscal Effects of Land Use Changes

Until recently, most communities looked upon new construction and the new residents it accommodated as attractive additions to the local tax base. True, some types of development, such as trailer parks and apartment buildings, were looked on with suspicion, but the general feeling was that if growth was good for the local private economy, it would swell municipal coffers as well. Now the pendulum has shifted, and citizens and their elected representatives emphasize the public service burden that new developments will impose.

The concern is particularly acute in suburbs, where families with school-age children make up a high proportion of new residents, and in rural areas where second-home developments are springing up. In the latter case, the new residents are demanding levels of public services far higher than those which rural townships have traditionally provided. Added police protection, garbage collection, better roads, and even such urban amenities as traffic signals seem to accompany this kind of growth. A town father in one Vermont community claims that newcomers even insist that roads be cleared of fresh snow immediately, night or day. "People don't go to sleep like they used to," he says.[14]

Mitigating growth's impact on the demand for local services are the declining number of children per family and increased state and federal sharing of education and welfare costs. On the other hand, two decades of inflation and interest rates that have reached levels far higher than in the past have made the marginal costs of building and financing new capital facilities far higher than the average costs of what is already in place. Under the most common municipal practice, new residents pay the same amount for streets, schools, and utilities as do long-time residents, even though the cost of the new infrastructure greatly exceeds that of the facilities that had been built in the past.

Empirical evidence on the fiscal effects of growth is mixed.[15] Often the results of the analysis seem to depend on whether the study is produced by the developer, by the municipality, or by some citizen group wishing to exclude growth. Methodological and measurement problems include estimating the characteristics of new residents, their incomes, and their tastes for public services; measuring the excess capacity of existing public facilities; guessing at future construction costs and municipal bond interest rates; and predicting long-term and secondary effects of growth. For example, highways are generally not widened incrementally as individual new developments are built, but as a result of congestion due to cumulative growth. Allocating the appropriate proportion of the cost of highway improvement to a single new subdivision is difficult indeed.

Despite the problems with these studies, interest in measuring the fiscal effects of growth is high. Citing a national survey of fiscal impact studies, one recent study reported that "During the 1970's the technique emerged as an almost universal large scale development accompaniment—either volunteered by the developer or required by the municipality."[16] Public resistance to local tax increases, which was dramatized by the passage of California's Proposition 13 and similar legislation in 1978, should keep local governments acutely conscious of how new projects affect their revenues and expenditures.

In a sense, the new skepticism about the fiscal impact of growth is merely a more sophisticated version of what has long been called "fiscal feudalism." Communities compete for the shopping center, with its high property and sales tax generation, and shun the trailer park, which requires services but contributes much less in taxes. They court the builder of expensive homes and discourage the builder of low-cost housing. Perhaps the only change that has occurred is an enlargement of the types of development that are considered fiscal drains. Now, even the expensive single-family home is suspect.[17]

The competition of local governments for tax revenues has reached ludicrous heights in places where functional economic units are broken up into a multitude of jurisdictions. In northern New Jersey, for example, the tiny borough of Teterboro virtually zoned out people, while zoning in an airport and industries. As a result, the town had about two dozen residents, a single public school student backed by some $75 million in assessed valuation, and the second lowest tax rate in the county.[18] In the Los Angeles area, the industrial city of Vernon (230 residents, 50,000 jobs) has done much the same, as have the aptly named City of Industry and City of Commerce.

If, as we have suggested, the number of types of development considered fiscally desirable has diminished, we can expect localities to intensify their efforts to obtain these "acceptable" projects and to exclude the rest. The result, of course, is not only an inequitable distribution of

the tax burden, but a tendency to bend environmental and other standards when necessary to entice a coveted project.

Degradation of the Natural Environment

The litany of environmental damage caused by poor land use is a long
and familiar one. The destruction of wetlands on Long Island, the
eutrophication of lakes in Florida, and the scarring of hillsides by strip
mining are common fare to the reader of environmental magazines and
the daily newspapers alike. One might suggest that the real problem lies
not in the cases of obvious devastation, which are often overstated, but
in the steadiness and irreversibility of the seemingly more minor damage.
For example, for every river that is grossly and unattractively polluted
by man's use of the shoreline, there are dozens that are attractive to look
at but manifestly unsafe to drink. Where the worst cases are often due to
some easily identified public or corporate excess (the strip mine or the
paper mill), the damage caused by piecemeal and individually innocuous
development may be both equally bad and far harder to repair or remedy.

When we make irreversible changes in the natural environment, we
implicitly ignore the possibility that public tastes and needs will change
over time. The draining and filling of wetlands is a good example. Long
considered useless, unattractive, and even dangerous, swamps and tidal
marshes are now widely appreciated for their fascinating ecosystems and
for their significant contribution to the productivity of lakes and oceans.
Similarly, there is a growing appreciation for the rough beauty of the
desert landscapes of the West, once considered by most people as bother-
some impediments to cross-country travel.

Many environmental problems concern the interrelation of air, water,
and the land. Urban sprawl and splatter not only waste land and energy,
they also can contribute to air pollution.[19] Unwise agricultural practices
and careless construction and logging lead to the erosion of billions of
tons of topsoil yearly. Excessive withdrawals of water from underground
aquifers have caused saltwater intrusion and threatened the water supplies
of cities. Building seaward of the duneline has caused beach erosion in
many coastal areas, as well as needless risk to life and property. In all of
these cases, the pollution or environmental damage we observe can be
traced back to prior, sometimes subtle, changes in land use.[20]

Destruction of wildlife habitat frequently accompanies land use
changes. Even though bear, bison, turkey, and other formerly plentiful
species now enjoy protection from unregulated hunting, there is no
chance they will even approach their former ranges or numbers.

Dramatic conflicts between land use changes and environmental forces occur when areas with natural hazards are developed. Despite considerable federal investment over the years in flood-protection measures, the continuing urbanization of floodplains has caused flood losses to climb.[21] Large portions of the heavily developed Florida coast lie within the one hundred-year flood zone. And, in California, building has taken place directly astride the San Andreas earthquake fault. Development in hazard areas has been implicitly subsidized by federal insurance and disaster relief programs, which have reimbursed much of the monetary loss suffered by those who have built even where the hazard was obvious or predictable.[22]

Degradation of the Visual Environment

Much of the damage to natural environments that has occurred is unseen except by the expert. Obvious to all, however, is the decline of visual amenity, particularly in those urban and suburban places where most people spend the majority of their time. Indeed, it is quite possible that the public's objection to development is not based so much on calculation of fiscal costs and benefits, ideal conceptions of urban form, or even on its effects on natural systems, but simply on how such developments *look*.[23]

Billboards, gas stations, shopping centers, and fast-food outlets compete for the customer's eye in city and suburb. New, less-expensive building materials have freed the designers of commercial buildings from the constraints of brick, wood, and stone and have spawned a generation of structures in which the building itself becomes part of the advertising message. This message is to be read not at the leisurely walking pace of the downtown window-shopper, but at the pace of traffic moving along a commercial boulevard or even an expressway.

Their angles as yet unsoftened by trees and other vegetation, new residential developments are often quite unattractive compared with long-settled neighborhoods. Similarly, modern expressways, despite considerable efforts by some of their designers, continue to be more functional than esthetic. Undergrounding of new utility distribution lines is increasingly popular, despite the considerable added costs, but it has been estimated that replacing those overhead lines already in place would cost perhaps $150 billion.[24] Undergrounding of high-voltage lines in rural areas is exceedingly expensive and is done only occasionally.

Local regulations have long been used to improve the visual environment, even to the extent, in some communities, of requiring approval by an art jury of new residential building designs. A ride along any long metropolitan artery, say, Los Angeles' Wilshire Boulevard or Miami's Highway A1A, is convincing evidence of the unevenness of these restrictions from community to community. The mobile city dweller finds that, even though his own municipality may be one of the fortunate ones, the habitual tracks of his daily experience take him through a variety of visual environments, many of them distasteful.

Closely allied to the decline of visual quality has been growth's near total disregard for the unique or the historic. Over one-third of the 16,000 structures listed in the 1933 Historic American Building Survey have already been destroyed.[25] The unique character of whole cities such as San Francisco and New Orleans has been eroded by the ubiquitous office tower, which is functional, profitable, and lifeless. Distinctive nonurban environments also face the homogenization that development brings. Resort condominiums might be shuffled from Vermont to Colorado to the northern California coast and many would not notice the change. Their designs show little appreciation of the environments that have evolved in these places over the years. In some places, such as Martha's Vineyard, heated opposition to new development has arisen, not because of the quality of the development itself, but because it would erode the uniqueness of the place.

Limitation of Housing Opportunity

Despite considerable progress in removing the most blatant forms of racial and ethnic discrimination in housing markets, residential segregation by race, by income—or by both—persists. Soaring prices for new housing and local efforts at fiscal zoning have raised the price of entry in many suburban housing markets beyond the reach not just of the poor, but of many members of the working class as well. It is a rueful joke in many affluent suburbs that most of the employees of local government cannot afford to make their homes there.[26] A major culprit in the housing price rise has been the price of land which, according to the National Association of Home Builders, has risen from 11 percent of the selling price of the typical new single-family house in 1949 to 25 percent in 1977.[27]

Federally funded housing programs, meager as they have been, might have made it possible for some low-income people to reside among more affluent neighbors, were it not for the enormous difficulty of getting communities to accept the subsidized families. The newspapers of the late 1960s and early 1970s were full of stories of neighborhood efforts to prevent the construction of low- and moderate-income housing, even of the "scattered-site" variety. Frequently the rhetoric of the environmental movement was used to mask more fundamental issues of class and race.

Regulations aimed at raising environmental quality, lowering densities, and protecting sensitive or hazardous lands have themselves been accused of contributing to the housing cost squeeze. So have municipal efforts to shift the burden of providing public services from the taxpayer and onto the developer or new home buyer. When various levels of government implement these policies, they weigh costs and benefits for those already living within their boundaries. The interests of outsiders, including would-be residents, are rarely considered.

Gainers, Losers, and Speculators

The public is both horrified and fascinated by the workings of the land market. Land speculators are almost universally condemned, while at the same time, the public praises homeownership as an investment and eagerly snaps up pieces of the New Mexico desert. Still, speculation in land might be considered as socially neutral as speculation in rare paintings or in stamp collections, were it not for three important side effects.

First, the potential for public action, particularly with respect to permitted land uses, to produce enormous changes in land values has frequently perverted the public decision process. Nearly every fast-growing metropolitan area has had its zoning scandals, and nearly every state has built roads that led principally to some favored individual's property.

Second, land speculation has caused large amounts of land to be held idle, reducing the total output of society. Landowners who suspect that their land may be urbanized in the future are reluctant to make investments that would maintain or increase its productivity as farm or forest.[28] Often they maximize their flexibility by withholding it from *any* use. Because the form of future patterns of urban growth is uncertain, the land subject to this speculative influence usually amounts to many times the area that actual urban uses could ever absorb.

Finally, speculation has been blamed for helping raise the price of land for housing, farming, and other uses to historic highs.[29] Land has come to be regarded as a reliable hedge against inflation, and as inflation has increased so has the investment demand for land, including some widely publicized purchases by foreign nationals.[30]

Certainly not all of the recent sharp increase in housing prices has been due to land costs, but the proportion of the price of the average new home attributable to land costs has been rising steadily. Similarly, farmland prices that have little relationship to the current productivity of the land have made it difficult for aspiring young farmers to enter the business. A county extension agent in Vermont claims, "You can't make a profit by buying land at one or two thousand per acre, even if you plan to grow gold."[31]

Municipalities have considerable power for affecting land values, but this is mainly in the form of windfalls and losses caused by zoning and investment decisions. They have neither the power to tax those who gain by their actions nor the funds to compensate those who lose.[32]

The Size of Development Projects

The greatest single impetus to the "quiet revolution" generation of land use controls was undoubtedly the sheer size of the development projects that were being proposed. Size, by itself, does not necessarily make a project undesirable, but it does make a project's impacts on its surroundings more obvious and widens the zone over which the impacts may be felt. Between 1968 and 1972, highly favorable economic conditions and extreme optimism in the development industry caused a flood of proposed projects of previously unheard-of size.

In Florida's Broward (Fort Lauderdale) County, for example, the twenty-five largest planned or ongoing residential developments would have added 800,000 persons to the population—doubling its size. Two individual projects were each to contain more than 50,000 dwelling units and the smallest of the projects more than 2,000.[33]

In the New Mexico desert, a consortium of gas companies planned seven huge coal-gasification plants, each costing $400 million.[34] The Arizona strip mine that was to feed them, already the largest in the nation, was to be enlarged from 2,500 acres to nearly 30,000 acres.

Elsewhere in the country, sports stadiums, new communities (one survey counted more than 150), rural factories, thermal and nuclear power plants, regional jetports, amusement parks, universities, and other very large facilities were producing significant economic and environmental effects extending over large land areas and, often, across several political jurisdictions.

The simultaneous occurrence of huge projects and a heightened public awareness of the environment caused sharp controversies to arise around the country. The first response of policymakers was usually to require that project impacts be explicitly recognized and, if possible, quantified —the impetus to national, state, and local laws requiring environmental impact statements. A second response, which occurred mostly in places with the fastest growth and the largest proposed projects, was the beginning of direct state regulation of land uses.[35]

The large-project binge was to end even more suddenly than it had begun. The post-1973 energy crisis caused most utility companies to scale down their demand projections and shelve some proposed projects; the simultaneous building industry slowdown, particularly in the overheated condominium and second-home sector, caused the cancellation of still other projects. Governments, strapped for cash and stung by environmentalist criticisms, scaled down or deleted many of the largest watersupply, navigation, and highway projects.

But as business conditions improved, starting in 1975, some large projects continued to cause controversy. The Kaiparowits power plant, a 3,000-megawatt coal-burning generating station that would have produced electricity for southern California from a remote location in Utah, was not killed until 1976. The same was true of Dow Chemical's proposed $500 million petrochemical plant in California's Sacramento River delta. At present, controversy continues over coal and uranium mines in the West, over oil refineries and offshore drilling facilities on the Atlantic coast, gambling casinos at Lake Tahoe, and new power plants in remote and scenic locations.[36]

The future of large-scale development in the housing industry is still uncertain. To date, developers have been quite cautious, preferring to spread business risks over a multitude of smaller projects. Virtually no new towns or large second-home developments have been begun since 1974. The building industry is quite an adaptable one, however, historically subject to shifting trends and enthusiasms. The half-billion dollar expansion of Disney World, for example, announced in late 1978, immediately revived the enthusiasm of Orlando developers, only recently preoccupied with overcapacity and bankruptcies. Since development of large-scale projects has some definite advantages for the larger firms in the industry, it is too early to assume that this form of development has disappeared.

It is unlikely that size itself is bad. In fact, large projects lend themselves to careful design, cautious review, and the planning flexibility made possible by single ownership. They bring land use issues to the public attention in a dramatic way that slow marginal changes do not. Ideally, they might be seen as opportunities for the public to improve and to redirect growth.

Unfortunately, it is this very size that has caused so many of these opportunities to be lost. The costs and benefits of large projects are spread over great areas and among several political jurisdictions, but it is only by chance that the spatial distribution of benefits coincides with the distribution of costs. To date, the general practice in this country has been to give the power to regulate land uses to the jurisdiction containing the project, not to all those affected by it. Thus, we find some large projects approved even though they impose substantial costs on other jurisdictions, while other projects are rejected even though they would confer substantial regional benefits. Moreover, many of these projects are so large and so complex in their effects that their evaluation is far beyond the analytical capability of the local governments that now bear the responsibility for regulating them.

Resistance to Change

Large projects are a symptom of the rate at which our society is changing. As the economy grows at a geometric rate, successive increments of growth become greater. Either this growth will be expressed in large, easily identifiable development projects or it will result in many smaller-scale projects whose cumulative impacts will be much the same. We are beginning to see many examples of public resistance not merely to the products of change but to change itself. This resistance extends to land use changes. In fact, people faced with disturbing political and social changes may find in their physical environment some last vestige of stability and may resist land use changes with special vigor.

Joseph Bodovitz, former director of California's Coastal Zone Conservation Commission, maintains, "If I were asked to suggest two books as indispensable reading for coastal zone planners, one of them would be Alvin Toffler's *Future Shock*. . . . Obviously I do not know what was in the minds of the 4.3 million Californians who voted for our State's coastal zone law, but I suspect that one major factor was the rapidity of change."[37]

Thus a final problem we face is the problem of change itself. Sometimes the change is physical—who has not lamented the loss of the vacant lot where one played as a child? Sometimes, the change is social—land use changes bring in newcomers with different customs, different incomes, sometimes different skin colors.

Perhaps the fervor with which people try to preserve the integrity of their environment is due to their having consciously chosen that environment. Developers are often mystified when projects embodying high standards of environmental protection and architectural quality are strenuously opposed by citizens. Areas once composed of single-family dwellings may be no less appealing to an outside observer than the same neighborhood converted to high-rise apartments. The new residents of the high rises may be more than satisfied with their environment. But the old residents, who originally chose the single-family neighborhood, are likely to resist the change.

Thus we return to the theme of chapter 1. Do people have an inherent right to determine the way in which land around them is used? And, if they do, how much of this right resides in the present residents of a local jurisdiction and how much in society as a whole?

We have seen that the public desire to do something about land use has roots in the many problems we see around us. We might now speculate about the land use pressures we will feel in the future, the roots of our future land use dilemmas.

Problems to Come

Predicting the future is a dangerous game. In some cases, social and economic forces have had such continuing momentum that trends first noticed many years ago are still with us today. The metropolitanization of the population was well underway in the 1940s; urban sprawl was decried in the early 1950s; the movement of the population toward amenity-rich places has continued for two generations. On the other hand, other trends have been obscure—the course of the birthrate; the mix of single- versus multifamily dwellings.

We can say with near certainty that the rate of new household formation from now until about 1990 will be the highest in history. The people who will form new families and who will, most probably, demand additional units in which to house these families, have already been born. Between 1960 and 1970, the number of persons reaching age twenty-five, an approximate threshold for household formation (and for purchasing homes) was 26 million. The 1970s have seen this jump to 36 million, while the 1980s will see a further increase to 41 million persons.[38]

During the 1990s the number of persons reaching age twenty-five will fall back to 34 million. And after the year 2000, this source of demand for land will again depend principally on the vagaries of the birthrate.

In all likelihood, the majority of these families will locate in metropolitan areas. Whether they choose the central city or a suburb is less certain. Forces leading to a resurgence of the central city include smaller families, improved public transportation, greater racial tolerance, falling urban crime rates, high energy costs, and the spread of some of the old big-city problems to the suburbs. Factors leading toward continued dispersion within the metropolis are the relatively lower costs of land assembly on the periphery, the fact that a good (highway) transportation system is already in place, the continuing dispersion of employment, and the rising level of average incomes.

A smaller, but growing, number of people will probably settle beyond the metropolitan fringe. Some will commute long distances into the city; others will work in the widely dispersed industrial plants that the interstate highway system has facilitated.

To some extent the mix of concentration and dispersion will depend on the land use policies that the suburbs and exurbs follow. Growth limits, development charges, and slow investment in infrastructure will raise the cost of building new housing in the suburbs, leading to infilling in the city and the renovation of existing structures.

Overall, the most likely outlook is for more diversity in both location and types of residential development than we have known in the past. Between the end of World War II and about 1970, growth typically took place in a sort of suburban doughnut, with a static and increasingly impoverished central city and a declining rural periphery. About 1970 differences became less pronounced, as rural areas began to grow again. Most recently, selected big-city neighborhoods have experienced a wave of residential renovation. The future promises a complex mix of locations and densities, with growth taking place partly as suburban expansion, partly as infilling in close-in suburbs, partly as exurban sprawl, and partly as central city infilling and renovation.

Amenity-rich locations are likely to continue to grow much faster than the average. Better educated and more widely traveled, the population has both the desire to move to locations with pleasant environments and, increasingly, the income to express this desire. In particular, the number of retired persons is expected to grow sharply. Weakened family ties and more liberal pensions should make older people a major factor in the housing market in popular retirement areas. Unlike job-oriented migrants, pensioners are free to gravitate toward places where the climate is moderate and the living costs low. This should add to the growth both of traditional retirement destinations, such as Florida and the Southwest, and of less fashionable but moderately priced havens, such as the North Carolina and Arkansas mountains.

Second-home demand has recently been picking up somewhat from its energy crisis doldrums. The potential market is still huge. Although the number of families having second homes jumped from 1.6 million in 1967 to 2.9 million only three years later, the proportion of households owning a second home is still only about 5 percent.[39] Even increases of a few percentage points in this figure would translate into enormous numbers of new units, concentrated in the limited number of areas of high amenity.

Demand for second homes seems to have shifted away from the resort-style development, with its common recreational facilities and relatively small lots. Many potential buyers are finding that they can buy 5 or 10 undeveloped acres for the price of a half-acre in a development; or that they can find a restorable farmhouse for the price of a condominium. The best located existing resort developments may continue to prosper, partly by "time-sharing," an arrangement that involves selling rights to use a jointly owned unit for a certain number of weeks per year.

There has been much debate over the future need for land to produce renewable and nonrenewable products. Some observers think that the United States will be drawn into a world food crisis within a decade, forced by moral as well as economic pressure to use its unmatched agricultural potential to export to starving third world nations. Similar scenarios may be foreseen for timber and for certain mineral resources. This could lead to some expansion of the land area devoted to these uses.

The future level of demand is only one element of the uncertainty. Also unknown is the exact composition of demand. Will Americans, for example, increase their consumption of beef as rapidly as they have in the recent past? Will hardwoods be increasingly substituted for softwoods in making paper? Will trees and shrubs be raised on huge "energy plantations" for conversion to alcohol or other liquid fuels? A final uncertainty remains as to whether commodity production is expanded by increasing the amount of land used for a given purpose or by using the same amount of land more intensively. Debate rages among foresters, for example, over the merits of increasing wood supply by cutting a greater number of acres annually or by investing in more intensive silviculture on the relatively smaller amount of land in the highest fertility classes.

One land-related crisis is already upon us, and seems likely to get worse. Drastic increases in housing prices have made it difficult for young people or others not already owning a dwelling to purchase one. If inflation continues at present rates, a significant redistribution of wealth might result. Current homeowners, who tend to be both older and wealthier than average, will improve their wealth position relative to nonowners. This could well have notable political impacts and may bring those persons most disadvantaged to seek a reorganization in the way new housing is built and financed.[40]

It is difficult to say whether the average size of residential or commercial developments will rise or fall in the future, or whether the average size of firms initiating such projects will change. On one hand, developers have become increasingly aware of the possibilities of capturing increases in land values created by their projects.[41] This would incline them toward building more planned-unit developments (PUDs), "mixed-use" developments, and new communities, where residences, commercial properties, and industries each help increase the demand for the other. Firms might also find economies of scale in planning, particularly when sophisticated (and expensive) environmental preplanning is required.

On the other hand, bitter and widely shared experience during the 1974–75 real estate recession convinced many firms that large projects involve high risks as well as great potential rewards. Firms have become particularly wary of the risks involved in installing expensive infrastructure in projects which may not be completely sold out for several years. These front-end costs are usually paid for with borrowed money, exposing the borrower to intolerable expense in the event of a sudden rise in interest rates. Moreover, as we shall see in later chapters, some developers are convinced that larger, more visible projects invite more stringent public scrutiny and regulation.

Demands for land for industry and for power production and distribution may be high, but the outlook is uncertain. Before the 1973–74 rise in energy prices, it was estimated that in the next two decades new high-voltage transmission lines would consume 3 million acres of new rights-of-way, while at least 225 new major generating stations would require hundreds of thousands of acres of prime industrial sites.[42] Since 1974 price-induced conservation has cut the annual growth rate of electricity demand from 7 percent to about half that figure. Nevertheless, even an optimistic forecast found that—without a significant new commitment to conservation—the United States must find sites for more than 400 new coal or nuclear power plants by the end of the century.[43] Moreover, new or nonconventional energy sources may involve significant new commitments of land—for strip mines, oil shale mines and processing plants, deepwater ports, oil refineries, geothermal and solar power plants, and coal-gasification works—engendering new kinds of land use conflicts.

Variations in pollution standards may become an important factor in the location of some industrial facilities. Much depends on whether standards are promulgated in terms of the purity of the effluent alone (treatment standards) or in terms of the effect of the effluent on the quality of the receiving medium (ambient standards).

Under a treatment standard, a potentially polluting industry would spend about the same amount on treating its effluent regardless of where it locates. Ambient standards, on the other hand, cause treatment costs to vary with location. The picture is further complicated by the prospective enforcement of air quality nondegradation requirements, which could severely limit the expansion of pollution-prone industrial and power plants in places where the air is still pristine.[44]

Demands for recreational land will probably continue to increase, although at some point today's extremely high percentage rates of growth will undoubtedly moderate. There is likely to be considerable conflict between different types of recreational uses, for outdoor recreation includes such varied, and sometimes incompatible, activities as family camping, snowmobiling, boating, hunting, operation of all-terrain vehicles, nature study, and wilderness hiking.

In general, we can expect that there will be even more conflicts among land use preferences in the future than we have already experienced. These conflicts will not be among land use aggregates—in table 2-1, Fischman's projection of future land requirements shows that, despite significant growth in population and economic activity and great changes in the composition of industrial output, the demand for land in broad categories of uses may not be remarkably different at the end of the century from what it was at its midpoint.[45]

Table 2-1. Long-term Demand for U.S. Land
(millions of acres)

	1950	1960	1970	1980	1990
Open farmland, including pasture	884	888	909	842	789
Other grassland and range	193	168	130	112	89
"Commercial" forest	457	502	523	499	551
Recreation, etc. land	42	62	81	103	126
Urban and transportation land	51	63	66	74	82
Public installations and facilities	26	32	34	32	39
Total land requirements	1653	1715	1743	1661	1676
Total land availability	1904	2271	2265	2264	2263
Surplus (+) or deficit (−)	+251	+556	+522	+603	+587

In the aggregate, land required for urban or recreational use can simply be shifted from other uses or from our rather large supply of unused land.[46] The conflicts, however, will occur over individual parcels of land. The wilderness advocate will not willingly accept a tract of land in Idaho when land suitable for this use can be found in North Carolina. The fact that family campers or all-terrain vehicle enthusiasts also covet the North Carolina land will not necessarily persuade the wilderness lover to settle for a far-off substitute. Similarly, the New Jersey farmer will doubtless be unimpressed by the argument that land taken out of cultivation by urbanization in his state can easily be replaced by the produce of new lands in Alabama or Delaware.

As a result of these conflicting demands for the services of the same pieces of land, we can expect that rights connected with land will be increasingly exercised, privatized, and priced. When a parcel is devoted to one use, say, farming, other uses such as forestry, recreation or urbanization often must be excluded. But even when there is no inherent conflict among uses, owners will probably increasingly exclude unregulated use by others, partly for fear of vandalism and overuse, and partly because public use may create "prescriptive" rights.[47]

Goals for Future Planning

If the identity of our future land use problems is still in doubt, so much more so is the manner of their resolution. The area and the exact identity of the lands that will be given over to housing, devoted to agriculture, or reserved as wilderness will have to be determined through hundreds of thousands of individual planning decisions. We might ask, however, whether there are any general principles that we can apply in achieving an environment that will be more satisfying than the one we have already created.

Efficiency

One criterion might be that of efficiency. To some, this might mean allocating land to its "highest and best" use in an economic sense. One of the stated goals of our society is to achieve a high degree of economic prosperity, a purpose difficult to achieve if our land resources are not efficiently allocated. Efficiency, however, should be interpreted to include the consideration of externalities arising out of the use of land. It is doubtful that land is used efficiently if its owner can pass the costs of his air pollution or his erosion on to others. Nor is it efficient to allow builders to save on land costs at the expense of higher public sector outlays for the extension of water and sewer lines.

Equity

The outcome of land use planning should divide rights to land among members of society in an equitable fashion. In allocating other rights among its members, society does not demand equality. For example, significant differences in incomes are permitted and sometimes encouraged, with social welfare programs guaranteeing citizens a minimum level of living somewhat higher than the bare subsistence level. Similarly, an equity standard for land rights might not mean equal use of land by all but only some minimum amount of use. Thus, we might tolerate private beaches, provided that there was some minimum provision for public ones. Minimum standards for recreational land might even be legislated, but other aspects of environmental quality connected with land, such as density or visual quality, cannot easily be defined.[48] We undoubtedly will have to content ourselves with a vague statement of goals similar to the 1949 Housing Act's mandate to provide all Americans with a "decent home and a suitable living environment." Such a statement, although too imprecise to have any legal effect, would nonetheless remind the makers of specific land use decisions of their obligation to consider the interpersonal distribution of rights in land and of environmental quality in general.

An equity criterion will sometimes conflict with the efficiency criterion. The principal conflict involves the use of the price system as an allocative mechanism. It is probably most efficient to allocate, say, access to wilderness or to areas of unusual scenic beauty, by charging a price high enough to prevent overcrowding. In a society with very unequal incomes, however, prices would exclude not just those who have relatively weak preferences for the use of these places, but those who, despite their strong preferences, lack the income needed to pay the price.

Preserving Long-run Options

Some land use decisions involve essentially irreversible commitments of land to a particular purpose. Wetlands, once drained, cannot as a practical matter be restored to their former state. Land use decisions that foreclose future planning options should be taken with particular care, since society's goals and constraints may change significantly over time. Our descendents are in a sense the "new colonials," for the decisions we make today, particularly our land use decisions, determine the range of choice available to those who will succeed us.[49]

Providing a Diversity of Environments

People differ greatly in the kind of environment they prefer. The density at which they choose to live, their styles of architecture, and their interest in natural environments depend on their personality, on their education, on their position in the life cycle. One man's rolling farm landscape may be another's potential golf course. Even Los Angeles has its partisans.

Fortunately, we have enough land to satisfy nearly all of these diverse tastes, provided we plan intelligently. We must be careful, however, not to plan too much. A uniform and static environment, even though ecologically sound and esthetically pleasing, must not become our goal. Each state has its own traditions, derived from its topography, economic base, and history. Within the states, municipalities and neighborhoods offer widely differing environments. The ultimate products of our future planning should be diverse, capable of responding to new social forces and of satisfying new esthetics.

Introducing the Case Studies

This chapter has looked at the dissatisfactions we have found with our current system of regulating land use and with the results that that system has produced. We have already noted that a number of states have taken a new interest in exercising powers they have long delegated to lower levels of government. These new initiatives have ranged from the mildest tinkering with environmental and subdivision rules to bold programs of direct state control. The next three chapters will discuss three of the most significant of these—Vermont's Act 250, California's Coastal Commissions, and Florida's Environmental Land and Water Management Act. Each has been in operation for six years or more. They provide a wealth of information as to how state intervention in land use has worked in actual practice.

Notes

1. See Marion Clawson, *Suburban Land Conversion in the United States* (Baltimore, Md., Johns Hopkins University Press for Resources for the Future, 1972); and Irene Taeuber, "The Changing Distribution of the Population of the United

States in the Twentieth Century," in U.S. Commission on Population Growth and the American Future, Research Report, vol. V, *Population, Distribution, and Policy* (Washington, D.C., GPO, 1972) pp. 31–107.

2. R. O. Harvey and W. A. V. Clark, "The Nature and Economics of Urban Sprawl," *Land Economics* vol. 41, no. 1 (February 1965) pp. 1–9.

3. Even within the boundaries of large cities urbanized for many years there is a surprising amount of vacant or undeveloped land. Marion Clawson, *America's Land and Its Uses* (Baltimore, Md., Johns Hopkins University Press for Resources for the Future, 1972) p. 39.

4. Jerome Pickard, "U.S. Metropolitan Growth and Expansion, 1970–2000," in U.S. Commission on Population Growth and the American Future, *Population, Distribution, and Policy,* pp. 127–182.

5. William H. Whyte, Jr., "Urban Sprawl," *Fortune* vol. 57, no. 1 (January 1958).

6. For a quantitative assessment of some of these impacts, see U.S. Council on Environmental Quality, *The Costs of Sprawl* (Washington, D.C., GPO, 1974).

7. As public policy has made growth on the rural edges of suburban Fairfax County, Virginia, more difficult, building has increased markedly in the next county farther out. The commuter traffic generated there, of course, continues to pour through Fairfax County on its way to the city of Washington.

8. See U.S. Congress, House of Representatives, Committee on Agriculture, Hearings, *National Agricultural Land Policy Act,* 95th Cong., 1st sess., June 15–16, 1977; U.S. Department of Agriculture, *Perspectives on Prime Lands* (Washington, D.C., USDA, 1975); and John S. Rosenberg, "Preserving Farmland," *Country Journal* (February 1979) pp. 69–76.

9. R. Dideriksen, A. Hidlebaugh, and K. Schmude, *Potential Cropland Study,* Statistical Bulletin No. 578 (Washington, D.C., U.S. Department of Agriculture, Soil Conservation Service, 1977).

10. *Wall Street Journal,* December 28, 1977.

11. Market price differentials may not reflect important externalities. For example, cultivating prime land may produce less water pollution than does cultivating marginal land, but the social advantage is not reflected in relative land prices.

12. See A. Allan Schmid, *Converting Land from Rural to Urban Uses* (Baltimore, Md., Johns Hopkins University Press for Resources for the Future, 1968).

13. Robert G. Healy, "Agricultural Land Retention: Land Market Issues," chapter prepared for a forthcoming book on farmland retention to be published by the Soil Conservation Society of America.

14. "Vermont's Loveliness Causes a Developing Storm," *National Observer,* April 1973.

15. For representative studies, see Thomas Muller and Grace Dawson, *The Fiscal Impact of Residential and Commercial Development: A Case Study,* Urban Institute Paper No. 712-7-1 (Washington, D.C., Urban Institute, 1972); Boulder (Colo.) Area Growth Study Commission, *Exploring Options for the Future—A Study of Growth in Boulder County,* vol. 7 (1973); and George Sternlieb, *Housing Development and Municipal Costs* (New Brunswick, N.J., Center for Urban Policy Research, Rutgers University, 1973).

16. Robert W. Burchell and David Listokin, *The Fiscal Impact Handbook* (New Brunswick, N.J., Center for Urban Policy Research, Rutgers University, 1978) p. 257. The study presents a great deal of material on how such studies are performed, as does Thomas Muller, *Fiscal Impacts of Land Development: A Critique of Methods and a Review of Issues* (Washington, D.C., Urban Institute, 1975).

17. Some interesting models of municipal competition for a tax base are discussed and tested in Edwin S. Mills and Wallace E. Oates, eds., *Fiscal Zoning and Land Use Controls* (Lexington, Mass., D. C. Heath, 1975).

18. "Danger—Zoning," supplement to the Hackensack (N.J.) *Record,* Aug. 3, 1970.

19. The relationship is not a simple one. Dispersed patterns of development encourage greater automobile use, thus adding to the amount of emissions dis-

charged to the atmosphere. On the other hand, because the emissions are released over a larger area, *ambient* air quality may actually be improved relative to more concentrated development. See Frank P. Grad, A. S. Rosenthal, L. R. Rockett, J. A. Fay, J. Heywood, J. F. Kain, G. K. Ingram, D. Harrison, Jr., and T. Tietenberg, *The Automobile and the Regulation of Its Impact on the Environment* (Norman, University of Oklahoma Press, 1975) pp. 191–195.

20. For a compendium of the many ways in which development can affect natural systems, see Dale L. Keyes, *Land Development and the Natural Environment: Estimating Impacts* (Washington, D.C., Urban Institute, 1976).

21. One report showed continuing urbanization of floodplains in Denver and Kansas City, despite considerable recent flood damage. Earth Satellite Corporation, "Land Use Change and Environmental Quality in Urban Areas," report to the U.S. Council on Environmental Quality (April 1973).

22. The 1973 Federal Flood Insurance Act is a sharp break with this policy, requiring local floodplain zoning as a condition for insurance coverage and denying both insurance and disaster relief to new structures built in flood-prone areas.

23. Landscape esthetics in general, with some excellent American illustrations, are discussed in Christopher Tunnard, *A World With A View: An Inquiry into the Nature of Scenic Values* (New Haven, Conn., Yale University Press, 1978).

24. U.S. Federal Power Commission, *National Power Survey, 1970* (Washington, D.C., GPO, 1971) vol. I, p. 14-7.

25. John J. Costonis, *Space Adrift: Saving Urban Landmarks Through the Chicago Plan* (Urbana, University of Illinois Press, 1974) p. 4.

26. The housing cost problem, and some possible solutions, are discussed in U.S. Department of Housing and Urban Development, *Report of the Task Force on Housing Costs* (Washington, D.C., GPO, 1978).

27. *Wall Street Journal,* October 11, 1978.

28. Howard E. Conklin and William G. Lesher, "Farm-Value Assessment as a Means for Reducing Premature and Excessive Agricultural Disinvestment in Urban Fringes," *American Journal of Agricultural Economics* vol. 59, no. 4 (November 1977) pp. 755–759.

29. That there has been a considerable, and rather lengthy, boom in land prices is undeniable. See, for example, Max Ways, "Land: The Boom that Really Hurts," *Fortune* vol. 88, no. 1 (July 1973) pp. 104–109, 168–170; J. Thomas Black, "Land Price Inflation," *Urban Land* vol. 33, no. 8 (September 1974) pp. 28–29; Robert G. Healy and James L. Short, "New Forces in the Market for Rural Land," *Appraisal Journal* vol. 46, no. 2 (April 1978). The role of speculators in fueling that boom and, indeed, the precise role that speculation plays in the land market, is a subject of some dispute. For an enlightening discussion of how speculators operate, see Bruce Lindeman, "The Anatomy of Land Speculation," *Journal of the American Institute of Planners* vol. 42, no. 2 (April 1976) pp. 142–152.

30. Among the many press reports are Hal Rubin, "The Selling of California," *California Journal* (December 1978) pp. 409–411; and Lindley H. Clark, "Speaking of Business," *Wall Street Journal,* February 27, 1979. See also U.S. Department of Agriculture, *Foreign Investment in U.S. Real Estate* (Springfield, Va., National Technical Information Service, 1976) PB 258 073; and Gene L. Wunderlich, *Foreign Ownership of U.S. Real Estate in Perspective* (Washington, D.C., U.S. Department of Agriculture, Economics, Statistics and Cooperatives Service, 1978) ESCS 24.

31. Rutland (Vt.) *Daily Herald,* Oct. 22, 1973.

32. The use of so-called subdivision exactions, in which developers make a payment to the city for permission to develop, is becoming more common, but it is unlikely that the courts would permit them if they exceeded the direct costs of providing the property with public services.

33. "Broward: From Boom to What?" supplement to the *Miami Herald,* May 1974.

34. *Los Angeles Times,* Oct. 21, 1973.

35. For example, Rosenbaum points out that interest in comprehensive state laws regulating large-scale development has been greatest in northeastern states where

large coastal industrial and commercial projects have been proposed and in western states where energy development has been rapid. Nelson Rosenbaum, *Land Use and the Legislatures* (Washington, D.C., Urban Institute, 1976) pp. 46–47.

36. *The New York Times,* March 12, 1979 (coal); *Wall Street Journal,* Nov. 11, 1978 (uranium); *Washington Post,* Feb. 4, 1978 (Tahoe); *The New York Times,* Aug. 9, 1977 (Utah power plants).

37. Bodovitz, "The Coastal Zone: Problems, Priorities and People," address to the Conference on Organizing and Managing the Coastal Zone, Annapolis, Maryland, June 13–14, 1973, p. 5.

38. Calculated from data in U.S. Bureau of the Census, "Projections of the Population of the United States, 1977–2050," *Current Population Reports* P-25, no. 704 (July 1977). Household formation rates have been even further increased during the present decade by increases in the number of the aged and divorced. Impacts of households on the demand for land also depend on incomes and consumer preferences.

39. U.S. Bureau of the Census, *Census of Housing, 1970,* vol. I, pt. 1 (Washington, D.C., GPO, 1972).

40. Ironically, the most visible political manifestation to date has been a "property tax revolt" by those who already own homes but are resisting the higher taxes that result from inflated home prices.

41. Compare, for example, the recent development of Florida's Disney World with that of the earlier (1955) Disneyland in California. In the California case, the success of the amusement park caused huge increases in the value of nearby land, which was not owned by Disney. In planning the Florida park, Disney purchased some 27,000 acres of land surrounding the amusement area.

42. Statement of Sen. Henry Jackson, *Congressional Record,* daily ed., Jan. 9, 1973.

43. U.S. Council on Environmental Quality, *The Good News About Energy* (Washington, D.C., GPO, 1979).

44. For a concise explanation of EPA's regulations governing nondegradation of air quality see National League of Cities, *Environmental Report* (October 1978).

45. Leonard Fischman, for Resources for the Future, 1972, alternative based on Series E population projection. The large increase in land availability in the 1950–60 decade reflects the admission of Alaska and Hawaii to the Union.

46. In particular, if there are opportunities for raising forest productivity through more intensive management, large amounts of land can be freed for other uses, notably recreation or wilderness preservation.

47. A "prescriptive" right or easement is one which is acquired by open and continuous exercise over an extended period of time. This concept or the related doctrine of "customary" use has been successfully used in California to ensure public access to beaches (*Gion* v. *City of Santa Cruz,* 465, P.2d 50, 1970) and in Oregon to enjoin private construction in the areas of dry sand between the vegetation line and the water's edge (State ex rel. *Thornton* v. *Hay,* 254 Or. 584, 595–599, 462 P.2d 671, 676–678, 1969). Even if opening up private land to public use does not create a legally enforceable right, owners may fear that it will create public expectations that may be expressed through future land use controls.

48. We might note that high-density areas include both Harlem and Park Avenue, while people live at low density in the Virginia hunt country and on New Mexico's Indian reservations.

49. See Edwin A. Bock, *The Last Colonialism: Governmental Problems Arising from the Use and Abuse of the Future,* CAG Occasional Papers (Bloomington, Ind., American Society for Public Administration, 1967).

CHAPTER THREE

Vermont—
Eight Years of Experience

VERMONT, ITS ENVIRONMENT largely unspoiled yet subject to intense development pressure, has now had eight years of experience with one of the nation's most comprehensive state land use laws. Only a decade ago the state actively wooed industry and tourism, styling itself "The Beckoning Country." In the late 1960s, having experienced its highest growth rate in one hundred years, Vermont began to have second thoughts about both the quantity and quality of that growth.

This concern led to the passage in 1970 of the Vermont Environmental Control Act (Act 250), which provided for direct district and state control of certain types of development and listed environmental and other criteria that these developments must meet. Act 250 also set in motion a process for additional statewide comprehensive planning. First, in 1972, came an "interim land capability plan." The following year, the legislature both extended and made more explicit the land use controls, and mandated an innovative tax on capital gains from land speculation. In 1974, after tumultuous public hearings, Vermont's legislature refused to pass the final step in the process that Act 250 had set up—a state land use plan setting density guidelines for the development of the entire state. Today, Act 250 is as potent as ever—and the land use plan has not been passed.

Vermont's experience has a dual significance. For one thing, the state now has had more than eight years' experience with a development permit system, set up by the state and administered through regional and state boards. No other state has so long a record of permit-granting experience. Equally important, Vermont's system of land use controls has been an evolving one, subject to legislative scrutiny and to intense public interest and debate. This progression has raised issues of state versus local control, property rights, fiscal and economic impacts, property taxation, and a host of other concerns sure to be debated again and again in other states making serious efforts to control and direct their growth.

Vermont's "Development Crisis"

Like so many land use problems, Vermont's began with transportation. Completion of new highways during the 1960s greatly improved the state's accessibility to the population centers of the northeastern seaboard. The ski areas of southern Vermont became only a 2½-hour drive from Boston and three hours from New York City. A four-season resort, Vermont became increasingly attractive to affluent buyers of second homes. Others came to stay, particularly the young, seeking a return to the soil or simply an unpolluted environment. New job opportunities kept the children of Vermont citizens from moving elsewhere in search of work. The state's population grew more during the 1960s (14.1 percent) than it had during the previous fifty years.

Although this rate of population growth was modest compared with that of such states as California or Florida, the distribution of growth magnified its effect. Particularly striking was the increase in proposed second-home developments in or near some of Vermont's small communities. For example, one vacation-home development, in the southern Vermont township of Wilmington, threatened to add 2,000 condominium units to an existing population of 1,200 people. A survey of Wilmington and the adjoining town of Dover, taken in 1969, found a total of seventy-three developers in business, one for every twenty-five residents.[1] Developments planned for these towns would have increased their summertime populations to ten times the June 1969 level.[2]

The proposed development of vacation homes on 20,000 acres owned by the International Paper Company near Stratton raised the possibility of similar development of other large corporate landholdings in the state. This growth, actual and potential, had several effects. Land prices soared. Farms that in the 1950s had sold for $50 an acre came to command $500 per acre or more. The assessed value of property in the state rose 12 percent in 1968, 16 percent in 1969, and 9 percent in 1970.[3] Lower-income Vermonters found that the only housing they could afford was a mobile home.

The part-time governments that had served small towns adequately in the past threatened to be overwhelmed by the public service demands of the new developments and their residents. Old rural highways that had not been maintained in years had to be improved so that development could proceed along the roadway.[4]

Full-time police protection became necessary to handle the increased crime and traffic. Since some vacation homes become year-round residences, local schools feared (perhaps unreasonably) an influx of new pupils.[5]

Some of the developments threatened to create environmental problems. Much of Vermont is underlain with bedrock covered with only a thin layer of topsoil. In some southern Vermont developments septic tank drainage from mountainside lots had already been leaching into water wells of lots farther below. By the middle of 1969 the state health department issued emergency subdivision regulations to deal with the situation. Erosion, the diversion of streams to create artificial lakes, and traffic congestion were also associated with the large developments.

Vermonters also were concerned about the impact of development on their way of life. Long used to low-density living and a rather stable social structure, they saw huge vacation-home communities as the first step toward making Vermont merely a northern extension of megalopolis. In addition to reducing the quality of life for residents, it was feared that second-home development would impair some of the state's qualities, such as its neat rural landscape and picturesque villages, that attracted tourists. Moreover, there was a question of political control. If even a fraction of the vacation homes became permanent residences, the original residents of the town might soon find themselves with a new political bloc in town meetings and local elections.

By the summer of 1969 most of these impacts were merely threatened. Although the rate of construction of dwelling units had more than doubled since 1965, the annual rate was still less than 2 percent of the standing stock.[6] With scattered exceptions, the large second-home developments were either just being subdivided or were still in the planning stage. A more immediate problem was taxes.

Vermont, although a poor state, supports a high level of public services. Taxes are among the highest in the country. The property tax is the major revenue producer, bringing in five times the revenue of the sales tax and twice that of the personal income tax. As land prices rose, land assessments (then set statewide at 50 percent of fair market value) and taxes increased dramatically. A 1969 reassessment in Wilmington more than doubled the township's tax roll, causing such a public outcry that the harried local assessment board resigned, and the governor was forced to intervene. One example of the type of complaint the assessment board was getting: a landowner complained about an assessment based on a value of $360 an acre while he, the owner, had 40 acres up for sale at $470 an acre. When the land was finally sold it brought an average of $625 an acre.[7]

Assessment at market value came to mean assessment at development value. Farmers, timber producers, and others who sought to use land in traditional ways found themselves bearing tax burdens out of proportion with the current productivity of the land.

There is some question, however, as to whether taxes alone were "forcing" them to sell to subdividers. A 1970 law, allowing taxation at use value provided that development rights were ceded to the state for a period of time, was not used. A 1974 law permitting tax stabilization contracts on farmland has been used only a dozen times.[8] Even in the mid-1970s, when development had continued to exacerbate farmers' tax problems and the operation of Act 250 had made land use controls seem less alien, there was strong resistance to the use of these laws.[9] Towns have been reluctant to lose the tax revenues, while landowners are unwilling to restrict the use of their property.

As the development boom proceeded, local governments were in most cases ill-prepared either to limit the amount of growth within their boundaries or even to control major aspects of its quality. None of the towns had a long-term capital budget; most did not have a zoning ordinance or a legally adopted town plan. The lack of full-time town executives or town planners frequently meant that the developer was far better prepared technically than the town zoning board, if any, that had to approve his proposal. One environmentalist remarked that it was just about impossible to hire a lawyer in southern Vermont who was not on some developer's payroll. In almost every town where there was a development, he said, the first move made by the developer was to put a selectman (councilman)—sometimes more than one—on the payroll.[10]

The State Government's Response

Southern Vermont's development crisis and a high degree of general interest in the environment resulted in a flurry of environmental legislation in the 1970 session of the state legislature. The Vermont Environmental Control Act created state land use controls and has been the basis for the subsequent permit and planning process.[11] The act set up certain state-administered environmental criteria that must be met by all projects beyond a certain size, including subdivisions of more than ten lots, construction of more than ten housing units, and development of commercial or industrial property of more than 1 acre. The act encourages local land use controls by raising the threshold for state review of commercial or industrial developments to 10 acres if the project is inside a town with local zoning and subdivision bylaws. All construction regardless of size at altitudes of more than 2,500 feet is also regulated. Government projects such as highways or public buildings are subject to the same rules as commercial and industrial projects.

The environmental criteria are administered by nine district environmental commissions, with appeal to the state environmental board (or, at the applicant's request, to the county superior court) and then directly to the state supreme court. The members of these boards are appointed by the governor.

Although the permit system was set up and is administered by the state, most decisions are made by the district commissions. These bodies are each composed of three members, usually citizens who hold no other state or local office. Each commission is responsible for passing on developments in an area encompassing about twenty to forty town governments. Five district environmental coordinators, all but one of them covering two district commissions, provide full-time staff assistance to the commissioners. The coordinators work in regional offices throughout the state.[12]

Permit hearings under Act 250 tend to be thorough but informal, emphasizing the settlement of differences by negotiation with the developer.[13] Technically, though, the hearing is an adversary proceeding, with the developer on one side and, on the other (if they make objection) the local selectmen, the local planning commission, state agencies, the regional planning commission, and *adjoining* property owners.[14]

In these proceedings, the state (usually represented by the agency of environmental conservation, an administrative agency distinct from the environmental board) is merely an advocate. According to Schuyler Jackson, former environmental board chairman, "Outside of resource protection, the state has not been an aggressive party to Act 250; it is the other parties—towns, and town and regional planning commissions, and citizen groups and property owners—that have made it work."[15] When state agencies appeared, Jackson added, they lost a number of times before both district commissions and the environmental board. In the recent Hawk and Pyramid cases, the state has assumed a more active role. These were exceptional, precedent-setting cases, however.

In its quasi-judicial capacity, a district commission must find, as a condition of granting a permit to a development, that the proposed project:

1. Will not result in undue water or air pollution
2. Has sufficient water for its reasonably foreseeable needs
3. Will not cause an unreasonable burden on an existing water supply if one is to be utilized
4. Will not cause unreasonable soil erosion or reduction in the capacity of the land to hold water
5. Will not cause unreasonable highway congestion or unsafe conditions
6. Will not place an unreasonable burden on the ability of a municipality to provide educational services
7. Will not place an unreasonable burden on the ability of the local government to provide governmental services
8. Will not have an undue adverse effect on the scenic or natural beauty of the area, esthetics, historic sites, or rare and irreplaceable natural areas
9. Is in conformance with certain statewide plans, which Act 250 required to be prepared
10. Is in conformance with a duly adopted local or regional plan or capital program.[16]

The permit applicant bears the burden of proof in meeting criteria 1 through 4, 9, and 10; opposing parties must prove their case under criteria 5 through 8. A permit may not be denied solely because it does not meet criteria 5, 6, or 7. For example, a district commission may find that a shopping center causes substantial additional traffic congestion, yet it cannot deny a permit on those grounds. The commission may, however, impose certain conditions on a developer under these criteria, such as making the builder of the shopping center install traffic lights or a deceleration lane on the adjoining highway.

Any statutory party to a district commission proceeding can appeal— the applicant, state agencies, and the relevant regional and municipal planning agencies and municipalities. Adjoining property owners, who may be parties to district commission proceedings, may appeal to the environmental board, but they cannot bring an appeal to the Vermont supreme court, a result of litigation that has not provoked a legislative clarification of Act 250 on this point.[17]

In the first four years of development under Act 250, criteria 1 through 8 figured most importantly when the district commissions and the environmental board reviewed applications. The Land/Tech and Haystack cases discussed below, for instance, were decided on the basis of water and sewer problems, traffic congestion, and esthetics.

In more recent cases criteria 9 and 10 have assumed greater importance. The land capability and development plan, passed in 1973 (see page 59), broadened the sweep of Act 250 review, especially in considering the fiscal and economic impacts of development.

The capability and development plan also added new criteria, making it more difficult to develop agricultural soils, forests, and mineral lands in ways that would interfere with these uses.[18] In 1978 the environmental board rejected an applicant's appeal and denied a permit for the subdivision into two-acre lots of 58 acres near Stowe. It was the first time a permit had been denied solely because the subdivision violated the agricultural land criterion. The board noted that the project "has not been planned to minimize the reduction of agricultural potential" by using cluster planning.[19]

Other new criteria involve energy conservation, the provision of public utility services such as electricity, and similar functional issues seemingly involved only in an indirect way with land use and environmental problems. According to the chairman of the environmental board, there was confusion about the applicability of these criteria just after their adoption, but now "it is routine—the commissions expect parties to come in with evidence on them."[20]

A closer examination of the permit process and selected cases indicates how Vermont's land controls work in practice.

Eight Years of Act 250

Statistical Overview

By July 31, 1978, after eight years and one month of Act 250 operations, 3,075 applications for land use permits had been made, roughly five-sixths for development and one-sixth for subdivision. Only ninety-two appeals from the district environmental commissions reached the environmental board; of these, thirty-nine resulted in permits, six were denied permits, and the rest were withdrawn or settled, removed directly to county court, or were pending. Just sixteen cases were appealed to the state supreme court. Of the total applications, only seventy-eight were denied, and about twice that number were withdrawn. The applications represented proposed development with a planned worth of over $800 million.[21]

The small number of permits denied or withdrawn understates the actual effectiveness of the law, since the commissions can attach many conditions to a permit. Virtually all of the permits, in fact, have been granted subject to one or more conditions.[22] For some controversial cases, a dozen or more conditions have been imposed.[23] Applicants have been required to change their method of sewage disposal, to reduce the density of development, to increase their setback from highways, to build culverts and retaining walls for erosion control, and even to change their architecture and the size of their signs.

The Act 250 process also serves as an administrative checkpoint, which makes sure the developer obtains from other state and local agencies required permits for sewage discharge, access to public highways, certification of water supply, and so forth. Although they have independent jurisdiction over many of these matters, in practice the district commissions have accepted the reviews of other agencies as evidence of satisfactory compliance with Act 250 criteria pertaining to the same subject matter.[24] For example, if a subdivider obtains a permit under the state's subdivision (health) regulations, commissions have found that the applicant has satisfied the sewage disposal and water supply requirements of the act. If a subdivision permit has not been obtained previously, an Act 250 permit may be issued on the condition that the applicant obtain one.[25]

State and municipal projects are also subject to Act 250 regulation, provided that they exceed the minimum size specified. Most of these come from the state's forests and parks department and the highway department. An environmental group once charged, in fact, that the highway department had planned to pave a section of forest road in segments, so that none would be long enough to fall under Act 250's acreage criterion.[26] Electric-generating plants and routes for transmission lines are not covered by the permit system, but are regulated by the public service board. The Act 250 process does extend, however, to electric-distribution lines longer than 2,200 feet, and district commissions have received a large number of applications for these.

Literally thousands of acres, particularly in southern Vermont, are exempt from Act 250 because they already had completed plans on file at the time of the law's passage. These projects are also exempt from the health board's subdivision regulations. Many have inadequate roads and sewage disposal. Environmental board administrator Kenneth Senecal points out that "Under Act 250 the burden is you prove it before you do it; in these cases they have to build the development, then the state has to prove it is polluting."[27]

There have been some attempts by developers to evade the provisions of the law on the grounds that their project was too large or too small to be covered. For example, subdivisions with lots exceeding 10 acres are exempt from the regulations. Signs along Vermont roadsides offering "lots—10+ acres" attest to the popularity of this idea.[28] On the other hand, commercial developers are tempted to create projects that are below the act's minimum-size threshold. For example, one landowner who wanted to build a gas station simply carved nine-tenths of an acre out of a larger tract and transferred it to a wholly owned corporation.

Another common arrangement has been for the owner to lease a lot below the statutory minimum to a developer and claim thereafter that he no longer has control over that lot.[29] The environmental board promises "vigorous enforcement" where the act is "willfully" avoided, but its power in these cases is limited.

A review of some of the more significant decisions of the district commissions and appeals to the environmental board shows a growing skill in applying Act 250's criteria and imposing appropriate conditions on developers, a greater attention to legalism, and increasing emphasis on the social and fiscal impacts of developments. The latter reflects in part the increased environmental sophistication of the developers, who now generally think through possible water and sewage problems before submitting their applications, and in part the increased quality of local and regional planning.

The environmental board has at times been more stringent than the district commissions and at times less so. For example, in one of the first cases brought under the act, a district commission required a proposed paper plant to return effluent of class-B quality to a stream that was itself of low C and D quality. The state environmental board eliminated this condition, which set a standard stricter than the state water quality law required.[30] Later that year, however, the environmental board fully backed the denial by another district commission of a permit to build thirty-eight vacation homes on a marsh that a University of Vermont professor described as one of the best natural bogs in the state.[31]

Act 250 and Second Homes

The application of Act 250 to the large second-home developments that it was primarily intended to control is best illustrated by three important permit cases—Land/Tech, Haystack, and Hawk.

LAND/TECH.   Land/Tech is a Massachusetts company that proposed a large recreational and commercial project near Stowe in 1971. Stowe, a central Vermont community of 2,400, is the center of one of the most popular skiing regions in the eastern United States and has come under great development pressure in recent years. Land/Tech's development was planned to include 167 condominium units, a 100-unit motel, gas station, shopping center, and large parking facilities. The $9 million development would be built on a 50-acre plot along the road connecting Stowe with the major ski area.

Although the developer applied to the district commission only for permission to build a portion of the condominium units, an environmental board ruling required that the commission consider the impact of the planned project as a whole. In testimony before the district commission, the project was vigorously opposed by the Stowe Planning Commission, the town's board of selectmen, and adjoining landowners.[32] They claimed, for example, that during peak winter ski periods traffic was already bumper-to-bumper from Stowe village past the area of the proposed development.

The town also claimed that the development would burden town services, although the developer said that his project, when completed, would generate roughly $150,000 in taxes annually. In exchange, he said, the development would only require town police and fire protection and disposal of garbage.[33]

Adjoining landowners, a hotel owner and a golf course operator, were particularly concerned about possible sewage drainage from Land/Tech's homes into their drinking water wells. All parties condemned the esthetics of the project, which they claimed would ruin their view of the surrounding mountains and would change the rural character of the landscape.

In February 1972 the district commission issued a permit, subject to having approval over signs and limiting the number of highway access points. The Stowe selectmen and planning commission appealed the decision to the environmental board, which overruled the district commission and denied the permit in February 1973. Crucial to this denial was its finding that the developer had failed to prove that the development would not result in undue water pollution. Test borings found the ground-water level was as high as 2 to 3 feet below the surface. The project would have generated 95,000 gallons of sewage daily, which would drain into the ground within 165 feet of another property's well.

The board also found, after viewing extensive traffic studies by the developer and by the town, that the project would cause excessive traffic congestion. This condition alone would not be cause for denial, however. The board failed to agree with the town that the project would place an unreasonable burden on municipal services, even though it would generate sixty-nine truckloads of garbage yearly, and would require the town to hire two more police officers, purchase two police cruisers, hire more waste disposal personnel, and rent another trash compacter.

The board also determined that the proposed development failed to meet criterion 8, the esthetic standard. Here, the board found that "Outside [Stowe] Village proper, the development of the Town of Stowe has been characterized by low density—The Land/Tech Corp. proposal is essentially different from the type of commercial and residential development that Stowe has experienced. . . ." The board asserted that this creation of a new high-density area outside the town center would have an undue adverse effect on the scenic and natural beauty of the area.

The record of the district commission proceedings and subsequent appeals runs to 1,300 pages. Testimony became so detailed that at one point Land/Tech's representative even specified the minimum and maximum height of the crabapple trees it would plant to screen the project from the adjoining golf course. The developer complained bitterly about the delay, which amounted to more than two years since the original application. In a letter to the environmental board he stated, "I simply cannot believe that the Vermont Legislature intended, by enacting the Environmental Act, that a developer would have to endure protracted hearings and expense in the tens of thousands, many times over, in order to obtain what should be merely conceptual approval to build in accordance with applicable law."

Land/Tech appealed the environmental board's decision to the state courts and simultaneously reapplied to the district commission for permission to build a drastically scaled-down version of its project. After a quiet period during the recession in 1974, Land/Tech began active negotiations with Vermont's environmental agency over its sewage disposal system.[34] The company ultimately won support for a project including ninety-six condominium units, tennis courts, a swimming pool, and a clubhouse. The motel, gas station, and commercial facilities were dropped from its plan, reducing the traffic burden and easing esthetic concerns. Noting that the 10 acres of Land/Tech's land bordering the major road would remain undeveloped, the district commission granted the company its land use permit in July 1978.[35]

HAYSTACK. Haystack is a Wilmington development that figured prominently in the 1969 "crisis" in southern Vermont. Shortly after Act 250's passage, the developer applied for a permit to subdivide 2,004 lots, to build 1,095 condominium units, and to construct a 700-unit hotel.[36] Several hundred lots had already been sold at the time of application, and the developer claimed that he was applying for an Act 250 permit, even though he believed his project, having been already begun, was exempt. The entire development had been designed before the passage of the law, a fact that would cause the developer considerable problems.

Haystack received one of the very first permits issued under Act 250. The firm was allowed to proceed with development, subject to some strict restrictions on sewage disposal, erosion control, water supply, and fire protection. After the permit was issued, a protracted controversy arose between the town of Wilmington and the developer over whether the conditions had been met. For example, in October 1972, the town manager wrote to the environmental board asking that Haystack's permit be revoked, claiming that the developer had broken off negotiations with the town for a joint tertiary sewage treatment plant, had not yet certified that the drinking water supply was sufficient, had abused surface streams, and had caused widespread erosion.

In the middle of 1972 the state water resources department informed Haystack that the state's policy was to avoid dumping even treated effluent into watercourses and that the state would limit effluent from all sources disposed in the Deerfield River to 500,000 gallons per day. The town of Wilmington claimed this entire allocation, even though it was far greater than the town's current needs. Haystack, which had been building its own sewage plant, was forced to propose a land-spray disposal system for its sewage. In the light of this limitation and the town's complaints about improper sewage disposal, the environmental board sharply limited the number of lots that could be built on in the development. Lot buyers found themselves with homesites which they were legally prevented from using, and Haystack's own land sales and construction program ran into difficulties.

Developments of this kind, often thinly capitalized, rely on the revenue from land sales to generate funds for land improvement and infrastructure. Lacking this volume of new business, the Haystack Corporation collapsed. Its major financial backer, Associated Mortgage Investors, Inc. (AMI), of Coral Gables, Florida, filed for bankruptcy protection and, in September 1974, filed a foreclosure suit against Haystack. Wilmington sued for $134,000 in back taxes, and the future for Haystack's few residents seemed bleak. In 1975, when 2,200 units of housing were to have been completed, 1,300 lots had sold but only 71 houses had been built and occupied.[37] The chairmen of the district environmental commission and the state environmental board told a reporter that they would never issue a similar permit today.[38] In the fall of 1978, after complicated disputes over land titles and financial responsibilities, AMI notified the district environmental commission that it was pressing its foreclosure motion on the two-thirds of Haystack's land and premises under its control, and that it would ask to have the permits transferred to itself or to the ultimate purchaser of the foreclosed property.[39] If the legal problems are resolved and the market for Vermont land recovers strongly, it is possible that several years hence some sort of Haystack community will be completed.

HAWK.   Since 1962 Robert C. Williams has been bringing the splendors of Vermont to purchasers of second homes. His Hawk Mountain Corporation, working in the White and Tweed river valleys, has slowly built 120 free-standing $100,000 homes on private hillside lots in Pittsfield, Rochester, and Stockbridge along Vermont Route 100. By carefully controlling the design, financing, and development of each Hawk community, and reaching affluent audiences through advertisements in *The New Yorker* and elsewhere, Williams took his company through the mid-1970s recession without the financial stress that wrecked Haystack.

But the fourth Hawk development proposal, in Pittsfield, encountered severe difficulties in meeting Act 250's original environmental criteria, and the newer standards embodied in the land capability and development plan. In January 1977 Hawk applied for a land use permit to develop 262 lots on a 585-acre parcel. The land is steep—85 percent of the slopes exceed 25 percent. The property borders both the Green Mountain National Forest and the White River, in which the federal government is trying to reestablish Atlantic salmon breeding grounds.

Hawk's application launched a two-year review process, complete with twenty-one hearing sessions and dozens of exhibits. The company's sewage plans, negotiated with the state environmental agency, were revised several times. Concern about erosion at the site—a serious problem if the White River's quality is to be maintained—produced a series of increasingly detailed, elaborate control measures. Hawk's developer even proposed to spread a cloth filter material over road cuts and fills in order to control runoff from exposed soil until plant cover rooted.

The Pittsfield (population, 300) town government opposed the project, even though fiscal studies prepared by the state planning office showed new tax revenues would exceed additional expenditures. Pittsfield residents, alarmed by the prospect of an eventual population of prosperous newcomers overwhelming and perhaps outvoting them, resisted the developer's argument that development was inevitable and economically necessary.

During the course of the hearings, several technical issues were resolved. A small utility that would serve part of the proposed Hawk community protested that it would be forced to purchase costly peak-hour electricity to do so. To ease the burden, Hawk offered to write covenants prohibiting electric heat and hot-water heaters in that part of the subdivision. Hawk also redesigned its project to reduce its impact on an adjacent deer-wintering area, and agreed to write deed covenants requiring residents to leash their dogs.

But when the district commission ruled on November 16, 1978, it found that Hawk had failed many of Act 250's environmental tests. The commissioners repeatedly found "the location of the proposed subdivision is critical," particularly because the steep, rocky site, with little soil, posed severe problems of water runoff, waste disposal, and erosion.

The commission also ruled against Hawk on esthetic grounds—much of the project would be visible from the scenic state highway when the hardwood trees in the area shed their leaves—and also because of the threat to the salmon habitat. In ruling on habitat and the use of the site for forestry, the commission noted that "The applicant owns other tracts of land in the area that would be reasonably suited" for subdivision, but that did not jeopardize aquatic or soil resources.

Hawk also failed a public facilities test—it was unwilling to pay for required road improvements that neither the town nor the state intended to undertake—and violated the regional plan for the area, which designated the site, by performance criteria, for primarily low-intensity or natural-resource uses.[40]

After a year of controversy, just half way through the district commission's review of the Hawk project, a reporter wrote, "Williams is bitter about it all. Act 250 is forcing everyone to build in a conventional way, he says. You have to answer all their questions at the outset, which means that you cannot devise innovative solutions to problems that arise midway through a project. Moreover, he says that there are almost hopelessly difficult bureaucratic problems."[41] Apparently impressed by the seriousness of these obstacles, Hawk did not appeal the rejection of its permit application. If it intends to develop the site in the future, the company will have to redesign its plans—and begin the Act 250 review process all over again.

EFFECT OF ACT 250.   Both the Land/Tech and the Haystack developments were planned luxury developments, far more expensive than many second-home developments built elsewhere in the country. Nevertheless, it is undeniable that each would have had some environmental impact and would be very large in relation to an existing town. In one case, development was completely prevented until the project was dramatically redesigned, and in another it was slowed drastically. In these and similar cases, Act 250 seems to have been quite successful in limiting the proliferation of huge second-home developments that had helped spur the act's passage. The review of Hawk, involving a developer and a project superior to Land/Tech and Haystack in quality and anticipation of problems, demonstrates that Act 250 will require even greater consideration for the natural and human setting of second-home communities.

Some Gaps in the Law

Act 250 is not so effective in restraining commercial strip development along highways, another worrisome problem in Vermont. The 10-acre minimum size for Act 250 review of commercial or industrial projects exempts most motels and gas stations on the approaches to towns. Even where the act can be applied, commercial establishments tend to find it easier than second-home developments to conform to the environmental protection provisions. For example, two shopping centers were approved along the highway outside Brattleboro (population, 13,000), even though the regional planning commission felt that such centers would depress economic activity in the downtown business district. The district commission did impose restrictions on architecture, setback, and signs that significantly improved the appearance of the development, but these conditions do not change the centers' impact on the physical form of the town.

Two shopping centers located across the street from one another on the outskirts of Rutland (population, 19,000) were also granted Act 250 permits. Here, too, the commission found it relatively easy to prevent the erection of objectionable signs and to limit soil erosion from parking lot runoff but could not come to grips with the problem of growth itself.

In 1978, however, the nationally publicized Pyramid Mall case suggested that Act 250 could apply to these larger issues as well.[42] At stake is the continued viability of a concentrated town center when challenged by sprawling commercial development outside the municipal limits, a battle being joined in many other states.

On July 20, 1977, the Pyramid Companies, a New York-based shopping center developer, applied for a permit to build a retail mall with nearly a half million square feet of space, Vermont's largest and only regional shopping center. It was to house eighty-two stores and twenty restaurants at a 97-acre site. The land, now a hayfield, is at an interstate highway interchange in the rural town of Williston, 6 miles from Burlington, Vermont's largest city (population, 38,000). The district commission's denial of a permit, on October 12, 1978, was easily the most controversial decision yet made under Act 250's authority.

In considering the $20 million project's application, the district commission held two prehearing conferences with the interested parties, and forty-three public hearing sessions over more than a year. The major environmental issues concerned air pollution and runoff from the large parking lot, for which Pyramid then designed an expensive on-site secondary treatment and disposal system.

Other issues arose for the commission under criteria 5 through 7. Pyramid maintained that it was responsible only for traffic congestion in the immediate vicinity. The district commission disagreed, holding the mall responsible for highway congestion on highways leading to it. On the fiscal side it was estimated that the mall would attract so few new families to the area that additional demands on Williston's school system would be minimal. But for Burlington the erosion of the tax base caused by the migration of retailing from downtown to the mall would so reduce revenues—by a half million dollars yearly—as to "place an unreasonable burden on the ability of the City of Burlington to provide municipal and governmental services,"[43] a violation of Act 250's criterion 7.

The legal basis for rejecting the mall, however, derived from the capability and development criteria on the costs of scattered development and public facilities (highways), and from the violation of relevant plans for the land. The commission found that the development "is not physically contiguous to an existing settlement" and that the additional costs for public services and facilities "outweigh any tax revenue and other public benefits of the development."[44] In reaching this important conclusion, the commission explained that in adopting the 1973 capability and development criteria "the General Assembly determined that scattered developments must pass a stricter test than those which merely expand existing settlements."[45] Pyramid failed the test because the mall could not "pay its own way either by generating tax revenue to pay for the extra cost of public facilities or alternatively by providing public benefits, such as increased employment opportunities."[46]

The commission also broke new ground in its review of the town and county plans for the area. It ruled that the mall violated the Williston town plan, despite three votes by the town planning commission finding the mall in conformance. It also ruled that the mall violated the Chittenden County plan, which designated the site for industrial use.

Pyramid appealed to the environmental board on November 8, 1978, and exercised its right to have its appeal heard before the county superior court. Since the hearing is *de novo,* the commission's precedent-setting rulings will be reargued, and will likely wind up in the Vermont supreme court. The ultimate outcome of these deliberations will determine whether Act 250 can govern such development.

Meanwhile, the case has had other significant effects. Its duration and sophistication put the district commission to an extreme test. To present crucial fiscal arguments, the state planning office commissioned Thomas Muller, of the Urban Institute in Washington, D.C., to make a study of the mall's effects on the state. Hammer Siler George Associates, also of Washington, prepared an analysis at the regional and county level for the Chittenden County Regional Planning Commission, and Rutgers' George Sternlieb prepared a city impact study under contract to Burlington. The case represented the state-of-the-art nationwide in assessment of the impacts of growth.

The case also caused some concern about the ability of citizen commissioners, working part-time, to handle such long-lasting, demanding controversies. The Vermont Natural Resources Council was not alone in noting that "The burden was particularly acute on the three-member District Environmental Commission."[47]

Appraisal

The consensus among state officials and other observers is that so far Act 250 has done little to reduce the absolute amount of growth in Vermont but has significantly improved the quality of development. The effect on the amount of growth is debatable, since there is no way of knowing how growth would have proceeded in the absence of the law. Several planned developments have not taken place, but unrealized plans have always been characteristic of the development industry.[48] The law may have discouraged some developers; and in cases such as Land/Tech, project sizes were cut.

We do know that in the first year under Act 250 (1970) there was a noticeable drop in construction from the growth trend of earlier years. The act coincided, however, with a general economic recession and the administration of the state health department's subdivision regulations, making it impossible to attribute the drop to Act 250 alone. By 1971 residential construction activity again rose, with a particularly sharp increase recorded in 1972, and another, smaller one in 1973.[49] The pace of building in the years since has varied with the condition of the national economy; experience in New Hampshire, Vermont's neighbor state, has followed Vermont's pattern closely.[50]

Act 250 has almost certainly raised the cost of building vacation homes in Vermont, partly by imposing delays and uncertainties, but mainly by imposing stringent environmental standards. For example, large developments in places with thin, rocky soils may be forced to build expensive tertiary sewage treatment plants. High costs of site preparation mean that expensive units, some costing $100,000 or more, are built on the land. In practice, district commissions have required so much information from developers that they have had to markedly improve the quality of their site plans. For example, for one large recreational–residential complex it was estimated that it cost at least $100,000 to do the groundwork leading up to the formal presentation of fact at the district commission hearing. For that hearing, the applicant had to have pinpointed building lots, roads and their grades, water supply lines, types of structures and their designs, sewage systems and water system details, financing arrangements, and even the legal setup of a homeowners' association, if there was to be one.[51] The environmental board later adopted a rule to ease the burden on developers facing such massive costs before beginning the Act 250 review process. Developers may ask to have hearings held on the criteria in "such sequence as the applicant finds most expedient and practicable." In essence, the board invites developers of controversial projects to see whether they comply with criteria 9 and 10 before going on to prepare detailed, expensive specifications for road grades, sewage treatment systems, and so forth. In the opinion of environmental board staff, "More developers should take advantage of the procedure."[52]

One of the goals of Act 250 was to encourage local governments to enact zoning ordinances and adopt town plans. Criterion 10 specifically requires that a proposed development be consistent with a duly adopted town or regional plan. Stowe town officials, for example, might have defeated Land/Tech at the district commission had they adopted a local or regional plan. They had not.

Since 1970, there has been a noticeable increase in plan adoption in some areas. As of November 1977 there were plans adopted in 220 of Vermont's 311 cities, towns, and incorporated villages. (There were also 181 permanent zoning ordinances and 69 municipal subdivision regulations, also a notable increase.)[53] Whether these plans are effective depends upon their contents. The Brattleboro shopping centers, despite the opposition of the regional planning commission, were actually in conformance with the commission's own land use plan.

Successful passage through the Act 250 permit process, of course, does not exempt a developer from existing local controls. For example, a proposal for a 198-unit apartment complex in Shelburne was approved by the district commission but successfully opposed by the local planning commission and selectmen.[54]

The environmental board has responded administratively to some problems, not fully resolved in the law, of both small and large developers. To allow the district commissions to focus attention on the most important proposals, the district coordinator may ask the commission to certify that a small project has no significant impact under the ten criteria, and may then issue a permit. The procedure is used frequently, particularly in the busiest regions where the district commissions face the heaviest workload.

At the other extreme, the largest projects are screened by interested state agencies to uncover possible problems or the need for permits, through the Act 250 Interagency Review Committee. This group formed informally in 1971 and was recognized by a directive of Gov. Deane C. Davis in 1972. The group is important because there is substantial overlap, never resolved legislatively, between "the generally more inclusive Act 250 criteria and the more specific standards and guidelines applicable to the programs of the various agencies."[55] Though the committee has served as a clearinghouse, there is some disappointment with it because participating agencies act upon their own legal mandates and seem uninterested in formulating broad, interagency positions on issues that spill over jurisdictional lines. While the meetings help to identify unresolved environmental problems in the early stages of project applications, a

mechanism for combining or better coordinating overlapping requirements awaits further legislation.

Capability and Development Plan (1973)

Although Act 250 provided strong immediate regulatory powers, it
also called for the environmental board to draw up a series of three
plans, which would then be approved by the governor and the state
legislature. Once adopted, these plans would have the force of law. The
first of these, the Interim Land Capability Plan, adopted in 1972, was little
more than a statement of general policies and a series of maps showing
which areas of the state had physical limitations to development, were
unique or fragile, or were especially suited to agricultural or forest use.
Act 250 required that subsequent plans be consistent with the interim
plan and neither the environmental board nor the legislature then was
ready to make any irrevocable planning decisions.

The second, the Land Capability and Development Plan, had considerably more content. It was proposed by the environmental board in
1972, extensively revised, and approved by the legislature in 1973 as a
set of general policy statements and additions to Act 250.[56] We will
discuss the provisions of this capability and development plan in some
detail, then discuss the third, or land use, plan.

The heart of the capability and development plan, as finally adopted,
is a series of amendments to the original Act 250 criteria. Several of these
clarify the act's environmental criteria (see page 45).[57] For example, a
project would be found to contribute to undue water pollution if it pollutes
the watershed of a public water supply or an aquifer-recharge area. This
interpretation is consistent with what had always been the commissions'
actual practice. The new amendments merely spell out the requirements
so that both developers and commissioners know what is expected of
them.

The capability plan goes beyond such clarifications; it also greatly
strengthens the planning power of local communities by forbidding the
state to either grant or deny a permit if its action would be inconsistent
with a local plan or capital budget, *unless* the proposed development will
have a substantial impact on surrounding towns or involves an overriding
state interest. Thus the state cannot stop towns that want to do so from
specifically planning for major growth, so long as the effects of development are confined within the borders of the town.[58]

What is potentially the most important section of the capability and development plan requires the commission to consider the impact of a proposed development on the ability of a town or region to provide public services. Under the original Act 250, a commission could place conditions on a developer that would mitigate this financial burden, but could not deny a permit for that reason alone. Under the new amendment, if the town has adopted a capital improvement program, the burden of proof that public facilities are adequate falls on the developer.

This provision gives towns the ability to directly control the amount and rate of their growth by timing the construction of public facilities.[59] As one environmental group put it, "The plan gives local government a tool for protecting itself from bankruptcy, if it cares to use it."[60]

In practice, not many of Vermont's small cities and towns have been able to make use of these powers. For an extraordinary case, such as the confrontation in Burlington over the Pyramid Mall, the local government may assemble or pay for detailed expert advice on the fiscal impacts of development. But most of the local governments are simply too small and have too few resources to make the effort.[61] In fact, the chairman of the environmental board thinks that even though many more communities have zoning than did before Act 250, some are not adopting zoning and subdivision controls or plans because they prefer to rely on the Act 250 review process instead.[62]

The capability and development plan did not become law without considerable public discussion and controversy. Public interest was stimulated by a Ford Foundation-financed project in which a copy of the proposed plan was mailed to each of the state's 150,000 households in advance of a series of hearings attended by 3,000 people. The plan went through more than twenty drafts as it was modified by both the hearings and by the state legislature. A group of property owners, organized in the largely rural northeastern part of the state, but ultimately reaching into ten of Vermont's fourteen counties, spent several thousand dollars on a series of ten radio advertisements against the plan; for example:

"The bureaucrats in Montpelier are trying to push through a capability and development plan. It would virtually destroy the rights of free men that Ethan Allen fought for. . . ."

"It will keep light industry out of a whole lot of Vermont . . . its real goal is to give the bureaucrats complete control over all rural land in Vermont."[63]

The issue was considerably confused by the inclusion of a proposed state zoning map with the draft of the capability and development plan that was mailed throughout the state. This map, part of the third, or land use plan, was both vague and, through a printer's error, almost illegible. The map was soon discarded, and the environmental board decided to put off its consideration until the 1974 session of the legislature. Despite the controversy surrounding it, the capability and development plan passed the legislature by a comfortable margin in April 1973.

The Vermont Land Use Plan

The Act 250 criteria and the capability plan are regulatory rather than indicative. The developer must set out in detail what he is going to do, and the district commission reacts to his plans. The third plan mandated by Act 250, the land use plan, was intended to indicate to the developer where growth would be encouraged and where it would be limited. Act 250 specifies that this plan would "determine in broad categories the proper use of the lands in the state whether for forestry, recreation, agriculture or urban purposes, the plans to be further implemented at the local level by authorized land use controls such as subdivision controls and zoning."[64]

The land use plan was inherently more controversial than the Act 250 permit procedure. By 1974, when it first came before the legislature, there had been about 1,700 permit applications under Act 250; the land use plan would classify, at least in a rough way, tens of thousands of parcels. Landowners who had only the vaguest thoughts of developing their land would suddenly take a strong interest in the uses that the plan permitted them. As an influential state senator put it, "When you're talking about regulation, you're talking about regulating the big, bad outside developer; when you talk about a plan, you're affecting all of the land in Vermont."[65] Moreover, the land use plan could cause substantial changes in property tax assessments (this will be discussed in detail below).

Vermont's land use planners worked feverishly during the summer and fall of 1973 trying to put together a land use plan in time for the 1974 meeting of the state legislature.[66] Act 250 gave them little guidance as to what the plan was to contain. The act requires that the plan "shall consist of a map and statements of present and prospective land uses . . . which determine *in broad categories* the proper use of the lands in the state" (emphasis added). Thus it was ambiguous whether the plan must be sufficiently detailed to show a use for each parcel of land in the state. It was equally uncertain whether the uses which were mapped would have the legal force of a zoning map.

After lands had been categorized, Act 250 provided that the boundaries could be changed only by petition to the environmental board and after a public hearing. This cumbersome process would make it very difficult to implement a plan based on mapping individual parcels.

Another important issue confronting the planners was the relation of the land use plan to local zoning. There is great support in Vermont for the principle of local control, yet much of the land has been neither locally zoned nor planned. Some means had to be found to force towns to plan and zone if the state was not to do it by default.

The land use plan also involved decisions about whether to emphasize tourism or second-home development. Arthur Ristau (then state planning director) claimed, "Vacation homes and tourism are on a collision course in Vermont," adding, "I think tourism has more to offer on an economic basis in the long run."[67] Underlying this view is a concern that vacation homes may become permanent residences, placing a severe service burden on Vermont's small communities.

After going through a number of drafts, the first "official" version of the land use plan was approved by Gov. Thomas Salmon and sent to the legislature in January 1974. The plan called for most of Vermont's growth to take place in existing cities, towns, and villages, at densities similar to those already prevailing there. When growth was planned for rural areas, it should take the form of cluster subdivisions or new communities. Vacation homes, said the plan, should also be clustered and subject to the same restrictions as permanent residences. Lands suited for agriculture, forestry, or mineral extraction, or lands with scenic or recreational potential should be put to uses that maximize this potential.

These principles were to be implemented by classifying all of Vermont's land as "urban," "village," "rural," "natural resource," "conservation," "shoreline," or "roadside." Within urban and village areas, growth could be accommodated at high densities, but rural lands would generally be developed with one building on 5 acres or more, natural resource areas with one building on 25 acres or more, and conservation lands with one building on 100 acres or more. Along shorelines and roadsides very large lots (200- and 400-foot frontage, respectively) would usually be required.

Local governments were to have a year to draw up plans for the development of the land within their borders. Conservation areas would be mapped by the state and subject to the state's density limits, but townships would have some leeway both in designating the boundaries of the other areas and in violating the density guidelines. The local plans would have to be approved by the secretary of development and community affairs, who would consider the comments of adjoining towns, regional bodies, and state agencies, and then determine whether the proposed local plan would "further the purposes and provisions of the state land use plan." Any party dissatisfied with the secretary's decision could appeal it to the environmental board and to the courts. But, in the end, if a town failed to prepare an acceptable plan, the state could step in with its own enforceable plan.

The proposed law was complex and not easily understood by the public. But its general outlines were clear. The state would map and control all development in conservation areas, mainly sparsely populated mountain and forestlands covering about a third of the state.[68] For the rest of Vermont, local governments would have to come up with plans generally acceptable to the state—or the state would do the job itself.

The proposed land use plan was sent to the legislature on January 8, 1974, where it was taken up by the house natural resources committee. The committee immediately began working with an attorney to turn the proposal, which was in narrative form, into the legal language of a bill. The land use map, a preliminary attempt by the state planning office to assign all of Vermont's lands to a particular category, was not to be available for another month.

The winter of 1974 was a time of great uncertainty in Vermont. The energy crisis, then at its height, not only squeezed local supplies of gasoline and heating oil, but also choked off the usual midwinter flow of skiers from outside the state. The woes of the recreation industry were made even worse by unusually light snowfall—the third straight year of poor skiing conditions. Its market depleted by high interest rates, the construction industry was also in a slump. These concerns did not mean that Vermonters had lost interest in protecting their environment, but they did cause them to take a new interest in the confused condition of the state's economy.

Early 1974 also found Vermont legislators concerned about the concentration of power in the state's overall environmental agency. Although the lawmakers refused to pass a measure repealing the state's controversial ban on no-deposit beverage containers and actually strengthened Act 250, they sent state shoreline and floodplain zoning bills to an early death. A newspaper described the bills as "victims of what boils down to more an anti-bureaucratic sentiment than a disregard for the environment."[69]

In addition to the state's general climate of uncertainty, the proposed land use plan faced two specific obstacles—an almost universal confusion as to its exact provisions and a new surge of interest in local control.[70] Local governments, which in the days just before Act 250's passage had "literally howled for help" from the state,[71] had become more planning-minded in the intervening four years. Local selectmen and planning commissioners now demanded the chance to make their own plans, unencumbered by the strict guidelines proposed by the state. As one man described a version of the plan, "While this plan has been ballyhooed by Montpelier as giving local control to towns under state guidelines, it in fact and deed takes planning decisions completely away from the towns and gives it to the bureaucrats in Montpelier. The towns can only recommend. Montpelier will decide."[72] The speaker of the house said the plan had been concocted "in the stratosphere of the elite."[73]

When the land-classification maps finally appeared, Vermonters learned more about what kind of future the planners were suggesting for the state. More than half of the state's land area was to be placed in the "natural resource" classification with suggested densities of one unit per 25 acres. Another third would be "conservation" lands, with one unit per 100 acres. Nearly all of the state's growth would occur on about 20 percent of the land area, with by far the largest amount being within towns and villages. Planners pointed out that, even under these density ceilings, Vermont could accommodate an additional 1.7 million people, more than two and a half times its current population and far more than any foreseeable population projection.[74]

The Fate of the Plan

In putting the proposed plan into legal language, the house committee weakened it considerably. Even in weakened form, it met considerable public opposition when the committee held its public hearing. According to Governor Salmon, "The plan was denounced as a Communist plot, a socialist plot, the work of 'traitorous whoremasters,' and the cause of nearly all Vermont's development and economic ills. It was blamed on New Jerseyites, this governor, former Gov. Deane Davis, the devil, state bureaucrats, planners and a bevy of architects. Law and order during the hearing were maintained by the narrowest of margins."[75]

Particular objection was made to the density limits in rural and natural resource areas. As one landowner claimed, "To put it succinctly, neither we nor countless others presently not farming the land are going to the expense of keeping it neat and cleared if its potential market value is jeopardized or destroyed. The sole reason we keep our land cleared is because we may one day wish to sell it." Of the plan's goal of concentrating new development in existing towns and villages, he said, "[As rural dwellers] we would not forsake view, privacy, or quiet for the racket all night in a village. That is precisely why we moved out."[76]

The opposition brought out by the hearing proved to be a fatal blow. By general consensus, the house committee agreed that a land use plan should not be legislated in 1974.

Governor Salmon later acknowledged the role that confusion and lack of public involvement had played in defeating the 1974 plan.[77]

The climate for passage did not improve in the next session. The soft market for second-home developments persisted and deepened, lasting, in fact, until the spring of 1977; and the 1975 version of the land use plan had a similar fate. It was replaced in legislative committee with a version that emphasized local control and removed the state's power to prepare plans for local governments that failed to do so themselves. But eventually even this version was killed by a unanimous (11–0) committee vote. In 1976 the Vermont house first defeated and then narrowly passed a watered-down version of the land use plan, but it was killed in the senate agriculture committee.[78] Since then, Governor Salmon has left office, and it has become accepted that a state land use plan is politically dead.

The failure of the land use plan does not necessarily mean that the state has turned against planning or even against state control. Polls taken during the 1974 legislative term showed that some 60 percent of those questioned favored a statewide regulatory land use plan.[79] Moreover, Act 250 emerged from the 1974 legislature unscathed and, in fact, somewhat strengthened.[80]

Currently, attention is focusing on ways to give some forecasting power to the regulatory Act 250 process by bringing better local and regional planning into permit hearings, as called for by Act 250's criterion 10 and the capability and development plan. Officials from the state planning office have been meeting regularly with the thirteen regional planning commissions to improve their work.[81] In August 1978, Gov. Richard A. Snelling established a Conference on State–Local Intergovernmental Relations to consider problems such as the "need to improve local government services provided by state agencies and the capability of regional planning and development commissions to respond to local needs." The conference will recommend means to improve the technical and management assistance available to local officials.[82] By such measures, the state planning office hopes to enable local governments to participate in Act 250 proceedings more knowledgeably. Such steps are not a substitute for the land use plan envisioned in Act 250, but they are evidence that the state continues to be interested in finding politically acceptable means of augmenting public control over development and change of Vermont's land.

Innovations in Tax Policy

Land Policy and Tax Policy

Land use policy seems almost inevitably to involve issues of tax policy. Even as the land use plan was dying in the house natural resources committee in 1974, the chairman of the ways and means committee was proposing to hold hearings on the plan's implications for the property tax.

In Vermont, land, at least theoretically, is taxed on the basis of its current fair market value, regardless of its current use.[83] We have noted that the dramatic rise in the price of undeveloped land in the last decade has doubled or even quadrupled the tax bills on many of Vermont's farms and woodlands. Farmers and forest operators claimed that they could not pay these taxes from their current operating income and were being forced to sell their land to subdividers.

One northern Vermont newspaper editorialized that:

> The value of undeveloped land in [the town of] Waterbury had risen by 300 percent while the value of all property, including buildings, had increased, on the average, by only 86 percent. Translated into the arithmetic of the tax bill, this means a calamitous shifting of the tax burden from buildings onto the very land which everyone in Vermont seems to believe should be preserved these days.
>
> The specifics of the story are enough to make an environmentalist weep: the taxes on commercial sprawl and trailers will probably decline; the local fish and game club is considering selling its 30 acres because taxes have doubled in one blow to over $700; other large landowners are under the same pressure and one selectman has sarcastically remarked that they should pay a visit to the local realtor soon.[84]

Vermont policymakers have been wrestling since 1968 with ways to relieve the property tax burden on farms and timberlands, land uses which not only improve the attractiveness of the landscape, but are associated with a highly prized way of life.

The simplest proposal was to tax land at its value in its present use, regardless of how much it could be sold for to a developer. Although this would reduce the taxes of the farmer and the forester, it would aid the land speculator even more, for much speculative land is being held idle and has very little current use value. To prevent this abuse, a number of states have established contracts with landowners by which tax concessions are granted provided that land is farmed for a specified number of years. But these contracts are frequently abused, too, since besides appealing to "legitimate" farmers, they also subsidize speculators who hold land not yet ripe for development. These landowners simply become contract farmers until they are ready to develop.

The legislature reached some agreement on necessary tax measures in 1973, when it adopted property tax credits and an innovative capital gains tax on land sales (see below). And debate over what further measures to take was broadened by the state planning office and the governor. A report by the state planning office on the future of farming in Vermont proposed that land be taxed at use value, except for commercial and industrial property and vacation property owned by nonresidents. The revenue loss would be offset by a capital gains tax on unimproved property and on vacation homes.[85]

The report recognized that reducing property taxes benefits current farmers but does not deal with the high cost of land to new farmers or farmers who are expanding their operations. Thus the report suggested that in addition to the tax plan, the state purchase the development rights to tracts of prime farmland, creating a new class of land whose value would be set by its agricultural value rather than its development value. New farmers could much more easily afford this "ex-rights" land. The 1978 legislature did not adopt a proposal along these lines "to facilitate the granting of conservation easements and the conveyance of development rights," but may reconsider it in the future.[86]

As we have mentioned, property taxes are intimately connected with the land use plan. If a state zoning map were to classify a parcel of land for agricultural or conservation use, its tax burden should drop accordingly. If the new restrictions on the parcel were reflected in a drop in its value, the current system of taxation at market value would produce a corresponding reduction in tax burden. On the other hand, landowners might believe that the classifications could be changed if there were sufficient pressure to develop, much as in the case of current municipal zoning. Then market value would continue to be above agricultural or timber value, and taxes would be higher than those under a use value system.

Strict state zoning might also severely reduce the tax rolls of some Vermont towns, which have swelled as the price of undeveloped land has risen. The land use plan might therefore have to provide for compensatory payments by the state to towns where the land reclassification was especially great.[87]

These issues have been mooted by the failure of the state to adopt the land use plan. Given the unpopularity of state zoning, there is little likelihood that property values would be depressed below their market value in this way. But even in the absence of the land use plan, other property tax issues persist.

Farm and Forest Use Value Taxation

Late in 1973 Governor Salmon unveiled a comprehensive system of tax incentives for farm, forest, and other open lands. Taxes on plots smaller than 100 acres would be reduced as long as the land was left undeveloped. The reductions would be greatest for landowners with the lowest incomes—those making more than $20,000 yearly would get no benefit. Farmers would get a special tax break—property taxes could not exceed 6 percent of their gross receipts from farming. Large parcels of open land could also qualify for tax reductions, but only if the owner agreed not to develop the land for fifteen years.[88] This rather bold proposal was virtually ignored amid the controversy over the 1974 land use plan and failed to become law.

But taking advantage of Vermont's improved economic condition, the 1978 legislature enacted a long-discussed use-value taxation measure similar to those in many other states.[89] Beginning in April 1980 farmers and owners of managed forestland may apply for taxation at current use value, rather than at fair market value. Eligible forestlands must be under a ten-year forest-management plan. Qualifying lands that are subsequently developed or subdivided into two or more parcels, regardless of whether a change in use actually occurs, are then taxed at fair market value, and are subject to a "land use change tax" equal to 10 percent of the fair market value of the property.

The proceeds from this tax are earmarked for a "use tax reimbursement fund" to replace tax revenues lost by Vermont towns. In 1978 the legislature appropriated $400,000 to establish this fund, noting that annual appropriations of $3 million would be needed to support the fund by the time payments begin in 1980.[90]

Property Tax Credits

Rising property values have also raised tax bills on dwellings, although usually by far smaller percentages than is the case for undeveloped land.

In 1973 the Vermont legislature passed a unique measure which links property taxes *on the principal dwelling of state residents* to the owner's income. Taxes on a home and up to 2 acres of land around it are limited to 4 percent of the owner's income for incomes less than $4,000 per year, and up to 6 percent for yearly incomes over $16,000.[91] The total amount of the tax credit cannot exceed $500 per household.

By being limited to persons living in Vermont for the entire tax year, the credit scheme clearly reflects the legislature's intention to discriminate between Vermont residents and persons owning vacation homes in Vermont. This theme of "Vermont for Vermonters" is a recurring one in Vermont's land use legislation. It also appears in the state's capital gains tax on land.

Capital Gains Tax on Land Sales

In 1973 Vermont also became the nation's first state to impose a special capital gains tax on the profits from land sales. Ostensibly a measure to provide revenue for the property tax credit scheme, the law may complement the effect of Act 250 in slowing the pace of subdivision and development. Moreover, although it is too early to be sure, this may be the first concrete expression of a new public attitude about whether individuals have the right to gain from increases in the value of their land.

The tax must be paid on gains on sales or exchanges of land held by the seller for less than six years. Gain allocable to the land is taxable, but gain allocable to any buildings on the site is exempt. The tax distinguishes between Vermont citizens and outsiders: Gains on the site of a taxpayer's principal residence are exempt from the tax within certain limits, but gains on vacation-home parcels are not. Gains on vacation properties owned by Vermont citizens *are* subject to the tax if properties are sold within the time limit.

The amount of tax depends on the percentage gain achieved and the length of time the seller has held the land. Rates (table 3-1) range from 60 percent, for sellers who make gains of more than 200 percent in less than a year, to zero for sellers who hold their land more than six years. This cutoff period means that the typical farmer, who usually has held his land for a very long period, will be unaffected by the tax when he sells. The subdivider, on the other hand, who depends on rapid turnover, will be subject to a relatively high rate of tax.

Under the governor's original proposal, the tax would have applied to gains on sales of land held less than ten years. Real estate interests

Table 3-1.   Vermont Land Gains Tax Rates

Years land held by transferor	Increase in value (%)		
	0–99	*100–199*	*200 or more*
	Rate of tax on gain		
Less than one year	30	45	60
One year, but less than two	25	37.5	50
Two years, but less than three	20	30	40
Three years, but less than four	15	22.5	30
Four years, but less than five	10	15	20
Five years, but less than six	5	7.5	10

mounted a heavy lobbying effort to defeat the bill and a compromise was reached imposing the six-year limit.

The tax is ultimately paid by the seller, but the actual transfer of money is made by the buyer to the state. Land buyers are required to remit 10 percent of the purchase price to the state after the sale is made. The seller then applies to the state for a refund or makes an additional payment, depending on his tax liability.

The tax became effective May 1, 1973. By the end of its first full year of application, the tax had raised some $1.3 million, well below the $2 to $3 million expected when the bill was adopted. One key factor in the relatively small amount of money raised was the almost wholesale transfer of land that took place just before the new tax became effective. During April alone, some $57 million worth of Vermont was sold, the highest single month for recorded transfers in the state's history.[92] Tax officials suspected that many of these sales involved dummy transfers at inflated prices in an attempt to establish a higher basis price and avoid the tax. One case involving this stratagem has been successfully contested by the state.[93]

The tax yielded even less in subsequent years. It produced only $860,000 in fiscal year 1975; two years later, when the building recession affecting speculative subdivisions in Vermont was still severe, the tax brought in $660,000. Revenues climbed about $50,000 in the next year.[94] Some of this decline in tax collections reflects the sluggish economy in Vermont, which lasted until spring 1977.[95] In a slower economy, there are fewer land sales, and because parcels held for more than six years are exempt from the tax, collections decline more as the period of owner- ship lengthens. But some of it must be attributed to legislative changes in the land gains tax, which have progressively broadened the exemption available to Vermont residents. The original act exempted from the tax 1 acre on which a taxpayer made his principal residence. In 1974 the legislature exempted holdings up to 5 acres, and extended the exemption from sellers of such properties to purchasers as well. Subsequent sessions allowed builders who buy land, erect a house, and sell it to a new owner for use as a principal residence, to qualify, too, and the 1978 legislature increased the exemption for qualifying sellers, purchasers, and builders to 10 acres or, where local zoning requires larger lots, up to as many as 25 acres.[96]

Governor Salmon claimed at the time of enactment that the tax would slow rapid subdivision growth and allow the land use plan to operate.[97] Jack Veller, a member of the environmental board and a real estate agent, disagreed. He claimed that the tax would generate less income than expected and would spur sales of land in smaller parcels, encouraging development. Veller reasoned that farmers, no longer able to find speculators who would buy and hold their land in large units, would build houses on land that might remain undeveloped if a large investor bought it.[98]

A speculator talked about moving his operation to New Hampshire, which has few controls. "Nobody in New York City wants to talk with me any more about Vermont land," he said. "*The New York Times* has a big Sunday piece on 'Vermont Gets Tough on Land Sales,' and they hear about the capital gains tax, and that's it. For land speculators, Vermont is dead. And if that is what they wanted, the capital gains law is working."[99]

In fact, it is difficult to judge whether the new tax has been successful, for its two purposes—to raise money and to dampen land speculation—are mutually contradictory. By the end of the tax's first year, the value of land sold in Vermont was at about its "normal" (and historically high) level. A slight lag behind the usual pattern of sharp increases in the value of sales from year to year was probably caused more by the tight money market than by the tax law.[100]

Developers as well as speculators are deeply affected by the tax, since many subdivide and sell their holdings within one to three years of purchase. The tax law does not distinguish between gains from subdivision and gains made by reselling large plots, and, in percentage terms, subdivision frequently produces the largest profits. An executive of the 5,500-acre Quechee Lakes development complained, "We think the tax is both unfair and possibly illegal. We are thinking seriously of taking the matter to the courts."[101]

One group of developers did sue the state, claiming that the tax was discriminatory and was passed with procedural errors. The Vermont supreme court denied both contentions and affirmed the constitutionality of the tax, adding, "We find no reason, therefore, that the legislature could not have acted to restrict land speculation by means of the land gains tax structure, within its constitutional powers."[102]

Conclusion

Vermont's system for state regulation of land is among the most comprehensive in the nation. It includes a permit procedure, performance standards, property tax relief, and a capital gains tax on land sales. Although the state zoning proposed in the land use plan has not materialized, and states such as Oregon appear to have gone beyond what Vermont has accomplished in this area, other innovations may be tested in the future.

The backbone of the system is the nine district commissions, each made up of three unpaid citizens appointed by the governor. The performance standards that these commissions enforce are part of the law itself. Appeals may be made to the state environmental board and to the courts.

Local governments are encouraged to plan for developments below the minimum size regulated by the state law and to take part in adversary proceedings before the district commissions and the environmental board. State agencies, particularly those concerned with pollution control, also give testimony at permit hearings.

After eight years of experience with state land control in Vermont the consensus view is that it has been more effective in improving the quality of development than in stopping it outright. Given the tremendous increase in second-home development elsewhere in the United States over the last decade, however, one suspects that Vermont's strict controls may have led to far less growth than would have otherwise occurred. In particular, its controls may have saved Vermont from the proliferation of the shoddy (though somewhat lower-priced) developments that have sprung up in the mountains of other northeastern states.

Vermont's land law has proved to be more effective in regulating second homes and suburban tracts than in stopping commercial sprawl. But the emphasis of Act 250 is shifting, and the land use permit process is proving to be adaptable. The law weathered the severe recession of the mid-1970s, and is now being applied not only to the revived market for vacation homes and ski areas but also, increasingly, to projects involved in the state's effort to diversify its economy. Most new commercial and industrial growth is likely to build upon the nucleus of such facilities around

Burlington, and the review of the Pyramid Mall indicates the increased local and regional sophistication that is becoming the norm in considering such projects. All residential, commercial, and industrial development covered by Act 250 must now conform as a matter of course to the law's environmental requirements, particularly concerning water pollution and erosion. Having established this minimum standard of performance, localities that choose to do so are now evaluating projects on broader criteria, including the preservation of agricultural land, energy conservation, the costs of utility services, and even social and fiscal impacts that seem to extend greatly the initial requirements of Act 250. The city of Burlington's aggressive role in the Pyramid case, and the participation of regional planning commissions from the entire far-flung secondary market area of the mall, indicate that the Act 250 process is bringing regional and state perspectives to bear on local projects. The work of the district commissions in conducting rigorous reviews of the Pyramid and Hawk applications on so many legal and technical criteria indicates that the Act 250 process is accommodating these new demands.

Finally, Vermont developers may have changed with the times. One coordinator feels that there are fewer denials of permit applications now because developers, recognizing the precedents set in Act 250's first eight years, are presenting better designed projects, or are improving them as necessary during the review process.[103] Another response, in line with experiences of comparable agencies in other states, is that the environmental board finds itself in court more frequently and more quickly than in earlier years.[104]

Perhaps the most interesting feature of Vermont's experience is that the policy has evolved over time. The lawmakers have moved from the strictly regulatory approach of environmental standards, to modifying incentives by a capital gains tax and by property tax abatement, and then to considering indicative planning for the growth of towns (long-term capital budgeting) and for the overall development of the state (land classification).

This evolution continues. Vermont's land tax policies are likely to be modified still further in coming years. And given the apparent political distaste for a state land use plan, some changes in government structure or resources may be advocated to bring about some of the same results. The Pyramid case may have revived public interest in the Act 250 process in much the same way the International Paper Company's proposed development of 20,000 acres hastened the act's adoption. As more citizens come to appreciate that through Act 250 local and regional plans can have legal, not merely advisory, effects, the environmental board chairman thinks that "The next step might be to legitimize those plans by coming up with regional councils parallel to the Minneapolis–Saint Paul Metropolitan Council."[105]

Whatever comes of these ideas, they indicate clearly that the process begun by the passage of Act 250 has not been concluded. The permit program is working, even when it incorporates new criteria or applies to new kinds of development. For the future, then, the question is not how to revamp Vermont's land regulatory process, but whether it can continue to evolve as the process itself uncovers new kinds of issues.

Notes

1. Rutland (Vt.) *Daily Herald,* July 17, 1969.
2. John Marshall, Jr., "The Efficacy of Act 250: The Evolution of an Environmental Law" (Montpelier, Vt., Environmental Planning Information Center, May 1971).
3. State of Vermont, Agency of Administration. *Biennial Report of the Commissioner of Taxes, 1972* (Montpelier, 1972). Seasonal homes were estimated to be worth $459 million in 1971, an increase of 114 percent in four years. See also M. I. Bevins, "Impact on Taxes of Second Homes," *Vermont Farm and Home Science* (Winter 1974).
4. Two towns that tried to turn these roads into "trails," which require no town maintenance, were sued by landowners. Rutland (Vt.) *Daily Herald*, Jan. 4, 1973.
5. According to David Heeter, then of the Vermont State Planning Office, estimates of the proportion of vacation homes converted to permanent dwellings ranged as high as 15 to 30 percent. Rutland (Vt.) *Daily Herald*, Aug. 10, 1973.
6. F. W. Dodge Co.)housing starts); U.S. Census of Housing, 1970 (housing stock), cited in *Vermont Facts and Figures* (Montpelier, Vermont Department of Budget and Management, 1973).
7. Rutland (Vt.) *Daily Herald,* May 21, 1969.
8. Communication from John McClaughry, received December 6, 1978.
9. In Hartland, a small town on I-91 surrounded by examples of new development, soaring assessments, and rising prices paid for small properties, four proposals for this kind of use value taxation of open land were quashed by the townspeople by a vote of 302–146, on May 25, 1976. See Barbara Villet, "One Town's Battle for Open Space," *Country Journal* (January 1977) pp. 35–40.
10. Justin Brande, chairman of the Vermont Natural Resources Council, quoted in the Rutland (Vt.) *Daily Herald*, Aug. 11, 1969.
11. A description of the administrative framework set up by Act 250 as well as the text of the act itself may be found in Fred Bosselman and David Callies, *The Quiet Revolution in Land Use Control* (Washington, D.C., GPO, 1971).
12. Since 1977 two coordinators—there had been seven around the state—have worked out of the environmental board's Montpelier offices, helping the busiest district commissions or those with the most difficult applications, thus distributing the uneven workload of the different regions more reasonably. Interview with Peter B. Meyer, Environmental Board, Montpelier, Vt., Sept. 6, 1978.
13. An interesting account of a routine Act 250 permit hearing may be found in Phyllis Myers, *So Goes Vermont* (Washington, D.C., Conservation Foundation, 1974) pp. 19–20.
14. In practice, some district commissions have allowed anyone who could demonstrate that he would be affected by a proposed project to become a party to the proceeding, with full rights to appeal. In a case in Stowe, for example, a person who

was not an adjoining landowner but who owned land on a town road that would have to be improved as a result of a proposed project was allowed to become a formal party. Telephone interview with Canute Delmas, District V environmental coordinator, June 28, 1974.

In June 1975, to comply with a state supreme court ruling, the environmental board adopted a new policy limiting the participation of those who are not official parties to Act 250 proceedings. District commissions may deny standing to most state residents, and owners of land abutting proposed projects must state specific objections and cite anticipated damages.

15. Schuyler Jackson, remarks to the Conservation Foundation Conference on State Land Use Planning, Chicago, March 1974.

16. The capital program provision was added in 1973. See text pp. 59–60.

17. See the discussion in State of Vermont Environmental Board, "Report to the Governor on the Administration of Act 250" (Montpelier, December 1976), photocopied, pp. 11–15. The litigation and statutory changes in standing rights of property owners, both in hearings and appeals, are analyzed by David G. Heeter, in Daniel R. Mandelker, *Environmental and Land Controls Legislation* (Indianapolis, Ind., Bobbs-Merrill, 1976) p. 338*n*, and p. 384*n*. See also note 14 above.

18. Prime agricultural soils, for instance, may be developed solely if development is the only way in which the owner can realize a "reasonable return on the fair market value" of his land, and only then if the development affects the land and adjoining parcels as little as possible.

19. Findings of Fact, Conclusions of Law, and Order on Application No. 5L0444 (Environmental Board, Montpelier, July 21, 1978). The developer has appealed to the Vermont supreme court.

20. Interview with Margaret P. Garland, Montpelier, Vt., September 6, 1978.

21. Vermont Environmental Board, "Statistics on Act 250 Applications from June 1970 through July 31, 1978," mimeographed. The number of denials overstates the number of projects actually stopped completely. As of August 18, 1977, according to a report by environmental board executive officer Kenneth Senecal, of 71 applications denied permits since 1970, only 40 did not ultimately receive permission; the others, revised, were approved. The Land/Tech case is one such example.

22. Telephone interview with Schuyler Jackson, Vermont Environmental Board, April 4, 1975.

23. A random sample of permits showed that conditions most frequently were imposed under criteria 1 (air and water pollution), 4 (erosion), 5 (traffic congestion), and 8 (esthetics). Permits were most frequently denied under criteria 1, 4, or 8. William Colgan, "A Preliminary Report on a Survey of Act 250 Applications" (Montpelier, Vermont State Planning Office, 1973).

24. Under the board's rules of procedure, it is "the preferred practice" that applicants submit all the needed environmental permits or certifications when they begin the Act 250 review. An alternative procedure allows the applicant to apply for the land use permit first—so he will not have to undertake very costly design and engineering before knowing whether he can get an Act 250 permit—but he then must make an affirmative case on each relevant aspect of his proposal to the district environmental commission during its hearings.

25. State of Vermont, Agency of Environmental Conservation, *Land Use and Development: Vermont's Environmental Programs* (Montpelier, 1972).

26. Rutland (Vt.) *Daily Herald*, July 13, 1973.

27. Interview, Montpelier, Vermont, July 2, 1973.

28. Bosselman and Callies, *The Quiet Revolution*, p. 81. Armstrong observes that sales of 10- to 20-acre parcels of forest land "assumed a marked upward swing with enactment of Vermont Environmental Act 250." Frank H. Armstrong, *Valuation of Vermont Forests, 1968–74* (Burlington, University of Vermont Department of Forestry, 1975) p. 6. A modification to Act 250 in 1974 made it more difficult to use this strategem, but it persists. The chairman of the environmental board, Margaret P. Garland, hopes a legislative change in the subdivision law can be devised to close the loophole. Interview, Montpelier, Vt., Sept. 6, 1978.

29. State of Vermont, Agency of Environmental Conservation, *Land Use and Development*, app., p. 10.

30. Rutland (Vt.) *Daily Herald,* July 28, 1970.

31. Marshall, "The Efficacy of Act 250." In 1972 the district commission approved a revised version of this same development, with extra safeguards to preserve the vegetation of the bog.

32. Land/Tech file, Vermont Environmental Board.

33. Rutland (Vt.) *Daily Herald,* Sept. 28, 1972.

34. Telephone interview with Paul Nergaard, district environmental coordinator, Sept. 6, 1978.

35. Land use permit for application no. 100036 (revised), District Environmental Commission no. 5, July 7, 1978, and accompanying Findings of Fact and Conclusions of Law.

36. Haystack file, Vermont Environmental Board. The application fee for this development was over $5,000. Fees are set at one-tenth of 1 percent of a development's value of proposed construction, plus $5 per subdivided lot.

37. Richard Wien, "The Collapse of a Development," *Country Journal* (June 1975) pp. 48–55.

38. Ibid., p. 51.

39. AMI letter in district environmental commission Haystack files; interview with Deborah J. Sisco, district coordinator, North Springfield, Vt., Sept. 7, 1978.

40. Information on the Hawk development comes from interviews with Peter B. Meyer, environmental coordinator, in Montpelier, Sept. 6, 1978, and Deborah J. Sisco, district coordinator, in North Springfield, Sept. 7, 1978; from reading the Hawk file at the district environmental commission's North Springfield office; and from District Environmental Commission no. 3, Order denying application no. 3W0246 and accompanying Findings of Fact and Conclusions of Law.

41. Hamilton Davis, "Vermont's Hawk: Endangered Species?" *The New Englander* (January, 1978) p. 60.

42. See *The New York Times,* May 9, 1978; *Business Week,* Oct. 30, 1978; *Environmental Action,* Nov. 4, 1978; *The New Englander,* Sept. 1978; and the syndicated newspaper columns of Neal R. Peirce appearing in, among other places, *The Hartford Courant,* June 19, 1978, and Oct. 24, 1978. All deal with the Burlington mall, and some discuss other, similar controversies of center cities competing against outlying malls. Generally, see Clifford L. Weaver and Christopher J. Duerksen, "Central Business District Planning and the Control of Outlying Shopping Centers," *Urban Law Annual* vol. 14 (1977) pp. 57–79.

43. District Environmental Commission no. 4, Order denying application no. 4C0281 and accompanying Findings of Fact and Conclusions of Law, p. 25.

44. Ibid., p. 39.

45. Ibid., p. 43.

46. Ibid., p. 42.

47. Vermont Natural Resources Council, *Vermont Environmental Report* (Montpelier, October 1978) p. 1.

48. For example, dozens of developers in the Dover area have filed permit applications but have not followed through with them. Interview with Kenneth Senecal, executive secretary, Vermont Environmental Board, July 2, 1973.

49. F. W. Dodge construction statistics, cited in *Vermont Facts and Figures* (Montpelier, Vermont Department of Budget and Management, 1974). Nonresidential construction fell well below its 1968–70 level after the passage of Act 250. There is ordinarily a great deal of fluctuation in this kind of construction.

50. In 1974 residential and nonresidential construction both declined sharply— some 20 percent—with the onset of recession. Nonresidential construction resumed in 1975 and has grown steadily since, while residential construction did not take off again until 1977, which became its best year in a decade. F. W. Dodge statistics were provided by George Donovan, Agency of Development and Community Affairs. From 1970 through 1974, housing starts in New Hampshire, which does not have

anything like Act 250, followed the Vermont trend almost exactly. In 1975 and 1976, Vermont starts rose and then fell slightly, while New Hampshire's fell and then rose. While the Burlington area is growing vigorously, there is nothing in Vermont to compare to the manufacturing development boom (and the associated new housing) in southern New Hampshire—around Nashua and Manchester—as firms expand over the state line to escape "Taxachusetts."

51. Rutland (Vt.) *Daily Herald,* Feb. 13, 1973.

52. Environmental board rule 13F in "Environmental Board Regulations Annotated: Supplemental Rules and Table Updates Effective February 1, 1978" (Montpelier, 1978) p. 8. Interview with Margaret P. Garland and Peter Meyer, Montpelier, Vt., Sept. 6, 1978.

53. Letter from Bernard D. Johnson, assistant director, State Planning Office, Oct. 25, 1978.

54. Bosselman and Callies, *The Quiet Revolution,* p. 85.

55. Environmental Board, "Report to the Governor on the Administration of Act 250" (Montpelier, December 1976) p. 8. See also Darby Bradley and Richard A. Mixer, "Act 250 and the Control of Soil Erosion and Sedimentation in Developing Areas in Vermont" (Burlington, Vt., Lake Champlain Basin Study, Jan. 1, 1978) pp. 22–24.

56. John McClaughry, one of the leading opponents of the Act 250 regulatory and planning processes, maintains that the 1973 capability and development plan—nineteen policy statements and amendments to the permit criteria—is not really a "plan" at all, and that it does not satisfy the Act 250 requirements for this second of the three proposed plans. Letter, Oct. 24, 1978.

57. The plan also contains a long set of state "planning principles" for land development and settlement patterns. In another section of the plan, however, the district commissions and environmental board are specifically forbidden to use the principles as criteria in evaluating permit applications.

58. Of course, the concept of "overriding state interest" could be given a very broad interpretation by the state.

59. The use of a capital improvement budget for controlling the timing of growth is often called the Ramapo plan after the city of Ramapo, New York, which passed such legislation in 1969. The Ramapo ordinance was upheld by the New York Supreme Court in 1972. This method of growth control has been given much attention by fast-growing suburbs in many parts of the country.

60. *The Land Capability and Development Plan in Plain English* (Montpelier, Vermont Public Interest Research Group, February 1973).

61. Interview with Bernard D. Johnson, Montpelier, Vt., Sept. 5, 1978.

62. Interview with Margaret P. Garland, Montpelier, Vt., Sept. 6, 1978.

63. As quoted in Rutland (Vt.) *Daily Herald,* Feb. 21, 1973.

64. 10 Vt. Stat. Ann. Ch. 151, 6043 (1970).

65. Sen. Arthur Gibb, remarks to Conservation Foundation Conference on State Land Use Planning, Chicago, March 1974.

66. The work was split between the environmental board and the state planning office, sometime rivals, who did not always agree on either the plan's format or its policies.

67. Rutland (Vt.) *Daily Herald,* Aug. 10, 1973.

68. For a view of the "conservation areas" from the point of view of the Vermont forest owner, see Frank Harris Armstrong, "The Importance of Being Sam," *American Forests* vol. 80, no. 7 (July 1974) pp. 8–11.

69. Burlington (Vt.) *Free Press,* Feb. 8, 1974.

70. David G. Heeter discusses the disagreements between the environmental board and the state planning office and the resulting confusion, in *Environmental and Land Controls Legislation* (see note 17 above), pp. 356–358, and 362–366. An Act 250 critic sees the confusion as, in part, deliberate, to conceal the state's intentions from citizens. See John McClaughry, "The New Feudalism," *Environmental Law* vol. 5 (1975) pp. 675–702.

71. Gibb, remarks to the Conservation Foundation Conference.

72. William G. Staats, Jr., letter to the editor, Brattleboro (Vt.) *Reformer,* March 4, 1974.

73. Burlington (Vt.) *Free Press,* March 14, 1974.

74. David G. Heeter, "Some Basic Comparisons Between the State Land Use Plan and Town Plans and By-Laws" (Montpelier, Vermont State Planning Office, June 1974), mimeographed. The author also compared growth allowed under the state plan with that permitted under current town plans and by-laws in three Vermont counties. Densities permitted under these local laws would allow their populations to grow by more than 1300 percent.

75. Salmon, remarks to the Conservation Foundation Conference.

76. Statement of J. W. Batchelder of Chester, Vermont, circulated to members of the legislature, Feb. 20, 1974.

77. Burlington (Vt.) *Free Press,* March 21, 1974.

78. David Heeter, in *Environmental and Land Controls Legislation* (see note 17 above) p. 370.

79. Rutland (Vt.) *Daily Herald,* March 30 and March 31, 1974.

80. The legislature enacted a measure to require Act 250 permits whenever more than five lots were to be sold at public auction. McClaughry, "Feudalism," p. 686. It also refused to repeal the 1973 land gains tax.

81. Interview with Bernard D. Johnson.

82. State of Vermont Executive Department, Executive Order no. 20, Aug. 23, 1978.

83. In practice, local assessors often include an "ability to pay" element in their assessments. Moreover, farmland assessments notoriously lag behind changes in the land's market value.

84. Saint Johnsbury (Vt.) *Caledonian–Record,* June 1973.

85. Benjamin Huffman, *The Vermont Farm and a Land Reform Program* (Montpelier, Vermont State Planning Office, July 1973).

86. Letter from Rep. Norris Hoyt, April 6, 1978.

87. One rough estimate of the impact of a land use plan on the tax rolls of five southern Vermont towns found reductions in tax base of only 1 to 8 percent. This might, moreover, be offset by increases in the value of parcels where the plan does permit development. Memorandum from Ralph Monticello, economic analyst in the Vermont State Planning Office, to Arthur Ristau, director of the Vermont State Planning Office, June 27, 1973.

88. Rutland (Vt.) *Daily Herald,* Sept. 14, 1973.

89. Bernard D. Johnson attributes the bill's passage in 1978 to the improved economy, which eased pressure on local budgets and made state payments to affected localities feasible. Interview, Montpelier, Vt., Sept. 6, 1978.

90. Vermont's law calls for the state to make up all lost revenues, but if the state fund should be insufficient, it is to be prorated to the qualifying towns, with the difference to be made up by the taxpayers whose land is assessed at use value. If this happens, the owners are free to terminate use value taxation without being subject to the land use change tax.

91. Vermont General Assembly, H.155 (1973).

92. *Vermont Times,* July 1973.

93. Interview with James Kendall, Vermont State Tax Office, June 28, 1974.

94. Telephone interview with Henry Ferry, Vermont State Tax Department, Land Gains Division, Sept. 12, 1978.

95. Information on the building slump comes from the interview with Henry Ferry; interview with Margaret P. Garland, chairman, Environmental Board, Montpelier, Vt., Sept. 6, 1978; and F. W. Dodge Company construction statistics provided by George Donovan of the Agency of Development and Community Affairs, Montpelier, Vt.

96. Information on legislative changes is from the interview with Henry Ferry, and the text of Act 240, approved April 17, 1978.

97. Rutland (Vt.) *Daily Herald,* July 14, 1973.

98. *Vermont Times,* July 1973.

99. Ibid.

100. The impact of Vermont's land gains tax on land prices and on the character-istics and investment behavior of land purchasers is the subject of an ongoing study by R. Lisle Baker and Stephen Andersen for the Environmental Law Institute, Washington, D.C. Results were not available in March 1979. Baker has speculated that "the amount of land transferred is likely to decline since both the supply and demand impacts of the tax cut in the same direction." He also expects to find that with fewer land transfers, land market intermediaries—bankers, brokers, lawyers—will lose real income, and that prices of developable land will fall. See his "Taxing Speculative Gains—The Vermont Experience," paper presented to A Conference on Tax Policies to Achieve Land Use Goals, University of Southern California Law Center, Los Angeles, February 10–11, 1978, photocopied. The theoretical analysis under-lying this study is spelled out in R. Lisle Baker, "Controlling Land Use and Prices by Using Special Gain Taxation to Intervene in the Land Market: The Vermont Experiment," *Environmental Law* vol. 4 (Summer 1975) pp. 427–480.

101. *Los Angeles Times,* Aug. 13, 1973.

102. *Andrews* v. *Lathrop,* 315 A.2d 860 (1974).

103. Interview, Peter B. Meyer, Sept. 6, 1978.

104. The supreme court has affected standing before the Act 250 review bodies (see notes 14 and 17 above) and has ordered some denials of permits reversed but has generally upheld the act and its administration. It has challenged environmental board rules, procedures, and declaratory judgments more often than the substance of permit decisions.

105. Environmental Board Chairman Margaret P. Garland, who has been in-volved with Act 250 since before its passage, thinks that the Pyramid case and the governor's emphasis on improving local government capabilities, coordinated by his state planning office, might have such an effect. Interview, Sept. 6, 1978.

CHAPTER FOUR

California—
"Saving the Coast"

CALIFORNIA'S EXPERIENCE with direct state control of land use was begun not by action of the legislature, but by vote of the people. On November 7, 1972, the state's voters approved a citizen-originated ballot initiative giving powerful state and regional commissions control over nearly all forms of construction along its entire 1,072-mile coast. For the succeeding four years, the coastal commissions made binding decisions on some 25,000 separate development permits, while simultaneously preparing a plan for the long-term management of the coast. That plan was the subject of months of active consideration during the 1976 session of the state legislature. The result, the California Coastal Act of 1976, has created a complex new state–local partnership for coastal protection, with the coastal commissions reviewing and certifying local plans and ordinances for their conformity to state coastal policies.

The 1972 initiative reflected widespread public dissatisfaction with local land use controls, for California had long given local governments considerable potential power to plan and zone. Its passage, confirmed by the legislature's later endorsement of coastal controls, was a recognition that the coast, a near-priceless recreational asset and symbol of the California way of life, has come to be considered a resource of statewide, rather than just local, concern.

"Where's the Beach?"

California's decision was not a response to a single outrageous development or even to a single set of problems. Perhaps it would be foolish to expect such a simple explanation in a state with 20 million people and over 1,000 miles of coastline. Specific local issues did fuel support, particularly organized support, for the ballot measure—high-rise beachside condominiums in San Diego and Los Angeles, oil drilling off Santa Barbara, and second-home construction north and south of San Francisco. These issues involve real and important threats to the coast, and we will attempt to enumerate them fully.

Nevertheless, the support of state coastal regulation by 55 percent of California voters was probably based primarily on vague fears and feelings which did not attach to any specific coastal issue. Proponents of the ballot proposal gave wide circulation to a cartoon showing a group of people dressed for beach activities—surfers, divers, fishermen, and children. "Where's the beach?" read the caption.

People had come to realize that, even if the beach itself had not disappeared, a number of rights which they had come to regard as public property were not public at all. As development proceeded, private individuals built on oceanfront lots which the public had used for parking. Hotels were built on scenic bluffs. Power plants were proposed, and sometimes built, that were visible for miles along an otherwise undeveloped coast. Increased residential density along the coast put pressure on curbside parking spaces. And all of this was quite legal, consistent with the exercise of existing private property rights and with local zoning.

It had dawned on the California public that its rights to use the beach were for the most part limited to the land actually in public recreation areas—in 1972 this amounted to about 250 miles, or less than 25 percent of the shoreline. Along much of the rest of the coast access was limited by fences, by buildings, or by topography.

California's spectacular population growth, higher incomes, and increased interest in outdoor recreation made demand for coastal recreation increase far faster than the state's modest additions to the beach park system. In 1971 the state department of parks and recreation estimated that to acquire even a 100-foot-wide strip of undeveloped beach property along the southern California coast could cost more than $400 million, while a similar strip in northern California could cost $240 million.[1] By contrast, the last park acquisition bond issue, passed in 1964, had provided $150 million for all parks for the entire state. And even purchase of a narrow strip of beach frontage would not solve problems of access, views, parking, and density.

Unlike, say, the Oregon coast or North Carolina's Outer Banks, California's coastline is not just a vacation area. Although portions are remote and undeveloped, the California coast includes some of the most valuable and intensely developed urban land in the world. Statewide, over 80 percent of the population lives within an hour's drive of the coast. Moreover, the immediate coastal zone, where ocean breezes tend to disperse air pollution, has become increasingly attractive as a place to live in the more urbanized, highly congested parts of the state. But unlike East Coast cities, where urbanization has overpowered the immediate natural environment, beach and city have long coexisted, albeit uneasily, in California. Long Beach's strand, for example, lies directly adjacent to that city's downtown office district.

By the late 1960s, however, competing demands on the coastline had begun to collide almost daily, while a rising interest in the environment brought new focus on the fragility of the coastal ecology. From San Diego in the south to Crescent City in the far north, the sheer rapidity of the change in land use and its cumulative effect on the recreational use of the coast became an issue.

In older neighborhoods such as San Diego's Ocean Beach and Los Angeles' Venice, the change was the conversion from old single-family homes to large, even high-rise, apartments. This involved not only dramatic increases in density, but a quantum jump in the cost of housing. Neighborhoods where students, the aged, the youth culture, and families of modest means could afford to live within walking distance of the sea began to be dotted with high-priced, luxury condominiums. Often the clearance of older units was aided by urban renewal funds, as cities clamored for the tax revenues that new construction would bring. Current residents protested to local government but were often ignored.

Along still-undeveloped parts of the coast, the subdividers were at work. In southern California large ranch holdings that had preserved miles of coast from development for a hundred years were being developed into planned communities. These were not merely recreational communities, but new urban areas, complete with industry, shopping centers, and office buildings. Farther north, on the Carmel coast, artichoke fields were being converted to building lots. And just outside of San Francisco, commented one reporter, "The big ranches are being purchased by ambitious developers, and at Half Moon Bay the little boxes are already sprouting side by side, with red real estate pennants flapping in the breeze."[2]

In some cases, the changes involved beach access. In Sand City, a town of only 220 residents near Monterey, local officials approved a 600-unit apartment complex on a 1-mile-long stretch of beach. This project, which would have closed off a beach previously enjoyed by the 500,000 residents of the Monterey area, was stopped only when the public raised such an outcry that the financial backers pulled out. Peter

Douglas, who was instrumental in drafting the coastal legislation, lamented, "Sand City was able to make that decision in complete isolation, even though it affected the entire area."[3]

Farther north, large second-home developments along the Sonoma and Mendocino coasts threatened to cut off miles of beach from public access. Sea Ranch, a "quality" development about 100 miles north of San Francisco, made an arrangement with county officials that shut off public access along more than 10 miles of beach. In California, all lands below the mean high tide line belong to the state, and the state constitution expresses emphatically that laws protecting the right of public access to them shall be given the most liberal possible interpretation. In exchange for a tiny piece of parkland, the county supervisors made it almost impossible for the public to exercise this right at Sea Ranch.

Near Malibu, just outside Los Angeles, except for the 6 miles (out of 26 miles) of coast that were publicly owned, a newspaper report noted that the "beachgoer is confronted by a wall of homes, fences and signs which block access to the state-owned beach below the mean high tide mark. Above all else Malibu is a mass of signs which symbolize the ongoing war between local property owners and visitors. The signs come in all sizes, shapes, and phrases. Their net effect is to continuously command the visitor to keep out, citing various county ordinances as their authority."[4]

Other changes were environmental. The coast was the site of several large power plants, including seven of California's eight then planned or operating nuclear units. Despite some of the most stringent air and water quality controls in the nation, they added a load of nitrogen oxides to the air or thermal discharges to the water. The ocean was also a convenient dumping ground for sewage effluent. A single treatment plant in Los Angeles discharged 340 million gallons of partially treated sewage daily into Santa Monica Bay. A local diving enthusiast claimed that, as the plume increased over time, the kelp beds which shelter much of the bay's marine life receded in its path.[5]

California's estuaries and coastal marshes, tidal nurseries for much of the ocean's life, had been especially subject to development. The National Estuary Study reported that of the twenty-eight sizable estuaries that existed in southern California at the beginning of the century, fifteen have been modified either slightly or moderately, ten have been altered drastically, and three have been destroyed. The study observed that "Bays, lagoons and estuaries are being filled for commercial and industrial purposes, and they are being polluted by industrial and domestic wastes. Housing developments cover much of their shoreline and bluff areas. They are being covered by silt resulting from poor and inconsiderate upland management practices. They are being filled, drained, or cut off from tidal circulation for agricultural and vector control purposes and by land development schemes."[6]

Since the early 1950s oil derricks appeared off California's coast, and ranks of pumps were found along some of its beaches. In a few cases, the oil companies went to considerable expense to disguise their handiwork—off Long Beach the drilling is done from artificial islands complete with palm trees and illuminated waterfalls. The 1969 Santa Barbara oil spill, however, was still fresh in the minds of many Californians. At several points along the coast, oil companies and utilities were planning offshore facilities for unloading oil and natural gas from Alaska. Tankers up to ten times as large as any seen before along California's coast might ply this potentially dangerous route. Before the passage of the coastal initiative, the state had some control over drilling but none at all over the location of supertanker ports.

There are some common threads to be found in these land use changes. Most did not involve the creation of new private property rights. Owners were simply finding it profitable to do what they had long had the legal right to do. Land economist Marion Clawson has commented that "Land use changes in the future are going to be made with increasing difficulty; many persons have substantial interests in maintaining present land uses. The number of persons who neither own nor use the land now, nor propose to do so in the future, but who nevertheless assert an interest in its use, is rising sharply."[7] California voters, who had long felt that they "owned" scenic views, open spaces, deserted beaches, even simply clean water, found that others considered these part of their own property—and the time was ripe for development.

Local governments along the coast generally enforced some kind of land use control, often including zoning. But these controls, reasonably enough, sought local objectives. The promotion of industry and commercial attractions meant new business opportunities for local residents and a welcome addition to the tax base. Local politicians were eager to take credit for any action that would reduce the burden on the homeowner. Like local governments everywhere, coastal cities seek a balanced tax base, encouraging activities that will bring in more tax revenue than they demand in public services.

Thus, by the end of the 1960s a rising demand to preserve the "statewide interest" in coastal land confronted a governmental structure that was unwilling or unable to assert that interest. Out of this came three unsuccessful bids for coastal laws in the state legislature and, in 1972, the coastal initiative.

Proposition 20

Bills to regulate coastal development were unsuccessfully introduced in the 1970, 1971, and 1972 sessions of the California legislature. Three times they passed the assembly, only to die before reaching the floor of the senate. In 1971 a coalition of environmental groups from all over the state, the California Coastal Alliance, formed to actively press for a coastal law and soon claimed that over 1.5 million people were receiving Alliance information, either directly or through participating groups.[8]

As legislative sessions came and went, these environmentalists became increasingly bitter at the uncompromising stand of the business and commercial interests lobbying in Sacramento. Oil and power company representatives, they claimed, were so confident of defeating any coastal bill that they would not even discuss the matter with the Alliance or with the legislators who had introduced the bills.[9] As the legislative effort seemed about to fail for the third time, the Coastal Alliance resorted to an old California tradition—the ballot initiative.

The initiative has a long, often distinguished, and sometimes zany history in California. In 1972 alone, voters were asked to legalize marijuana, restore the death penalty, and outlaw a grape boycott. By June of 1972 the Alliance, after a whirlwind campaign, had secured 418,000 valid signatures and placed the coastal initiative on the ballot. It was assigned the twentieth position among the twenty-two proposed laws on the ballot and became known as "Proposition 20."

Proposition 20 is differentiated from most other land laws in the United States in that it was wholly written by environmentalists. It was nonetheless not a statement of an uncompromising position. Its authors, most of whom had previous experience in politics, wanted to produce a law that would appeal to the needs of the public, survive court challenges, and not unnecessarily offend the legislature or local politicians. They were aware that less than a year before, an initiative proposing extreme pollution controls had been soundly defeated at the polls.

The authors of Proposition 20 took as their model for coastal regulation the San Francisco Bay Conservation and Development Commission (BCDC), which since 1965 has regulated development along the shoreline of the bay. The BCDC formula was to create a single-purpose agency that would prepare a conservation and development plan to be submitted to the legislature. While the plan was being prepared, development could proceed only if it received a permit from the commission. This permit power would last only for a limited time—the legislature would decide what was to come next.

In the case of the BCDC, the environmentalists had won a singular victory. When the San Francisco Bay plan was finished in 1969, the legislature accepted it with only a few amendments, then gave the BCDC permanent permit power to implement its own plan.[10]

Proposition 20 proposed the creation of six, twelve- to sixteen-member regional coastal commissions, evenly divided between representatives of local (county and municipal) government and "public" members appointed equally by the governor, senate rules committee, and the speaker of the state assembly.[11] Over these regional bodies would be a state commission, with six public members and six delegates from the regional commissions. It would act as an appeal body from actions of the regional commissions. The commissions would have until the end of 1975 to prepare and submit to the legislature a plan for the conservation of the coastal zone. This coastal zone was quite broadly defined to stretch from 3 miles out to sea inland to the highest elevation of the nearest coastal mountain range.[12]

While the commissions were preparing the plan, they would have the power to veto or modify all forms of development in the water area of the zone and in the 1,000-yard strip of land just inland from the water's edge.[13] Such a wide permit area included, of course, not only the state's beaches but such heavily developed real estate as downtown Santa Monica, San Diego's Mission Bay, and the Los Angeles–Long Beach harbor. The only tidal or coastal area exempt from the permit process was that part of San Francisco Bay already regulated by the BCDC.

Where state permit processes in such states as Maine and Vermont are limited to controlling developments of, say, 10 acres or more, the California Coastal Commissions' powers would cover almost all construction, filling, dredging, and discharge, save only maintenance dredging of existing navigation channels and minor (less than $7,500) improvements to single-family homes. Coastal permits would be required in addition to, and would not substitute for, existing types of governmental permissions, such as building permits, subdivision filings, or local zoning approvals. State agencies, such as the highway department and the state colleges, as well as local governments, were not exempt from the permit requirement. Their projects were treated in much the same way as those proposed by private developers.

In deciding on permits, the commissions would have to find that a development would have no substantial adverse environmental effect and would be consistent with "the maintenance, restoration, and enhancement of the overall quality of the coastal zone environment, including, but not limited to, its amenities." Developments were also to be consistent with the "continued existence of optimum populations of all species of living organisms" and the avoidance of "irreversible and irretrievable commitments of coastal zone resources."[14] To make the permit process even more stringent, a two-thirds majority of a commission would be required to approve dredging or filling of estuaries or bays, developments on agricultural land and those that would reduce the size of a beach or interfere with access to the water, and certain other types of projects. This requirement, moreover, was for a two-thirds majority of the commission *membership,* not just two-thirds of those attending a given meeting. An absent member would in effect be a vote against granting a permit.

Two novel features of the initiative were perhaps indicative of its origin as a citizen-drafted measure. One was the exceptionally strict prohibition of conflict of interest among members of the commissions. The initiative provided for fines or imprisonment for commissioners who participated in decisions in which they or their family had a current or even a prospective financial or employment interest. The second feature was the encouragement of public participation, not only in the planning process but in the permit procedure as well. For example, if a permit was granted by a regional commission, any person "aggrieved" by its approval could appeal to the state commission. And any aggrieved person could appeal the state commission's decision to the courts.[15]

The coastal commissions, like the original BCDC, were to have only a temporary existence. But, again like the BCDC, the commissions' plan would recommend a means of implementation to the legislature. Perhaps, thought the environmentalists, the permit/plan/permanent agency sequence that had been so successful in "saving" San Francisco Bay could be extended to California's entire coast.

The Proposition 20 campaign was a David and Goliath contest between the Coastal Alliance and the San Francisco public relations firm of Whitaker and Baxter, which spent some $1.1 million on behalf of such development interests as Standard Oil of California, the Irvine

Company, Southern Pacific Land Company, and Pacific Gas and Electric. According to *Los Angeles Times* reporter, Phil Fradkin, "The main issue in the campaign was the veracity of Whitaker and Baxter."[16] The developers mounted a billboard campaign urging voters, "Don't Lock up the Coast—Vote No on 20." Bob Moretti, speaker of the state assembly, called the billboard message "out-and-out fraud."[17]

Pacific Gas and Electric, the major northern California electric utility, called Proposition 20 "an essentially elitist piece of legislation for the benefit of a small minority of our citizens."[18] The AFL–CIO and the building trades unions also opposed Proposition 20, although some unions, including the southern California United Auto Workers district, supported it. The League of California Cities voted 123 to 74 to oppose the initiative, and the mayor of Long Beach commented, "Everything I have labored for for twelve years in office will come to a screeching halt if it passes. This is a very vicious piece of legislation."[19] On the other hand, the measure was endorsed by many city councils, including those of Los Angeles, San Diego, and Sacramento.

One crucial endorsement was that of the *Los Angeles Times,* which had editorialized in favor of the coastal bills in the legislature and now printed a strong statement in support of the initiative. The Coastal Alliance mounted a major volunteer campaign.[20] In Orange County, for example, where more than a million votes were at stake, Alliance volunteers called every voter twice.

The debate over Proposition 20 generated far more heat than light. Opponents claimed that the initiative mandated a no-growth policy, confiscated private property, would be disastrous for the economy, and would actually reduce beach access. Their discussion of these issues, however, rarely got past the level of sloganeering. The Coastal Alliance, on the other hand, had to spend more of its time correcting the confusion raised by its opponents than on the underlying problems of the coast itself.

On election day, November 7, 1972, California voters approved Proposition 20 by a 55 to 45 percent margin. The measure passed in thirty-two of California's fifty-eight counties, but these included all of the populous counties around Los Angeles, San Diego, and San Francisco. In Santa Barbara County, scene of the 1970 oil spill, the measure garnered 62 percent of the vote, but in Humboldt and Del Norte counties along the far north coast, it failed miserably.

An analysis of voting patterns in 334 California cities found that Proposition 20 tended to be supported in places with high levels of education and (although the statistical association was weak) with high levels of per capita income. The initiative did relatively poorly in places with high proportions of political conservatives and with large numbers of laborers and construction craftsmen. Distance from the coastline did not appear to influence how a city's electorate voted.[21]

Permit Administration: "Everything But Glaciers"

Permit regulation of coastal development began on February 1, 1973. For the next four years the regional commissions, operating under the mandate and policies of Proposition 20, processed 24,825 permit applications. Over 800 regional decisions were appealed to the state commission. Commission meetings, often filling an eleven-hour day and spilling over into the next day, were some of the best attended of any public body in California.[22] Particularly remarkable was the range of types of development considered—a consequence both of the diversity of the coastline and of Proposition 20's broad definition of development. One state commissioner, reflecting on his experience during those years, remarked that, "The coast is 1,100 miles long and there is every kind of pressure on us. The only thing we didn't have to deal with is glaciers."[23]

The permit process was intended to serve three distinct functions. Most important, it would protect the coast from incompatible development while the coastal plan was being prepared. Second, information uncovered in the course of permit consideration would result in a better, more "realistic" plan. Finally, it was hoped that the immediacy of debate over actual land use controversies would heighten public interest in coastal issues and lead to greater public participation in all aspects of the coastal program. The permit process, claimed state commission executive director Joseph Bodovitz in a 1973 speech, would be "an excellent education in planning" for both commissioners and the public.[24]

The permit process proved to be exactly that, as the state and regional commissions began to amass a body of permit experience that one researcher has likened to a "common law of the California coast."[25] Although individual permit decisions do not set precedents in a strict courtroom sense, policies developed from the earliest days of the permit process carried over to the coastal plan and are even now the basis for regulatory action by the commissions.[26] Commission staff members have sometimes sought to minimize the long-term importance of the permit process, depicting it as a kind of holding action pending completion of the coastal plan and, since 1976, pending completion of coastal planning by local governments.[27] Such a stance tends to belittle the importance of the permit process, for it has not only been a source and a mirror of evolving coastal policies but also the primary means by which the coastal commissions have to date actually affected coastal development. The commissions' permit record therefore deserves our detailed scrutiny.

Appointments to the commissions alternately delighted and enraged Proposition 20's proponents. Appointments to regional boards in San Diego, the south central coast (Ventura, Santa Barbara, San Luis Obispo), and the north coast were heavily in favor of development; those appointed to the boards just to the north and south of San Francisco were more in favor of protecting the environment. The crucial South Coast Commission, which controls development in Los Angeles and Orange counties, was evenly (and sometimes bitterly) divided between the two factions. The state commission, however, was solidly conservationist. This lineup, with a conservation-oriented, generally unified state commission and a varied group of regional bodies, has persisted to the present time.

A survey of commissioners found that of the fifty-six who responded, 64 percent had voted for Proposition 20 and 36 percent against. Of the twelve state commissioners, eleven had voted for the initiative.[28] The state commission and its staff have been heavy with alumni of the BCDC. Melvin Lane, publisher of *Sunset* magazine and chairman of the state commission, was the chairman of the BCDC; another state commission member had helped draft the BCDC legislation. Both the executive director and the chief planner for the state coastal commission had held identical jobs in the BCDC.

The Exemption Question

One of the first problems faced by the coastal commissions was the question of exemptions for ongoing projects. Proposition 20 had made an attempt to be retroactive to April 1972, but legal opinion was clear that any construction begun prior to November 8, the day after election day, was exempt. Opinion differed, however, on the status of construction begun between November 8, 1972 and February 1, 1973, the date the permit system was set up. For many months, the commissions held that all projects that had not received a building permit (or other "final discretionary approval") before November 8 were not exempt from the law and had to apply for a permit.

Eventually, however, the California Supreme Court ruled that permits were not required if "substantial lawful construction" had started before February 1, 1973. The court reasoned that using any earlier date would

have meant a *de facto* construction moratorium during the period between the passage of the act and the beginning of the permit process,
causing "serious economic dislocations not contemplated by the act."[29]

The question of exemptions is a technical one, but not a minor one.
The South Coast Commission alone approved 140 claims of exemption,
involving construction valued at $2.4 billion. Commissions found exemp-
tion cases particularly frustrating in that their decision had to be based
solely on the date on which "substantial" construction started, and they
could give no consideration whatever to whether the project was environmentally sound.

Moreover, complicated questions arose in the case of projects with
several interrelated phases. For example, must an urban renewal agency
which cleared land for construction several years ago now apply for a
coastal permit to build on it?[30] Or must the developer of an interdepend-
ent planned-unit development secure a permit to build those sections
that were not underway when the initiative was passed?[31] In one Orange
County case, a developer graded scores of acres shortly before the permit process went into effect, then claimed that if he were not allowed to
build, the graded land would erode into the sea. He was not exempted.

A Permit Overview

It was in decisions on development permits that the coastal commissions first began to face the real problems of the coast. From the beginning, the state commission interpreted its powers broadly, used them
decisively, and counteracted an initial timidity on the part of the regional
commissions. A deluge of permit applications confronted the commissioners from the moment they took office, and the load was never to
slacken in the ensuing years. Since the commissions were statutorily
bound to dispose of an application within a fixed period of time, their
hallmark became rapid, unequivocal decision-making. Many unsuccessful permit applicants would accuse the commissions of being arbitrary,
inadequately informed, or inconsistent. But no one could call them inde-
cisive.

The number and complexity of the applications caused the commissions
to rely heavily on staff reports for information and recommendations, yet
in most cases the commissioners themselves, not the staff, made the
important policy choices.[32] Staff, particularly at the state level, eventually
became very proficient at extracting the "significant coastal issues" posed
by a particular project and summarizing them for the commissions'
consideration.

Both because of the heavy permit load and because of a genuine interest in making the regulatory process accessible to the general public, the coastal commissions adopted informal, nonlegalistic procedures.[33] The procedural goal seemed to be to put the ordinary citizen objecting to a project on an equal footing with the developer's cadre of expensive lawyers, architects, and expert witnesses.[34] Because Proposition 20 had granted virtually unlimited standing to appeal disputed projects to the state level, there were initial fears that a small group of citizen activists could tie up the process and bring development to a standstill. This never happened, in part because of citizen restraint, and in part because the state commission demonstrated early that it would reject frivolous appeals out-of-hand.[35]

One can broadly characterize the coastal commissions' record of permit administration as the faithful implementation of an unusually strict and uncompromising legal mandate. Projects that threatened major environmental damage, that would urbanize previously pristine stretches of the coast, or that would adversely impact coastal agriculture were rarely approved. Other projects were allowed to proceed subject to extensive, and often costly, conditions. Nevertheless, the Proposition 20 years by no means saw a total moratorium on building along the coast.

Of the first 15,025 permits processed by the regional commissions, 488, or 3.2 percent, were denied. The state commission denied 262 on appeal. Adjusting for double-counting (permits denied on both levels), it can be estimated that fewer than 4.5 percent of the total number of permits applied for were ultimately denied.

Because so many permit applications were to build a single-family home or for other small projects, one might argue that the value of coastal construction approved is more relevant than the actual number of permits approved. No statewide figures on value of permits are available. But we do know that the South Coast Regional Commission (which handled two out of every five permits processed statewide) denied 13.5 percent of the applications, by dollar value, that it acted upon. The figures are $2.03 billion of construction approved; $318 million denied.[36]

In addition to the relatively small number of permit denials, the coastal commissions affected development in two principal ways. First, once developers learned that the commissions were applying the law strictly, they simply did not submit applications for projects that were almost certain to be denied. This was particularly true for very large projects on previously open land and for large-scale land divisions. There is no way to document these "discouraged projects," other than to note that several multi-hundred-acre tracts of land held by developers in 1972 were still undeveloped in 1978, despite six years of very strong consumer demand. One can point, for example, to the Irvine Company's 3.5 miles of coastline in Orange County, one of the nation's hottest housing markets. During the Proposition 20 years, Irvine did not file for permits for this portion of its holdings, having decided to work with the commissions and with local government on a comprehensive plan that might later be submitted as part of a local coastal plan.[37]

A second way in which the coastal commissions influenced development was by approving permits subject to conditions. Conditions might include such modifications to a project as reduction in density, increased use of buffers around sensitive areas, dedication of a public accessway, reduction in the bulk or appearance of a structure, or change in the method of sewage disposal. The state commission, which in its rulings on appeals set policy for the regional commissions, illustrates the important role that conditions played in controversial cases. In a sample of 77 appeals, 4 percent were approved as submitted, 43 percent were denied, and 53 percent were approved subject to conditions.[38]

The record of permit conditions, the pattern of approvals and denials, and the commissions' thousands of hours of debate over permits provided a strong indication of the commissions' policy direction, one which was reflected in the coastal plan and in the 1976 Coastal Act, and which even now is being implemented as the commissions review local plans. There have been some waverings, false starts, and inconsistencies, but most of the basic policies were forged quite early and were refined, rather than reversed, as time went on.[39] The following pages will discuss major coastal issues and policies, giving the major emphasis to actions of the state commission and the busy South Coast Regional Commission.

Beach Access—In Its Broadest Sense

Beach access, in its strictest sense as the legal right of the public to physically reach the publicly owned ocean shore, proved to be less of an overriding issue than the Proposition 20 campaign had indicated. Few developers were so bold as to propose projects that would actually fence off portions of the beach. Undoubtedly, knowing that the commissions would disapprove such projects was a deterrent. Access in its strictest sense became an issue primarily in two parts of the coast—in toney, densely developed Malibu and along parts of the sparsely settled shoreline north of San Francisco. In Malibu, the coastal commissions were confronted with applications to build single-family homes on vacant lots directly along the water's edge. In many cases, these lots represented the only way the public (sometimes with the necessary help of a hole in a fence) could gain access to the water. Over howls of protest from Malibu property owners, the coastal commissions required builders of new single-family homes to leave open corridors at the side of their lots, so as to permit public access to the beach. Moreover, in addition to this "vertical" access to the beach, the commissions often also exacted "lateral" access, an easement allowing the public to use most of the sand area between the house and the water's edge.[40]

In Marin and Sonoma counties, the access problem was somewhat different. There, very large pieces of private property, formerly ranchland, had been subdivided before 1972 into "closed gate" recreational subdivisions. Here, requiring an individual permit applicant to dedicate an easement would not solve the problem, as the public would have to traverse dozens of individually owned lots in order to reach the water. In one case, the huge Sea Ranch development, the commissions attempted to hold individual permits hostage in order to pry overall grants of access from the development's property owners' association.[41] In another, the commissions exacted individual grants of access, with the idea that these can eventually be connected in a way useful to the public.[42]

Beach access has more frequently been invoked in more subtle ways, involving parking, traffic congestion, "visual access," and other issues affecting the convenience of public access rather than its legality.

In the urban areas, where beach use is heaviest, beach access and use is determined mainly by parking. As shoreline neighborhoods have changed from single-family residences to apartment buildings, the available curbside parking spaces have been increasingly preempted by residents. Among the first permits to be denied by the south coast commission were several for duplexes in an oceanfront neighborhood in Newport Beach. The city of Newport Beach had required one parking space per unit, a ratio that clearly would have involved residents parking their extra cars on the narrow and congested streets. At subsequent meetings the commission approved duplexes that had two or more off-street parking spaces per unit and came up with a rough standard requiring two spaces per unit plus one guest parking space for each ten units. The state commission also adopted this ratio as its standard. Interestingly enough, the city of Newport Beach, which had protested the original permit denials, eventually changed its local ordinance to require 2-for-1 parking.

Strict parking requirements such as these usually also mean a decrease in density. Rather than devote a larger proportion of his lot to parking, the builder typically builds fewer, larger (and more expensive) units. Thus the parking standard that makes it easier for a middle-income person to park at the beach makes it more difficult for him to afford to live there.

Perhaps the heart of the access issue is the question of whether the beach should be primarily a place where a fairly limited number of people can have homes, a place for public recreation, or a place where a natural environment is preserved and protected. The commissions recognized all three as legitimate uses of the coast and tried to find policies that would result in some balance between them. Several issues are involved in finding that balance.

First, should residential use of the coast be encouraged at all? The commissions certainly approved their share of condominiums, but in several cases indicated that, if given a choice, they would prefer hotels to apartments, reasoning that hotels and other commercial facilities serve a greater number of people with the same amount of construction. Similarly, the state commission blocked the demolition of a small waterfront amusement park, which was slated to be replaced by a condominium. Executive director Bodovitz commented, "A use that would provide the most opportunity for the public to enjoy the benefits of being near the water ought to take precedence over a use, housing, that would limit the waterfront to a smaller number of people."[43]

A second issue is whether low-income people should be able to continue to live in the coastal zone, despite market pressures that have tended to force them out. More than a dozen appeals to the state commission raised this issue. The commissions have been eager to preserve the dwindling supply of low-cost housing along the coast, but have found it difficult to find legally and economically viable ways to do so. Permits were denied in both San Francisco and San Diego for projects that would have replaced low-cost housing with industry.[44] In several cases, the commissions have required developers to set aside a modest number of units in a new condominium for low-income or elderly tenants, occasionally granting the developer a density bonus for so doing. In still other cases, the commissions have simply refused to allow the demolition of older, but still sound, low-rent units. These cases are significant, yet they have been exceptions in a general commission policy of allowing, albeit reluctantly, the redevelopment of transitional urban neighborhoods with new structures and somewhat higher densities.[45]

A final aspect of the access problem is that increasing beach access sometimes conflicts with the commissions' other goals of protecting the marine environment and improving the quality of development. For example, increasing the public's use of an undeveloped piece of shoreline threatens the destruction of any adjoining tide pools by souvenir-hungry beachgoers. Beachside trailer parks, restaurants, or campgrounds may be more unsightly than low-density, luxury residences, yet they make the beach available to a greater number of people of more varied incomes.

Here again the commissions have gone both ways. The state commission approved (with conditions) a campground for recreational vehicles opposite the beach at Malibu. The staff report read, "This appeal poses one of the most important policy questions yet to come before the commission: should uses of land in the coastal zone that benefit many people have preference over uses that benefit a few? . . . Many Californians who will wish to use and enjoy the coastal zone may not be able to afford to live permanently in it. Thus, landowners and developers should be encouraged to provide increasing opportunities for Californians of all levels of income to enjoy coastal areas."[46] Two months later, the commission turned down a proposal by the state department of parks and recreation for a beachside campground for recreational vehicles. Here the project would actually have paved over part of the beach—and the alternative was not residential development, but simply continued use as open, day-use beach.[47]

In their search for standards governing which types of activities should have priority in locating near the water's edge, the commissions have postulated the useful concept of "coastal relatedness." This means giving preference to those activities which have a need, or at least a substantial advantage, in being close to the ocean. Thus, at least in theory, the commissions have frowned on locating new shopping centers, office buildings, and freeways within the coastal zone while looking with favor on such "coastal-related" projects as commercial fishing docks and view-oriented restaurants.

The commissions have acted on a number of cases involving what they call "visual access." Proposition 20 required a two-thirds majority to approve developments which "substantially interfere with or detract from the line of sight toward the sea from the state highway nearest the coast." This provision is particularly important north of San Francisco, where rocky headlands rather than beaches are the main pull for visitors. This became yet another issue in the Sea Ranch controversy. At Sea

Ranch, several hundred vacant, already subdivided lots covered the coastal terrace that sloped between the coastal highway and the sea. If large houses were built on some of these lots, they would substantially interfere with the view of anyone driving down the coast. Moreover, the developer had planted 50,000 pine seedlings to screen the development from the roadway. As these grew taller, they too would block visual access. Said commission executive director Bodovitz, "If nature takes its course at Sea Ranch, a motorist will feel that he is in the midst of pine forest and not know that the ocean exists."[48]

Over the years, the commissions have taken several approaches to problems of physical and visual access at Sea Ranch. They have denied permits for houses that would block views, and allowed others only if their size was reduced. For a time, the commissions required anyone who wished to build a home at Sea Ranch to deposit $1,500 into a fund that was to be used to buy access and preserve views. At present, commission policy is simply to deny new permits until the Sea Ranch Association agrees to conditions on access, building siting, and removal or trimming of trees.

Elsewhere, the commissions have tried to secure visual access by reducing the height of buildings, by pulling them back from the edge of scenically prominent bluffs, and by requiring developers to place structures on a lot so as to avoid creating a "Chinese wall" of buildings with little or no space between them.

Density and Growth

We have already looked at the density of beachside development as one of the determinants of beach access. The commissions have also been dealing with density as a land use issue. Although Proposition 20 was an expression of the voters' concern with the "loss" of the beach, the law mandated the commissions to control change in the entire coastal zone, beachside or not. Some of the citizen organizations which had supported Proposition 20 were as concerned with high rises, neighborhood change, and the loss of open space as with the deterioration of the beach environment. Thus, the coastal commissions have become part of the debate over the rate and form of urban growth that has been engaging planners, environmentalists, and local governments throughout California and the nation. Issues of growth and density took very different forms in urban and rural portions of the coastline. Within cities, the commissions had to decide how to deal with coastal neighborhoods in transition to more intense forms of development. For example, in Redondo Beach, a heavily urbanized community in Los Angeles County, the neighborhood on the bluffs above the beach has for some years been changing from single-family homes to luxury apartments. There was considerable local opposition to this dramatic increase in density. Just as the South Coast Commission was debating a permit application for a ten-story condominium in this neighborhood, a slate of "slow-growth" advocates won a local council election. Almost immediately, the coastal commission denied the permit for a ten-story building and made it clear that four stories would be the maximum permitted in that area.[49]

In other transitional areas such as San Diego's Ocean Beach and Los Angeles' Venice area, the commissions were willing to turn down large apartment buildings that would set new density precedents, but not to halt building altogether. The test generally was whether the proposed building was in character with surrounding structures. As in the Redondo Beach case, the commissions gave special weight in their decisions to expressions by the electorate, such as San Diego's height limit and Santa Monica's slow-growth council slate, and to actions of local government, such as the proposed downzoning of Venice. In the case of San Diego, a 30-foot height limit, passed by local voters, was used by the state coastal commission as the basis for denying a permit for a building designed before the law was passed.[50] This same policy of allowing infilling— except where it would block coastal views and access—but being very reluctant to allow dramatic changes in neighborhood character, was also implemented in smaller urban places, such as those found along the coast of San Luis Obispo County.

In yet another decision, the state commission limited growth adjacent to an historic area. Mendocino is an old redwood-lumbering village on scenic headlands 150 miles north of San Francisco. The entire town of 1,500 has been placed within an historic preservation district. The commission rejected an application to build a forty-five-unit motel there, even though it would be outside the historic district and was admittedly well designed. The commission found that the project was simply too large to be consistent with the scale of the historic town, where the largest lodging place has only twelve units. The commission suggested that visitors would be better accommodated in the larger town a few miles up the coast.[51]

The commissions' authority over the location of roads and sewers, as well as their mandate to protect agricultural land, gave them considerable power to control the expansion of some suburban fringe areas. This was dramatically expressed when the state commission cut the capacity of an Orange County sewage outfall, reducing the potential population growth of an area stretching 20 miles inland.[52] The sewer system, as approved by local government, was designed to serve a population of 220,000 by the year 2000. At the time, slightly more than 50,000 persons lived in the area. The coastal commission limited the outfall's capacity to 174,000 persons, expressing a concern for the declining air quality in the region. The project required a coastal permit because the effluent, which already was to meet very strict water quality standards, would be piped through the permit zone to the ocean.

In Carlsbad, a rapidly growing area in northern San Diego County, the regional commission denied a permit for a freeway-connector road that would have permitted hundreds of homes to be built in fields formerly devoted to commercial flower growing. Similarly, in areas near Santa Barbara, the state commission allowed some expansion onto agricultural land contiguous to built-up areas, but refused to grant permits for water and sewer connections to leap-frog subdivisions.

The commissions' most obvious impact on the form of coastal growth has been to prevent the subdivision, and hence the development, of large parcels of land in undeveloped portions of the coast. They have given several reasons for doing so—to protect open space for its scenic value, to keep land in agriculture or grazing, to avoid water pollution from individual septic systems, and to keep the oft-times narrow coastal highway from being crowded beyond its capacity. In places with high scenic or recreational value, moreover, the Proposition 20 commissions foresaw eventually recommending that the land be purchased for addition to the state park system. Prohibiting subdivision or erection of structures would keep this future option from being foreclosed. On at least two occasions, commissions denied permits for single-family homes on multiacre properties, claiming that the areas were designated by the parks department as priority areas for acquisition.

When the commissions prohibited any development at all on large tracts, either inside or outside of cities, they almost invariably did so "to preserve planning options pending completion of the coastal plan." After 1976, they continued much the same policy, citing both their new legislative mandate to concentrate development within already developed areas, and the fact that final disposition of these properties could not be made until local coastal plans were certified. Such severely restrictive policies might seem to skirt the edge of inverse condemnation or "taking," yet courts have frequently allowed such strong action when it was imposed temporarily during a period of plan preparation or revision.[53] Still unresolved, even today, is the question of how much development will be

EMORY AND HENRY LIBRARY

ultimately allowed on these parcels and how California's courts will respond.[54]

In their permit administration, the coastal commissions actively intervened to affect the form and character of development in urban, suburban, and rural places, showing a strong preference for development that did not differ markedly from what was already in place nearby. Despite their strictness, they allowed a substantial amount of construction—easily more than $3 billion worth—within the coastal zone, including some building directly adjacent to the shoreline. Although the commissions operated at a time of concern over the *rate* of development (as in Ramapo, Petaluma, and elsewhere), they did not intervene explicitly in that controversy, permitting virtually any development that could meet the tough criteria of Proposition 20.

The Natural Environment

The coastal law is commonly thought of as an "environmental" law, yet direct damage to natural systems was not the focus of most permit cases. A sample of appealed permits showed that 23 percent raised issues of landslide or erosion, 17 percent issues of water quality, 16 percent sewage or septic tank issues, and 6 percent air quality concerns. By contrast, 43 percent of the appeals raised visual (view or esthetic) issues, 40 percent raised issues of public access and recreation, and 37 percent raised parking or transportation issues.[55] The lesser frequency of strictly environmental concerns in California permit cases as contrasted with Vermont, Florida, and elsewhere is probably the result of the high level of pollution regulation and site development standards that existed in California prior to Proposition 20.

Among the more significant cases was the Orange County sewage outfall which we have already mentioned. In approving this permit, the South Coast and state commissions imposed water quality standards higher than the already strict limits required by the regional water quality board. Commission members felt that this treatment standard would encourage reuse of the water, making the outfall necessary only to balance supply and demand. One member, a marine biologist, went so far as to say that waste waters should be treated to a condition where they *enhance* the productivity of the receiving waters, citing Proposition 20's mandate to restore as well as protect marine life.[56] In a number of cases involving possible pollution from individual septic systems, the coastal commissions either denied permits or granted them subject to detailed conditions on the design and monitoring of waste disposal. The commissions were particularly sensitive to the protection of California's remaining coastal wetlands. In an appeal of a San Diego Commission decision, the state commission approved a 380-unit condominium near one of the last remaining lagoons in San Diego County, but only after cutting the size of the project in half and pulling the development 300 feet from the water's edge.

The commissions did allow interference with a natural lagoon environment for what they considered a higher goal—"farming" the sea. A Monterey County company was allowed to use a saltwater lagoon for raising oysters, clams, and other shellfish, even though there was some evidence that this activity might interfere with the use of the lagoon by migrating birds.

One provision of Proposition 20 caused the commissions to regulate an activity not generally covered by state land use laws—"the removal or logging of major vegetation." At first glance, such authority might be thought irrelevant to coastal protection, yet for hundreds of miles of northern California coastline, uncontrolled logging would threaten visual amenity and impair water quality. The commissions decided a number of logging cases, usually allowing cutting, but with conditions requiring buffer zones around streams, on erodable slopes, and in scenic areas.

Overall, the record of the commissions in protecting natural environments was quite good. In some ways, this environmental task was rather easy, for stopping pollution is no longer a politically controversial policy, and public officials are becoming accustomed to placing the burden of proof on the potential polluter. Moreover, in most cases an applicant was able to figure out some way to mitigate environmental impacts, yet still complete his project. Much more difficult and complex environmental tradeoffs had to be made in a small but important group of applications, those involving energy developments.

Energy and the Coastline

During the first few months of the commissions' existence, most observers would have predicted that energy-related projects would consume a great deal of their attention. On industrial drawing boards at that time were plans for conventional and nuclear power plants within the coastal zone, for terminals, tank farms and refineries for Alaskan oil, terminals for potentially dangerous liquefied natural gas, and offshore drilling off Malibu and in the ill-starred Santa Barbara channel. Only a fraction of the projects then contemplated actually reached the commissions. Most fell victim to the recession, post–energy-crisis cuts in demand projections, and state–federal regulatory squabbles that did not directly involve the commissions. A handful of energy cases were considered and provided many of the elements of controversy—tradeoffs between economic and environmental goals and between conflicting environmental objectives; impacts that were exceptionally expensive or impossible to mitigate; applicants enraged at regulatory complexity; and environmentalists fearful of a sellout.

In the first major energy case, both the South Coast Commission (voting 10–1) and the California State Commission (voting 9–1) approved a $92 million modernization of a Southern California Edison plant near the Los Angeles harbor.[57] Edison seldom operated this old plant, built before air pollution standards went into effect in 1947, but the company claimed that rising energy demands would make it necessary to run it far more frequently in the future. Modernizing the plant would add pollution to the coastal zone but would let Edison make less use of "dirtier" plants elsewhere in the Los Angeles basin. This early decision demonstrated that the coastal commissions were not unalterably opposed to coastal energy facilities and that they took a comprehensive, rather than an exclusively coastal, view of resource protection.

More hotly debated was an application for an $850 million expansion of the San Onofre nuclear-generating plant on the coast north of San Diego.[58] The proposed project involved building two 1,140-megawatt reactors immediately adjacent to the existing nuclear plant. By the time the San Onofre proposal was submitted to the coastal commissions, it had gone through a long series of hearings before agencies with other responsibilities and had received permits from all of them—the U.S. Atomic Energy Commission (AEC), the California Public Utilities Commission, the California Water Resources Control Board, and so forth.

The proposal was first submitted to the San Diego Commission, which approved it by a 9–1 vote. Several environmental groups then brought an appeal to the state commission. Much of the opposition was based on radiation dangers—an issue legally reserved to the AEC and beyond the power of the commissions to consider.

In its public hearing on the appeal, the state commission heard utility executives testify that the additions were vital to meet southern California's growing demand for electricity, particularly since natural gas and low-sulfur oil were in short supply. They argued that the project would be consistent with the coastal law because the site on which it would be built was already dedicated to the generation of nuclear power. Moreover, the environmental effects had been considered by several state and federal agencies and found acceptable. Regulatory delays had already pushed the project four years behind its original schedule, which meant that the utilities would have to burn an additional 70 million barrels of fuel oil that otherwise would not have to be consumed.

Opponents countered that many scientists have questioned the wisdom of the entire nuclear program with respect to disposal of radioactive wastes and the possibility of catastrophic accident. But aside from safety, the project would be an unwise and irreversible commitment of coastal resources. Construction would destroy a half-mile of sandstone bluffs and canyons, carved into unique and beautiful patterns by the action of wind and sea. The staggering amount of seawater needed to cool the reactors would carry with it plankton, which includes the eggs and larvae of many marine organisms. Subjected to heating and mechanical stresses, as much as 90 percent of the living material so "entrained" in the system might die.

In December 1973 the commission met for a vote. Pressure on the commissioners to approve the project was enormous—before them were telegrams from a U.S. Senator, members of Congress, and state officials, urging approval. The commission staff recommended denial. According to their report:

> From the beach below . . . there are the towering bluffs, carved and patterned by wind and water; the sound of the surf; and the silent, twisting canyons. This combination provides an experience virtually unique along the Southern California coast. And, just as nobody would propose to carve a power plant into Yosemite's Half Dome, the staff does not believe that anyone should destroy the bluffs and canyons at San Onofre. Our society is not yet so poor that we must chop down our cathedrals for firewood.[59]

The staff recommended that the project be redesigned—using a different kind of cooling system and a new type of reactor that requires less cooling water—and relocated, about a half-mile inland.

Utility spokesmen said they found these proposals unacceptable. In terms of time, the alternatives would take years. New approvals would have to be sought from many agencies and the cost, they asserted, would be in the hundreds of millions of dollars.

Because the project would require the closure of a section of beach during construction, approval required a two-thirds vote. The vote was six in favor and five opposed; the application was denied. A newspaper account described the utility officials as "obviously shocked and dazed."[60]

Southern California Edison issued a statement claiming the denial "will compound unemployment as well as the energy shortage. It threatens to make the resulting economic and personal repercussions a continuing part of the lives of Californians."[61]

Then the negotiations began. Pleas to reconsider its decision came to the commission from many directions, from the Federal Energy Office to the San Diego Chamber of Commerce. The utilities continued to refuse to consider moving the reactors off the coast, and after a month of negotiation, the commission agreed to reopen the case. The "compromise" solution would allow construction, but would reduce the area of bluffs destroyed to two-tenths of a mile, limit future expansion at the site, and require a study of the effects of cooling water on marine life by an independent board. If the study found environmental damage, the cooling system would have to be redesigned. The utilities claimed the conditions would cost at least $40 million.[62]

In February 1974 the commission accepted this new proposal by a 10–2 vote. A reporter described the conditions as "the strictest levied by any state agency on a nuclear power plant built in this country."[63] The environmentalists who had brought the appeal were not appeased. Their attorney commented, "Compromise is one thing; complete capitulation is another."[64]

The coastal commission chairman later observed that the toughest thing about the San Onofre decision was the commission's lack of authority to consider safety and safeguards. "If we had that authority," he continued, "I think it is very unlikely that any such plant would ever get approval from our commission."[65]

In later energy cases the commissions continued to implement a policy of allowing coastal facilities provided that most environmental impacts were mitigated. This was true in another (fossil) power plant case, an oil refinery expansion, and an onshore facility serving an offshore oil field.

A final controversial case, debated in 1975–76, found the state commission exacting major conditions but refusing to ban outright a new source of energy supply. The Exxon Corporation applied for a permit for a facility in Santa Barbara County to collect oil and gas produced by offshore wells, process it onshore, and pipe it back out to a near-shore terminal for loading onto tankers.[66] About 200 tanker trips yearly might be required, presenting a potential for a major oil spill. The state commission staff suggested that the tankers could be eliminated if Exxon were to join with other companies producing oil in the area and build a pipeline directly to Los Angeles-area refineries. Exxon balked, citing both the estimated $47 million added cost and the many uncertainties involved. The commission, voting 9–2, granted the company a permit for a temporary terminal only, insisting that studies be done on the economic and environmental feasibility of the pipeline option.

Some Permit Lessons

During the Proposition 20 years (1973–76) the coastal commissions became involved in permit controversies involving every conceivable land use issue. Demolition of an old structure would bring up historic preservation or the displacement of poor tenants. An application for a backyard swimming pool might elicit a condition that it be solar heated so as to save scarce natural gas. Building on a bluff would involve argument between geologists and neighbors over whether the structure was safe. In one bizarre case, the commission was asked to rule on whether artist Christo Javacheff should be allowed to build a 24-mile-long steel-and-canvas "running fence" across Marin County headlands. (The state commission refused to grant a permit—Christo built the temporary fence anyway.[67])

It was quite apparent from their permit decisions that the commissions were taking an extremely broad view of what "coastal" resources were and what types and locations of development could affect them. In part, this was explicitly mandated by Proposition 20, which had a very broad definition of development and which created the wide 1,000-yard permit zone and an even larger zone that was to be governed by the coastal plan. In part, the broad view reflected the commissioners' own inclination, for they made little effort to give less detailed scrutiny to projects relatively far from the shoreline and occasionally introduced interpretations of the law—as in the case of low-cost housing and energy conservation—that were not specifically mentioned in the statute.

The fact that the law was applicable to projects much smaller than those typically regulated by state land use laws was a mixed blessing for the commissions. They did find that some such projects could have substantial impacts on the coast. For example, the commissions were presented with applications for single homes along totally undeveloped stretches of coastline, applications for homes several times the size of those which surrounded them, and others that presented serious sewage-disposal issues. The commissions also came to appreciate the "cumulative impact" that a concentration of individual small and medium-sized projects could have. The chairman of the South Coast Commission recalled that in early 1973 his commission approved numerous multistory buildings in Redondo Beach, one at a time. An aerial photograph showed that the buildings were to be erected in the same vicinity. "We suddenly realized," he said, "that we were planning another Miami Beach."[68]

On the other hand, the sheer number of projects resulting from this low threshold threatened to exhaust the commissioners (miraculously the system never actually broke down), and the limited time devoted to each permit caused many applicants to feel that they had not been given a fair chance to defend their project.

The law's application to state and local government projects was a similar mixture of advantage and disadvantage for the commissions. Many of these government projects, particularly large urban renewal developments and highways, presented at least as many coastal issues as did similarly sized private projects. Moreover, one researcher has concluded that the coastal commissions had a lasting impact on state bureaucrats, helping them "see the coast as a geographic entity, rather than simply in terms of their own functions."[69] At the same time, the rough handling given the pet projects of some local governments created a reservoir of hostility and mistrust that the commissions even now must face.

One important indirect effect of the Proposition 20 vote was to convince the state parks department of the strong demand for coastal recreation. After 1972 more than 90 percent of state park-acquisition funds were spent within the coastal zone.[70]

The Coastal Plan

The ultimate duty of the coastal commissions under Proposition 20 was not to grant permits but to prepare a plan for the permanent use and protection of the California coast. The plan was to be submitted to the 1976 session of the state legislature for consideration and action. It was to contain both policies for the coast and a recommended way of implementing them, for the Proposition 20 coastal commissions, and their regulatory powers, were to go out of existence ninety days after the legislature adjourned.

The temporary nature of the permit authority was a calculated gamble by the authors of Proposition 20. In part, they were influenced by the success of the BCDC, in which a temporary permit system, with strong participation by local officials, resulted in a permanent plan that was acceptable to localities, the legislature, and the environmentalists. More important, Proposition 20's authors feared that a permanent coastal agency, set up by initiative, might eventually prove even less responsive to citizen concerns than had local city councils and zoning boards.

A Comprehensive Plan—One Element at a Time

State commission director Bodovitz had a rather clear vision of how the planning process might take place. Its debt to the BCDC experience was unmistakable. What was needed, he asserted, was neither more research nor more specific plans for the coast, but a set of policy decisions. As he argued in one early speech, "We already know more about the coastal zone than we've thus far been willing to act upon."[71] Like the BCDC plan, and paralleling the coastal commissions' approach to the permit process, the coastal plan was to feature active commissioner involvement, massive public participation, and strong resource-protection policies. As did the BCDC plan, the coastal plan would contain both broad policies and maps showing specific places where they would be applied. But at no time was there the intention of making the plan a detailed state zoning map of the coast.

Although the final product was a comprehensive plan, it was put together from nine distinct topics or "elements," adopted sequentially. Eight of these were composed of problem analyses and policy decisions on a particular aspect of coastal resources or coastal development: marine environment, coastal land environment, geologic hazards, energy, recreation, appearance and design, transportation, and intensity of development. Another, which was not considered until all the other elements had been adopted, contained the crucial recommendations for future government powers and funding needed to carry out the plan.

For each element, the same adoption process was repeated. First, the state commission staff drew up a detailed background paper, containing an analysis of the problem and tentative policy recommendations. These were sent to the regional commissions, which held public hearings and workshops and then adopted the element, adding whatever "regional amplification" was needed to cover local conditions or problems. Then the state commission collected the six regional versions of the element, held still more hearings, and voted on statewide policies. Each regional commission (at least in theory) dealt with the same element at the same time, maximizing press coverage and making it easy to see whether the overall planning program was keeping up with its demanding schedule.

This step-by-step approach to planning drew some early criticism from those who felt that it slighted the great interconnectedness of coastal problems.[72] Bodovitz and his planners defended it as the best way to encourage participation by commissioners and the public. "One of the lessons learned from much of the land and water planning of recent years," he said, "is that comprehensive plans with their long summaries and multiple appendices are rarely understood by the public and infrequently adopted by the decision makers. So, necessity virtually dictates that effective planning be done one element at a time."[73]

By design, the first three topics were the least controversial. It had been hoped that by first reaching agreement on how to protect the coast's natural systems, commissioners would find common ground that would carry over into the consideration of such controversial questions as intensity of development and the role of energy facilities on the coast. There is no evidence that such consensus was actually produced—members of the South Coast Commission, for example, were described by one participant as "philosophically as far apart in the last element [of the plan] as in the first."[74] But taking the easiest elements first enabled the commissioners to avoid early public confrontations that might have foredoomed the plan.

The time schedule for the planning effort was unusually tight. Throughout 1974 the regional commissions adopted one plan element almost every month, all the while trying to keep up with their monstrous permit load. By March 1975 the first eight elements had been completed, and they were bound together as the first, preliminary version of the coastal plan.

Given the time pressures, most planning bodies would undoubtedly have settled for a staff-written plan, with a few token public hearings and commissioner discussions. Not so the California coastal commissions. The chairman's letter transmitting the plan to the legislature described it as evolving out of "public participation in resource planning on a scale unmatched in California."[75] It is difficult to argue with his statement when one considers what the commissions did: hundreds of informational meetings and 259 regional public hearings held on the plan elements; 15,000 copies of the preliminary plan distributed; more hearings (described by one observer as "an orgy of public participation") attended by 6,000 people in sixteen counties; 25,000 copies printed of the lengthy final plan.[76] In addition to using public participation to comment on policy choices, the commissions used it as a major source of information. Natural scientists from government agencies, universities, and interest groups were used as voluntary "technical reviewers," and served as the commissions' primary means of checking the scientific soundness of their recommendations. Local governments, too, were encouraged to comment as part of the participation process—other than some informal staff consultations, local planners had no other role in preparing the coastal plan.

What effect did all this participation have? For one thing, large numbers of participants thought that their views had been given fair consideration.[77] The argument that the plan, like the coastal initiative itself, had its origin in popular sentiment was to be a potent one in subsequent legislative debate. Participation also probably reinforced the commissions' inclination to take a broad view of coastal resources. Although some development interests and local governments criticized the inclusion of broad policies on agricultural land, energy conservation, and low-cost housing, other participants strongly identified those as important coastal concerns. Participation also helped the commissions see potential implementation problems. For example, a draft policy on public access was refined after public comment to take specific account of who would maintain accessways and of conflicts between access and natural resource protection.[78]

Overall, the commissions gave considerable weight to public sentiment that suggested strengthening the amount of resource protection, that broadened the scope of "coastal" problems, or that pointed out specific implementation problems. Having much less impact was the not inconsiderable testimony that voiced general opposition to the scope of regulation, that demanded compensation for regulatory action, or that suggested that coastal policy making be returned to local government or state functional agencies.[79] The state commission in particular seemed to operate from the assumption that Proposition 20 had called for a plan that was broad and highly oriented to the protection of coastal resources. The legislature, not the coastal commissions, was believed to be the appropriate forum for making tradeoffs and compromises.

The plan that emerged from all of this activity—in December 1975, precisely on schedule—was an attractively presented 443-page report. It contained detailed discussions of coastal issues and 162 numbered policies for dealing with them. The plan asked that these policies be applied in a coastal zone that generally stretched five miles inland, but was extended even farther at points to include stream valleys and prime agricultural lands.

It took a comprehensive view of coastal resources, devoting eight full pages to agriculture, fifteen pages to energy conservation and alternative energy sources, and 2½ pages to air quality.[80] Literally dozens of times, the plan told other state agencies specific things to do to ensure that their activities did not harm coastal resources. In the case of the state energy commission, it even recommended a vast increase in authority, asking that the legislature empower the energy agency to control not just power plants (as it then did), but all major energy production, transmission, and processing facilities statewide.

The plan's resource-protection policies were strong ones, consistent with those developed in the course of permit administration. Unlike the terse "environmental Ten Commandments" contained in Vermont's Act 250, the coastal plan's policies were complex and sophisticated, filled with implementation criteria, review procedures, and calls for studies of specific issues for which knowledge was sparse. The agricultural land policy is a good example. Strongly protective of farming, it nevertheless presented detailed criteria governing the circumstances in which farmland could be used for urban expansion. Moreover, the policy explicitly recognized that land regulation alone could not ensure the survival of coastal agriculture. It therefore made recommendations on property taxes, agricultural research, studies of local farm economies, and even mentioned the possibility of direct state aid to farmers.

In addition to the general policies, the plan contained more than 200 pages of geographically specific discussions of problems and policies. (One example: "Cleone Acres, Mendocino County. Do not allow strip development in undeveloped areas along Highway 1 north of Cleone Acres.") Maps were presented in the plan as well. They did not indicate zoning or intensity of use, but specifically identified areas of special resource value.

The centerpiece of the plan was its recommendation for implementation. The "powers and funding" element was the last prepared, so late in fact that not all the regional commissions had a chance to vote on it. A variety of approaches to applying coastal policies were suggested in the first discussion draft, but the preponderance of opinion (including influential support by the Coastal Alliance) was that actual implementation of land use controls should be returned to local government, provided that some way could be found to bring local regulation into line with the strict policies contained in the coastal plan.[81]

The plan's recommendation was for a complex mixture of state and local control. Local governments would have three years to bring their land use plans and regulatory ordinances into line with coastal policies. Compliance would be enforced by having the local plans reviewed and certified by both state and regional coastal commissions. And until a locality's plans had been certified, state and regional control would continue much as before. Moreover, a permanent state commission would be created to hear appeals from local decisions (in a limited range of cases) and to oversee periodic revisions to the local plans. The recommendation was thus for a distinct shift from the interim regulatory system set up by Proposition 20. From an institutional standpoint, it called for a much more important role for local government. In terms of regulatory method, the plan recommended moving from case-by-case permit review to reliance on policy standards and before-the-fact designation of permitted uses.

The Legislature Responds

When the BCDC's plan was submitted to the legislature in 1969, the lawmakers passed a very brief bill making the bay agency permanent and declaring that the plan had legal force. Enactment of the coastal commissions' plan was not to be so easy. Soon after the coastal plan was released, legislative leadership indicated that they wanted to consider the plan in full detail, and were unwilling to simply endorse it by reference. Thus January 1976 found legislative staffers frantically trying to rework the plan's policies into the format of a legislative act. It was given the number A.B. (for Assembly Bill) 1579—not coincidentally, 1579 was the year in which Sir Francis Drake first set foot on the California coast.

The lineup of interests supporting and opposing the coastal bill was not vastly different from that which occurred over Proposition 20. The Sierra Club, the Coastal Alliance, the League of Women Voters, local environmental groups, and a few local governments were among its supporters; the California Chamber of Commerce, Association of Realtors, and the County Supervisors' Association were among its opponents.[82] Two new organizations also appeared: PACE (an acronym for People, Access, Coastal Environment), which lobbied for strong policies on access and on low-income housing; and CEEB (Council for Environmental and Economic Balance), a coalition of large firms and trade unions.

Unlike the Proposition 20 days, however, the emphasis of both sides was on negotiation rather than inflammatory rhetoric. Opponents of the bill were aware that a then-secret CEEB poll had revealed surprising citizen support for strict coastal regulation. As a result, all but the most adamant foes of coastal controls took the position that some kind of coastal bill had to emerge from the legislature. The alternative was another initiative and the possibility that the Proposition 20 system might be made permanent. The environmentalists, on the other hand, were not at all sure that they had the strength to mount another successful initiative. Since the coastal plan was exceptionally strong, supporters felt that they had some room for compromise.

The legislative twists and turns taken by the coastal bill have been chronicled elsewhere.[83] Its passage took eight months. During that time it absorbed several hundred separate amendments, was defeated by a single vote in the Senate Finance Committee, was redrafted and dramatically resurrected (with the new number S.B. 1277), and was passed in the final week of the legislative session. On the day it finally passed, the bill's future remained in doubt until negotiators, who had huddled all day in the governor's office, sent an urgent message to the floor of the legislature announcing some final compromises.

The new coastal act incorporated the most important features recommended by the coastal plan. First, it contained, with only minor changes, the plan's basic implementation principle of state review of local land use plans and regulations. Until these "local coastal programs" were certified, a process expected to take until 1981, development within the coastal zone would continue to be regulated by state and regional coastal commissions.[84] Second, the plan's long list of general and specific policies was shrunk to twelve pages of "coastal resources planning and management policies," but many of these were strong indeed. Finally, even after all the local plans had been certified, a permanent state coastal commission would continue to hear citizen appeals of local action on certain large or strategically located projects.[85]

The differences between the coastal plan and this "California Coastal Act of 1976" point up the major focus of legislative debate. The wide proposed coastal boundaries were pulled back toward the water's edge. The new regulated zone extends generally 1,000 yards inland, but with "bumps" reaching farther inland to encompass streams and wetlands and "dents" shrinking the zone in built-up urban areas.[86] Legislators were unsympathetic toward the argument that broader swaths of coastal farmland required protection, expecting to deal with that issue in a comprehensive farmland retention bill scheduled for consideration the following year. (The farmland bill failed to pass in both 1977 and 1978.)

Many changes between the plan and the law concerned the relationship of the permanent coastal agency with other agencies of state government. Proposals involving regulatory overlap were firmly refused, but the new law allowed the coastal agency great power to review other agencies' *development* activities.[87]

The Coastal Act also contained several technical provisions increasing the power of local governments. Perhaps the most important was a provision that after 1981, half the membership of the permanent state coastal commission would be composed of local elected officials.

When the Coastal Act was signed in September 1976, environmentalists hailed it as a major victory. True, the legislature had not actually accepted the coastal plan. In fact, that document, with all its resource maps and detailed policies, had no legal effect whatever. But many of its most important features had become part of the new law.

One prominent environmentalist enthusiastically proclaimed that the new law was "the strongest piece of land-use legislation in the nation."[88] Other observers, viewing the law's complexity and the newly central role of local government, were more cautious. University of California researcher Stanley Scott termed the law "a sort of uneasy compromise between local government supporters and conservationists."[89]

After the Coastal Act

The 1976 Coastal Act created new coastal commissions, with a new mandate and new standards. Many of the Proposition 20 commissioners initially received appointments to the new California Coastal Commissions (dropping the appellation "conservation commission" had been one of the legislative compromises).[90] But by early 1979 most of the dominant personalities of the Proposition 20 years, including all the BCDC alumni, were gone from the state commission and its staff. Members of the current state commission include a geologist, a businesswoman, a union official, a political science professor, a rancher, two city councilmen, three "citizen activists," and a former state senator.[91] Chairman of the state commission is Bradford Lundborg, a Santa Rosa physician who had formerly served on the North Central Regional Commission.[92] The new executive director, Michael Fischer, had been executive director of the North Central Commission and had had experience both as a local planner and in noncoastal planning at the state level. Such experience was considered essential, given the new commissions' close working relationship with local governments and the need to secure voluntary cooperation from peer agencies in the state bureaucracy.

One innovation has been the addition of three nonvoting members to the state commission, representing the State Lands Commission, Business and Transportation Agency, and Resources Agency. These persons— generally delegates sent by the agency head—say comparatively little during commission meetings, but are relied on to present agency views and to inform their agencies of important commission decisions.

Drafting the Local Coastal Programs

Although the coastal commissions continue to process permits—applications have been running at a rate slightly higher than in Proposition 20 days—their most important function is the encouragement and review of local planning efforts. These local coastal programs (LCPs) are to consist of two stages. First, each of the fifty-three cities and fifteen counties within the coastal zone will prepare a land use plan based on the policies contained in the 1976 Coastal Act. Then, jurisdictions must adjust their zoning and other ordinances so as to implement the policies. Both stages must be approved by state and regional coastal commissions, which also are supplying funding and interpretive guidelines elaborating on the act's broad policies.

The relationship between local governments and the coastal commissions has not been a particularly happy one. One reason is the political tensions involved, for the coastal act is forcing many localities to do something that, as one regional commission staffer put it, "They don't believe in to begin with." This is complicated by the fact that while the day-to-day technical work is being done by local and commission staff planners, the groups that have ultimate decision-making power, namely, local elected officials and members of the coastal commissions, have had very little direct contact. Mutual suspicion is high.

Another reason is inherent in the task itself. Local planners in California are accustomed to preparing either broad policy declarations designed as community consensus or very specific zoning maps and physical plans. A local coastal program is something different, a policy plan with a direct tie to implementation. For example, in its land use phase, a local coastal program must deal with the intensity of use of particular pieces of coastal property, something much more concrete than is normally done in a local general plan.

The result has been called by one researcher "the specificity controversy."[93] Local governments are afraid that specific parcel-by-parcel use designations will make the plan too inflexible. How, they ask, can they anticipate exactly what a developer will be interested in building years in the future? The coastal regulators, for their part, know that their permit authority will be strictly circumscribed once the local plan has been approved and are eager to "nail down" environmental gains so that they cannot later be dissipated by development-minded local authorities.

Funding has also been an issue, although it is one that has both favorable and unfavorable implications for local coastal planning. During the 1978–79 fiscal year, the state commission has made available to local governments $3.5 million to pay for planning, most of it federal money obtained under the national Coastal Zone Management Act. Local governments complain that the amount is inadequate, given the extent of planning problems they must consider—ranging from beach erosion control to low-income housing—and the paucity of local data specific to the coastal zone. Some cynics, however, believe that if given more money, local governments would needlessly prolong the process, postponing hard decisions. The 1978 property-tax-reduction initiative (Proposition 13), on the other hand, placed many local planners' jobs in jeopardy. With state funding available for coastal planning, localities may be encouraged to give that work higher priority and thereby avoid laying off employees.

The coastal commissions' planning strategy has been to encourage a few localities, particularly small jurisdictions somewhat sympathetic to coastal planning, to submit their LCPs early as an example to others of how to do it. As executive director Fischer puts it, "We need some success stories, and we need some prototypes."[94] By the end of 1978, reported the commission, 82 percent of the affected local governments were "actively involved in their coastal planning."[95] Seven plans had been given at least informal review by state or regional commissions and one, for the tiny north coast town of Trinidad, had been given official, albeit conditional, approval.

If the ability of local governments to produce adequate plans is still in question, so is the capacity of the commissions, with their limited staff, heavy permit responsibilities, and lack of familiarity with local planning, to adequately review them.[96] Some observers argue that the commissions must cut their long list of coastal concerns down to a few key priorities— beach access, coastal-relatedness, rural sprawl, for example—or concentrate on a few areas, while allowing local governments more flexibility in less "critical" matters or locations. Others believe that the essence of the coastal commissions' work to date has been their comprehensive view of coastal resources and that no detail should slip through the process unscrutinized.

The state commission predicts that most of the local programs—both plans and implementation measures—can be certified by the July 1981 legislative deadline.[97] Others are not so sure, observing that the only sanction faced by a local government that does not obtain certification will be continued permit regulation by a state commission due, after 1981, to number six local elected officials among its twelve members. In the meantime, says a state commissioner, local officials can use the permit process to blame the coastal commissions for denying projects they do not themselves have the political courage to deny.

Current Coastal Issues

Most of the policies now being implemented by the coastal commissions, both in reviewing plans and in judging permit applications, are very similar to those we have described in our discussion of the Proposition 20 years. The commissions have not backed away significantly from their earlier strong stands nor have they the ability, under the 1976 act, to develop entirely new policies. Nevertheless, certain types of issues seem to have gained particular prominence since 1976.

One of them is what to do about existing small-lot subdivisions in scenic or environmentally sensitive parts of the coast. As executive director Fischer put it in a talk to a large group of southern California property owners: "Three places are now causing us the most [regulatory] problems: Mendocino County, Big Sur and the Santa Monica Mountains. All are rural, all are world renowned, and all are fantastically beautiful. All have a large supply of existing small undeveloped lots, limited highway capacity, and very high recreational visitor demand."[98] No real solution to the problems of those places, Fischer continued, would be possible until the relevant local governments had prepared their local coastal programs.

Unfortunately, the local programs are no panacea. Whether the final decision is made by a coastal commission or by local government, the underlying problem remains the same—what can be done about lots subdivided in times of lesser environmental concern, and now owned by individuals who feel strongly that they have a legal and moral right to build a structure?[99]

One possible solution, used by the state commission in several permit appeal cases, is requiring persons who own multiple adjoining lots to combine them into a single building site, reducing density from existing lot patterns of five or six units per acre to one or two units per acre.[100]

This idea has led to more complex forms of density transfer as well. In one 1978 decision, the state commission allowed a property owner to subdivide a parcel in the developed portion of Malibu into three building sites, in exchange for extinguishing the development potential of and dedicating to open space fourteen small lots he owned in a more remote section of the Santa Monica Mountains.[101] In yet another case, the state commission was faced with an application to build six houses on twenty contiguous parcels totaling four acres. Because of steep slopes, the commission ruled that no more than two houses could be accommodated on the site. But, in addition to granting the developer permission to build the two houses, the commission compensated him for his reduction in development potential by granting him two additional "transferrable development credits." The owner soon sold one of his credits for $35,000 to someone wishing to create an additional building site in a more developed part of Malibu.[102]

An intriguing tool for lot consolidation, particularly of splintered rural land with agricultural potential, is the California Coastal Conservancy. Created by a companion bill to the 1976 Coastal Act and given $10 million by the state, the Conservancy can acquire, resubdivide, and resell land; restore degraded coastal wetlands; purchase buffers around sensitive areas; and manage land dedicated for coastal access. A representative of the coastal commissions sits on the Conservancy's five-member board. One proposed project would consolidate seventy lots or more in a Sonoma County subdivision, concentrating units on about 10 percent of the land.

Another recurring issue for the coastal commissions has arisen from their policy of requiring dedication of public access as a condition for permitting new construction on beachfront lots. Property owners have complained that the commissions require them to dedicate an easement extending from the high-water mark to as close as five feet from their dwelling, exposing them to noise and vandalism. A class action lawsuit has been filed by a group of property owners in an attempt to overturn the policy. The commissions, for their part, maintain that they are simply enforcing the access requirements of the 1976 Coastal Act and the basic beach-access guarantee in California's constitution.

Low- and moderate-income housing has continued to be the subject of many permit cases as well as an issue in several jurisdictions' local coastal programs. By giving density bonuses, reducing parking requirements, or simply requiring that developments include a small percentage of subsidized units, the commissions have since 1976 provided for about 600 units of family or senior citizen housing. The commissions have also asserted that the 1976 act's requirement for full access for low- and moderate-income households gives them authority to bar the conversion of rental apartments to condominiums or stock cooperatives.

The commissions' overall permit record under the 1976 act has been quite similar to that under Proposition 20. Statewide, 93 percent of permit applications have been approved, with about 7 percent of all regional decisions appealed to the state body.[103]

As if the combined load of permits and LCPs were not enough to occupy the commissions, the state commission has also undertaken a number of specialized tasks mandated by the legislature, including designating 260 miles of coastline as "unsuitable" for power plant construction, drawing up coastal forestry guidelines to be implemented by the state forestry board, and evaluating sites for a planned liquefied natural gas terminal. In mid-1978 the state public utilities commission, which has final authority over such a terminal, gave preference to the site ranked third by the coastal commission.

Energy issues also figured in delaying the coastal commissions' certification to enter the "implementation phase" under the federal Coastal Zone Management Act. Action by federal coastal zone management officials was delayed pending resolution of a suit by oil producers, who contended that the California program did not adequately provide for national energy needs. But a federal court sided with the commissions, and by the end of 1978, the federal coastal zone management administrator could announce certification of the California program, "the most visible coastal program in the nation and likely to remain so."[104]

This federal endorsement of their program is a welcome event for the commissions at a time when they face a variety of problems. Internally, the commissions are finding it difficult to maintain the enthusiasm that had fueled them during the first heady years of implementing the coastal initiative. The permit load continues to be heavy, leaving commissioners exhausted from seemingly endless agendas. Staff, too, finds that the immediate pressures of permit work take time away from the complex job of helping local governments prepare their local coastal programs. "Even our planning director gets involved in permits," complains one overworked regional staffer.

Citizen participation has also fallen off since the Proposition 20 years. "Some citizens are tired, or frustrated," says a state commissioner, "some have moved on to other issues. Whatever the reason, the fire is gone, and citizen supporters are not nearly as active as before."[105]

In seeming parallel to the decline in participation, press attention to the commissions has fallen off. Much of the notice the commissions receive highlights delays, housing costs, and the commissions' impacts on individual property owners.[106]

More than forty bills introduced in the 1979 legislative session would directly affect the commissions. "Not one of them," notes commission staff director Fischer wryly, "proposes to *expand* our powers."[107] Among the most threatening are proposals to reduce the inland reach of the commissions' authority and bills that would exempt all single-family homes from permit review, even where construction would block beach access or coastal views.

The commissions hope to head off such moves by supporting legislation to increase state funding for access purchase, exempt single-family homes on serviced lots that are both off the beach and within incorporated areas, and make minor adjustments in the permit zone. The Sierra Club has given these proposals guarded support, fearing that otherwise more drastic changes in the Coastal Act are possible.[108]

Conclusion

California's coastal program has been the boldest effort to date in state land use regulation. Endowed by the original ballot initiative with an exceptionally strong legal and political position, the coastal commissions—particularly the state commission—aggressively implemented the law. California courts, traditionally tolerant of innovations in planning, allowed the commissions great flexibility. The volume of development permits processed and the diversity of land use issues that were raised and dealt with are unrivaled by any other state land use program, coastal or noncoastal.

During the period 1972–76, the coastal commissions demonstrated that, given strong legal authority and the will to use it, a state agency can make a visible difference in the amount, location, and quality of development. Created at a time of rapid and destructive coastal development, the coastal commissions dramatically reduced the rate of damage to coastal resources, without resorting to a blanket building moratorium. They demonstrated that coastal development does indeed raise issues of greater than local concern, among them public access, view protection, retention of productive farmland and low-cost housing, prevention of sprawl in rural areas, and the location of energy facilities and of state infrastructure. The commissions also showed that an unprecedented amount of citizen participation can be allowed without sacrificing planning deadlines or causing frivolous objections to bog down the regulatory process.

Perhaps most important, the commissions showed that vigorous interim enforcement need not so alienate the public or the legislature that they refuse to extend or continue the controls.

These accomplishments were purchased at the expense of some damage to the feelings of local officials and substantial costs to some coastal landowners, a legacy likely to cause the commissions some problems in the future.

Since 1976, the commissions have been faced with the even more complex task of consolidating their early successes. It is simply impossible to say whether the coastal protection gains made during the Proposition 20 years will be retained or slowly dissipated.

One major uncertainty is whether planning techniques are sufficiently well developed to enable the commissions to move smoothly from project-by-project regulation to anticipatory planning for future development. The 1976 Coastal Act contains a number of strong, clearly stated policies. But ahead lies the job of applying those policies to tens of thousands of individual parcels of land in order to regulate construction that may not even be proposed until years into the future. The California coastal program is thus on the frontiers of urban and regional planning not only in its ambitious goals but also in its methods.

A second uncertainty arises from the requirement that this complex task be done in collaboration with local governments, many of them unwilling partners. Moreover, by 1981, half the members of the state commission must be appointed from the ranks of local elected officials. Because to date the state commission has been dominated by strongly conservation-minded people, a change to greater local government influence could substantially change this still-evolving program's orientation.

Yet another uncertainty stems from the fact that widespread public mistrust of government regulation in general has not excepted the coastal commissions—perhaps the most vigorous of California's regulatory bodies. "The public image of the Coastal Act," laments one state commissioner, "is not that it is protecting the environment or protecting access, but that it is another example of government overregulation." This perception may make it difficult for the commissions to withstand future legislative attempts to whittle their authority.

It is perhaps a measure of how difficult land use problems really are to note that despite the commissions' strenuous regulatory actions, and despite the 1976 legislative endorsement of so many of the coastal plan's recommendations, the protection of the California coastline is not assured. In retrospect, the 1976 legislative "victory" seems to be merely a milestone separating one phase of a protracted political and legislative struggle from the next.

Notes

1. California Department of Parks and Recreation, California Coastline Preservation and Recreation Plan (August 1971), cited in California Legislature, Joint Committee on Open Space Lands, *State Open Space and Resource Conservation Program for California* (Sacramento, 1972) p. 29.

2. San Francisco *Chronicle,* May 30, 1971.

3. "California's Vanishing Coastlands," article circulated by California Coastal Alliance.

4. *Los Angeles Times,* Feb. 8, 1970.

5. Interview with Donald May, Hermosa Beach, Sept. 23, 1973.

6. U.S. Department of the Interior, Bureau of Sport Fisheries and Wildlife, *Southern California Estuaries and Coastal Wetlands: Endangered Environments* (Portland, Oreg., BSFW, January 1972) p. 5.

7. Clawson, address to National Land Use Policy Conference, Des Moines, Iowa, Nov. 18, 1972.

8. For a fuller account of the formation of the Coastal Alliance and the struggle to enact Proposition 20, see Janet Adams, "Proposition 20—A Citizens' Campaign," *Syracuse Law Review* vol. 24, no. 3 (Summer 1973) pp. 1019–1046; and William J. Duddleson, "How the Citizens of California Secured Their Coastal Management Program," in Robert G. Healy, ed., *Protecting the Golden Shore* (Washington, D.C., Conservation Foundation, 1978) pp. 5–14.

9. Peter Douglas, "Answers to Arguments Raised Against the Coastline Protection Initiative" (August 1972) p. 9, flier in files of the California Coastal Alliance.

10. For an excellent study of the BCDC experience, see Rice Odell, *The Saving of San Francisco Bay* (Washington, D.C., The Conservation Foundation, 1972).

11. Officially, Proposition 20 (the coastal law) is the California Coastal Zone Conservation Act, and the state commission is the California Coastal Zone Conservation Commission. The text of the law is contained in California Public Resources Code, § 27000 *et seq.*

12. In southern California, where the coastal mountains are discontinuous, the zone extended 5 miles inland or to the crest of the mountain range, whichever was shorter.

13. The permit zone contained about 500,000 acres of land, one-half of 1 percent of the state's total land area.

14. California Public Resources Code, § § 27402 and 27302.

15. Compare this procedure with, for example, that prescribed by Vermont's Act 250, which requires that parties to commission permit hearings must be local or regional governments, planning commissions, or adjoining property owners.

16. Interview, Los Angeles, Sept. 17, 1973.

17. Quoted in the *Los Angeles Times,* editorial, Sept. 25, 1972.

18. Pacific Gas and Electric, undated policy statement.

19. *Los Angeles Times,* Oct. 19, 1972.

20. By this time the Coastal Alliance had grown to include more than 1,500 participating organizations, ranging from the League of Women Voters and the Sierra Club to the Aquajets Skin Diving Club.

21. Robert Deacon and Perry Shapiro, "Private Preference for Collective Goods Revealed Through Voting on Referenda," *American Economic Review* vol. 65, no. 5 (December 1975) pp. 943–955.

22. During the Proposition 20 years, the busy South Coast Regional Commission met weekly for up to fifteen hours at a time. Other commissions, including the state commission, met once or twice a month. At present, mainly because of an extremely high permit load, the state commission has a two-day meeting, twice a month.

23. Rimmon Fay, quoted in *Los Angeles Times,* July 12, 1978.

24. Bodovitz, "The Coastal Zone: Problems, Priorities and People," address to the Conference on Organizing and Managing the Coastal Zone, Annapolis, Md.,

June 13–14, 1973, p. 5. My own evaluation of how well the permit process fulfilled each of these expectations may be found in Healy, ed., *Protecting the Golden Shore,* pp. 67–95.

25. Paul van Seters, "The California Coastal Zone Conservation Commissions: An Exercise in Pragmatic Administration," (Berkeley, Center for Law and Social Policy, University of California, 1976). Unpublished manuscript.

26. Healy has argued elsewhere (*Protecting the Golden Shore,* pp. 79–86) that the lessons of the commissions' permit regulatory experience go far beyond the relatively general policies that were incorporated into the coastal plan or the 1976 Coastal Act. Significantly, current coastal commission regulations provide that one criterion for certification of local coastal programs is their "consistency with applicable commission decisions."

27. For example, remarks of current state commission executive director Michael Fischer to public meeting in Malibu, Calif., Dec. 7, 1978.

28. *Los Angeles Times,* Feb. 12, 1973.

29. Majority opinion of the California Supreme Court in *San Diego Regional Coastal Commission* v. *See the Sea, Ltd.* San Diego Superior Court No. 340206, 4th CIV 12650. See *Los Angeles Times,* Aug. 23, 1973; Aug. 24, 1973; and Oct. 11, 1973.

30. The state coastal commission refused to exempt the Redondo Beach urban renewal agency, even though it had spent $38 million on parts of its project before the coastal law went into effect. A superior court judge ruled that those parcels for which the agency had specific plans were exempt, even though construction had not yet begun. The remainder of the project must obtain permits. *Los Angeles Times,* Oct. 12, 1973.

31. In most of these cases the coastal commissions refused an exemption unless a building permit for the specific parcel had been obtained.

32. This was true of the planning activity as well. Sabatier found that "A rather careful analysis [of three plan elements] reveals that none of the three commissions examined could be said to have been improperly dominated by their staffs." Paul Sabatier, ed., "The Development of the California Coastal Plan: Influence, Information, and Inter-regional Variation," (Davis, Calif., Division of Environmental Studies, University of California, Davis, 1976) p. IV-18. Unpublished manuscript.

33. Proposition 20 contained a number of features that promoted public participation in both planning and the regulatory process. But in the end, it was probably the personal commitment of many commissioners to the ideal of participation, as much as the legal mandate, that made citizen involvement such an important part of the California program.

34. Of course, because the law applied to small developments as well as large, sometimes one found an inexperienced permit applicant, with no legal help, confronted by citizen activists who had become "expert" in objecting to projects.

35. For an evaluation of the citizen role in the appeal process see Duddleson, in *Protecting the Golden Shore,* pp. 22–25. Another recent study, based on statistical analysis of regional commission decisions, concluded that "most of the time citizens did not avail themselves of the opportunity to participate in the public hearings held by the Coastal Commissions, but when they do participate, they are effective." Judy B. Rosener, "Democracy and the Administrative State: Can Citizen Oversight Make Bureaucrats Responsive?" Paper prepared for presentation to the American Society for Public Administration, Baltimore, Maryland, April 1–4, 1979.

36. Of the 357 applications denied by the South Coast Commission, 129 (worth $99 million) were resubmitted and later approved. South Coast Regional Commission, *Permit Status Report,* Dec. 31, 1976.

37. A land use plan for the property, approved by local government, is now before the regional commission for certification.

38. Paul Sabatier, "State Review of Local Land Use Decisions: The California Coastal Commissions," *Coastal Zone Management Journal* vol. 3, no. 3 (1977) p. 288.

39. One important exception—a significant number of permits involving large areas of open land were denied "temporarily" to "preserve planning options."

40. Under the California constitution all areas below mean high tide are already public property. The commissions have learned that obtaining an easement is only part of the solution to the access problem. Some public agency must accept the easement, post and maintain it, and protect the property owner from vandalism and rowdiness by persons using the accessway.

41. In this case, involving the Sea Ranch development, the property owners have not yet relented. See Appeals 133-73; 84-74; 416-78.

42. Appeal 395-78.

43. Minutes of the state commission meeting of Jan. 9, 1974.

44. Appeals 51-73 and 178-74.

45. The state commission has been especially strict, however, with developments that use state or federal money to subsid.ze projects catering to high-income people. It used this reasoning to turn down a large hotel in a publicly built marina and an expensive condominium in a beachside urban renewal project.

46. Appeal 163-73.

47. Appeal 236-73.

48. *Los Angeles Times,* October 18, 1973.

49. South Coast Commission meetings of April 30, 1973, and May 31, 1973.

50. Appeal 34-73.

51. Appeal 161-73.

52. Appeal 29-73; reheard as Appeal 61-76.

53. Citations of cases upholding the commissions' authority in this regard, as well as a critical look at the commissions' general success in the courts, may be found in Michael M. Berger, "You Can't Win Them All—Or Can You?" *California State Bar Journal* vol. 54, no. 1 (January–February 1979) pp. 16–23.

54. Often, the commissions will not have to choose between the stark alternatives of no development or unrestricted building. The very s:ze of some parcels may allow use of cluster zoning or other forms of density tradeoff. Another option would be to transfer development rights from rural parcels to other parcels contiguous to existing built-up areas. Moreover, it is quite possible that courts will rule that lands on which agriculture can be profitably practiced may be restricted to that use, despite the existence of more lucrative development options.

55. Sabatier, "State Review" pp. 266–67.

56. Statement of Rimmon Fay, member of South Coast Commission, before the state commission, June 20, 1973.

57. Appeal 82-73.

58. Appeal 183-73.

59. Appeal 183-73, staff recommendation, p. 2.

60. *Los Angeles Times,* Dec. 6, 1973.

61. Ibid.

62. *Los Angeles Times,* Feb. 18, 1974. An interim report of the marine study, released in 1979, found some damage to marine life but did not recommend changes to the plant's cooling system.

63. *Los Angeles Times,* Feb. 21, 1974.

64. Ibid.

65. Letter of Melvin B. Lane to Robert G. Healy, Oct. 9, 1974.

66. Appeal 270-75.

67. C. Tomkins, "Onward and Upward with the Arts," *New Yorker* vol. 53, no. 6 (March 28, 1977) pp. 43–46.

68. Donald Bright, quoted in *Los Angeles Times,* July 23, 1973.

69. John S. Banta, "The Coastal Commissions and State Agencies: Conflict and Cooperation," in Robert G. Healy, ed., *Protecting the Golden Shore* (Washington, D.C., Conservation Foundation, 1978) p. 129.

70. Interview with Robert Cooper, supervising land agent, state department of general services, December 1976.

71. Bodovitz, "The Coastal Zone," p. 4.

72. See Robert G. Healy, *Land Use and the States* (1st ed., Baltimore, Md., Johns Hopkins University Press for Resources for the Future, 1976) p. 92.

73. Bodovitz, "The Coastal Zone," p. 8.

74. Interview with Robert Rooney, former chairman of the South Coast Commission, January 1976. The hope that implementation experience would change participants' minds may have been doomed from the start. An intriguing survey (taken in the fall of 1977) of nearly 500 respondents who were connected in some way with the commissions' activities found that their overall evaluation of the commissions' performance depended more on initial predispositions (whether they had voted for the initiative) and judgments about the desirability of the commissions' activities in selected areas than they did on perceptions of how well the commissions achieved their statutory objectives. Daniel Mazmanian and Paul Sabatier, "Policy Evaluation and Legislative Reformulation: The California Coastal Commissions." Paper prepared for delivery at the Policy Implementation Workshop, Pomona College, Claremont, Calif., November 16–17, 1978.

75. Letter of Melvin B. Lane in California Coastal Zone Conservation Commission, *California Coastal Plan* (Sacramento, State of California, 1975).

76. Duddleson, in *Protecting the Golden Shore*, p. 33. In his essay, Duddleson describes the active role taken by citizens in all phases of California's coastal effort.

77. Rosenbaum found that a sample of "active participants" in the California program expressed greater satisfaction with the commissions' planning choices than did participants in three other state land use programs. See Nelson Rosenbaum, *Citizens and Land Use Policy* (Washington, D.C., Urban Institute, 1978). Clark found that thirty out of thirty-nine scientist-reviewers whom he surveyed thought the weight given by the commissions to their input had been "strong" or "adequate." John Clark, "Natural Science and Coastal Planning," in Robert G. Healy, ed., *Protecting the Golden Shore* (Washington, D.C., Conservation Foundation, 1978) p. 196.

78. See Duddleson, in *Protecting the Golden Shore*, pp. 39–40.

79. As we will see, as a result of public input the plan called for the future coastal agency to share *implementation* powers with state and local agencies. Policies, however, were to be firmly in the hands of the coastal agency.

80. As an example of the plan's specificity: offroad vehicles used in coastal areas were not to "result in noise levels that exceed 65 dBA at a distance of 50 feet from the noise source." As an example of its broadness of scope, the plan urged that the relevant state agencies revise utility rate structures to "more accurately allocate the increased costs of peak load production...."

81. For a discussion of how this policy evolved, see Duddleson, in *Protecting the Golden Shore*, pp. 42–45.

82. The California League of Cities, although it pressed for specific modifications to the bill, was generally supportive.

83. Duddleson, in *Protecting the Golden Shore*, pp. 48–60.

84. The regional commissions were initially scheduled for elimination in 1979, but a 1978 amendment to the act extended them until June 1981.

85. Among such projects are those within 300 feet of a beach or coastal bluff, those within 100 feet of a wetland, and major public works projects and energy facilities.

86. The maximum inland reach of the coastal zone is five miles.

87. There is one exception, however. The Coastal Act removes the coastal commissions' authority to set the location of new power plants, but allows the state commission to designate areas where the state energy agency may *not* permit them.

88. Larry Moss, executive director of California Planning and Conservation League, quoted in Barbara J. Swain, "The New Coastal Commission, More Bad News for Developers," *California Journal* vol. 8, no. 3 (March 1977) p. 85.

89. Stanley Scott, "Coastal Planning in California: A Progress Report," *Public Affairs Report* (Berkeley, University of California, Institute of Governmental Studies) vol. 19, no. 3–4 (June–August 1978) p. 1.

90. Members of the new commissions were appointed using the same formula as under Proposition 20. For continu.ty's sake, the law provided that at least one-quarter of the members of the new commissions had to be members of the old ones.

91. Only three of the members of the state commission (December 1978) had been on the commission during Proposition 20 days, but another six had regional commission experience. One interesting phenomenon has been the increase in the number of women on the state commission from one in 1973, to two in 1975, and six in 1978.

92. Lundborg resigned from the state commission in March 1979, citing the time pressures that the post required. The commissioners elected Dorill Wright, mayor of Port Hueneme, to replace him as chairman.

93. Scott, "Coastal Planning in California," pp. 3–4.

94. Michael Fischer, statement at meeting of state commission, San Francisco, Nov. 29, 1978.

95. California Coastal Commission, *Biennial Report,* 1977–78.

96. Jens Sorensen, *State-Local Collaborative Planning: A Growing Trend in Land Use Management* (Berkeley, University of California Institute of Urban and Regional Development, forthcoming) app. I.

97. California Coastal Commission, *Biennial Report,* 1977–78.

98. Remarks of Michael Fischer, Malibu, Dec. 7, 1978.

99. This theme is emphasized in the name of one group of affected owners, which calls itself Citizens for Land Justice.

100. For example, Appeal 246-78.

101. Appeal 346-78.

102. Appeal 158-78. See also *Los Angeles Times,* Oct. 23, 1978.

103. Data for January 1977–October 1978, from California Coastal Commission, *Biennial Report,* 1977–78.

104. Remarks of Robert Knecht before the California Coastal Commission, Los Angeles, Dec. 13, 1978.

105. Judy Rosener, interviewed by William Duddleson, August 1978.

106. For example, late in 1978 considerable press coverage was given to the purported difficulties suffered by landowners who sought commission approval to replace homes destroyed in a fire in the Malibu hills. See also *Los Angeles Times,* July 12, 1978; and Tom Hazlett, "A Case of Coastal Piracy," *Inquiry* vol. 2, no. 7 (March 19, 1979) pp. 17–22.

107. Telephone interview, April 9, 1979.

108. *Los Angeles Times,* March 28, 1979.

CHAPTER FIVE

Florida— Harnessing the Growth Explosion

AT TIMES DURING THE 1970s, as many as 25,000 persons a month have moved to Florida. Drawn by the mild winters and abundant recreation, the newcomers have made Florida the nation's fastest-growing major state.[1] The development that has sprung up to accommodate them has placed severe pressures on a unique and sensitive natural environment. It has also stirred serious interest in controlling growth and in reducing its harmful effects. A major result of this interest is a state land use law, the Environmental Land and Water Management Act of 1972, whose passage and administration we will examine here.[2]

This law allows the state to designate "areas of critical state concern" and forces local governments to protect statewide interests when these areas are developed. It also allows a limited amount of state overview of very large developments, including the huge residential developments that have become a Florida specialty. These "developments of regional impact" are regulated by a complicated process involving local government, regional planning agencies, and the state, with the last becoming directly involved only in the few cases that are appealed. Several other laws affecting Florida's land were also passed by the 1972 legislature, and additional laws have been adopted in the years since then.

More than any other state, Florida has tried to reconcile the aspirations of strong local governments with regional and statewide interests in environmental protection. We have already seen how Vermont passed its state land law to come to the aid of township governments too small and unprofessional to do a proper job of evaluating the large new developments that were confronting them. Along California's coast, local governments were better prepared technically, but the voters, many of whom lived in other communities, simply did not trust them. Its law initially bypassed local government, emphasizing citizen enforcement and mandatory plans drawn up by the state and region.

Florida has included local governments in the process from the start. Its law, disappointing as some of its record has been, is a significant experiment in both land use control and in intergovernmental cooperation.

A New Kind of Growth

The rate and scale of Florida's recent growth is almost unimaginable. Only the most frenetic days of California's postwar expansion can compare to it. In 1973, for example, one out of every seven new homes built in the United States was built in Florida. Florida was hard hit by the dramatic nationwide falloff in housing starts that began early in 1974, particularly because the earlier building boom had left it with a considerable stock of unoccupied units. But the demographic and climatic factors that caused the state to grow so rapidly in the early 1970s were unchanged, and growth has resumed. Particularly rapid has been the growth of the Orlando area, where the development of Disney World stimulated the construction of 25,000 new motel and hotel rooms within a decade; and of south Florida's Gold Coast, stretching along the Atlantic from Miami to Palm Beach;[3] and of the retiree-oriented Sun Coast from Saint Petersburg southward along the Gulf. Massive and sprawling though this growth has been, it has concentrated in these few regions, attracted by the warm winter climate, or the ocean shoreline, or, for many, the employment opportunities generated by an expanding economy. Even as this growth explosion continues, other Florida counties, particularly in the northern panhandle, have been growing slowly or even losing population. This contrasting pattern—explosive coastal growth versus stagnation or decline in much of the state's interior—persisted or worsened as the 1974–76 recession halved the state's growth rate, if only temporarily.

New Types of Development

Florida's recent growth boom differed from the earlier California experience in a number of ways. For one thing, there was a far wider range of densities, with a tendency to emphasize densities toward the higher end of the range along the coasts. Although single-family houses are still popular, the high prices of land and building materials have made the town house, the residential cluster, and the garden apartment the predominant types. Along the coasts, the seemingly insatiable desire for oceanfront living has made possible the high-rise condominium, which stacks the largest possible number of people on a small (but very expensive) piece of land.

Another feature of Florida's expansion is the popularity of a new type of subdivision, the planned-unit development (PUD). These developments incorporate a variety of housing types, along with commercial sites, extensive recreational facilities, and sometimes even light industry. They can cover thousands of acres and house tens of thousands of people. Where urban areas once grew by the gradual accretion of many small tracts of homes and individual businesses, they now find much of their growth channeled into a handful of gigantic developments. The fast-growing Fort Lauderdale area could have doubled its population of 800,000 by the completion of only twenty-five projects proposed at the peak of the early 1970s boom, the *smallest* of which planned to house some 6,100 persons. The three largest were planned for over 100,000.[4]

New and Growing Markets

A significant portion of Florida's growth caters to the retiree or the second-home market. Unfettered by the usual need to live close to a source of employment, these purchasers are offered homes and homesites in huge planned communities in places that have been until recently virtual wilderness. We have already mentioned ITT's Palm Coast, which originally planned housing for 750,000 in tiny Flagler County (1970 population 4,500). An inventory of one hundred "new community" developments, involving 965,723 acres, found plans for 2,171,423 dwelling units to accommodate an estimated population of 5,808,407 new residents where only 151,224 people lived at the time.[5]

The speculative subdivision of Florida has, of course, been going on at least since the turn of this century. In the past, however, the property merely changed owners—the land itself was left untouched. Now, at least partly in response to federal and state land sales regulations, developers are installing roads, canals, drains, artificial lakes, and other facilities, even for lots that are unlikely ever to be built upon. The land is being urbanized even faster than it is being populated.

A Fragile and Unique Environment

All of this activity has been taking place in a state with a unique and complex natural environment. Florida's southern half, where most of the growth is concentrated, is the only area of tropical life in the continental United States. It contains birds, vegetation, soil types, and whole ecological systems found nowhere else in the country. The richness of this life belies its sensitivity to change. As elsewhere in the tropics, Florida's natural environment is dependent on a web of interrelationships, woven from the interaction of different forms of life (as in a food chain) or the interaction of living things and the land that supports them. In so delicately balanced a system, removal of one element can have serious and far-reaching consequences.

The key to much of Florida's natural life is water. Fresh water flows through the state in rivers, such as the Saint Johns and the Caloosahatchee. It settles in the great shallow lakes—Okeechobee, Apopka, Kissimmee. It spreads in a slow-moving sheet across the Everglades. Water stands for at least some part of the year in swamps and wetlands covering more than a third of the state. Below the surface of the land, water is also flowing. Under most of the state, at depths ranging from immediately beneath the surface to hundreds of feet below it, is a huge formation of water-bearing limestone known as the Floridan aquifer. It is the source of 90 percent of the water used in the state. Replenished by the slow seepage of surface water through the soil, it mixes the waters from various sources, one with another. Along the coasts, surface fresh and salt water mix to form estuarine systems, including the biologically productive areas in south Florida characterized by the red mangrove.

The problems that resulted when massive growth was imposed on the Florida environment are well known.[6] Just as water is a carrier and intermediary between components of the natural system, it became a means by which change in one part of the environment fostered still further changes. Pollution, flooding, saltwater intrusion, drought, and the spread of undesirable aquatic plants were among the results. Other results of growth have been urban sprawl, destruction of wildlife habitat, air pollution, areas devastated by phosphate mining and left unreclaimed, building on floodplains and areas prone to hurricane tides, inadequate recreation areas, and overburdened public services.[7] Rather than continue this litany, we might consider three typical, and important, groups of problems.

Crowding the Water's Edge

In Florida, as elsewhere in the nation, waterfront land is among the most desirable. The ideal seems to be a single-family home with boat slip alongside, but the price of land has made this inaccessible to all but a few. Instead, high-rise buildings are built along the oceanfront, not only in Miami but in many other communities along both coasts. An alternative to using the existing frontage more intensively is to create new waterfront land. "Finger" canals are dredged into the shoreline, with small canals radiating off larger ones, much as residential streets branch off boulevards. Dredge and fill can also extend the shoreline seaward, creating new buildable land from the shallow mangrove areas that edge Florida's southern flank.[8]

These new techniques have made it possible for more people to live on the ocean shore, but they have exacted an environmental price. The oceanfront high rises have destroyed the dunes and sea grasses that are part of the ecology of an ocean beach, accelerating the rate at which the beach erodes. The virtual disappearance of the sand beach along Miami Beach's hotel strip is a dramatic example. The Corps of Engineers estimated that 200 of Florida's 800 miles of ocean beach are critically eroded. Replacing the sand costs upwards of $500,000 a mile, and must be repeated again and again.[9]

Finger canals are often extended so far inland that the natural flushing action of the tides fails to be effective. Nutrient-rich runoff from lawns and seepage from household septic tanks pollute the stagnant water, killing all but the hardiest marine life and rendering the canals murky and unattractive. The filling in of mangrove areas and other coastal wetlands destroys the spawning and feeding area of many fish and marine creatures, including some of high value as game or food fish—snook, channel bass, pink shrimp, and tarpon, for example. And, perhaps most obviously, intense development along the shoreline threatens the scenery and the relaxed ambiance that most beach dwellers had moved there to find.

Building on the Wetlands

So much of Florida's surface is at least a seasonal wetland, that it is almost inevitable that these lands will receive some of the state's growth. The standard practice is to dig one or more artificial lakes, creating an attractive amenity feature and providing the huge quantities of fill dirt needed to build up the other low-lying parts of the site. Properly engineered, this kind of land alteration will not be too harmful. In some cases, however, lakes are dredged to depths of 30 to 40 feet, so as to maximize the amount of fill obtained. Beyond depths of 10 to 12 feet, sunlight cannot penetrate to the lake bottom. The natural cleansing process combining the effects of sun, oxygen, and aquatic plants cannot operate there. The lake can become polluted and eventually septic.

Deep cuts into wetlands also make it possible for surface water occasionally to mix, unfiltered, with the water of the underlying aquifer. In the natural system, wetlands retain rain close to where it falls. Runoff is purified by slowly seeping through the soil. When much of the site is filled in and surface water is channeled into large central water bodies, this natural purification system has no chance to operate. The filling in of wetlands has also contributed to local flooding and has destroyed wildlife habitat, including that of several rare or endangered species.

A Place Like Everywhere

Perhaps the most unfortunate effect of development has been its tendency to erase many of those things that have made Florida unique. Ranks of central Florida orange groves have been torn out, to be replaced by town houses. Sleepy coastal fishing camps have turned into bustling resort towns. Even the great swamps have lost some of their sense of remoteness and mystery. The billboards, the shopping plazas, the tracts of houses that pepper the landscape are, in fact, little different from their counterparts in New Jersey or Illinois. Florida, a place like nowhere else, is starting to become a metropolis, a place like everywhere.

The Birth of Land Policy

Having described these undeniable problems, we must put them in perspective. An uncritical reader of the many newspaper accounts of life and environment in Florida would probably by now have been persuaded that it is a state of eutrophying lakes and suffocated fish, its beaches awash with sewage and hedged in by condominiums, all overshadowed by the smoke from the muck fires of the Everglades. In fact, there is much in Florida that is still attractive. The best measure of its appeal is the number of tourists and new settlers it continues to attract.

The new, larger scale of growth presents new opportunities for planning, for it makes it feasible for a developer to hire a competent staff of physical planners and environmental consultants. It also allows the developer to build densely on the least sensitive part of his site, leaving floodplains, marshes, and wildlife areas undisturbed. Greater scale, moreover, makes it much easier to associate social, fiscal, and economic side effects with a specific development or project.

Most hopeful of all is the fact that the environmental degradation of Florida has not gone unnoticed by Floridians. Beginning in the mid-1960s several small groups of environmentalists began to publicize some of the more dramatic cases of man's interference with natural systems. They were aided by the nationwide surge of interest in ecology and in wildlife conservation, subject areas for which Florida provided a wealth of examples. At first, battle lines were drawn over specific development issues, chief of which were the Cross Florida Barge Canal, the Turkey Point nuclear power plant, and the proposed Everglades jetport. Each of these received national attention, and each was eventually resolved (more or less) in favor of the environmentalists.

Early in the present decade, it became common, and indeed fashionable, to question the value of growth itself. In part, this was a reaction to the rate at which Florida's growth was proceeding. In part, it marked a realization that piecemeal solutions to Florida's environmental woes were all but impossible. Florida became one of the leaders in local government attempts to limit or control growth. Building moratoriums were placed in effect in a number of south Florida counties and cities, including one that for a time covered 300 square miles on the western side of populous Dade County. In 1972 voters in Boca Raton approved the nation's first "population cap" ordinance, directing that the city, then having 32,000 inhabitants (up from a population of 992 in 1950), be rezoned to accommodate no more than 40,000 dwelling units, indicating an eventual population of about 100,000.[10]

The first stirrings of activity on the state level were felt around 1970. Until that time, the interest of Florida's state government in land use had focused on promoting development—attracting new industry, improving the highway net, encouraging the opening of new farmlands, and promoting the tourist industry. The state did have legislation regulating the dredging of wetlands and providing for a setback for coastal construction, but these laws were loosely enforced. Carter reports, "For the most part, official attitudes towards Florida's natural resources favored more or less unchecked private exploitation. Between 1955 and 1967 the [regulatory body] sold some 28,000 acres of state-owned submerged lands to developers. So freehanded was the cabinet in allowing dredging and filling, that in some instances entire estuaries were in danger of being converted into labyrinths of land fills and finger canals. . . ."[11]

The state did little to prod local governments to regulate the use of land—and most localities responded with a lassitude of their own. Florida was the last state in the union (in 1967) to make a general grant of zoning authority to its counties. (Before that time, many individual cities and counties had been given the authority to zone by special act.) As late as 1973, less than half of the counties exercised land use controls of any kind. And of these counties, several exercised controls only for areas along major roads or within a certain number of miles from the county seat. More than 50 percent of the state's land area was without local development controls of any kind.[12]

By the beginning of the 1970s, however, the new mood of at least a few of Florida's cities was matched by a new environmental responsiveness in the state legislature in Tallahassee. A 1967 reapportionment had freed the legislature from the domination of rural interests and had brought in new faces from the populous urban areas—precisely those places that were beginning to feel the growth squeeze.

A major step toward state involvement was a conference called by Gov. Reubin Askew, in September 1971, to deal with a serious drought in south Florida.[13] Most of the 150 experts and politicians who attended agreed that such water crises would occur again and again unless south Florida came to terms with its explosive growth. The discussion quickly broadened from a consideration of improving water management to ways to control the use of land. A task force was appointed by the governor to translate this concern into a bill for the 1972 legislature.

For a time, the task force considered some sort of comprehensive state land use plan, mapping those areas of the state that could allow development, and those where new building should be restricted. This approach was dropped in favor of one that would emphasize state intervention only in the "big cases"—that is, those involving large projects or particularly sensitive environments. Such an approach would keep state interference with local zoning to the necessary minimum.[14]

The big-cases approach is, of course, that taken by the American Law Institute (ALI) in its Model Land Development Code. The code is intended to modernize the standard zoning and planning ordinances dating back to the 1920s that have been adopted by most jurisdictions. It is no coincidence that a consultant to the Florida committee was Chicago attorney Fred Bosselman, associate reporter of the ALI committee that had begun drafting the code in 1968.

On the advice of Governor Askew, who did not want to present the legislature with too sweeping a revision of existing practice, the committee did not utilize the many provisions of the ALI code that deal with local planning and zoning procedures. Instead, it concentrated on the code's Article 7, which proposes methods for protecting nonlocal interests when land is developed.

The ALI's recommendations are based on a number of beliefs about the proper role of the state in regulating land use. First is the belief that only a minority of land use decisions involve significant state or regional interests and should be subject to state intervention. According to the code's drafters, "The decision whether a gas station should be located on the corner of Fifth and Main Street in Elyria, Ohio, can only be made intelligently in Elyria, not in Columbus or in Washington."[15] Second, where there are nonlocal considerations, the state should make policy, but should leave its implementation and enforcement to local governments. The state can protect against violation of its policies by providing for an appeal of local decisions. A third belief is that, while planning is desirable, land use problems are so urgent that regulation should not be put off until the state has prepared a comprehensive plan.

The Florida law, given the ambitious name Environmental Land and Water Management Act of 1972, contains many of the ideas and much of the language of the ALI code's Article 7. Two of the code's major concepts appeared to have an almost uncanny applicability to Florida's land problems. The ALI recommendation that a state regulate very large developments (called "developments of regional impact") seemed quite relevant to the "new kind of growth" we have already described. And the code's idea that a state designate some geographic areas as being of "critical state concern" appeared well suited to a state with so many places of environmental value and unusual fragility.

The law that emerged from the legislature (passed on the very last day of the session) was the result of a number of adaptations and political compromises. Where the ALI code would have a state administrative agency designate critical areas, the Florida law relies on one of that state's unique institutions—the Florida Cabinet. The cabinet is made up of six independently elected state officials—the attorney general, secretary of state, treasurer, comptroller, and the commissioners of education and of agriculture. Cabinet members each have their own political constituency, a situation that infuses their biweekly meetings with considerable public posturing and more than occasional controversy. Sitting with the governor, the cabinet acts in a number of executive and adjudicatory roles. In this case, the governor and cabinet would not only designate each critical area, but would also act as the appeal board governing "developments of regional impact."

Another change limited the total area that could be designated as critical to no more than 5 percent of the state, or 1.7 million acres. Moreover, before any land could be designated, the voters had to approve a $240 million bond issue for the acquisition of environmentally endangered lands. The voters later approved the bonds (by a margin of three to one), but the provision left a strong impression that the money was in some way tied to the critical areas program, causing some of those regulated to believe that the state should purchase, rather than just regulate, their land.

Finally, Florida decided to place major responsibility for asserting the nonlocal interest over large developments not in a state agency but in several regional planning councils. (This is mentioned in the ALI code as a possible option.) This choice seems similar to the regionalization found both in California and Vermont, but in practice, Florida has formed a system with much less direct state involvement than occurs in either of those two states. In the following pages we will describe this new system in detail and evaluate how it has worked.

Critical Areas

The Florida law allows the cabinet to designate three types of areas as being of "critical state concern." First are those areas "containing, or having a significant impact upon, environmental, historical, natural, or archaeological resources of regional or statewide importance."[16] Just considering the possibilities for "environmental" or "natural" areas points up the vast number of Florida acres that might qualify under this section —and the significance of the amendment limiting the total amount of land designated to 5 percent of the state. Aquifer-recharge areas, wetlands, unique ecosystems, and wildlife habitat all might be included.

Second are areas "significantly affected by, or having a significant effect upon, an existing or proposed major public facility or other area of major public investment." An obvious example would be the oft-proposed south Florida jetport. No matter what location was chosen, the huge new airport would be a magnet for hotels, offices, and other private development. Since noise-control considerations would undoubtedly dictate a location fairly far from existing urbanization, the jetport could introduce a hodgepodge of new private development into a remote, and probably unregulated, area. Designation of the lands adjoining the jetport as being of critical state concern would mean that growth would proceed under state-approved guidelines.

Finally, a critical area might be an area of "major development potential, which may include a proposed site of a new community, designated in a state development plan." New communities have been considered by many to be a key to allowing Florida to grow while avoiding sprawl and preserving environmental quality.[17] This section is a promising one, for it means that the state could positively encourage the development of certain sites, by designating them as critical and approving regulations that would make their development profitable. Unfortunately, this section could not be implemented until Florida had prepared the required state development plan, and this was not completed until 1978 (see below).[18]

Regulation of critical areas is a mix of state and local control. An area is designated by the Administration Commission (made up of the cabinet and governor), which defines the area and sets forth principles for its development. Local governments then have six months to adopt development regulations that comply with those principles. If the local regulations are not satisfactory, or the local government does not act at all, the cabinet and governor can adopt state regulations and give them the force of local law. In any case, the regulations are then administered by local government, under the eye of the Division of State Planning, which can bring the locals to court if enforcement is improper. The original law did not provide for interim controls to protect land that had been designated, but was not yet under regulation. A bill passed by the 1974 legislature substantially removes this loophole. But in setting up interim controls it specifically prohibits a temporary moratorium on developments.[19]

The Administration Commission does not move to designate a critical area until the area has been thoroughly studied by the Division of State Planning, a time-consuming process. Two years after the law's passage, only three areas had been officially designated, although more than sixty areas, ranging in size from 100 acres to 2 million, had been suggested for study. Additional designations have been delayed since then by constitutional challenges to the critical areas program, and by the realization that some of the local governments involved would be incapable of administering sophisticated critical areas regulations. (Nonetheless, in some instances, the state has improved land use processes without actually designating a critical area; see below). Hampered by lack of funds, the planners working on critical area designation have also found that they cannot recommend defensible planning principles without a detailed understanding of the natural system or other resources they are trying to protect.

The Big Cypress

Indeed, this was a major lesson of the first critical area to be designated, the Big Cypress Swamp. The Big Cypress is a virtually uninhabited area of more than one million acres of ponds and grasslands lying just to the north and west of the Everglades National Park. It serves as a recharge area for the underlying aquifer, provides a vital source of water to the mangroves forming the western edge of the park, and is a significant wildlife area in its own right.

Some of the Big Cypress has been drained for farmland, but most lies idle, undisturbed except for occasional logging or ranching. Despite its remoteness, however, hundreds of thousands of acres have already been subdivided into 1- to 5-acre lots and sold to gullible investors. In parts of the Big Cypress the old joke about the "underwater Florida lot" is sometimes a reality.

Speculative lot sales can not only defraud the public, they can also damage the land itself. One development company in the western Big Cypress has crisscrossed its 113,000 acres with a network of drainage canals and unpaved roads. These so-called improvements have scarred the landscape and created serious drainage problems. Ironically, although some 73,000 lots had been sold by 1973, only a few dozen families had completed houses there. Elsewhere in the Big Cypress, another developer planned a city of 30,000, an undertaking that would require a great deal of drainage and earth moving.

Collier County, which is the local government for most of the Big Cypress, nominally controlled land use there, but, as Carter observes, its planning activities until recently were "a sham or an absurdity."[20] Conflict of interest was rampant, with some county officials responsible for land use decisions having direct ties to the land developers.

Worried about the effects of Big Cypress development on the water supply of the Everglades Park and prodded by south Florida environmentalists, the federal government had for some time been considering the purchase of 570,000 acres as a national freshwater preserve. In 1973 Florida tried to induce Congress to act, earmarking $40 million of the $240 million land acquisition bond issue for purchase of lands in the preserve. Late in 1974 Congress authorized $116 million to buy the rest of the preserve. By late 1978 more than half of the preserve lands had been purchased, and Congress had authorized an additional $40 million of federal funds to complete the program.

The Big Cypress is a good example of the limits of purchase as a means of regulation. Despite huge contributions from both federal and state governments, the purchase area covers less than half the Big Cypress, leaving several important natural areas unprotected.[21] Clearly, the Big Cypress is a place that might be regulated as a critical area.

In the summer of 1973 the Big Cypress was designated as Florida's first critical area, not by the governor and cabinet, but by a special act of the legislature. This not only meant a speedier designation, but also meant that the area would not be counted toward the 5 percent acreage limit. State planners, rather than the local governments, were to draw up the regulations.

When the draft regulations were released and submitted to public hearing, local residents—and many legislators—were horrified. In their proposal, which they insisted was a draft meant to be revised, the planners interpreted literally the legislative mandate to regulate not just the purchase area, but other Big Cypress lands important to south Florida's ecology. The draft regulations covered more than 1.5 million acres, including 90 percent of Collier County. As Myers describes the local reaction:

> Everywhere massive new development would be prevented and allowable development closely regulated. There were restrictions on burning, ditching, filling and dredging, destroying vegetation, building new drainage facilities, pumping groundwater, and road-building. Allowable site coverage ranged from 5 to 20 percent and all structures had to be built one foot above the 100-year floodplain. State officials say they consulted with local officials in developing the regulations, but local officials insist otherwise.[22]

Hearings in the Big Cypress area were "packed, tense, and hostile."[23] Some of the legislators present admitted to the crowd that they had not realized what was in the bill when they had voted for it. The planners drastically revised their recommendations, limiting them to those that could be clearly defended with environmental data. When the Administration Commission approved final regulations (voting 6–1) in November 1973, the area included only the lands to be purchased for the preserve itself and a 285,000-acre buffer zone around them.

For the lands covered, no more than 10 percent of the site can be disturbed, and only 5 percent covered by an impermeable surface. Destruction of mangroves and salt marsh grasses is flatly prohibited, as are finger canals and drainage works that let fresh water escape into the ocean.

According to state planners, except for a couple of complaints about road building, development activity is quiet in the Big Cypress.[24] The regulations are enforced by the county, which has turned down some development. Public acceptance of the controls, moreover, apparently is far greater than the sentiments expressed at the public hearings would indicate. A straw vote taken along with local elections in February 1974 found voters favoring both federal purchase of the preserve and critical area controls in the buffer zone by a margin of nearly 3 to 1. Collier County has since adopted some stringent zoning controls.

The Green Swamp

The planners were more cautious in their recommendations for the second area designated, central Florida's Green Swamp. More than half this area is wetlands, forming the source of five major rivers. There the huge Floridan aquifer comes closest to the surface. Water permeating the soil recharges the aquifer and maintains the water pressure that makes it possible to pump water easily from the aquifer elsewhere in the state.

Like the Big Cypress, the Green Swamp has felt the first stirrings of development. Disney World is located only 10 miles from one of its edges, and the growth that this and similar attractions have brought to central Florida has spilled out even to the more remote areas. In the few years from 1968 until the area was designated, more than 43,000 acres in the Green Swamp were registered with the Florida Division of Land Sales.

Before even submitting the Green Swamp area to the cabinet for designation, the state planners prepared a report describing the environmental resources of the swamp and detailing its function as a recharge area. Mindful that this time any lands designated would be subject to the 5 percent (1.7 million acre) limit, they suggested that only 316,000 of the 800,000 acres be protected, emphasizing that part which was at once the most valuable for aquifer recharge and most threatened by intense development. Two sets of hearings were held in the area, even before the recommendation was submitted to the cabinet.

In July 1974 the governor and cabinet voted 4–3 to designate 323,000 acres of the swamp as a critical area. After local governments failed to satisfy the state's principles for protecting the area, the division of state planning drew up regulations for local implementation. There has been relatively little development in the area since then, but the regulations were set aside in court on procedural grounds.[25]

The Florida Keys

New issues arose when the Florida Keys were proposed for critical areas protection. The keys are the first critical area containing a great deal of urbanization. They also contain a local environmental movement —a citizens association presented the cabinet with a 2,200-signature petition asking for critical area designation.

The keys, ninety-seven low-lying islands stretching 130 miles into the Gulf, were described in the state's predesignation report as "beginning to suffer, at least partially, from their own success.[26] About a million tourists visit them yearly, and some 56,000 people live there. The whole area was fast becoming an unattractive strip of billboards, trailer parks, and commercial sites, its single highway congested and its water supply strained by growth. On the drawing boards was a new threat—the high-rise condominium. The state's report described the impact of tourist and residential growth not only on the area's delicate environment, but on its public services as well. The single water pipe that linked the keys and provided most of their water supply had been inadequate for years. The highways and bridges between the islands badly needed repair. Facilities for proper disposal of sewage and of solid wastes were almost nonexistent. "Proposed public investments," said the report, "may cost more than a *quarter of a billion dollars* of state, federal, and local money in the next five to ten years simply to meet the demands of the existing and 1985 populations."[27]

The keys are another striking example of the failure of a local government to protect a resource that is of statewide and, indeed, national value. Said environmentalist Raymond Dasmann, "The county authorities [in Monroe County] have thus far been badly remiss in providing the leadership that the keys so badly need. Controlled up to now by the Key West voters, the county commission has been oriented toward the urban problems of that city and inclined to approve anything in the outside area that would bring money to the county."[28]

Early in 1975 the governor and cabinet traveled to the keys, where they held a ten-hour hearing on critical area designation before a crowd of eight hundred. They found a divided audience, with much of the opposition coming from those living in the keys' only large town, Key West. On April 15, they voted 5–2 to designate the whole island chain. They rejected a proposal that Key West be exempted from the regulations and accepted most of the suggestions of the state planning staff. Local governments on the keys were to prepare plans and zoning maps, based not only on protecting natural values but on increasing the cost-effectiveness of public investments. Developers of large and medium-sized projects were to submit a "community impact assessment statement" to the local government when proposing their projects, so as to ensure the availability of public services.

As an added inducement to local government, the governor and cabinet asked state agencies to identify sources of possible federal and state aid in financing needed services, and to help local governments in drawing up appropriate regulations. The regional planning council also worked on the project and secured aid.

The Division of State Planning feels that although its technical assistance arrived a little too late, the local governments did an excellent job of drafting regulations. Monroe County and the cities of Key Colony Beach, Layton, and most of Key West prepared their regulations and adopted them before the deadline for Administration Commission action.[29] Since then the Division of State Planning has reviewed several hundred local development orders under the regulations, resolving most problems through conferences and appealing only once to the governor and cabinet (the local decision was upheld).[30] In all, says the official responsible for seeing that localities comply with the regulations, "Monroe County has done an extremely commendable job."[31] Elections have removed some of the public officials who were hostile to the designation, replacing them in some instances with leaders of the citizen groups favoring state protection.[32]

This change in political attitude may be very important to the critical areas program. On November 22, 1978, the Florida Supreme Court, ruling in *Cross Key Waterways* v. *Askew,* found the administrative designation of critical areas under the 1972 law to be an unconstitutional delegation of legislative authority. The ruling did not affect the Big Cypress, which had been designated by a special legislative act, but struck down the Green Swamp and Florida Keys as areas of critical concern.

Outgoing Governor Askew, who had cited the 1972 law as one of his chief accomplishments, called a special legislative session. To overwhelming editorial support around the state, the legislature passed a law designating the two affected critical areas, using the boundaries and land development regulations that had been in effect, until July 1, 1979. Under the law a joint legislative committee was established to make recommendations on how to designate critical areas in the future. The committee report was due by March 15, 1979. The new governor, Robert Graham, who as a state senator led the fight to pass the Environmental Land and Water Management Act, established a task force on how to protect the existing critical areas and to designate new ones. And state environmentalists petitioned the supreme court to clarify its ruling; they hope that some administrative mechanism will satisfy the court, so that future designations need not be approved by the legislature on a case-by-case basis.

The future of the keys is uncertain. Environmentalists and state planning officials think that the political climate has changed sufficiently so that the worst environmental and land use abuses will be prevented even without state protection. In this view, critical area designation administered a necessary jolt to local governments, compelling them to clarify their procedures; and the electorate agreed.[33] But others believe that with the completion of road, bridge, and water supply improvements (in February 1979 voters approved a $53 million expansion of the aqueduct), the keys will be reopened to booming development.[34] A compromise may take place, whereby most of the keys area will be redesignated, perhaps excluding Key West, which is already developed and subject primarily to disputes over historic preservation.

Evaluating the Critical Areas Program

Many observers now feel that the critical areas program has stalled and that no new designations are likely. Environmentalists and, surprisingly, even some who were instrumental in passing or administering the 1972 law, criticize the leadership of the Division of State Planning for being too timid politically to designate additional areas.

There are other, less political reasons for not designating critical areas, and the division's response to them does indicate its continuing interest in making the law work. As was already noted, the fact that the state comprehensive plan was not completed until 1978 prevented designation of any economic development areas—an action which might have won the program political support, especially in the panhandle.

In one case, along the upper Suwanee River, the expansion of phosphate strip mining threatened to pollute the water of downstream users. The state moved to designate the mined land as a critical area, then relented when the mining company offered to refrain from mining 10,000 acres lying in the river's floodplain. According to a state planner, it is unlikely that the county governments involved would have pressed for this kind of concession—one of the counties has a population of only 7,800, of whom 40 percent of the adult men work at the mine.[35]

Another study area—a barrier island off the Atlantic coast—was dropped when the two county governments there decided to form a council of governments and work out their own land use controls.

In another area—the Apalachicola River and Bay system—the state planners' determination to go beyond remedial designations, where crises had already arisen, collided with the local governments' inability to administer the necessary programs and regulations before development problems began. The impending completion of an interstate highway, the beginning of industrial development, and the first large residential project threatened to overwhelm local authorities and to ruin downstream fisheries.

In the state's view, the growth was not so massive as to precipitate a crisis, as it had in the keys. Moreover, 80 percent of existing land was used for agriculture and forestry—uses exempt from critical areas regulation—and the local administrative machinery was inadequate or nonexistent. Instead of designating the area, the state helped to establish a thirty-one-member committee with representatives from state agencies, regional planning councils, county governments, businesses, and conservation groups. This committee has helped improve local land use skills—a new regional council was formed, planning efforts were begun, and disputes over the residential development were resolved—and has made state expertise accessible. Should the need arise, the state could designate the area later, but for now, state planners think they are achieving similar results without formal critical areas designation.[36] This approach also may be tried in the Charlotte Harbor area on the southern Gulf coast, where enough lots have been platted to accommodate 1.9 million new residents, seriously threatening valuable, shallow coastal waters.[37]

John M. DeGrove, who helped to write the 1972 law, praises state intervention "short of actual designation." He sees it as a useful accommodation to the political and other problems of the critical areas program.

One of these fundamental difficulties—gathering information—is encountered even in the nondesignation approach, but without the pressure of statutory time deadlines. When a land use agency issues permits for projects, if it is so inclined, it can require the developer to provide any information needed to judge the environmental or other impacts his project will have. This is sometimes hard to achieve in practice, but at least the burden of proof usually falls on the person wishing to change the environment. Before designating critical areas, however, the regulators must furnish all the information. Moreover, they must implicitly bear the burden of proof that development, of whatever kind, will prove harmful to some statewide interest. It is a time-consuming, expensive, and inexact procedure.

It is because of such implementation problems that DeGrove thinks, "The state policy part of the act—critical areas—would be unhealthy even without the courts. The local initiative part of the act—developments of regional impact—is healthy." And it is there that Florida's land use act is producing something like a growth-management policy for this rapidly changing state.[38]

Developments of Regional Impact

The provision of the ALI model code dealing with "developments of regional impact" was meant to be applicable everywhere in the country. It seems especially appropriate, however, that Florida should adopt this language, for so many of the developments proposed there are large in size and far-reaching in effect. According to the Florida law, a project is of regional impact if it affects the citizens of more than one county. Rules adopted by the Administration Commission (and approved by the legislature) early in 1973 give specific content to this vague definition.

A development of regional impact (DRI) might be:

An airport

A racetrack or sports stadium

A power plant larger than 100 MW[39]

A high-voltage electrical transmission line crossing county borders

A hospital serving more than one county (hospitals of fewer than 100 beds are exempt

A manufacturing plant or industrial park providing parking for more than 1,500 cars

A mine disturbing more than 100 acres annually

A large port facility or oil storage tank

A postsecondary educational campus having more than 3,000 students

A shopping center covering more than 40 acres or providing parking for more than 2,500 cars

A housing development, mobile home park, or subdivision larger than 250 units (in the least populous counties), or larger than 3,000 units (in the most populous ones).[40]

By relating the minimum project size to a county's population, the definition takes account of the fact that a housing development of 250 units would have a major impact (and would be an uncommon event) in tiny Glades County (population, 4,200), but would be almost unnoticed in Dade County (population, 1.5 million).[41]

Five major actors are involved in the disposition of a DRI application: the developer, the local government, a regional planning council, the state planning agency (Division of State Planning), and Florida's governor and cabinet, acting together as the Land and Water Adjudicatory Commission. In contrast to the permit processes in Vermont and California, which take place largely independently of local government, Florida's law makes local government the linchpin of the entire proceeding. There is, in fact, no state permit at all. The developer's final goal is a "development order" issued by local government following a state-mandated process and stating what he can build and what conditions he must meet.

The DRI process is activated when a developer makes an application for his project. Unlike critical areas designation, the DRI decision involves state reaction, not state initiative. The process does not start when an area is thought ripe for development, nor when new infrastructure makes building more attractive, nor when a state plan indicates that a particular area should grow more quickly. A DRI begins only when a developer proposes to build a particular project in a particular place.

As had been the case before the 1972 law was passed, developers base their decisions as much on the availability of land as on its suitability for development. The scarcity of large parcels within existing urbanized areas almost invariably forces developers to areas that are marshlands, wetlands, recharge areas, or environmentally sensitive zones. Says Florida environmentalist William Partington, "Obviously you can buy a lot of wetlands cheaper than land that's high and dry."[42] When the developer writes up his DRI application, he has already determined what he wants to build on his site. In his application, he attempts to show that the social and environmental resources at his location can support the proposed use. Says Partington, "It really should be the other way around—look at the site and determine its limiting factors." This would require, of course, that the regulatory authority have technical data on hundreds of thousands of parcels of land. It is a problem similar to that involved in assembling the information needed for the designation of critical areas.

The application that the developer submits must contain the answers to scores of questions about the environmental, economic, and fiscal impact of his project. Often running to hundreds of pages, and accompanied by a fairly detailed site plan, it costs a few thousand dollars to $75,000 or more to prepare, but represents advance planning and data gathering that may reach hundreds of thousands of dollars. Most of this planning would have to be done anyway before the project was built. The DRI process probably forces the developer to make specific plans, such as water and sewer studies, much earlier in the course of his project than would otherwise be the case. If the project is disapproved, of course, this front-end investment is lost.

The completed application is submitted to the local government, which schedules a public hearing for no sooner than sixty days after the filing. Most DRIs would have to go to local public hearings in any case, since they involve changes in zoning or are planned-unit developments. In a few instances, though, they are built on land already zoned to the intended use, and would have escaped public hearing entirely were it not for the state law. The local government usually combines the DRI hearing and the local zoning hearing into a single proceeding.

If the DRI happens to be located in a town or county that has no local zoning or subdivision controls, the local government has ninety days to adopt them.[43] If local government chooses not to do so, the developer can build without further ado.

When the developer submits his application to the local government, he also sends a copy to the appropriate regional planning agency. This is a multicounty council of governments, with a governing body made up of county (and sometimes city) officials, supported by a staff of from six to two dozen professionals. There are now eleven of these, covering all of Florida's counties. Membership, however, is voluntary, and not all counties belong to the council covering their region. Volusia County, for example, which includes Daytona Beach, is not a regional council member. Most were built up from existing regional bodies, set up in the 1960s to do regional planning and A-95 review or to promote economic development. A few were created specifically to handle DRIs.

The regional planning agency (council) has fifty days to review the developer's application, to prepare a written critique of it, and to make a recommendation that local government approve, deny, or modify the project. Until mid-1974, a council had only thirty days to make its recommendation, an impossible situation that caused most councils to take desperate and ingenious measures to gain more time. Even fifty days is little enough time to evaluate such questions as the biological effects of a sewage system, the effect of development on endangered species, or the public service demands of future residents of a project that may take twenty-five years to complete.

The regional recommendation goes back to the local government, in time for the public hearing. By law, the recommendation is based on whether the development will have a favorable or unfavorable impact on the region's environment, resources, and economy, on public facilities, and on the availability of adequate housing reasonably accessible to people's place of employment.

Local government need only "consider" the regional findings and recommendations. It may accede to some or part of them, denying the application or imposing conditions on the developer. It can, and sometimes does, ignore them completely. On the other hand, a developer may face few criticisms of the regional impact of his proposal, yet find that local government objects to local impacts that were given little weight in the regional recommendations. In practice, regional council staff reports evaluate a good number of purely local impacts, such as the demand for schools and other public facilities. The regional *recommendations* are more closely limited to regional questions.

If local government approves, it issues a permit called a "development order." At this point, state and regional governments can use their only real weapon—the right to appeal to the Adjudicatory Commission. An appeal may be brought by the Division of State Planning or by the regional planning agency. If the development has been turned down, or if he finds the conditions imposed in the development order are too harsh, the developer can appeal. Unlike in Vermont, an appeal cannot be brought by a local government adjoining, but not containing, the proposed project.[44] If a local government objects to a project lying within another city or county, it must persuade the regional planning council to carry, and pay for, an appeal. Moreover, unlike in California, private citizens have no right to appeal.[45] Once an appeal is initiated, however, a materially affected adjacent government can intervene in the proceedings.

Thus, Florida's DRI process is a mixture of regional evaluation, local control, and state review. The process takes place under rules drawn up by the state, and the Division of State Planning is kept informed of the progress of each DRI application. But until an issue comes to the cabinet on appeal, the state remains in the background. The regional council is directly involved from the start, but its power, except for the appeal power, is one of persuasion rather than compulsion.

Even though it stays in the background on individual DRI applications, the Division of State Planning plays an increasingly important role in establishing the rules for the process. The land use law empowers the division, on request, to issue a "binding letter of interpretation" to determine whether a proposed development is a DRI subject to review, a development below the DRI threshold, or a vested development exempt from review.[46] The division also rules whether changes in previously vested projects are now subject to DRI review.

A 1978 court ruling significantly broadened these powers. In the *Port Malabar* case, the General Development Corporation challenged some binding letters affecting its projects. The court held that the "presumptions" of regional impact established by the 1973 rules did not confine the division "to a mechanical chore of counting dwelling units or making other quantitative calculations."

Instead, the division may find that a project smaller than the numerical threshold for DRI review is so located as to require the developer to undergo review anyway. The division may also find that a large project is exempt, for the same reason.[47] Finally, the division is empowered to aggregate "ostensibly separate" development proposals to require DRI review of a developer's several, subthreshold projects.

It is the dispersion of power that makes the DRI process so significant an experiment in intergovernmental relations. It is also what makes the process unusually difficult to evaluate. Florida is a state with 67 counties and 390 cities. Like the eleven regional councils, their governments vary widely in objectives, in staff quality, and in the philosophy of the officials who run them.

There have been cases in which regional councils passed over regional impacts for short-range political ends. There were others in which the conscientious efforts of the regions were blatantly ignored by development-minded local governments. In still others, unwise projects were turned down after regional recommendations pointed out the problems the projects would create. We find case after case in which design improvements were made in response to the DRI review. In the pages to come, we will discuss some examples drawn from Florida's experience, not so much to judge the performance of Florida's units of government, but to show how the system works, where it succeeds, and where it fails. These cases arose in the first years after the law took effect (on July 1, 1973), during which four-fifths of the applications for DRI approval through mid-1978 were made, and when the patterns for reviewing DRIs were established.

The Number and Scale of DRIs

Five years after DRI review began, 266 applications for development had been submitted. Almost 60 percent were for residential projects, proposed to contain over 965,000 housing units; of these, permission was granted to build 500,000 units. Withdrawal by developers of applications for development approval accounted for far more of the "lost" units than did denials or conditions attached to permits by government agencies. The other major categories of DRIs were shopping centers (thirty-two), transmission lines, office parks, and projects for 171,670 acres of phosphate mines. Of the 179 DRIs finally acted upon by local government through mid-1978, 13 percent were approved, 79 percent approved conditionally, and 8 percent denied.[48] About thirty applications were withdrawn; about half as many escaped review when the counties in which they were located failed to adopt land use regulations.

During that period, thirty-eight local decisions were appealed. In about half the appealed cases, negotiations resulted in changes to the project, and the appeal was dismissed. A handful of appeals was dropped for lack of standing or because the application was withdrawn, and six appeals were still pending. Only four of the appeals actually reached the Adjudicatory Commission, and in only one case (Three Rivers, see page 150) did the commission reverse local approval of a project. Negotiation and compromise, rather than forceful cabinet-level decision-making, seem to characterize the DRI appeal process.

These cumulative figures conceal one of the most important changes in the process, the precipitous decline in DRI applications since the first year of project review. In 1973–74 some 140 applications were received. They included proposals for 632,000 residential units, enough to house 1.8 million people. Eighteen regional shopping centers were also proposed, with 5.5 square miles of floor space.[49]

In the second year, DRI applications decreased to sixty-nine, and by the fourth year there were only eleven applications. The total did not climb until 1977–78, when twenty-two applications were received. From the more than 600,000 units proposed in the first year, the total sank to 26,000 residential units proposed in 1976–77.[50] This means that DRI-sized developments collapsed even more severely than did Florida's building industry as a whole.[51] In retrospect, it is clear that the DRI process came into effect at the peak of Florida's second great land boom of this century (the first occurred in the 1920s), and that the number of DRI applications in the first year represented feverish activity and an eagerness to break ground so intense that many developers unnecessarily applied for DRI review, further inflating the first-year figures.[52]

The rate of project approvals is very much in line with the permit experience of other states, where outright denial is a relatively rare event. The crucial question is to what extent the conditions imposed have removed the problems that the proposed developments would otherwise pose. We know that in its first year, the DRI process approved projects containing some 367,000 residential units, while denying projects containing a total of only 7,000. We do not know, however, exactly how many units were cut from those projects that were given conditional approval. Moreover, even this figure might be misleading, for developers often apply for higher densities than they actually expect to obtain, then give up some units in the course of bargaining with local governments.

Inspection of regional council files reveals cases in which conditional approval substantially removed the problems threatened by the project's initial design—and other cases in which the conditions were inadequate. Conditions have tended to address environmental problems, particularly those related to water supply, and problems connected with the adequacy of public facilities. They have almost always been concerned with making growth more acceptable, rather than with limiting its extent. It has been suggested that some conditional approvals may impose conditions so onerous as to amount to *de facto* denial. This appears relatively insignificant, for although several developers have appealed denials, only one developer has appealed a conditional approval. Since most appeals are negotiated to a settlement, it is difficult to say who "won" or "lost."

Three Rivers—The First Appeal

The first case to be decided by the cabinet on appeal provides some excellent examples of the "regional impacts" with which the 1972 law was intended to deal. Three Rivers was a planned residential community, proposed to be built on a 5,800-acre tract of open land in central Florida's Lake County, about 20 miles north of Orlando. When completed in the 1990s, the project would have housed 50,000 people in 18,000 dwelling units.

Located on the outer edge of the booming Orlando metropolitan area, Lake County has yet to garner much of the development that has so recently changed the face of Orange, Osceola, and Seminole counties, which form the central nucleus. Lake County commissioners looked with delight at the taxes and employment opportunities that Three Rivers could bring into the county. The developer promised "an environmentally inspired, totally planned community [where] our subsidiaries work in harmony to acquire strategic property, meet exacting design and planning criteria, and then market and/or develop the best possible product."[53]

Since the DRI cutoff for Lake County was 750 units, the Three Rivers project was clearly required to go through the approval process. When its application was evaluated by the East Central Florida Regional Planning Council, two classes of regional problems began to stand out. The first concerned the project's impact on the Wekiva River, which borders the Three Rivers property on one side. The river had previously been proposed for designation as a "scenic and wild river" worthy of inclusion in the state's scenic rivers program. The council found the developer's plans for disposing of sewage and storm runoff too vague to assure that the Wekiva's waters would not be polluted. Moreover, just the sheer magnitude of the project would inevitably alter the quality of the recreational experience. The developer countered that his sewage plans would meet state standards and that he would leave a 200-foot greenbelt of natural vegetation between the project and the river.

More easily quantified was Three Rivers' impact on Seminole County, just across the river. Unlike Lake County, Seminole had had its full share of the Orlando area's recent growth—and then some. County officials looked with suspicion on new developments, particularly ones they felt would burden local public services. To them, Three Rivers was a traffic generator, as well as another thirsty community drawing down the region's water well field. Traffic from the new city would be "twice the volume that Walt Disney World experienced on its busiest day."[54] It would be necessary to replace the two-lane road connecting Lake and Seminole counties with a six-lane highway. Seminole would get some of the problems, but none of the taxes.

Swayed by Seminole County's arguments and by political pressure from those in opposition, the regional council recommended against the project. Lake County then held its public hearing—and issued a development permit. The regional council's objections were virtually ignored. Lake County claimed that, on its own initiative, it was already imposing the strongest conditions ever required from a project in the county's history. The planning division director of the regional council countered, "The simple fact is that while the conditional use permit may be sufficient for Lake County, it isn't for the regional interest involved—the name of the game has changed—local implementation is desired, encouraged, and supported *as long as it adequately considers the overall regional interest* —they haven't."[55] To the surprise of many, including its own chairman, the regional council voted to underwrite an appeal.[56]

Lake County officials were angry, and the county attorney charged that the regional council was trying to make his county a recreational area for the larger counties.[57] The developer was also unhappy, having already spent over $200,000 on planning. His chief planner complained that the DRI process unfairly penalized those who tried to build large, planned projects instead of piecemeal ones. "If we didn't come in [with a new community]," he said, "we could have, under existing Lake County zoning, put in one unit per acre right along the river, using septic tanks— just as they have now across the river in Seminole County."[58]

In any case, the appeal was made, with the regional council soon joined by the Division of State Planning. For a time, the state considered simply buying the property for parkland, but it balked at the $12 million price tag. This figure, the property's appraised value, was double what the developer had paid only two years before. Some observers speculated that the developer had hoped all along to get development permission, then sell the property to the state—at a price reflecting its new-found development potential. With the state having rejected purchase, the appeal went before a state-appointed hearing examiner. He allowed arguments not only by the developer, the state, and the regional council, but by Seminole County as well. His report agreed with the county's contention that Three Rivers would cause an unreasonable traffic burden. He also found that the developer had simply not furnished enough information to ensure that the project would not cause water pollution. The examiner wrote, "While it would be unduly burdensome and probably technologically premature to require a developer to have available complete detailed engineering plans and specifications for a twenty-year development at the outset of the development, it is equally contradictory to expect a regional planning agency to fulfill its statutory obligation of evaluating the project without having access to the underlying information necessary to the performance of that obligation."[59] He recommended that the project be denied a permit. The developer, he suggested, might reapply solely for the first five-year phase, presenting detailed plans of what this phase would entail.

In October 1974 the Adjudicatory Commission voted 5–0 to accept the hearing examiner's report. The first DRI appeal had ended in a victory of regional over local interest.

The site remained vacant late in 1978, and no new development application had been received. Three Rivers, one of only four appeals actually voted on by the governor and cabinet, and the only case in which the local government's decision was reversed, helped to establish the credibility of the DRI process early on. The undeveloped area remains a powerful reminder that, at least in some ways, a potent new law controls the largest Florida developments.

Doral Park—The Regional Council Takes a Chance

The regional councils are not always so tenacious in bringing appeals. The South Florida Regional Planning Council is considered to be among the "toughest" of the eleven councils, with a staff that provides a thorough fiscal and environmental workup on each project and a governing council that tends to back up its staff. In the case of Dade County's Doral Park development, however, the council was unwilling to act decisively on a project that presented clear environmental problems.

Doral Park is a luxury, golf-oriented PUD (proposed for 16,000 residents) in western Dade County on the edge of the Everglades. In order to build up the low-lying land for building sites, the developer proposed to dig a chain of twenty-one lakes, each 40 feet in depth. In lakes this deep, sunlight cannot penetrate to the bottom, making the natural purification process much less effective. More important, the lakes would cut into the top of the Biscayne aquifer, the source of Miami's water supply. If the lakes ever became polluted, their waters could contaminate the aquifer itself. The staff recommended denial of the project, which the regional council chairman called "a very dangerous gamble with the basic water supply of South Florida."[60]

The county officials who sit on the regional council, however, split on the project, five in favor, five opposed. The Dade County commission held its hearing. It cut the project's density somewhat but allowed it to go ahead, despite the unsolved water quality problem. The regional council, mindful of the cost of an appeal and of the seven appeals it had outstanding, decided to let the matter rest.

Unlike Three Rivers, Doral Park did not find one county outraged at the spillovers from a project in another jurisdiction. Pollution of the aquifer was only a long-range possibility, rather than a quantifiable certainty. The regional council decided to take the chance; however, the risk was deferred by the recession, and Doral Park was among the vast majority of residential DRIs postponed for years. By mid-1978 site improvements had begun, but no actual construction on the project was reported.

Lake Ola—The Power of Local Government

It is important to remember that while Florida has many weak local governments, some that have been found to be corrupt, and still others that are simply hungry for development, it also has a number of cities and counties that pay close attention to the negative impacts of development—particularly when these impacts are felt within their own borders. An example is Lake Ola, a project which passed regional review, only to be turned down at the local level.

Lake Ola was another PUD, this one involving 1,265 units in Orange County, close to the Lake County border. The regional council voted conditional approval, but when the project came to local public hearing, some 150 citizens turned out to protest. The project, it seems, violated the county's own master plan, placing high-density development in an area that did not yet have the needed public services, and the county commissioners denied development permission.[61]

Ironically, the developer filed an appeal of the county decision, and tried to use the regional approval to overturn his local defeat. His reasoning suggests an interesting twist to the DRI process. Although the Florida law makes no mention of so-called developments of regional benefit,[62] local refusal of a power plant's, industry's, or airport's DRI application might be appealed by the regional agency or the state, on grounds that the location was optimal from the regional standpoint. The cabinet then might—if the political climate were right—force the local government to accept the project.[63]

In this case, inconclusive legal maneuvers and the recession left the development in limbo. When building revived, the project (in less ambitious form) emerged as a more conventional development, not subject to DRI review, and was approved by Orange County.[64]

Belcher Oil—Energy as a DRI

One of the few DRIs that has not involved a housing development or a shopping center was the proposal for building Florida's (and, at that time, the nation's) first offshore port for unloading supertankers. Miami's Belcher Oil Company proposed a docking platform 24 miles off the state's western coast, capable of handling crude oil carriers too large for any U.S. port. The oil would be taken by pipeline to a proposed $200 million refinery on Tampa Bay and converted to low-sulfur fuel oil for Florida's ever-hungry electric plants.

Evaluation of Belcher's DRI application found Manatee County, site of the refinery and potential recipient of $2 million yearly in property taxes, pitted against adjoining jurisdictions worried about oil spills and air pollution. The major objection of the regional council was the paucity of information about Belcher's specific plans. One observer called the application "just a glossy real estate promotion brochure" and speculated that Belcher wanted to get development permission only to resell it to some major refiner. Belcher countered that detailed engineering studies would cost millions—far too much to spend without some assurance that the project would be approved.

Despite a regional turndown, the Manatee County commission voted to issue a development order. The regional council then voted to appeal, although with some misgivings as to how much an appeal might cost. The regional council was joined by a number of other "intervenors," including three counties, three cities, some individuals, and the state's pollution control agency. The legal status of these additional parties was uncertain, but the state officer appointed to hear the appeal took the position that "anyone who wants to can come along."[65]

Its position undercut by a voter referendum opposing the refinery, Belcher withdrew its application in November 1974. The right of individual counties to have "standing" in the DRI process has been denied in court rulings since.[66]

DRI Issues

There is continuing discussion in Florida about what kind of project should properly be called a development of regional impact. The current regulations fail to cover such significant projects as highways, hotels, commercial strips, and the opening up of new areas to piecemeal development. In one important case, an appeals court agreed with the Division of State Planning that a 9,000-acre well field in Pasco County, meant to serve Pinellas County and Saint Petersburg, was *not* a DRI because it was covered by the act establishing water management districts, and not by the Environmental Land and Water Management Act.[67] Another example was a proposal to build four, forty-story buildings on a small island off Miami. Under current rules this 1,000-unit project would not have been *nearly* large enough to qualify as a DRI.

Others worry about the cumulative impact of many small projects. Some regional agency staffers estimated in 1974 that current DRI thresholds were capturing as much as 50 percent of the development in their region, but there was no way of confirming this figure with objective data.[68] Given the realities of development financing during and after the 1974–76 recession, the proportion of total development covered by DRI review is probably much less than this now.

Another recurrent issue is enforcement. The state has no staff assigned to make sure all projects of DRI size apply for permits. Since projects are built, and often planned, in stages, a project may not cross the DRI threshold for several years. The Division of State Planning intends to prosecute developers who violate affidavits stating that they will not expand their project in the future, but there is no current process for keeping track of a project's build-out.[69] Moreover, the state does not check into whether developers comply with the conditions imposed by their development order. This duty falls to local government, which may not have been eager to impose the conditions in the first place. An attorney claims that there have been few complaints about noncompliance. He admits, however, that the state merely responds to complaints by citizens and local governments and makes no effort to actively seek out possible violations beyond sending out an annual questionnaire to developers.[70] The regional planning councils, which often negotiate conditions with developers, are equally restricted in their oversight of projects.

There is evidence that a huge number of potential building sites have been exempted from DRI review by the law's very liberal provision of "vested rights." Where California's coastal law requires that a building permit or similar specific approval have been obtained before the effective date of the law, Florida allows vesting of projects that are in much earlier stages of planning and approval. Amendments passed by the 1974 legislature even further widened this loophole.

For example, Disney World, the magnet that has transformed the Orlando region into a hotel and service industry boomtown, was given wide-ranging powers by incorporating itself as the Reedy Creek Improvement District in 1967. In October 1978 it announced a half-billion-dollar expansion, which is likely to attract more millions of visitors and to make each tourist prolong his stay. The entire project is exempt from DRI review because it is vested; Disney is considered a model developer, but if it were not, the state would have no course of action. And the new Orlando boom, which began within hours of Disney's announcement, is likely to be in small developments outside of DRI reviews.

One study of the DRI process found that in the first three years and ten months under the law, 228 applications for binding letters of interpretation to establish vested rights were received by the Division of State Planning; 204 projects were vested entirely or in part.[71] It is not surprising then that although there was much litigation over vested rights in California, there has been virtually none at all in Florida.

The Division of State Planning has recently brought some of the more troublesome vested projects under DRI review by negotiating agreements with developers. The prototype agreement was made with ITT's Palm Coast. Shortly after Palm Coast began selling lots, it encountered prob-

lems in obtaining canal-dredging permits. The division and ITT negotiated an agreement to do at least conceptual planning for the whole
project, and to submit future development plans to DRI review when
appropriate. In 1974 and 1975 a Flagler County grand jury found evidence of technical violations of the Florida platting law and suggested
that the project's vested status might be investigated by the state. By 1977
ITT had changed its management, reduced Palm Coast's size dramatically, and changed its emphasis from land sales (40,000 lots were sold)
to community development. An agreement signed that August initiated
a conceptual planning process, now under way, by which state agencies
are reviewing the initial plans and becoming familiar with land use and
environmental issues that will arise when Palm Coast begins submitting
DRI applications in 1979.[72] General Development Corporation signed a
similar agreement for its projects throughout Florida.

The DRI process has done little to involve individuals and citizen
groups in project review. Projects of this size ordinarily go to public
hearing in the course of zoning changes, even without the requirement
of the DRI law. Information brought out by the regional council's review
is useful to those who might oppose a particular project, but Florida's
organized environmentalists are not numerous enough to take full advantage of this new asset. The relatively short time that elapses between initial
application and final decision on the development order means that *ad hoc*
groups have little time to organize against a project at the scheduled
hearing.

DRI review seems better suited to addressing the objections of neigh-
boring *governments* in the region than those of citizens. To the extent that
the interests of citizens and their governments coincide, this will not be
objectionable. It does appear that DRI review better answers the kind of
technical and financial questions that concern governments (How much
new sewer capacity will this project demand?) than the more subjective
questions that concern many citizens (How will growth affect the quality
of the human environment?). In recent sessions, the legislature has
shown no interest in remedying these shortcomings.

A Question of Expectations

Florida's DRI process can be evaluated only in terms of the expectations one holds for it. A conservative view might be that the DRI review
exists to allow regional and state interests to be asserted over those
projects so large that their effects spill over jurisdictional, in this case

county, boundaries. Rather than allow a single affected jurisdiction to assert this interest, the DRI process requires that the injured party persuade a majority of county governments in the region to make objection to the proposed project and, if that does not effect changes, to bring an appeal.

If the objective is this modest, we might judge the DRI process a success. We have seen how in both the Three Rivers and Belcher Oil cases, clearly defined spillovers (traffic congestion, air pollution) caused jurisdictions affected by the proposed development to be heard—and to be supported in an appeal. Before the 1972 law, these objections could not have been made so effectively. DRI review has been called "a process without a policy," but if the goal is solely to avoid spillovers, process alone may be all that is required.

Some observers maintain, moreover, that in the course of reviewing DRIs, policies have evolved. In two significant Broward County cases, for instance, the county followed the regional council's urgings and approved development orders with stringent requirements for low- and moderate-income housing, a significant accomplishment.[73]

If we set our goal somewhat higher, however, the record of DRI review becomes considerably less impressive. Many Floridians had had such high hopes. By providing a thorough impact study of the large developments that were so changing the face of Florida, they hoped DRI review would lead to increasingly sensitive and careful development. Here, too, DRI has had its successes:[74] density has been slashed in several south Florida PUDs; shopping centers have been greatly reduced in size or turned down completely; a mangrove area was saved from destruction south of Fort Myers; and public access was assured along an Atlantic Ocean beach.

But at least as numerous as these successes have been the failures— the projects allowed to go forward even though ill-conceived and ill-located, with environmental problems left uncorrected, or even unappreciated. These failures may be traced in great part to two fundamental weaknesses in the DRI process.

Regional Weaknesses

The first of these is the inherent weakness of Florida's regional planning councils. Creatures of the local governments that compose them, they have no independent political base. The councils themselves (as distinct from their professional staffs) are made up largely of local elected officials. This, said the director of the Tampa Bay Regional Planning Council, "puts the council in the awkward position of biting the hand that feeds it."[75]

To be sure, a side effect of the DRI review has been a general encouragement of regionalism. Before the process went into effect, less than half of Florida's counties were participating members of regional councils. Three of the regions had no council at all. Now all of the regions have a council, staffs of existing councils have expanded, and most counties and some cities are participating. Perhaps most important, the councils for the first time have a responsibility to perform that involves them in major, immediate development decisions.

But it would be idealistic to assume that a county commissioner sitting on a regional council is instantly transformed into a person who consistently sets regional above local good. Since he is still accountable only to the electorate—and the special interests—of his home county, an astute politician is just as likely to trade favors with commissioners from other counties. As one regional council staffer complains, "These politicians just can't see past county lines—I guess things just haven't gotten bad enough yet."[76] His sentiment is echoed repeatedly by staff planners who see their objections to projects ignored or even suppressed for political reasons.

A planner who recently left the Orlando area council explains, "The law focused attention on the fact that there is good and bad in development. It said, 'Let's expose the facts and make some conscious decisions.' The hidden hope of the law was that local government officials would adopt the same . . . thought process," both in local zoning decisions and in their role as regional planning council members. He thinks that the act has educated officials about the desirable and destructive aspects of all development decisions, but has not altered the politics of development decision making. "The classic retort to regional council recommendations heard throughout the state," he says, "is, 'Every man has a right to go bankrupt.' " This philosophy has underlain "attitudes toward land development in Florida since the 1800s."[77]

A commissioner from a powerful central Florida county flatly admits as much: "I can guarantee you that we can get any project approved by our regional planning council. We wouldn't have to say a word—they know there would be polar bears in the streets of Miami before they got another favor from us."[78] We might note that in the case of both Three Rivers and Belcher Oil, the county pushing for the project's approval was one of the less powerful members of the regional council.

One analyst thinks that these political considerations are ruinous to the Florida DRI process. He writes that the composition of the regional planning agencies represents "a serious obstacle to effective state and regional participation in the DRI decision-making process. . . . Collections of local governmental officials in regional guise but ultimately accountable politically only to their local constituencies realistically cannot be expected to produce effective advocacy for state and regional interests."[79]

County commissioners who sit on the regional councils seem most responsive to environmental concerns when they come from a local constituency that is itself concerned about the effects of growth. Seminole County, which pushed the Three Rivers appeal, has one of the state's most aggressive local programs for making developers offset the public service costs of their projects. South Florida's environment-minded regional council, moreover, is dominated by representatives of the Gold Coast counties, which first spawned the state's slow-growth movement. It is not surprising to learn that the South Florida Regional Council, aided by an attorney who has been closely involved in developing the state's land use laws, has been far more aggressive about appealing local development orders than any other council.[80] It may be for this reason that several south Florida counties—those west of Miami, and to the north of Broward County—have split away from the South Florida Regional Council and joined or formed others they can control more easily.

As a result of these political differences, most observers agree that the councils vary tremendously in quality. Staff work, says one, ranges from "ill-prepared to extremely competent and well versed" in understanding the development process and its effects.[81] The staffs are hard-pressed; it is unusual for a regional council to have even one person working full-time on DRI review. Appeals increase the burden, and must be paid for from general funds available to the councils.

Contracts that provide for review of water and natural resources problems in DRI projects by regional water management districts (created by a 1972 law) are improving the technical quality of the regional council reports. Compared to the $500,000 that the Division of State Planning divides among the eleven regional councils for DRI review activities, the South Florida Water Management District alone has a budget of $25 million, a huge technical staff, and a genuinely regional outlook. The district shows no hesitation in pointing out flaws in the DRI process, noting, for instance, that by focusing solely on DRIs, the regional councils overlook regionwide growth and do not consider serious locational problems when developments are sited in important water-resource areas.[82]

Some thoughtful observers hoped—and still do—that the powerful water districts, and not the regional planning councils, would be charged with DRI review.

When they appeal local DRI rulings, the regional councils maintain their control over the final conditions placed on projects. The appeals process has evolved into a forum for negotiating with developers for additional conditions, usually desired more by the regional council than by the local government. The first five years have resulted in just four rulings by the Adjudicatory Commission but in at least eighteen negotiated settlements. And overall, only about 20 percent of local DRI decisions have been appealed.[83] Clearly, both regional councils and state government have been emphasizing persuasion and have been quite conservative in their attempts to modify local decisions.

Local Resistance

Even when the regional councils act decisively, the DRI process faces a second obstacle, the resistance of local governments. Since the regional recommendations are only advisory, local government may choose to accept them only partially, or to ignore them completely.

The technical review done by the regional council staff has almost certainly improved the factual basis for local decision making. Local interests opposing projects have been quick to use this material in the mandatory public hearings. Nevertheless, local response to these critiques continues to depend on the local government's initial predisposition toward growth. Seminole County's commissioners, for example, have asked to see the full regional staff reports on projects there, unfiltered and untempered by any political decisions by the regional council.[84]

A planner in a more growth-oriented county, on the other hand, finds that "The county commissioners don't always review the 4,000 pages that are presented to them—and even when they read them they have many biases."

The Adjudicatory Commission, by its review of appeals, is the one power that could change local practice, but it has scarcely done so, overruling local development approval only in the Three Rivers case. The ALI code proposed an important role for an administrative agency in reviewing DRI appeals. But the governor and cabinet, distracted by other duties, rely on hearing examiners when an appeal forces its way to their attention. In effect, the nonjudicial state-level review anticipated by the ALI drafters—such as is exercised by the Vermont Environmental Board, under Act 250—has not appeared in Florida.

No appeals have yet been pursued to overturn a local government's rejection of a project with positive regional benefits. "Perhaps the most significant disappointment of the DRI program, as it has been administered," says a lawyer who was the first administrator of the law, "is that [this] balanced perspective envisioned in the ALI code has never been achieved."[85] Developers naturally resent this skewed situation.

It should not be too surprising, therefore, that the DRI review has not brought about a revolution in local land use control. The law, after all, mandates neither reforms in local planning practice nor state standards that new projects must meet.[86] There *is* evidence that DRI is having a longer-term effect of exposing the more backward counties to sophisticated analysis of the fiscal and environmental impacts of major developments. Even the most growth-oriented local official cannot fail to be impressed by studies that point out a project's public service demands or the flood hazard that may arise when a wetland is filled in. Everywhere in Florida developers are being made to answer questions that, before DRI review began, would simply have never been asked. Apparently local officials also value these aspects of DRI review; when a "one-stop shopping" bill to simplify permitting came before the 1978 legislature, it proposed that DRI review be consolidated with requirements for water consumption and dredge-and-fill permits. For the first time, Florida's associations of county commissioners and city governments joined the regional councils and the Division of State Planning in a coalition to remove DRI from the bill.[87] Some local jurisdictions are even adopting the questions on the DRI review form for use in their own evaluation of projects that fall below the DRI threshold. One calls such projects "mini-DRIs"; another, "developments of county impact."[88]

The Developers Respond

Developers find the DRI review an expense and an aggravation, but not much of a hindrance unless their project is turned down or appealed. The practice of making local issuance of a development order coincide with local proceedings on the project's zoning change or PUD approval has kept delay, ever the bane of developers, to a minimum. Many developers do complain that the regional councils demand needless information and cavalierly reject the expert opinion of the developer's traffic consultants or sanitary engineers. One consulting planner complains that the regional councils "have twenty-two-year-old kids criticizing a developer who has been around forty years." Many of the questions that are asked, adds a colleague, concern problems, such as school financing, that are local rather than regional in scope.[89]

The law permits the regional planning council to rule that a DRI application is incomplete and to request more written information. The developer may comply or insist that his original application is complete. This process prevents the regional council from delaying an application until the developer complies with its requests.

A Seminole County developer feels that having to spell out the fiscal impacts of his project made him an easy target for stiff local development fees. The development order for his 4,000-unit project contains fifty-six separate conditions, many requiring him to install and pay for expensive public facilities. He charges that a competitor could build the same number of units in many scattered apartment houses without having to absorb these public costs.

A planner who once worked for a regional council sympathizes with this complaint. He says that economic data are not available in several regions, and that an antideveloper bias results. It is easier to quantify the approximate costs of new development—road improvements or higher school enrollment—than it is to predict the new revenue that such development will contribute. In a project proposing to house 50,000 persons over a decade, he asks, who can predict the mix of retired to working residents, what their incomes are, where they will shop, and what locality will get their sales taxes? Nonetheless, he thinks the process does discourage the completely speculative investments in land development projects that have so often scarred Florida without ever meeting community needs.[90]

As a result, developers evade DRI review by designing smaller projects. An environmentalist maintains, "The thresholds for DRI review are becoming . . . limbo bars under which developers are ducking."[91] Although he could point out that the economic climate no longer favors huge projects of the sort launched in 1973 and 1974, an attorney who represents developers says the law causes delays and administrative difficulties that tend "to encourage the avoidance of it. The fact that there are not large numbers of projects indicates that people avoid it if they can. Few would volunteer to go through it."[92]

Undoubtedly the biggest problem that developers are having with the DRI process is that it binds them to long-range plans, denying them the chance to change their projects to fit rising costs and changing markets. Early in the DRI process, at least two developers claimed that because of changed conditions they could no longer live with the terms of their development orders.[93] Voicing a similar concern, Three Rivers' developer argued that "to demand a firm commitment to the type of waste treatment facility which will be employed for a project to be completed twenty-five years from now deprives a New Town concept of one of its most important advantages."[94]

At least in a technical sense, this problem was relieved by a 1977 amendment to the law. Developers holding DRI development orders are allowed to modify their projects so long as they do not make a "substantial deviation" from the terms of the order. Among specific changes allowed are an increase of 5 percent, or 200 dwelling units, whichever is less; a decrease in the number of units; a reduction of 5 percent or 50 acres in open space, whichever is less; an increase in open space; or, a change required by environmental agency or water management district permits.[95]

It is expected that the procedure will be greatly used by many developers who never built the DRIs that were approved in 1973–74. It is not yet known how the process will work since the determination of substantial deviation is the responsibility of local government.

Nonetheless, developers are not completely appeased. The DRI process itself tends to be discouraging, some say, because it forces developers to speculate about conditions too far into the future. According to one attorney, the process "forces the developer to be speculative, then criticizes the hell out of him for doing it."[96]

As a general matter, environmentalists praise the DRI portion of Florida's land use law. "If nothing else," one says, "it has forced the developers to buy some pretty good consultants instead of just going into an area and completely wrecking it." He feels that they have gained from the process, too. They are learning to avoid wetland sites, to build with nature when necessary to allow water to go into recharge areas rather than building expensive canals, and to donate swamps to the public. In some instances, he says, developers have learned about water, sewage, and traffic problems they might otherwise have overlooked at their peril.[97]

In turn, the development community is no longer united in opposition to the law. In 1972 only one corporation assisted in drafting the Environmental Land and Water Management Act. John DeGrove thinks that while "most are not really happy with the way the law is working out," they favor a state framework for development as protection against arbitrary local action. That is, they favor the concept, if not its implementation.[98] Some suggest that "the DRI process may not be needed at all in its present form once the Local Government Comprehensive Planning Act [see below] comes on line."[99] This suggests continued resistance to, and perhaps even a new attack on, the process in the legislature. Given the vagueness of many local plans, environmentalists will surely oppose such arguments.

Overall, the DRI process has "put to the test the art of intergovernmental decisionmaking," says James W. May, the state official who administers the 1972 law, and helped the state and local governments gain perspective regarding other's needs. As in California, where regulation by permit preceded planning, DRI review, says May, "gave us the opportunity for experience-based decision making" as Florida began to promote local and state planning.[100] What use Florida makes of that opportunity remains to be seen.

Toward a Comprehensive Land Use Program

The framers of Florida's 1972 land use law were well aware that regulating critical areas and large private developments could not, even in the best of circumstances, solve all of the state's land-related problems. Some progress had already been made, particularly in the protection of beaches and wetlands. A 1967 law required that before the state could issue a permit for dredging or filling in a wetland a biological survey must be taken to determine the environmental effects. The disposal of state-owned tidelands, from that time on, was much more closely regulated. In 1970 the legislature enacted a law which limited the degree to which new buildings could encroach on Atlantic and Gulf Coast beaches.

The 1972 legislature passed more legislation than just the Environmental Land and Water Management Act. A Comprehensive Planning Act created a new agency charged with preparing a long-range plan for the development of the state.

We have already mentioned the $240 million land acquisition bond issue, placed on the ballot by the 1972 legislature and overwhelmingly approved by the voters. By 1978 all these funds had been spent or committed to buy pristine habitats with unique natural features. A 50,000-acre ranch in Osceola County, containing pine and cypress woods and Kissimmee River wetlands, was purchased, as were 28,000 acres of woods bordering the Saint Johns River for 15 miles in Orange County.[101]

Recognizing that a great deal remained to be done, the 1972 legislators also set up the Environmental Land Management Study (ELMS) Committee to suggest further policy directions. While the committee was deliberating, only one significant new land law was passed, the Florida Electrical Power Plant Siting Act of 1973. This law, similar to those in several other states, requires utilities to give the state ten-year forecasts of their power-generating needs and their plans for future sites. These sites would then have to be certified by the state's pollution control board, with input from the Bureau of Comprehensive Planning in the Division of State Planning.

Many expected great things from the 1974 legislature. The ELMS Committee had proposed several new laws, chief of which was a Local Government Comprehensive Planning Act. It had become apparent that, if the philosophy of the 1972 law had been to leave considerable power in the hands of local government, then these governments would have to be goaded, or even forced, to plan for their future development. Previous laws had *permitted* local governments to prepare comprehensive plans. The ELMS Committee proposal would have the state *require* that each local government come up with a comprehensive plan within three years. Once adopted, no local zoning ordinance could be in conflict with the plan, and no development that was in conflict could be approved.

As one member of the committee put it, "This legislation does not dictate to any city or county in Florida the specific answers to its particular problems. Planning is not an exact process. How the citizens of Pasco County wish to plan their future way of life may be very different than the legitimate desires of the citizens of Okeechobee County. But, if passed, this legislation does remove the alternative *not to plan at all*. . . ."[102] The proposed law authorized $50 million in state aid to finance this planning, with the money raised by doubling the documentary surtax on real estate transactions.

Also before the legislature was a bill setting a growth policy for the state. The bill, a pet project of the retiring speaker of the state house of representatives, would not be a hollow policy declaration, but was to be supported by implementing measures—a $12 million study of the state's carrying capacity, impact fees for new developments, and an inventory of the state's resources. Still other bills before the legislature would have set a statewide building code, tightened controls on coastal wetlands, and allowed the state to use eminent domain to purchase environmentally endangered lands.

The legislature approved almost none of this. Some bills passed one house, only to die in committee in the other. A thirty-one-page growth policy statement cleared the house, but was pared to only two pages in the senate. In the end a ten-page compromise was agreed to. It made a few bold statements, including the declaration, "It shall not be the state's policy to stimulate further growth generally, but to plan for and distribute such growth as may develop . . . [and] the desired kind, rate and extent of growth shall be primarily determined by the carrying capacity of natural and man-made systems of an area."[103] Measures to implement these policies, however, were totally lacking. The carrying capacity study, for example, was left unfunded.

Florida's 1975 legislature took the step it had rejected in 1974 and voted overwhelmingly to require local governments to prepare comprehensive plans. Those that failed to do so within four years would have them prepared (at local expense) by the state. The state has the power to comment on, but not to change, plans prepared by local governments. These plans are intended to do more than grace the planners' shelves. After they have been adopted by local government, "all land development regulations enacted or amended shall be consistent with the adopted comprehensive plan."[104] "In effect," says one observer, "the legislature is insisting on a minimum level of home rule."[105] Significantly, the 1975 law, unlike the 1974 version, removed state funding for the mandated local planning.

The legislature also passed a New Communities Act, which allows developers of such projects to obtain status as special districts, giving them certain governmentlike powers to tax, issue bonds, condemn land, and provide public services. This privilege requires that the developer obtain both county permission and DRI approval as well as provide a specified amount of low- to moderate-income housing units.

These laws exhausted the legislature's interest in land use questions until 1978, when two bills were passed. One weakened Florida's proposed coastal zone management program,[106] and a second, the Private Property Rights Act, established a court procedure for determining when denial of certain environmental permits, including DRI development orders, entitles a property owner to compensation from the state. The law is based on the ALI code and provisions of the English Town and Country Planning Act of 1971.[107]

The record of implementing these bills has been as mixed as the legislature's performance in passing them. Although the New Communities Act establishes a mechanism for developers to pass along their front-end costs for infrastructure to their customers, it has, for all practical purposes, been entirely ignored. Given the potential in Florida for managing rapid development through large, well-planned projects, this failure is disturbing.

Preparation of the state comprehensive plan was delayed by uncertainty about how to cover the daunting breadth of the legislative mandate for the plan, which was to "provide long-range guidance for the orderly social, economic, and physical growth of the state." What emerged after four years of drafting, public hearings, and skirmishes with the legislature, was the Florida State Comprehensive Plan, a document containing fourteen "elements" on topics such as agriculture, education, land development, and social services.[108]

The plan primarily identifies existing laws and programs, suggests studies on how to improve them or to coordinate their application to common problems, and poses goals against which to evaluate government actions. The 1978 legislature permitted the governor to make the plan an executive tool, but as an advisory document only, except where already authorized by law, and removed the section of the law making the plan "effective as state policy." What is left is a document and a process for review of state agency programs and budgets. Implementation of the plan has begun; its future role depends upon future governors, who are free to use the plan—or ignore it—as they wish, and upon the legislature, which must respond to any requests for new laws.

Under the Local Government Comprehensive Planning Act, 457 counties and cities and three special districts were required to designate planning agencies by July 1, 1976. Only five cities failed to do so, and in these cases the county government then assumed responsibility. The local governments then had three years to draw up plans. By the fall of 1978, 102 governments had submitted plans or parts of them to the state for review. Many, if not most, localities are expected to need at least one of the two year-long extensions the law allows before submitting their plans.

A complete plan is required, by statute, to contain sections on land use, traffic, waste and water, conservation, recreation and open space, housing, intergovernmental coordination, and utilities. Larger governments are required to complete more elements.

The plans received so far vary widely in quality. Sanibel, the famous sea-shelling island off the Gulf coast, prepared an expensive, sophisticated plan based on model natural systems and carrying-capacity analysis. Miami, on the other hand, submitted a map as its land use element, and failed to adopt any of the supporting documents underlying it as parts of the plan.[109]

In reviewing the plans, state planners look chiefly at the relationship between state and local comprehensive plans and the consistency and feasibility of the local plans. Local governments are not currently required to forward their final plans, as adopted, to the state, so there is no systematic way to monitor their reaction to state-suggested revisions of the plans. However, the state is pressing for such a requirement to be restored to the law.

To date, too few plans have been completed to evaluate the local governments' comprehensive planning process. The system will not be completely in place until 1981. There is no way of knowing what local governments will do to implement the plans, nor is the state empowered to compel them to do so, or even to oversee local performance. Most persons familiar with the course of land development in Florida expect local governments uninterested in controlling growth to be little changed by the process; and some expect tough plans to be subjected to frequent litigation.

Conclusion

Florida's recent venture into state land use control is at once exciting and frustrating. It is exciting because the state, which combines extremely rapid growth with an especially vulnerable natural environment, has faced the problem of intergovernmental relations head on, welding a complex partnership of local, regional, and state authorities. It is frustrating because this dispersion of power has meant that nonlocal interests are too frequently unprotected and because local governments have not all accepted the challenge to improve their own performance.

The Florida philosophy, embodied in the Environmental Land and Water Management Act of 1972, is that the state should take part in land use decisions only when the character of the land involved (a critical area) or the character of the proposed project (a development of regional impact) requires the protection of a statewide or regionwide interest. In this it is quite similar to both the ALI's Model Land Development Code and the federal land use legislation that failed to pass the 1973 and 1974 Congresses. Even where there is such a nonlocal interest, the state guides, persuades, and reviews, while actual administration of the controls is left to local authorities.

After five years' experience, it can now be seen what a useful—but limited—tool DRI review is. The DRI process, in concert with new laws on dredge-and-fill operations, for example, makes it unlikely that any grossly damaging land subdivisions or new communities will despoil more of Florida's coast. For other major developments, DRI review provides a useful negotiating tool so that nonlocal interests can be accommodated, by attaching conditions to development orders. Developers now expect to confront these conditions, and local officials are learning how to use them, so the major actors have been educated by the process.

But DRI review is a tool of the last war. The development boom that it attacked is over. Florida may continue to add over one hundred thousand units of housing each year, but not a half million. As development takes place in smaller increments, as fast-food restaurants stretch along more highways, Florida's special qualities erode, and DRI review can do nothing about it.

To deal with this cumulative change, some sort of "growth management" is advocated by many Florida land use experts. But here the record is mixed, too. The process of critical areas designation is bogged down, and it has not been utilized to locate new economic development. The state's comprehensive planning process is unlikely to affect the siting of new development. Much depends upon the willingness of county government to take charge of the land use control system. Several of the more urban, sophisticated counties are beginning to do this,[110] reemphasizing the ultimately subordinate role of state government in Florida's ongoing transformation.

Notes

1. Between April 1970 and July 1976, Florida's population grew by 1,573,000, or 23 percent. The growth rates of Arizona (26.7 percent), Alaska (25.6 percent), and Nevada (23.7 percent) were higher, but the absolute number of people added to all three states combined equaled only 673,000. It is expected that after the 1980 census, Florida will have two additional members in the House of Representatives, again matched only by California and Texas. The migration rate cited, for 1973, fell during the subsequent recession, but the average rate during the 1970s approached 20,000 per month.

2. Formally, the law is Ch. 380, Florida Stat. (1972).

3. In a single Gold Coast county (Broward), for example, more living units were authorized in 1973 than were authorized that year in the entire state of New Jersey. See "Broward: From Boom to What?" special supplement to the Miami *Herald,* May 1974.

4. Ibid., p. 13.

5. Many of these projects, of course, are lot-sales schemes that will never house anyone; and others failed or were delayed or reduced in size during the recession. See "New Community Developments in Florida," *Florida Environmental and Urban Issues* (March 1974) p. 8. INFORM's report on Florida wetland subdivisions, which studied nine projects (including Palm Coast), ranging in size from 9,900 acres to 118,118 acres, projected a combined population of 1,542,400, of whom only a tenth would reside at the (now scaled-down) ITT project. See *Florida Environmental and Urban Issues* (November 1977) p. 10.

6. There is a vast literature on Florida's environment and its problems. Among the most useful works are Luther Carter, *The Florida Experience: Land and Water Policy in a Growth State* (Baltimore, Md., Johns Hopkins University Press for Resources for the Future, 1975); Raymond Dasmann, *No Further Retreat* (New York, Macmillan, 1971); William R. McCluney, *The Environmental Destruction of South Florida* (Miami, University of Miami Press, 1971); and various issues

of *ENFO,* the newsletter of the Environmental Information Center of the Florida Conservation Foundation.

7. Surprisingly, the fiscal impacts of growth, while the subject of some discussion, are not perceived as being so crucial as they are in other fast-growing areas. Property taxes are still low in Florida, particularly when compared with those in the northern cities from which many migrants come.

8. Changes in U.S. Army Corps of Engineers regulations and Florida law sharply reduced such activities after 1975.

9. *ENFO* (July 1974).

10. The cap was overturned in circuit court in *Boca Villas Corporation* v. *City of Boca Raton,* 45 Fla. Supp. 65 (15th Cir., 1976), and has been appealed to the Fourth District Court of Appeals. The judge did not reject the concept of growth caps, but found that Boca Raton had acted arbitrarily, without any professional or scientific study. See Daniel W. O'Connell, "Florida Planning and Zoning Case Law: 1974 to Mid-1978," *Environmental Comment* (August 1978) p. 12. Neither side has pressed for resolution of the appeal, and the city and developers are reaching an informal accommodation. The 1978 population of Boca Raton was 54,000. Interview with James C. Nicholas, Florida Atlantic University, Boca Raton, Oct. 9, 1978.

11. Carter, *The Florida Experience,* p. 46.

12. Ernest R. Bartley, "Status and Effectiveness of Land Development Regulation in Florida Today," in Environmental Land Management Study Committee, Conference on Land Use, Miami, June 11–12, 1973, *Summary Report* (Tallahassee, ELMS Committee, 1973) pp. 8–9.

13. For a detailed account of the conference and the subsequent drafting of the 1972 land use bill, see Carter, *The Florida Experience,* ch. 5. The legislative struggle over the bill is recounted in Phyllis Myers, *Slow Start in Paradise* (Washington, D.C., Conservation Foundation, 1974).

14. Note that Hawaii, which takes the comprehensive mapping tack, has only a handful of local governments with which to contend.

15. American Law Institute, *Model Land Development Code.* Proposed Official Draft (Philadelphia, ALI, April 1975) p. 289.

16. Citations are from Florida Stat. (1972 Supp.) 380.05.

17. Many Florida developers, particularly the largest ones, like to style themselves as new community builders, even when they have to stretch the term considerably.

18. See Daniel W. O'Connell, "Existing 'New Community' Policy and Legislation in Florida, 1973," in Environmental Land Management Study Committee, Conference on New Communities, Miami, July 15–17, 1973, *Summary Report* (Tallahassee, ELMS Committee, 1973).

19. Amendment to Ch. 380.05, Florida Stat. (1974).

20. Carter, *The Florida Experience,* p. 231.

21. Ecologically, it would be preferable for the preserve to protect wetlands and recharge areas throughout the swamp, leaving the highlands in private hands. Landowners have objected, however, that scattered private inholdings would have little value and that the government could easily deny access to them. The purchase program will assure continued supplies of water to the Everglades National Park and southwest Florida estuaries.

22. Myers, *Slow Start in Paradise,* pp. 22–23.

23. Ibid., p. 23.

24. Telephone interview with Bernie Hyde, Division of State Planning, Oct. 6, 1974. This was verified in an interview with James W. May, chief, Bureau of Land and Water Management, Division of State Planning, Tallahassee, Oct. 11, 1978.

25. The state had not complied with statutory time limits in adopting the regulations. O'Connell, "Florida Planning and Zoning Case Law," p. 13. The case was *Postal Colony Co., Inc.* v. *Askew,* 348 So. 2d 338 (First District Court of Appeals, 1977).

26. Florida Division of State Planning, *Final Report and Recommendations for the Proposed Florida Keys Area of Critical State Concern* (Tallahassee, Division of State Planning, December 1974) p. 2.

27. Ibid., p. 41.

28. Dasmann, *No Further Retreat,* pp. 125–126. In 1974 two seats on the county commission were won by candidates taking a strong antigrowth, anti-high-rise position.

29. Stephen Fox, "Florida's Areas of Critical State Concern: An Update," *Florida Environmental and Urban Issues* (April 1978) p. 8.

30. Interview with James W. May. Though the state may review all local development orders, it may move to exclude minor projects.

31. Ibid.

32. One limited survey found citizens generally in favor of designation, and officials, particularly in Key West, opposed—a finding confirmed by subsequent election returns. The study also showed that local governments found the state's technical assistance to be too little, too late. See James C. Nicholas and Carol C. Crawford, "Areas of Critical Environmental Concern: A Case Study." Paper presented to the Southern Regional Science Association Annual Meeting, Richmond, Va., April 1976.

33. Interviews with James W. May, and with Charles Lee, vice president, Florida Audubon Society, Maitland, Oct. 5, 1978.

34. Interview with Barry Peterson, executive director, South Florida Regional Planning Council, Miami, Oct. 10, 1978.

35. Interview with Bernie Hyde.

36. Fox, "Florida's Areas of Critical State Concern," pp. 8–10.

37. Interview with James W. May.

38. Interview with John M. DeGrove, Florida Atlantic University, Boca Raton, Oct. 9, 1978.

39. While the rules still define power plants as DRIs, the 1973 Electrical Power Plant Siting Act established a separate review process for such facilities. The legislature has not passed the technical amendment removing power plants from the list of DRI projects, but they are not reviewed as DRIs. Interview with James W. May.

40. The list we present here extracts from and simplifies the official list, which may be found in Florida Department of Administration, Administration Commission, "Land Planning," in *Rules* (Tallahassee, Florida Department of Administration, 1973) ch. 22F-2, pt. II.

41. We might note that this kind of definition speaks more to local impact than to intercounty spillovers. In practice, however, this approach is probably more efficient than the alternatives. A flat statewide minimum would mean that every urban apartment tower would be a DRI, while a definition without a numerical standard would be difficult to administer.

42. Interview with William Partington, executive director, Florida Conservation Foundation Environmental Information Center, Winter Park, Feb. 21, 1974.

43. Alternatively, the state could, during this period, designate the site as a critical area and require the adoption of local regulations.

44. See note 66, below.

45. It has been suggested that citizens might gain "standing" to appeal by invoking Ch. 403, § 412 of Florida's 1971 Environmental Protection Act. Telephone interview with Gilbert Finnell, then at Florida State University School of Law, Tallahassee, Aug. 29, 1974. To date, this has not happened.

46. The South Florida Regional Planning Council has already challenged the division on one such case. The division denied the council standing to argue that a series of marinas in Biscayne Bay were in fact part of a single large project and thus clearly subject to DRI review. Memo written by Barry Peterson to regional planning council executive directors, Oct. 9, 1978, and appended correspondence from the division, Sept. 13, 1978. The regional council is pressing the issue in court.

47. *General Development Corporation* v. *Division of State Planning,* 353 So. 2d 1199 (First District Court of Appeals). As of January 19, 1979, the division had found five projects over the quantitative DRI standard to be exempt from DRI review, and one smaller project to be subject to DRI review. Memorandum from James W. May with attached proposed rules 22F-1.16 and 22F-1.31, Estimate of Economic Impact.

48. Figures provided by Tasha Buford, Bureau of Land and Water Management, Division of State Planning, Tallahassee, from the division's "Developments of Regional Impact: Summary of the First Five Years, July 1, 1973 Through June 30, 1978" (Tallahassee, 1978). Mimeo.

49. Figures are taken from *Developments of Regional Impact—A Summary Report for the First Year* (Tallahassee, Florida Division of State Planning, September 1974).

50. See note 48, above.

51. DRIs are built over many years or even decades, so the number of units approved each year vastly exceeds the number of building permits issued for the same project each year. In 1972, 283,000 permits were issued; in subsequent years, 267,000 (1973), 111,000 (1974), and 48,000 (1975). These figures of course include permits for projects smaller than the threshold for DRI review. U.S. Department of Commerce, Bureau of the Census, *Statistical Abstract of the United States 1977* (Washington, D.C.) p. 775.

52. Interview with James W. May. May fears that the subsequent retrenchment may have gone too far. Banks may be unwilling to finance the large-scale projects that provide the greatest opportunities for careful, superior planning and environmental protection.

Another indication of the severity of the crash caused by overbuilding may be found in employment figures. As of June 1975, coastal zone unemployment in the counties from Miami north was 13.4 percent; two-thirds of the job losses were construction related. See James C. Nicholas, "Economy of the South Florida Coastal Zone," *Florida Environmental and Urban Issues* (December 1975) pp. 11–12.

53. Advertisement by Major Realty Corporation, *Fortune,* vol. 89, no. 2 (February 1974).

54. Carl Gosline, then planning director of East Central Florida Regional Planning Council, quoted in Miami *Herald,* Dec. 13, 1973.

55. Carl Gosline, notes in Three Rivers project file, Dec. 18, 1973. Significantly, the council's policy committee tried to fire Gosline five months later for what they considered his overly aggressive review of projects.

56. After Lake County had issued its development order, the regional planning council chairman had commented, "I doubt very seriously that an appeal would pass. Most of the member commissioners involved feel that the council has had its say and most have the attitude that zoning is a local matter." *Orlando Sentinel,* Jan. 8, 1974. Days later the council voted 21–4 to appeal.

57. Christopher Ford, quoted in Eustis (Fla.) *Lake Region News,* Jan. 16, 1974.

58. Interview with Jim Klement, Major Design Corporation, Orlando, Feb. 21, 1974.

59. Report of C. McFerrin Smith III, quoted in the Orlando *Sentinel,* Sept. 7, 1974.

60. Harvey Ruvin, quoted in the Miami *Herald,* Jan. 8, 1974.

61. Although Lake Ola was denied on the basis of noncompliance with the county master plan, the first DRI in Orange County, Granada, was also not in compliance, but was approved. According to a former regional council staffer, "I think it shows that it all depends on who the developer is and knows. When the land use plan does not show the 'right' density for the 'right' developer, the plan becomes a flexible guide to be changed to fit the situation. When the plan shows a different density than that proposed by an 'out-of-favor' developer, the local officials use the plan to deny the project." Personal communication, Nov. 20, 1974.

62. This is another category of the ALI model code.

63. One critic doubts that this will ever happen. In his view, the state has interpreted the law so that DRI review exists alongside local zoning decisions, rather than taking precedence over them. Thus, localities could let projects to which they object—low-income housing is the favorite example—go through the DRI process, but still deny them needed zoning changes. See Thomas G. Pelham, "Regulating Developments of Regional Impact: Florida and the Model Code," *University of Florida Law Review* vol. 29, no. 5 (Fall 1977) pp. 818–819, and 851.

64. Interview with Carl Gosline, Stottler Stagg & Associates, Orlando, Florida, Oct. 4, 1978.

65. Telephone interview with Scott Wilson, executive director, Tampa Bay Regional Planning Council, Sept. 18, 1974.

66. The relevant cases are *Sarasota County* v. *Beker Phosphate Corporation,* Fla. App., 322 So. 2d 655, and *Sarasota County* v. *General Development Corporation,* Fla. App., 325 So. 2d 45.

67. *Pinellas County* v. *Lake Padgett Pines,* 333 So. 2d 472 (Florida Second District Court of Appeals, 1976). See the discussion in Pelham, "Regulating Developments of Regional Impact," pp. 799–800.

68. Joseph M. Thomas and George Griffith, "DRI," *Florida Environmental and Urban Issues* (April–May 1974) p. 3.

69. Interview with Barry Lessinger, Division of State Planning, Tallahassee, Feb. 19, 1974.

70. Telephone interview with Louis Huebner, Division of State Planning, Oct. 10, 1974. A recent study of the enforcement of wetlands laws found that more evasions of regulation occurred in Florida than in North Carolina or Maryland. See National Wetlands Study, "Preliminary Report: North Carolina Case Study" (Washington, D.C., The Urban Institute, October 1978) p. 10. Nonetheless, in other respects, Florida's wetland enforcement procedures are highly innovative. See Nelson Rosenbaum, "Enforcing Wetlands Regulations." Speech presented to the National Wetlands Symposium, Lake Buena Vista, Florida, Nov. 7, 1978, pp. 4–7.

71. Pelham, "Regulating Developments of Regional Impact," footnote 88, p. 807.

72. Interviews with James W. May and Wade L. Hopping, who were involved in the negotiations for, respectively, the Division of State Planning and ITT.

73. The projects are the 84 South development and the Arvida Corporation Indian Trace community. Interview with John M. DeGrove.

A former chief of the Bureau of Land and Water Management disagrees, arguing that "no matter how effective the DRI process becomes, it will remain only a process. As such, it will not provide policy, but will collect and synthesize impact data for policymakers. DRI review should, therefore, be viewed as a tool to implement state growth policies incorporated in a state land development plan." See Robert M. Rhodes, "DRIs and Florida's Land Development Policies," *Florida Environmental and Urban Issues* (February 1975) p. 16.

74. Most of these successes have been a result of negotiation with the developer rather than the direct application of power.

75. Interview with Scott Wilson.

76. Interview, Feb. 22, 1974.

77. Interview with Carl Gosline.

78. Interview, Feb. 25, 1974. The commissioner points out that although each county has an equal vote on the regional planning council, his county has considerable influence with the state legislature and in the state association of county commissioners. His county also contributes a disproportionate part of the regional council's funds.

79. Pelham, "Regulating Developments of Regional Impact," p. 814.

80. For an analysis of the South Florida Council's deliberate use of appeals to force negotiations and developer concessions in the development order, see Jon M. Ausman, "Chapter 380 Mandated Actors, Actor Interactions, Roles and Relationships in Southeast Florida: Six Studies" (MPA thesis, Florida Atlantic University–Florida International University Joint Center for Environmental and Urban Problems, August 1976).

81. Interview with Charles Lee.

82. Resource Planning Department, Central and Southern Florida Flood Control District, "Report to Governing Board on DRI Activities and DRI Procedures" (West Palm Beach. November 1974). The Flood Control District, now renamed the South Florida Water Management Distirct, publishes annual summaries of its DRI and other land policy reviews.

83. Figures provided by Tasha Buford, Division of State Planning (see note 48).

84. The county planning director emphasized, however, that most of this information would have been obtained by the county even without the DRI process. Interview with Roger Neiswender, Seminole County planning director, Feb. 23, 1974.

85. Letter from Robert M. Rhodes, Tallahassee, Dec. 7, 1978.

86. As we will see below, reform of local planning was to be the principal recommendation of the Environmental Land Management Study (ELMS) Committee.

87. Interview with James W. May.

88. See Alan S. Gold, "Dade County's Entry into the Quiet Revolution," *Land Use Law and Zoning Digest* vol. 28, no. 1 (1976) pp. 5–9.

89. Interview with members of an Orlando planning firm, Feb. 21, 1974.

90. Interview with Carl Gosline.

91. Interview with Charles Lee.

92. Interview with Wade L. Hopping, Tallahassee, Oct. 12, 1978.

93. Telephone interview with Linda Frazier, Division of State Planning, Sept. 17, 1974. The 1977 amendments allow the state, regional councils, and developers to agree on how to process DRIs—in increments, with a master plan and subsequent phases, or all at once—providing some needed flexibility.

94. Letter from James E. Slater, counsel for the Major Realty Co., to the Lake County Board of Commissioners, Jan. 3, 1974.

95. Florida Stat. 380.06 (7) (g)–(i).

96. Interview with Wade L. Hopping.

97. Interview with William Partington, Oct. 4, 1978. See note 42 above.

98. Interview with John M. DeGrove. See also Daniel H. Dennison, "The DRI Process: A Developer's View," *Florida Environmental and Urban Issues* (December 1975); and James W. May's response, "The DRI Process: A State View," *Florida Environmental and Urban Issues* (April 1976).

99. Interview with Wade L. Hopping. The point is given theoretical support by Pelham, in "Regulating Developments of Regional Impact," pp. 826–828. He suggests that regional council review of DRIs should not duplicate the local plan, but instead focus on the consistency of each DRI with local, regional, and state plans.

100. Interview with James W. May.

101. Federal investigators are examining possible bribery, kickbacks, and other fraudulent practices in the land-purchase program. See "U.S. Is Investigating Florida's Environmental Deals," *The New York Times,* Feb. 17, 1979, pp. 1 and 44.

102. Presentation of James H. Shimberg to Governor Askew and others, senate chamber, Dec. 20, 1973.

103. H. Con. Res. 2800 (1974).

104. Local Government Comprehensive Planning Act of 1975, § 12.

105. Daniel W. O'Connell, "Local Government Comprehensive Planning Act of 1975: An Introduction to House Bill 182," 1975.

106. Senate Bill No. 2-D (ch. 78-287) rejected outright a proposed coastal zone management plan submitted to the legislature by the Department of Environmental Regulation. The law "expressly rejected" the department's proposal to "divide areas of the state into vital, conservation and development" zones, made local government participation in the program voluntary, and required the new coastal program to be based on existing authority without extending "additional regulatory authority to any governmental body" except as provided in the bill.

107. See the analysis by Robert M. Rhodes, "The Florida Property Rights Law," *Land Use Law and Zoning Digest,* vol. 1 (new series), no. 1 (January 1979) pp. 5–7; and also his article, "Compensating Police Power Takings: Chapt. 78–85, Laws of Florida," *Florida Environmental and Urban Issues* (October 1978).

108. A scholarly observer of the process notes that "considerable compromise in the formulation of goals, objectives, and policies was apparent . . . as planners sought consensus among policy advisory group members. A large number of rather general noncontroversial policy recommendations evolved as much by judgment by consensus as from objective evaluation of alternatives." See Tilden Curry, *The State Comprehensive Plan: An Evaluation of Its Relevance to Public Decision-Making*

and State Planning Methodology (Ph.D. dissertation, Florida State University, Department of Urban and Regional Planning, August 1978) p. 212.

109. Interview with Robert Kessler, senior planner, Bureau of Comprehensive Planning, Division of State Planning, Tallahassee, Oct. 12, 1978.

110. Luther Carter stresses the importance of these county actions. See his "Dade County: The Politics of Managing Urban Growth," *Science* (June 4, 1976) pp. 982–985. See also the article by Gold, "Dade County's Entry into the Quiet Revolution." For discussions of Broward County and Hillsborough County planning, respectively, see *Florida Environmental and Urban Issues* (April 1978; December 1978).

Collier County, using a provision for transfer of development rights, has persuaded the Deltona Corporation (whose Marco Island development is the despair of environmentalists and wetlands experts) to shift 374 units from 112 acres of wetlands to two smaller upland sites. Neno J. Spagna, "Transfer of Development Rights: The Collier County Experience," *Florida Environmental and Urban Issues* (February 1979) p. 16.

CHAPTER SIX

Alternative Approaches to State Land Use Control

VERMONT, CALIFORNIA, AND FLORIDA have each evolved a distinctive new system of state land use control. The states differ in their major land use problems, in the way local and regional governments participate in the process, in the extent of citizen participation, and in the role of a written plan. Each state, however, has in common the principle that certain kinds of land use changes should involve the guidance or approval of a level of government representing a broader than local constituency.

A number of states have programs based on this principle already legislated and operating. Nearly every one of the fifty states has been at least considering them.[1] The programs—operating and proposed—are a diverse lot. Some have been influenced by prospective national land use legislation or by the American Law Institute's (ALI's) Model Land Development Code. Other programs have borrowed from those states that were early pioneers.[2] Often programs stem directly from the nature of the land use problems experienced by the state and take advantage of institutions, occasionally unique ones, already existing in the state's governmental structure.

We might outline some of the alternative approaches taken by the states by looking separately at two characteristics of their programs: first, what types of land or what types of activities are thought to be of more than local concern—that is, *what* does the state control? And second, what is the structure of the system set up to protect this more than local interest—that is, *who* decides?

What Does the State Control?

Critical Areas

A number of states have designated certain areas or classes of land as being of "critical state concern," and requiring some form of state intervention or oversight to ensure their protection. These may be individual areas of great scenic value, such as the Florida Keys, North Carolina's Outer Banks, or certain wild and scenic rivers. They might be areas of historic significance or lands necessary for the survival of endangered animal (or even plant) species. We have already seen that Florida made this approach an important part of its land use program, although, as we have noted, the critical areas are not to exceed 5 percent of the state's land area. Colorado, Maryland, Minnesota, Nevada, North Carolina (in coastal counties), and Oregon have also established mechanisms for designating critical areas.[3] The federal Coastal Zone Management Act of 1972 also requires participating states, in preparing coastal area management plans, to designate areas "of particular concern" for special protection. By the end of 1978, more than a dozen state plans had qualified for continuing federal support.[4]

A specific area considered "critical" by a state is New York's huge Adirondack Park, where 3.7 million acres of privately owned land are interspersed with 2.3 million acres owned by the state. In 1973 New York's legislature approved strong state-administered controls over the private lands in the Adirondacks, claiming that the state has "an obligation" to provide a land use framework, "which recognizes not only matters of local concern but also those of regional and state concern."[5]

A similar effort to protect and manage New Jersey's million-acre Pine Barrens began with a federal–state partnership in 1978. The federal government agreed to provide 75 percent of the funds—up to $3 million for planning and $23 million for land acquisition—for a Pinelands National Reserve. A commission consisting of seven local government representatives, seven gubernatorial appointees, and a representative of the Department of the Interior will prepare a plan and regulations for the entire area, while recommending which most sensitive areas (perhaps only 5 percent of the total) should be acquired.[6] In the meantime, New Jersey's governor has by executive order temporarily limited new construction there.

A bi-state approach was tried at Lake Tahoe, one of the world's highest, deepest, and clearest lakes, which is visited by 15 million tourists annually.[7] In 1969 California and Nevada, whose border bisects the lake, formed the Tahoe Regional Planning Agency, a commission made up of local government representatives from each state, gubernatorial appointees, and a nonvoting federal member (federal lands cover more than 60 percent of the Lake Tahoe basin).

The Tahoe agency has been severely hampered by the fact that a majority of both state delegations is needed to turn down projects. And three out of each state's five votes are cast by local government. As a result, high-rise gambling casinos have been erected on the Nevada shore and thousands of lots subdivided on the California side. Air and water pollution, traffic congestion, and esthetic degradation have followed.

California's dissatisfaction with the performance of the Tahoe agency has led it to seek a revision of the body's charter.[8] In late 1978 agreement was near on amendments that would require a majority of both state delegations to *approve* new development. Like the new Pine Barrens scheme, it also involved an infusion of federal money—in this case for federal purchase of key casino sites. But Nevada lawmakers seemed reluctant to assent to the change, leading one influential California congressman to threaten to seek designation of the Tahoe region as a national recreation area.

The most common application of the critical areas approach is to designate a particular type of land, rather than a specific area, as critical. Wetlands,[9] shorelines, aquifer-recharge areas, beaches, and floodplains are among the areas most frequently cited. State programs protecting wetlands, lake shores, and floodplains are common in the Midwest, where more comprehensive programs of state land use control are not well advanced. Vermont, befitting its identification as the Green Mountain state, has given special protection to areas higher than 2,500 feet. Virtually all of the states having ocean coastlines have begun some form of coastal zone management program.[10] By passing Proposition 20, California officially declared its entire coastline to be an area of state concern, finding it "a distinct and valuable natural resource belonging to all the people."[11] Washington's designated "shorelines of statewide significance" include not only its entire ocean coast, but also ninety-three rivers and sixty-two large lakes.[12] Some of these laws anticipated the federal coastal management program in 1972; the money it made available encouraged most of the other states to participate, or to bring their programs into conformance with the federal legislation.

Other areas that may be considered of state concern are those involving natural hazards, including earthquake fault zones, areas of high fire danger, and places with unstable or easily eroded soils.

Land may be considered critical because of its productive potential or its natural resources. Prime agricultural land can be given special protection from development, as it is under the permit criteria of the Vermont Environmental Board and the California Coastal Commission. Alternatively, positive incentives may be given to keep farmland in production. In 1956 Maryland passed the first law providing for preferential tax assessments for farmland, and since that time more than forty other states have followed suit. Managed woodlands and timberlands in the most productive land quality classes also qualify for tax breaks or protection in some states.[13] Recently, some of the highly urbanized New England states have begun buying "development rights" to farmland. New Jersey, Massachusetts, and Connecticut each appropriated $5 million to see whether farmers would sell development easements to the state. Regulatory means to achieve the same results have been established in Oregon and debated in California.[14] The Wisconsin Farmland Preservation Act of 1977 extends tax credits to owners of farmland and conditions the amount and continuation of the credits on each county's adoption of planning and zoning measures.[15] Federal legislation to support these experiments with as much as $450 million has also been proposed; it was not approved by Congress in 1978.

Open or Unzoned Lands

The state may wish to exert direct supervision over the use of land outside of urban areas, either because the land is undeveloped or because it is not planned and zoned by local government. Frequently the land is both undeveloped and unzoned. Colorado and Oregon are among the states paying particular attention to such lands. Both states have required city or county plans to be drawn up for the state's entire land area, most of which had been previously unregulated.[16] Oregon's Land Conservation and Development Commission, in fact, determined that "Urban growth boundaries shall be established to identify and separate urbanizable land from rural land," so that development will be contained.[17] Maine's Land Use Regulation Commission, created in 1969, oversees a huge area—10.5 million acres, some 51 percent of the state—consisting of unorganized townships and plantations. Its comprehensive land use plan, authorized in 1971 and adopted in 1976, divides the land into protection, management, and development zones. To protect the northern woods, the commission declared its policy was to "encourage new development in existing developed areas; promote orderly, balanced growth adjacent to these areas, and allow well-planned development in other areas."[18] The legislature accepted the commission's zoning standards based on the plan in 1977, and the zoning process is now ongoing. The commission reviews applications for development permits in all the areas under its jurisdiction.

Implicit in this approach is the idea that, while local government may be doing a good job of regulating the very limited area subject to its control, the statewide interest requires land use controls even in areas that are remote or lightly populated. On occasion the state may take over direct control of these open lands. Hawaii's state land law calls for dividing the entire state into four types of districts: urban, rural, agricultural, and conservation.[19] Land in the urban district is subject only to local regulation, while the state oversees development in the remaining areas. The Adirondack Park plan also divides land into districts, with the state imposing the heaviest controls in nonurban areas.

Developments of Regional Impact

Another common approach looks to the size and impact of the development rather than to its location. The size of a development that is considered "large" or "of regional impact" varies from state to state. In Vermont, where most local government units are very small, state and regional boards control residential developments with ten units or more. Maine's 1970 law regulates housing developments larger than 20 acres in size.[20] In Florida, a development does not come to the attention of the state until it has more than 250 units (in the least populous counties) or more than 3,000 units (in large counties, such as Dade). The Adirondack Park Agency's standards for regional impact also depend upon the type and location of proposed developments.

Particularly in the Adirondacks, Florida, and Vermont, land use laws were enacted in the face of proposals for enormous housing developments, sometimes including thousands of units. We have discussed in earlier chapters how projects of this size, popular in the early 1970s, have not really recovered since the 1974–75 recession. Higher land and interest costs make it unlikely that they will return soon. Instead, the cumulative impact of many smaller developments may become a more pressing land use issue. Under rigid numerical standards, such as those used in Florida, much of this development may escape the state's review.

Vermont and Maine regulate commercial and industrial developments on the basis of acreage (1 acre in Vermont; 20 acres or buildings including over 60 thousand square feet of space in Maine), but most state programs are based on the type of activity proposed as well as its size. In Delaware, for example, all new heavy industry is excluded from a coastal zone extending as much as 12 miles inland. Light manufacturing is allowed only after securing a permit from a state board.[21] In Florida, state permits are required for shopping centers, airports, factories, and other uses, usually with a cutoff depending on building area, number of employees, or number of parking spaces provided.

Since 1969 twenty-five states, including such diverse places as Connecticut, Kentucky, Maryland, New Mexico, and Washington, have enacted state controls over the location of electric power plants. As of March

1978 these agencies had received a total of seventy-six permit applications, twenty-five of them for nuclear plants.[22]

Closely related to the regional impact idea is the concept of a "key facility." Here the emphasis is not on the size of the project per se, but on its growth-inducing effects. Major highways, airports, university campuses, and reservoir and irrigation projects have again and again generated growth on the lands surrounding them. Where strict water pollution laws have been enforced and the ability to dispose of effluent is a major barrier to growth, new sewage treatment plants and trunk sewer lines have become key determinants of growth patterns. Although some key facilities are built by the private sector (for example, large factories and ski areas), they are more frequently the result of public investments.

Several attempts have been made by states to coordinate their infrastructure investments with planning goals, but these have had little success thus far. A comprehensive policy for public investment planning was also an important part of Vermont's proposed land use plan (1974) and the privately sponsored California Tomorrow Plan (1972).[23]

Land Uses Affecting Public Investments

Looked at from one perspective, public investments are the levers of growth, generating new land uses and new private economic activities. In many cases, however, public investment follows growth rather than leading it. A state might wish to intervene in private land use decisions either to protect the value of existing public investment or to minimize the demands for new public infrastructure.

A proposed Georgia law which would designate certain specified parts of the state as "vital areas" mentioned at several points that a particular area was the scene of "major public investment."[24] Florida's regulation of private lands in the Big Cypress area was undertaken mainly to protect the water supply of the Everglades National Park. Similarly, floodplain regulations can be used to reduce the need for public disaster relief, laws limiting "premature" subdivisions can eliminate demands to extend public services to remote areas, and erosion controls can reduce the need to dredge public reservoirs and waterways.

The explosive growth of arid areas around Denver, Phoenix, San Diego, and Los Angeles raises the prospect of multibillion-dollar water projects to serve new populations.[25] Opposing unnecessary state investments were reports prepared by state planning offices in California and Massachusetts. Though not backed up by any legislation or regulatory power, these plans had as their goal renewing and reusing existing urban infrastructure, and locating new growth on "vacant and under-utilized land within existing urban and suburban areas and presently served by streets, water, sewer, and other public services."[26]

Developments of Regional Benefit

Certain types of development, including airports, prisons, landfills, and public housing projects, produce benefits for an entire state or region, but are frequently unwanted by local communities. Localities invoke their own plans and zoning regulations to exclude these uses, delaying needed projects and forcing them to locations that are (from the regional standpoint) suboptimal. Poor communities, in particular, seem to get more than their share of such projects. In other cases, environmental damage is done because the places most suited to the proposed project have rejected it locally.

The state may wish to step in to ensure that nonlocal interests are at least considered when locations for this kind of development are chosen. At present there are few state mechanisms for doing this. Massachusetts' 1969 Housing Appeals Law, often referred to as the "Anti-Snob Zoning Law," set up a state board to review cases in which proposed government-subsidized, low- or moderate-income housing developments are denied requested rezoning or other required local approval. The appeals body may overturn the local decision if it is not "reasonable in view of the regional need for low- and moderate-income housing." By its sixth year of operation, the committee had overturned local decisions against housing in thirty-one of thirty-three cases, for a total of 4,222 units, 420 of which have been built and occupied. One observer notes that the housing appeals agency has "survived numerous legal challenges to its constitutionality and annual attempts at repeal or other weakening legislative changes," while producing a "small yet significant track record in actual housing built, occupied, or under construction."[27]

New York's Urban Development Corporation, a state agency, was originally given the power to build public housing projects without the approval of local government. In 1973, after the corporation proposed to build 100 low- and moderate-income housing units in each of nine suburban Westchester County towns, the state legislature quickly provided for a local veto. Theoretically, the Florida state government can override a community veto of large developments through the "development of regional impact" process, but this power is not being exercised.[28] Maine's state board of environmental protection has a similar power under the 1970 Site Location of Development Act. It has not been used to impose a project on an unwilling community.

Where special opportunities arise for developments of regional benefit, states may create specific land use authorities. In 1968 New Jersey established the Hackensack Meadowlands Development District to take control of nearly 20,000 acres of marshes and wetlands located only three miles from Manhattan. Fourteen local governments included part of the meadowlands, which were used primarily for dumping garbage. Under a seven-member commission, a plan was drawn up for the area in 1970, designating half the land for industry and business, one-sixth for housing, and the rest for open space. The commission also has powers to assemble land and issue bonds. So far, sports facilities and a hotel have been built, and plans are being drawn up to accommodate a population of 125,000 and nearly 200,000 jobs.[29]

Dealing with Specific Problems

A final approach, one that has been used by virtually all of the states, is to deal with specific land use problems. Pollution of water supplies from improperly designed septic systems can be avoided by passing and enforcing state health regulations. A critical environmental area can be protected by purchasing it for a park. These piecemeal approaches often continue even in states which have embarked on more comprehensive land use programs, bringing complaints by developers over the multiplicity of permits that must be obtained. On the other hand, some states, including Michigan and Wisconsin, have forged rather broad programs of state land controls out of just such bits and pieces of narrow-gauged environmental controls, without ever passing a "comprehensive" state land use law.

Who Decides?

Once a state has decided which lands or which kinds of problems should be "controlled" by the state, it must make even more controversial decisions as to how that control should be exercised and with whom it should be shared. This is a question that can be discussed as a problem in organization theory or administrative science, and profitably so. But it is also a question of power—of political power and, for the individuals involved, of personal power.[30] The diversity of ways in which states control or influence land use decisions results not just from ideal conceptions of how certain tasks should be divided, but from the interplay of public and private interests, each trying to increase or maintain its authority.

This struggle can be a very good thing. Local governments, fighting the state's efforts to intercede in land use decisions, may be forced into effective planning for the first time. In the very act of trying to retain their powers over land use, they may find themselves more willing than in the past to exercise them. We have argued, however, in chapters 1 and 2, that even the most honest and capably administered system of local control will sometimes fail to protect nonlocal interests in prospective land use changes.

Our survey of how power might be divided can be seen as a list of choices for the states, one to be looked at in the light of the strength and responsiveness of existing institutions and the realities of politics. In considering these alternatives, one should constantly ask—how is the nonlocal interest exercised and protected?

State Zoning

Only a handful of states have attempted "state zoning," that is, outlining on a map the prescribed or the prohibited uses for large areas of land. Not only is this strenuously opposed by local governments, but it is seen as a direct attack by landowners, who rush to see how the state has classified their particular parcel. Only in the special circumstances of Hawaii, the Adirondack Park, Maine, and (to a small extent) Delaware, has state zoning proved to be politically acceptable. The speaker of Iowa's house of representatives jokes that "We would have trouble putting a map through the Iowa legislature that outlines our present counties."[31]

Hawaii, the first state to engage in comprehensive state land control of any sort, chose the state zoning approach and remains its foremost practitioner.[32] Facing the prospect of an explosive urban expansion sprawling onto the state's very limited supply of agricultural lands, the 1961 legislature created the Hawaii State Land Use Commission to zone all the lands of the state into three classes of use.[33] The commission's nine members are private citizens appointed by the governor.

Land classified as "urban" is intended to provide just enough room for the orderly expansion of existing settlements, particularly Honolulu, where most of the state's population is concentrated. Within the urban zone, control is exercised by local government, which can, if it wishes, impose its own, more detailed, zoning. On "agricultural" lands, the land use commission retains control, allowing uses other than farming only by special permit. The "conservation" lands, mainly steep slopes and water-sheds, are regulated by still another appointed state board.

This decisive classification occurred in a state used to highly centralized government and a minimum of local control. The twin goals of protecting agriculture and curbing urban sprawl were eagerly endorsed by the large sugar and pineapple companies, who owned most of the threatened farm-land and who feared that scattered subdivision would add to their costs of production.

The zoning system has been involved in frequent controversy, usually over the rezoning of land (by the land use commission) to more intensive use or the granting of special permits. Conservationists complain about piecemeal additions to the urban zone while other land, zoned for urban development, still lies vacant. Housing advocates blame the law for raising Hawaii's already sky-high housing prices and advocate massive rezoning to relieve the pressure. County governments, now experienced in planning, feel that the state zoning is an anachronism that has served its purpose. The commission itself has been called "an agency where politics has often seemed more important than planning."[34]

The charge that the commission has too frequently made ad hoc, politi-cally inspired decisions is reinforced by the fact that for most of its history its actions were not guided by explicit legislative objectives. In 1975, state lawmakers reacted to this criticism by binding the commission with a set of moderately specific policies, among them the charge to avoid significant adverse effects on agriculture, or on natural, environmental, and other re-sources; to make maximum use of existing public services; and to avoid scattered urban development.

The record shows that Hawaii's land use law has been relatively, but not completely, effective in stopping the urbanization of agricultural lands. In the first ten years (1964–74) after the initial mapping was completed—years of exceptionally rapid growth of both Hawaii's population and its economy—the urban district has been allowed to grow by some 30,000 acres, or about 25 percent.[35] Most of this land came out of the agricultural zone, but very little was land of the best quality.[36] Several cases of scat-tered development might be noted, including the approval of a new town in the heart of Oahu's fertile central plain and the location of resorts and tourist attractions in the conservation zones. Nevertheless, the law has had a striking effect on the pattern of Hawaii's growth, making urban expansion far more compact and orderly than it would have been without the law.

State zoning came to the 3.7 million acres of privately owned land in the Adirondack Park in 1973. Long a vacation spot for urban New Yorkers and a mecca for outdoorsmen, the Adirondacks had been until very recently untouched by the massive second-home developments such as those which have sprung up in the Catskills and the Poconos. Early in the 1970s, however, two proposed developments, involving 9,000 and 4,000 homes, respectively, indicated that the Adirondacks were no longer to be protected by their remoteness. Over the protests of local governments and many of the 120,000 permanent residents of the economically depressed towns within the park, the New York legislature, in 1971, set up a state commission to draw up a plan for the private as well as the public lands.

The plan represents a strong assertion of the environmental and recreational interests of the state as a whole over the local interest in economic development.[37] As passed by the legislature in 1973, the plan divides the private lands into six categories—hamlet, industrial, moderate intensity, low intensity, rural use, and resource management. About half the future growth would occur in the hamlet zone, at the edge of existing towns, and the rest at low density or in widely scattered clusters.[38] More than a million acres in the resource management zone are limited to one unit ("principal dwelling") for each 42 acres.

The plan placed permit power over all the zones in a state commission, the Adirondack Park Agency. Within the hamlet zone, some powers are shared with local governments. In the more restrictive zones, even minor projects have to secure a permit from the agency. Local governments can reclaim some of their lost powers in the higher-intensity zones by submitting an acceptable local land use plan to the agency. Even in that case, however, the agency retains permit authority over such uses as very large subdivisions, high rises, and airports. Because of the substantial authority retained by the state, and for numerous other reasons (including lack of resources, initial lack of interest on the part of the park agency in helping local governments plan, and fierce local hostility toward the agency) by late 1978 only five towns had recovered some permit review authority from the agency.[39]

As is the practice in local zoning, each zone has certain uses listed which are presumed to be "compatible" with the character of the zone. Unlike traditional local zoning, however, these uses are not entitled to a permit by right, but must also comply with environmental criteria before they are granted the state permit.

Both of the large projects that had helped create the concern for the park's future have been stopped. The parcels on which they would have been built have been placed into the most restrictive (resource management) category. The smaller of the two, proposed by a New Jersey developer and called Ton-da-Lay, would have been allowed by the plan under a "grandfather" clause, but the project was denied a water permit by the state Department of Environmental Conservation. The majority of the developments reviewed by the agency have been far smaller—individual homes, subdivisions of a few lots—a cause of continuing political opposition to the agency's existence. Researchers seeking clues to the environmental impact of the agency's treatment of such projects found it difficult to establish that adverse environmental effects were reduced.[40]

The yet incomplete zoning of Maine's unincorporated areas by the Land Use Regulation Commission arose from circumstances similar to those in the Adirondacks. The huge region contains only 12,000 permanent residents in an area the size of Connecticut, Massachusetts, and Rhode Island combined. The large timber companies that own much of the area will not be much disturbed by the commission, and other major development pressures are not present.

Delaware has state zoning in the sense that since 1971 it has controlled new industrial development locating on the Delaware River and Bay, on the ocean, and in a strip of coastal land ranging from a few hundred yards to 12 miles wide. The law prohibited new heavy industry and offshore bulk transfer facilities, and required other new manufacturing to obtain a permit before locating in the zone. It was passed in response to a proposal to locate a 200,000-barrel-a-day oil refinery on marshlands bordering Delaware Bay. Proposals for a superport, chemical plants, and even an artificial island for storing and transshipping coal threatened to convert the least developed portion of Delaware's coast to a replica of the industrial complex around Wilmington.

The law has effectively stopped the development of these energy-related facilities along the Delaware coast.[41] Although the law is quite simple in its prohibition of heavy industry, there have been arguments as to which industries are acceptable. In 1973, for example, an appeals board overruled the recommendation of the state planner (who administers the law) and agreed to consider a permit for a "light" chemical plant that would include four or five 25,000-gallon tanks and three 50-foot-high distillation columns.[42] As of October 1978, 102 projects had come up for some sort of state review; over 60 percent were found to be exempt from the law, and of the rest, none resulted in the denial of a permit. Most were expansions or changes of established nonconforming facilities in the zone.[43]

There has been continuing pressure from business and labor groups to soften the law's terms, and to allow prohibited uses so long as they meet environmental standards. Said the chairman of the Du Pont Corporation,

"You're not going to have a refinery coming in that is an ecological disaster. You ought to be able to establish standards and not let one in unless it can meet those standards."[44] Spokesmen from the building trades unions have claimed that the publicity the law has generated was scaring business away from Delaware. One testified that "With the number of people out of work [here], the state won't need beaches because no one will have money to get to them."[45] Other unions have supported the law or remained neutral.

Despite these criticisms, Delaware lawmakers have not moved to weaken the law. Proposals to do so have failed in every General Assembly session since 1971. In 1974 a proposal was introduced to eliminate the flat prohibition of heavy industry and offshore petroleum facilities and subject them instead to a case-by-case permit system. The measure failed in committee. On the other hand, the lawmakers refused, in 1973, to pass proposed legislation that would have extended state permit review to large commercial and residential projects within the coastal zone.[46]

The Double-Veto System

One of the most common forms of state land use control is what we might call the "double-veto" system. Here local government retains all of its existing power over development, submitting projects to the usual building permit controls, rezoning hearings, sewer connection permits, and so forth. But in addition to going through the local process, if any, a developer must secure a separate permit from a state or regional body. The consent of two levels of government is thus required for the project to proceed. Conversely, either of the two can withhold approval and "veto" the project. Either can also impose conditions on the project. Local governments may find it difficult, however, to impose conditions on projects which are built on land already zoned to that use, and which do not require more than routine building and occupancy permits.

Typical examples of double-veto systems are those of California, Vermont, and Maine and the coastal zone laws of New Jersey and North Carolina.[47] In each case, projects beyond a certain size, projects located in particular critical areas, or projects having both characteristics must secure a special permit from a state or regional commission.

The decision on the state or regional permit may come before or after the developer has gone through the local process. In Vermont, localities often prefer to have a developer go through the Act 250 process first, since the larger, more experienced staff available through the state can bring out technical problems that might otherwise be overlooked. Moreover, a town can use the Act 250 process to test the political reaction to a project. One Vermont official says, "Some towns use Act 250 as a way of denying development without taking responsibility for it."

In other places, including California, a developer must receive at least conceptual approval from local government before applying for a state permit. In general, double-veto processes tend to impose added costs on developers. Information required for a regional hearing may not be the same as that required by the local government. Developers are reluctant to proceed with expensive design studies or environmental impact statements unless they are sure that at least the general outline of their project is acceptable to both levels of government.[48] Moreover, delays are always costly in a business involving such high carrying costs.

A double-veto system minimizes state involvement in local planning and zoning. Thus it affords protection to localities that want to impose particularly strict standards on development or that wish to exclude certain types of development entirely. Even if an oil refinery or a landfill is acceptable to the state commission, the local government retains its preexisting right to zone it out.

In theory, double-veto systems give little incentive to local governments to improve their local land use controls. Such a system simply interposes a level of government that can consider a project's impact on state and regional interests—and perhaps say no. Actually, in state after state, the creation of a parallel state system of land use control has brought visible improvement to the existing local system. Local authorities seem to examine proposed developments with greater care when they know that the project will be subjected to a second, and very public, state-mandated scrutiny.

At times local governments are given some input into the state side of the double veto. In North Carolina, members of the coastal zone commission are appointed by the governor from a list nominated by coastal area governments. In California, and to a lesser extent in Maine, designated local representatives are a minority on the state or regional commissions. In Vermont, where district commissions are made up of citizen members, local government has special rights of advocacy and of appeal.[49]

Nonlocal Input into the Local Decision Process

An alternative to the two-level, double-veto permit system is to allow state or regional input into local decisions *while they are being made*. As we have seen, Florida's process for regulating "developments of regional impact" allows regional planning agencies to comment on applications for large projects, with the public hearing and disposition of the permit handled by local government. If the region or the state (or the developer) is dissatisfied with the outcome of the local decision, it can appeal to the Florida Cabinet. The regional agency requires the developer to produce considerably more information than was usually required by the local governments, but the fact that only a single hearing is needed makes the procedure much quicker than a double-veto system would be.

Under a 1974 Maryland law local governments must notify the state when they receive proposals for large developments or developments in critical areas. The state then may intercede as a party to local regulatory proceedings. It may not, however, veto the local decision. According to one Maryland official, the law offers the state "a formal procedure for giving advice" to local governments.[50]

By 1978, the state planning department had reviewed, analyzed, or testified in some 176 separate local matters, including 36 zoning cases. In one case, for example, a county denied an application for rezoning to permit a sand-mining operation after state planners testified that the project could adversely affect water quality, noise, and esthetics of a nearby area under study for a state park.[51]

State Guidelines and State Plans

Virtually all of the states, including some we do not usually associate with state planning, have some sort of regulation of procedures for local planning, and sometimes of its content. These range from the mildest requirements for the filing of subdivision maps, to state environmental standards, and in a few places, to actual state review of local plans.

What distinguishes this approach from the more direct approaches we have just discussed is that state intervention is, in this case, a onetime thing. A standard is set, a parcel of land is classified, perhaps with the state strongly overriding the wishes of local government. But once the plan is made or the regulation promulgated, actual regulation of land use changes is done by the local authorities. Only if the local government wishes to alter its state-reviewed or -approved plan, must it go through some form of the state clearance procedure again.

The relative power of state and local government in plan making varies from state to state.[52] The most familiar arrangement, and the one which gives the least power to the state, involves a state drawing up plans which contain large amounts of information and broad policies, but which have little or no regulatory effect. This kind of state map or policy might be termed a *guide plan.*

Here the state prepares a statewide comprehensive plan, setting general policy goals and perhaps even classifying individual parcels of land as to their suitability for development. Then the state uses moral suasion and wide publicity to induce local and regional governments to bring their plans into conformance with statewide goals. Connecticut's Plan of Conservation and Development (1974) took this approach. The plan tried to reconcile environmental planning with state land use policies, and then served as a (nonregulatory) guide for both state investment and local planning.

The Connecticut plan identified about a quarter of the state as "suitable for urban development," another quarter as appropriate for permanent open space, and the remainder as a "limited development" area, which would be mainly agricultural. A Connecticut official claimed that the plan should not be seen as a proposal for centralized state control, but rather as an influence on local planning decisions.[53] A similar effort was New York's State Environmental Plan (1973), which emphasized land use control as a way of protecting environmental quality.

New Jersey's guide plan, even while still in draft form, has recently been used as part of the basis of court decisions in which developers sought to build at higher densities than those permitted by local zoning. In one case, the court overturned the local zoning, ruling that the guide plan mapped the township as one of the state's future growth areas. In the other, local large-lot zoning was allowed to stand, because the entire township had been mapped as "prime open agricultural lands."[54]

Two of the most prominent guide-plan efforts may be found in Florida (see page 168) and Hawaii. The Hawaii State Plan, approved almost unanimously by the legislature in 1978, sets a series of "themes" and policies for the state.[55] Like Florida's plan, it is extremely broad in its subject matter, dealing not only with land use, population, and the environment, but also with health, culture, education, and public safety. Some critics have charged that its policies are so vaguely worded as to have little real effect—for example the plan makes only veiled and ambiguous reference to such controversial suggestions as setting limits on state population growth and redirecting growth from crowded Oahu to the outer islands.

The Hawaii plan's importance, perhaps, lies not in its policies but in its requirement that the decision-making process under the state land use law, as well as county general plans, conform to the state plan. State agencies, moreover, must prepare "functional plans" for such subjects as agriculture, housing, and transportation and submit them to the legislature. These, too, must conform to the overall policies of the state plan. A new policy council, with state, local, and citizen members, has been set up to oversee the process. There is thus a major opportunity for interagency and intergovernmental cooperation. Expectations, at least, are high, with the governor terming the plan "second in importance only to our state constitution," and the state's largest newspaper praising it as "more than mere words."[56]

If the guide-plan approach is comprehensive but optional, an approach we might term *standard setting* is limited in its scope, but regulatory and enforceable. Here the state sets standards for local planning and regulation. This is most frequently done through state subdivision map laws. Until recently, most subdivision acts merely required cities and counties to make sure that a subdivider filed a map with the locality and, perhaps, a copy with the state. More recently, some states have come to demand that substantive standards be met. In both Colorado and Oregon, the state requires that before a subdivision can be approved by local government, the applicant must demonstrate that sufficient water and adequate sewage disposal are available to support the use intended.[57] This is not an unimportant requirement in states such as these two, where the subdivision of arid lands is a major problem. In California, a 1971 law makes local approval of subdivisions contingent on meeting a whole list of environmental criteria.[58] Other California laws require that local general plans have specific elements covering land use, conservation, noise, and scenic highways —and that local zoning ordinances be consistent with the general plans.[59]

The final approach to state involvement in plan making has come to be called *collaborative planning*.[60] This increasingly popular procedure (it has been adopted by twelve states, six of them since 1974) combines some of the breadth of state comprehensive planning with some of the power of mandatory standards. Typically, the state establishes broad planning goals or policies, and then invites or requires local governments to incorporate them in their own plans. Florida's Local Government Comprehensive Planning Act, discussed earlier, is of this sort. The state law lists elements that must be included in local plans, and the state planners comment upon—but cannot force changes in—the local drafts.

Much greater powers are given to state planning authorities in other collaborative planning schemes. Under the California coastal law and the Adirondack Park Agency, local plans must comply with state standards. The state agency is empowered to review and reject local plans if they fail to be sufficiently rigorous. In California, all coastal communities are required to plan; in the Adirondacks, local action is voluntary and, as was noted, the incentives for doing so have apparently not been strong enough to bring about any meaningful response.

In one case, this sort of powerful review extends across an entire state. Oregon, where former governer Tom McCall long crusaded for better land use, is often considered to have a system of centralized controls. In fact, Oregon's principal state land use law, the Land Conservation and Development Act of 1973, is based on mandatory local planning, with cities and counties drawing up comprehensive plans within a framework set by the state.[61] The Oregon law, which has been described as "planning from the bottom up," required the state Land Conservation and Development Commission (LCDC), whose members are appointed by the governor, to publish statewide goals and guidelines. After that, local governments would have to bring their plans—and their land use ordinances—into conformance. Administration of the law has been greatly aided by favorable state court decisions, which, among other things, required that local zoning conform to local plans.

Adopted by the LCDC in late 1974, the state goals (with later additions there are now nineteen goals) and guidelines cover such diverse topics as housing, forestry, beaches and dunes, tourism, and the economy. The most important are the urbanization and the agricultural land goals. The urbanization goal requires that local governments designate urban growth boundaries, allowing room for planned year 2000 population growth. Then, under provisions of the controversial agricultural land goal, all good-quality soils outside the boundaries must be zoned for "exclusive farm use." Such land can be urbanized only if the local government can prove to LCDC that it is needed for nonfarm use or that it is already "irrevocably committed" to such use.

Not unexpectedly, many cities have wanted to include very generous amounts of land within the growth boundaries. The Willamette Valley town of Wilsonville, for example, proposed to draw its growth boundary to include about 10 square miles of in-production farmland. In that and other similar cases, the LCDC has refused to approve the local plan.

Counties, too, have tried to justify large acreages of open land outside the urban growth boundaries as needed for development, primarily for rural residential use. In one county, for example, local authorities proposed designating 65,000 acres of agricultural land for farming and 39,000 acres of agricultural land for residential, commercial, and industrial use. The LCDC has in the past given some indications that it will make local governments closely justify such designations, but the commission has yet to rule in several cases likely to be precedent-setting.

Another important LCDC goal requires local governments to encourage affordable housing. In pursuit of the housing goal, the LCDC refused in 1978 to accept the city of Saint Helens' zoning ordinances because neither multifamily dwellings nor mobile homes—both opportunities for lower-cost housing—were permitted anywhere in the city. Interestingly, the housing goal has been enthusiastically embraced by some Oregon environmentalists, who realize that local exclusionary policies could dash their hopes of concentrating growth within existing cities and towns. They have pushed LCDC and regional governments to enforce "fair share" housing policies and have even intervened on the side of a housing developer in an appeal to LCDC that overturned one city's six-month moratorium on new residences.

By early 1979, over 30 of the 278 local jurisdictions in Oregon had gained approval of their plans from LCDC. Primarily these were sparsely populated or slower-growing places, whose plans raised relatively few tough issues. As many as three more years might be required before all of Oregon's cities and counties will have gone through the process. LCDC's political standing was given a boost in 1978, when Oregon voters turned back, by a 61–39 percent margin, an initiative that would have repealed the goals and threatened to reduce LCDC to an advisory body.

In some instances, the state and local government collaborate in dealing with specific categories of land use concerns. Critical areas protection provides the clearest examples. Colorado's 1974 land use law allowed state input into local plan making, although the state has virtually no power to impose statewide interests on the local authorities.[62] As part of their comprehensive plans, local governments could designate "areas and activities of state interest." These included the usual array of critical areas (with such uniquely western additions as avalanche zones and dry wash flood channels) and key public facilities, but did not cover large private developments. The state could suggest to the local authorities that specific areas or activities be designated, but the local government was left free, after holding a hearing, to notify the state that its recommendations have been rejected. Even after designation, activities and areas of state interest would continue to be regulated by local government. The state Land Use Commission, which oversees the act, has had some success in forcing local governments (through court actions) to adopt appropriate regulations but the legislature has not passed strengthening amendments to the law and has even slashed the commission's budget. One planner said that since passage of the law, "The support for the commission has greatly decreased."[63]

Florida's critical areas program, which we have already discussed, allows for state designation of the areas and for binding state approval of local regulations to govern their use. Here the protection of statewide interests is quite strong, but is limited by the fact that the areas designated may not total more than 5 percent of the area of the state. As was noted, the degree of collaboration has varied, too: in the Green Swamp, the state drew up the regulations; in the Florida Keys, it accepted local recommendations.

The "Demonstration Effect"

The weakest level of state intervention is not really a power at all, but a form of influence. When either fear of state intervention or successful state implementation of a new regulatory technique leads local governments to voluntarily choose to adopt some sort of land use control for their own use, we have an example of the "demonstration effect." Most often, the effect is unintentional—the state acts, the local governments see a good thing—but it could, perhaps, be deliberate.

Instances of the effect have been discussed in earlier chapters. Some Florida cities, notably Clearwater, have legislated "little DRIs," treating important developments in their jurisdictions with review procedures or evaluative criteria suitably scaled down from the regional review of developments of regional impact. Dade County has done the same. In Vermont, the adoption of Act 250 environmental criteria for local zoning decisions is another example. More generally, the adoption by states of environmental impact statement requirements (in imitation of the National Environmental Policy Act) is now spreading further, to localities.

In some cases, the demonstration effect occurs because local governments are unaware of innovative land use tools until the state experiments with them. In others, the state's success in creating advanced land use measures emboldens the local governments which had wanted to go beyond rudimentary zoning, but which feared the political consequences. This may be the case in Florida, for example. It may be that the most lasting effect of the development of regional impact and critical area programs will be to inspire local action, encouraging the aggressive implementation of state-of-the-art planning.

In Massachusetts, the state Housing Appeals Law may be affecting the record of housing approved by local zoning boards of appeal. Says the state's chief housing official, "I think we are giving the localities the leverage they need to do things which they know are right but which are just not politically possible."[64]

Guiding Land Use Through the State Budget

We have already discussed the importance of state investment in such facilities as expressways, universities, and water and sewer projects in inducing regional growth and land use change. To the extent that this is true, states might use their investments to encourage people and activities to locate in one area rather than another.

Although it might seem a relatively simple task for the state to coordinate its own capital programs in some sort of long-range comprehensive plan, the reluctance of functional agencies (highway department, housing finance program, or water management agency) to relinquish their budget-making power and the absence of state land use plans against which to compare the budget, has made such coordination virtually nonexistent. Efforts at centralized, long-term budget planning in several large states have foundered because of the jealousy and suspicion of functional agencies. Detailed, highly professional functional plans—one thinks particularly of highways—are often much more specific and likely to be carried out than the vague land use plans with which they are not coordinated, but which they do so much to affect.

Recognizing the lack of such coordination within the budget process itself, development permit requirements in Vermont and the California coast govern public as well as private projects. Other states, including Maine and Florida, do not exempt government projects from permit requirements, but simply do not require a permit for many kinds of projects, such as highways and water resource developments, that are usually built by the public sector.[65]

Attempts to relate the construction of key facilities by the state to long-term land-planning goals continue to be made. Vermont's abortive land use plan (1974) contained a little-discussed section giving the state planning office power to pass on all major state or state-aided capital projects. Public utility capital projects would also be evaluated, with final power to approve or deny resting with the public service board. All of these projects were to be evaluated for their impact on furthering the policies of the land use plan.

The privately sponsored California Tomorrow Plan (1972) proposed that a state planning council prepare not only land use plans, but long-term and annual capital budgets, guided by a state infrastructure plan. If the governor's proposed budget, submitted to the legislature, differed

from that of the council, he would be required to explain the modifications.[66]

While not establishing, or even recommending, procedures for doing so,
the Massachusetts and California plans mentioned earlier called for better
coordination of state capital spending with urban revitalization programs.

States may influence land use decisions through their tax policies as well
as by their expenditures. In some cases, states set the ground rules for local
collection of ad valorem property taxes, including assessment ratios for
various types of property and exemptions for certain classes of property
owners. More important, through their policies on aid to local governments for schools and welfare, states have a great influence over how high
the local property tax will be. We have already mentioned that the level of
property taxes and the extent of their variation from one community to
another are powerful determinants of the location of new construction
and the maintenance of older buildings. Tax treatment of capital gains,
depreciation, and the deduction of interest costs are also important in-
fluences on private land use decisions, although federal tax laws are of far
greater significance than those of the states. The passage in 1978 of the
huge property tax cuts proposed by California's Proposition 13 revealed
some of the land use consequences of tax law dramatically.[67] Some local
governments, for example, quickly moved to impose expensive development fees on new lots to cover some of the government's infrastructure
and service costs that had been paid for by property taxes.

Among tax-related policies which states have considered are capital
gains taxes on profits from land sales, a uniform statewide property tax,
greater state assumption of school and welfare costs, and authorization
of local development impact fees.[68]

Other Positive State Actions

In addition to using the state budget to affect land use change, states
have several other opportunities to take direct and positive action. They
may purchase land outright, buy scenic easements or development rights,
subsidize certain desired activities, and even develop land themselves.

Currently, state and local governments own about 7 percent of the
nation's land. Of this, about a third (42 million acres) is state land open
to at least limited recreational use.[69] The states have recently been acquiring additional parkland at the rate of several hundred thousand acres
yearly.[70] But despite the willingness of voters to approve large bond issues
for state land acquisition, this method of land control is by its nature a
limited one.[71] It has been estimated, for example, that acquiring desirable

open space in California alone would cost in excess of $4 billion.[72] Today, the cost might be twice this figure.

Outright state acquisition need not be limited to parklands. Since 1971 Maryland's Department of Natural Resources has been authorized to acquire sites for future privately owned electric power plants. Financed by a surcharge on current electric bills, which raises about $5 million yearly, the program was designed to purchase three to eight sites, which will be resold when needed by the utilities. When sites are finally approved for use by the state, local zoning cannot be used to exclude a power plant. Thus far, one site has been purchased, and negotiations for a second are underway. An oversupply of generating capacity has caused Maryland utilities to temporarily lose interest in siting new plants and the initial site has not been used.[73]

It has often been suggested that the answer to the dilemma of limited state funds and soaring land prices is the purchase by the state of less-than-fee interests in land. For example, the owner of a strip of land on either side of a scenic highway might sell an easement to the state, giving up his right to erect structures or cut trees. This idea was used in the 1950s to protect views along Wisconsin's Great River Road and is the principal means of assuring shoreline preservation in Oregon's program to upgrade the Willamette River. We might expect the easement approach to work rather well in preserving the character of lands that are as yet untouched by development pressures. For these lands, the difference between market value and their value in some environmentally compatible use is small, and the price of an easement would, in consequence, be low.

Unfortunately, the lands that are most likely to be urbanized or otherwise developed already have price tags that reflect these intense uses. Here the price of an easement can be almost as high as the price of outright purchase. This proved to be the case on Long Island, where Suffolk County began purchasing farmland development rights for thousands of dollars per acre. The New Jersey and Connecticut development rights programs were, accordingly, begun as much more modest experimental programs with $5 million budgets in each state. It was estimated that, before interest costs, protecting much of each state's desirable farmland in this way would cost $1.7 billion in New Jersey and $500 million in Connecticut (in 1973–74 dollars).

Another, rather common, state policy is to subsidize desired land uses. More than forty states give preferential property tax treatment to farmland.[74] Many extend this subsidy to timberland and other open space as well. One approach is simply to ignore market value, and tax these lands on their value in current use. A variant requires that the subsidy be repaid if and when the land is developed. A few states require a contract be made between the landowner and some level of government, by which the owner agrees to keep the land in agriculture for ten years or more in exchange for a lower tax assessment.

Perhaps the most sweeping direct state involvement occurs where the state takes on some of the functions of the private developer. New York's quasi-public Urban Development Corporation (UDC) was created in 1968 to pursue the physical expansion and redevelopment of urban areas with the full range of development powers, from planning to construction to management. It can condemn land, if needed for its projects, and could, until this power was revoked in 1973, override local building codes and zoning ordinances. The UDC was intended to be self-sustaining, but it was authorized to raise up to $2 billion in working capital by selling tax-free bonds.

Much of the work of the UDC involves building federally subsidized housing and constructing community facilities for local governments. It also builds factories and commercial buildings, which it leases to private industry. Since its inception, the UDC has built more than 33,000 housing units, about half in New York City, the rest in urban areas throughout the state. It was also involved in building three new towns—Lysander, near Syracuse; Audubon, which will cushion the impact of a new state university campus outside Buffalo; and a new town–in town, Roosevelt Island in Manhattan's East River.

Despite the UDC's impressive size, the operations have only a minor impact on the structure of land use in New York. The three new towns, for example, were intended to have an eventual population totaling only 66,000, a small number indeed for the nation's second most populous state. Moreover, a basic UDC mission is to improve the physical environment for low- and moderate-income families and improve their job opportunities. This also has made the UDC quite dependent on federal housing-subsidy programs, which boomed in the 1960s and then declined. In February 1975, as New York City and the state foundered financially, the UDC defaulted on $135 million of its bond anticipation notes. The state legislature created a new agency to buy mortgages on UDC property, but while city and state building programs remained in a depressed condition, the UDC maintained a low profile. Only recently has the agency resumed large-scale development activity, concentrating less on low-income housing and more on industrial and commercial projects too large or complex for private developers to attempt.[75]

State Participation in Federal Planning Programs

Much has been made of the considerable land use planning authority that has been quietly amassed by federal agencies, notably by the Environmental Protection Agency (EPA). National laws governing air quality, water quality, solid waste disposal, noise pollution, and transportation have authorized broad powers over land uses that directly or indirectly contribute to environmental problems.[76] Although overall standards are usually set at the national level, EPA and other agencies have relied heavily on state governments for implementation. A good example is the Clean Air Act of 1970 (as amended in 1977) which requires that states draw up detailed plans for improving air quality where pollution is high and maintaining the purity of air where it is relatively unpolluted. These plans can involve substantial changes in transportation systems and in where new industries are permitted to locate. Another pollution control program with an impact on land use is the required long-term planning of sewage treatment plants, a vital utility that is an increasingly important determinant of the location of new housing. Planning programs established by the 1972 Water Pollution Control Act Amendments authorized hundreds of millions of dollars for state planning to control water pollution from factories, new housing, and such nonpoint sources as runoff from farms and parking lots.

Through these delegated federal powers, states may get both important new methods for controlling development and, in many cases, the funds necessary to pay for the task.

North Carolina—Putting It Together

It is often said that the opportunity for the states to experiment with new policies is one of the glories of a federal system of government. We have seen that despite the similarities that come from facing some of the same problems and despite the influence of the ALI's model code, the states have evolved a wide variety of approaches to controlling land use. A fascinating sidelight of this variety is the extent to which states have incorporated their own unique institutions into their land use programs. Florida, for instance, uses the elected Florida Cabinet as the final administrative appeals body in its state controls. California's coastal law was not only the product of the initiative process, but also reflects the state's long history of solving problems with single-purpose commissions. And in Iowa, a proposed state law (narrowly defeated in the 1974 legislature) would have made existing soil conservation committees the basis of statewide planning. Our survey of regulatory techniques has emphasized that variety but has perhaps neglected to show how several of these approaches might be put together into a comprehensive state program.

We might consider North Carolina, a state not in the vanguard of state planning efforts, but one which has given serious thought to its land problems. North Carolina's varied topography and diverse population mean that it faces an unusually wide variety of problems—coastal zone problems along the Atlantic shore, urban sprawl in the central Piedmont, second-home development in its western mountains. It is the tenth most populous state and is enjoying massive industrial investment, yet it has no cities with populations over 300,000. Local government, particularly county government, is often professional, though some say it is "not necessarily competent," particularly in the exercise of development controls.[77]

Long used to uncongested living and plentiful open space, North Carolinians are becoming aware that rapid growth has begun to challenge these amenities. Says James Hinkley, former assistant state planning officer, "The only time we feel real urban pressure is when we travel to Atlanta or Washington, or other metropolitan areas, on vacation or business. Then we only get a short taste of what it is like; this little taste makes us thankful that we live in North Carolina. . . . [But] we have been resting on our laurels. We are letting what has happened to our nation, from Richmond on up through the northeast, happen to us."[78]

To respond to these pressures, the executive branch of the government, in 1974, proposed four bills to begin a coherent program for the protection of state interests. The Coastal Area Management Bill would have required mandatory local land use planning in the coastal counties, with planning supervised and given final approval by a state commission appointed by the governor.

An almost identical bill would have created a commission for the twenty-four counties in the western mountains. Still another bill proposed a land policy council, composed mainly of the heads of state agencies. The council would classify all the land in the state as to its suitability for development and would assist local governments in preparing plans for their future growth. This bill was commonly thought of as being directed toward the urban sprawl in the Piedmont counties, although in fact it involved planning for the entire state. Finally, a fourth bill would have set up a state land conservancy corporation, which could purchase land for state use without the red tape that is usually attached to state purchase.

Already on the books in North Carolina are laws authorizing municipal zoning (1923), county zoning (1957), local subdivision regulations

(1959), state coastal dredge-and-fill permits (1969), and preferential assessment of open-space lands (1973). The state also has considerable authority over air and water pollution, and does a good job of regulating development in its coastal wetlands.[79]

These scattered bits of power, along with the four proposed bills we have described, would easily have given North Carolina the legal power to cope with its development problems and engineer whatever future its citizens desire.

The legislature, after taking pains to protect local control of land use, adopted much of what was put before it. It passed the Coastal Area Management Act and the Land Policy Act. It also established the land conservancy, but denied it real power or funding—in order to keep the Republican governor, a peculiarity in North Carolina at that time, or bureaucrats from doing anything the legislature might dislike. Commenting on the delicate politics involved, one planner says, "Why did they call it the North Carolina Coastal Area Management Act? Because they were afraid to have the word 'zone' appear anywhere in it."[80] Reflecting rural opposition, the mountain areas act was not passed in 1974, and died in committee in 1975.

Implementation of the laws has followed the careful course that marked their adoption. Under the coastal law, the governor appoints a fifteen-member commission, a majority of whom must be chosen from lists of nominees made by the county governments. The twenty coastal counties are required to plan. Municipal governments that meet certain qualifications may do so. Only one county failed to adopt a plan, and forced the state to plan for it. (Landowners in the county unsuccessfully challenged the law's constitutionality in court.) Following state directives, the heart of the local plans is a five-category "land classification," designating areas as developed, transition, community, rural, or conservation, on the basis of existing use, future need, and natural constraints. This classification was inspired by Hawaii's 1961 law, but the classifications lack the regulatory effect of the sort seen in Hawaii and the Adirondacks.

The state's review and approval of twenty county and thirty-two municipal plans, though guided by no tough statutory standards, resulted in the state repeatedly insisting that local plans be tightened. Other notable features of the planning process were $1.6 million in state aid to local governments for planning, and extensive public information efforts culminating in the mailing to each resident of a synopsis of the plan and classification map. In the fall of 1978, the coastal management program was approved to receive continuing federal financial support by the national

Office of Coastal Zone Management, making North Carolina the first southern state so recognized.

An early evaluation of the plans found those prepared in the most developed localities, where there was prior planning experience, to be far superior to those in the counties still seeking to attract extensive growth.[81] The same study found limited use of the plans by state agencies, and observers agreed that the coastal law provided little guarantee that the plans would be enforced or used. An executive order issued by the governor has more recently put pressure on state agencies to act consistently with the plans, and the law mandates that permits for development within areas of environmental concern be denied if projects are inconsistent with the plan.

Under another part of the law, the commission designated areas of environmental concern in the coastal zone, and in March 1978, began administering a permit process for development in those areas. Major developments, defined in terms such as those found in Maine's site location of development law—those that require major environmental permits, are larger than 20 acres, or involve large structures—require state commission permits. Some observers feel that procedural problems could hamstring the commission's permit process if it is taken to court, so the legislature may have to pass a corrective bill.[82]

Overall, the strategy under the coastal law has been an introduction to planning for localities where it had not been practiced. The state appeared to be saying, "We'll get people used to the idea, then maybe they'll get into implementation methods later."[83] Whether that happens, of course, depends upon the program's performance in the next few years; if the legislature is dissatisfied, it will not renew the program in 1981 when, under a "sunset" law, it is scheduled to expire.

The Land Policy Council's record of achievement is more mixed. By late 1976 it had prepared "A Land Resources Program for North Carolina," calling for statewide land classification, special treatment for key facilities and large developments, protection of fragile areas, and institutional improvements in the management of North Carolina lands.[84] One critic found the program overly ambitious, combining as it did parts of the land use laws of several states.[85] A bill was introduced in 1977 by one land policy council member to establish a state commission to oversee local land classification plans and to monitor large developments. It was defeated in the legislature because of the wariness of farm interests, the absence of any immediate threat to a visible resource such as existed on the coast, and the disinclination, after a recession, to discourage development in any way. In 1978 a greatly reduced council staff was studying ways to devise a more acceptable bill, focusing primarily on the control of public investment through local planning.[86]

North Carolina, by carefully cultivating local support, has been able to expand its capacity for responding to state land use issues. Its land use initiatives have not been nearly so forceful—or so effective—as those of Vermont, California, or Florida, but a state role is now well established in its institutional framework of land use control.

Yet, as we have seen in our case studies, the institutional framework is only the beginning. It provides a mechanism for allocating rights but tells us little about how that mechanism works in practice.

Chapter 7 deals with the issues that arise in setting up these new institutions and in applying them to actual land use decisions—the political rivalries, the economic effects, the social tradeoffs, and the planning goals. If this chapter has given us some recipes for a state regulatory process, the chapter to come hints at what might happen when we try to use them.

Notes

1. According to one survey, during 1974 only two of the fifty states failed to either consider, initiate a study of, or enact state land use legislation. *Land Use Planning Reports* vol. 2, no. 22 (July 8, 1974).

2. For an analysis of this "diffusion" effect, see Nelson Rosenbaum, *Land Use and the Legislatures: The Politics of State Innovation* (Washington, D.C., Urban Institute, 1976).

3. For citations and discussion, see Thomas J. Schoenbaum and Kenneth G. Silliman, "Coastal Planning: The Designation and Management of Areas of Critical Environmental Concern," *Urban Law Annual* vol. 13 (1977) pp. 19–23.

4. See ibid., pp. 16–17, for a discussion of the program.

5. State of New York, Adirondack Park Agency Act (1973) p. 3.

6. *Congressional Record* Oct. 12, 1978, pp. S. 18517–18519. See also, "Rustic Pine Barrens in Urban New Jersey Attracts Developers," *Wall Street Journal,* Aug. 8, 1978; and "U.S. Legislation Aids Effort To Save Jersey's Pinelands," *The New York Times,* Nov. 10, 1978.

7. See William E. Felts and Geoffrey Wandesforde-Smith, *The Politics of Development Review in the Lake Tahoe Basin* (Davis, Calif., University of California Institute of Governmental Affairs, 1973); Ginny McPartland, "Changing the Tide in the Lake Tahoe Basin," *California Journal* vol. 7, no. 1 (January 1976) pp. 9–11; and "Tahoe: What's Best for Troubled Tahoe," *Sunset* (June 1978) pp. 88–99.

8. California's dissatisfaction with the bi-state agency led it to revive, in 1973, an earlier agency, the California Tahoe Regional Planning Agency, composed of state and local representatives from the California side. In 1975 the California agency adopted, over objections of local government members, a growth-restricting regional plan covering two-thirds of the Tahoe basin. Among other things, it prohibits new subdivisions on the California side of the lake until 85 percent of present lots are built on.

9. State wetlands laws have been studied in depth by Nelson Rosenbaum under a National Science Foundation grant. Existing statutes are described in Rosenbaum's "Protecting the Nation's Wetlands: An Assessment of State Regulatory Statutes" (Washington, D.C., Urban Institute, 1978) Working Paper 1236-02; and by Rosenbaum and his colleagues in articles in *Environmental Comment* (July 1978). In

addition, a comparative analysis of state wetlands statutes may be found in Nelson Rosenbaum, "Statutory Structure and Policy Implementation: The Case of Wetlands Regulation," paper presented to the Policy Implementation Workshop, Pomona College, Claremont, California, November 1978.

10. A comprehensive overview of trends and issues in coastal zone management may be found in the massive collection of papers in Marc J. Hershman and James H. Feldmann, *Coastal Zone Management: Readings and Notes* (Seattle, University of Washington Institute for Marine Studies, 1979).

11. California Public Resources Code, Div. 18, Ch. 1, § 27001. Other critical area legislation in California included the San Francisco Bay Conservation and Development Commission Act (1965), the Suisun Marsh Preservation Act (1974), and the proposed A.B. 15 (1975), the last giving the state authority to prevent the urbanization of prime agricultural land.

12. Washington Shoreline Management Act (1971). Washington's law was the first fully accepted by the federal coastal zone management program. An early assessment of the act's effectiveness in the Puget Sound area (focused on the law's permit program, not its planning measures), found it effective in reducing environmental damage from development, but less so in securing public access to water and insisting that development be water related. Maureen McCrea and James H. Feldmann, "Interim Assessment of the Washington Shoreline Management Act," *Coastal Zone Management Journal* vol. 3 (1977) pp. 119–150.

13. Regional Science Research Institute, *Untaxing Open Space* (Washington, D.C., Council on Environmental Quality, 1976) pp. 11–21.

14. The best overview of farmland-preservation programs is Robert E. Coughlin, *Saving the Garden: The Preservation of Farmland and Other Environmentally Valuable Land* (Philadelphia, Pa., Regional Science Research Institute, 1977). A more recent report on some of these programs may be found in John S. Rosenberg, "Preserving Farmland," *Country Journal* (February 1979) pp. 68–76.

15. Peter W. Amato, "Wisconsin Hopes a New Land Law Will Preserve Its Farms," *Planning* (January 1979) pp. 10–12.

16. Oregon: O.R.S. 215.505 *et seq.;* and Colorado: C.R.S. 106-2-34, 1972 Supp., and C.R.S. 106-2-10. The Colorado law applies only to unincorporated county areas.

17. Oregon Land Conservation and Development Commission, "Statewide Planning Goals and Guidelines" (Salem, Ore., January 1, 1975) Goal 14, "Urbanization." The use of boundaries to designate developable and open areas appears to be more common in Europe. One notable example is discussed in William K. Reilly, "Thoughts on the Second German Miracle," *Conservation Foundation Letter* (August 1976).

18. Land Use Regulation Commission, "Comprehensive Land Use Plan" (Augusta, Maine Department of Conservation, 1976) p. 6. The commission also provides, in booklet form, its enabling legislation (Title 12, M.R.S.A., Chapter 206-A, section 681 *et seq.*); and its "Land Use Districts and Standards" (chap. X of its rules). Information on current activity comes in a letter from Frederick W. Todd, the commission's supervisor, land use planning, Dec. 13, 1978.

19. Hawaii Rev. Stat. Ch. 205.

20. Maine Site Location of Development Act (1970). Housing is interpreted as a "commercial" use.

21. Delaware Coastal Zone Act (1971).

22. John H. Williams, "Power Plant Siting Reform—Panacea or Purge," *Public Utilities Fortnightly* vol. 102, no. 10 (Nov. 9, 1978) pp. 21–26.

23. *The California Tomorrow Plan* (San Francisco, California Tomorrow, revised ed., 1972).

24. Georgia legislature, Senate Bill 557 (1974).

25. "As Water Supply Ebbs, Arizonans Are Fretting Over Economic Effects," *Wall Street Journal,* Dec. 28, 1977; "California Desert Now an Urban Frontier," *The New York Times,* Nov. 11, 1978; and "In California, Water Means Both Money and Politics," *The New York Times,* Dec. 17, 1978.

26. California Office of Planning and Research, "An Urban Strategy for California" (Sacramento, 1978) p. 10. Massachusetts Office of State Planning, "City and Town Centers, A Program for Growth: The Massachusetts Growth Policy Report" (Boston, 1977).

27. James C. Breagy, *Overriding the Suburbs: State Intervention in Housing Through the Massachusetts Appeals Process* (Boston, Citizens Housing and Planning Association, 1976). See also James C. Breagy, "Housing Appeals Statute Provides Massachusetts with Statewide Powers Over Local Housing Ordinances," *Journal of Housing* vol. 33, no. 11 (December 1976) pp. 548–550.

28. One critic doubts that it will be. See Thomas G. Pelham, "Regulating Developments of Regional Impact: Florida and the Model Code," *University of Florida Law Review* vol. 29 (1977) pp. 789–852.

29. A good short discussion of the Hackensack authority appears in *Large-Scale Development: Benefits, Constraints, and State and Local Policy Incentives* (Washington, D.C., Urban Land Institute, 1977) pp. 19–20 and 111–113. The commission's problems in accommodating housing are discussed in "Ex-Director Sees Growth Periled in Meadowlands," *The New York Times,* Nov. 17, 1978. Transportation problems are reported in "Where a Rush Hour Won't Be 60 Minutes," *The New York Times,* Dec. 10, 1978.

30. Dr. John M. DeGrove, director of the Florida Atlantic University/Florida International University Joint Center for Environmental and Urban Problems, has analyzed the administrative and political issues in numerous publications. His book, *The Politics of Growth and Land Management,* prepared for the Charles F. Kettering Foundation, should present these ideas at greater length.

Another political scientist, Frank J. Popper, addresses issues of political and bureaucratic power in "Land Use Reform: Illusion or Reality?" *Planning* (September 1974) pp. 14–19, and in a forthcoming study sponsored by the Twentieth Century Fund and tentatively titled "The Politics of Land-Use Reform."

31. Remarks of Andrew Varley to Conservation Foundation Conference on State Land Use Planning, Chicago, March 1974.

32. Additional material on Hawaii's experience with state zoning may be found in Fred Bosselman and David Callies, *The Quiet Revolution in Land Use Control* (Washington, D.C., GPO, 1972) pp. 5–53; Phyllis Myers, *Zoning Hawaii* (Washington, D.C., Conservation Foundation, 1976); Daniel Mandelker, *Environmental and Land Controls Legislation* (Indianapolis, Ind., Bobbs-Merrill, 1976) pp. 269–322; and Thomas H. Creighton, *The Lands of Hawaii: Their Use and Misuse* (Honolulu, University of Hawaii Press, 1978).

33. A 1963 amendment created a fourth classification, "rural," which allows residential development on half-acre lots. Its use has been limited to a few thousand acres on the Neighbor Islands.

34. Editorial in the Honolulu *Advertiser,* June 6, 1974. The last (1974) five-year boundary review found the commission shifting 5,438 acres into the urban category (about 38 percent of what landowners proposed) and 4,056 acres from urban to other categories. Hawaii State Land Use Commission, *Report to the People* (Honolulu, State of Hawaii, 1975). Among more recent decisions were a 1977 reclassification of 640 acres on Oahu for a tourist–commercial–recreational complex and a 1978 refusal to block a developer from building 740 houses next to the state's largest wetland.

35. Myers, *Zoning Hawaii,* p. 74.

36. Shelley Mark, "It All Began in Hawaii," *State Government* (Summer 1973) p. 191.

37. This is not to imply that support for state zoning came exclusively from outside the park. An organization called Citizens to Save the Adirondack Park, which included many Adirondack residents, actively supported strong state controls.

38. The similarity to the 1974 Vermont land use plan is not coincidental. There was some transfer of ideas through use of the same consultants and simple geographic proximity.

39. While a substantial number of local governments within the Adirondack Park have hired consultants or otherwise engaged in planning, local elected officials have been reluctant to actually adopt and implement plans. These issues are discussed at length in a study of the Adirondack Park Agency by Gordon Davis and Richard Liroff, conducted under the auspices of the Environmental Law Institute with funding provided in part by the National Science Foundation (forthcoming). Frank Popper also examines the political opposition to the agency in his forthcoming book, cited at note 30, above.

40. The analysis included review of permit files and visits to construction sites. See chap. 4 of the Davis and Liroff study.

41. The refinery found a new location along the Delaware River, near heavily industrialized Marcus Hook, New Jersey. Here, the refinery is required to obtain a New Jersey wetlands permit, but is in an area not covered by New Jersey's 1973 coastal zone law. Wilmington (Del.) *Journal,* June 21, 1973.

42. Decision of the Delaware Coastal Zone Industrial Board on application of DeGussa Delaware, Inc., Nov. 12, 1973. The company, however, never applied for a permit and decided instead to build in Alabama. Says a Delaware planner, "Delaware just didn't roll out the red carpet as Alabama did." Telephone interview with John Sherman, Delaware State Planning Office, Dec. 5, 1974.

43. Letter from Nathan Hayward III, director, Delaware Office of Management, Budget, and Planning, Nov. 9, 1978. Hayward administers the coastal law.

44. Washington *Post,* Feb. 5, 1974.

45. *Delaware State News,* Sept. 19, 1973.

46. The planning portions of the law and the final administrative definition of heavy industry have never been completed. State Coastal Zone Industrial Control Board and Office of Management, Budget, and Planning, *Coastal Zone Act Administration, June 28, 1971–June 30, 1977* (Dover, November 1977) p. 8. The law and other Delaware coastal legislation are examined in John L. Pedrick, Jr., "Land Use Control in the Coastal Zone: The Delaware Example," *Coastal Zone Management Journal* vol. 2 (1976) pp. 345–368.

47. California Coastal Zone Conservation Act (1972); Vermont Act 250 (1971); Maine Site Location of Development Act (1970); New Jersey Coastal Areas Facilities Review Act (1973); and North Carolina Coastal Area Management Act (1974).

48. In response to this complaint, Vermont's 1973 Capability and Development Plan amended Act 250 to allow the district commissions to make a determination as to whether a proposed project met criteria 9 and 10 (conformity with local and regional plans), before considering the other, more technical, criteria.

49. Frank Popper's political analysis of land use regulation examines this phenomenon generally, and concludes that it is a means by which local officials incrementally extend their influence over state agencies' use of their powers. See note 30 above.

50. Telephone interview with Edwin L. Thomas, Maryland Department of State Planning, Baltimore, April 17, 1979. Maryland's critical areas designation process has much the same purpose, since the state's proposed management guidelines are not binding on local governments.

51. *State Planning in Maryland, 1978* (Baltimore, Maryland Department of State Planning, 1978) p. 35; and *Notification Review Report, 1978* (Baltimore, Maryland Department of State Planning, 1978).

52. In most states, involvement of state government in plan making began in 1933–35, when the National Resources Planning Board encouraged states to set up planning boards. By 1936, every state but Delaware had one. But most boards produced more data than specific plans and, after World War II, many were replaced by state economic development agencies. See Mel Scott, *American City Planning Since 1890* (Berkeley, University of California Press, 1971) pp. 304–305, 357, and 411.

53. Brad Chase, office of state planning, quoted in *Land Use Planning Reports,* vol. 2, no. 8 (April 1, 1974). Later (1976) legislation created a formal process for

revising and updating the plans regularly, but made them advisory guides for state agency action only. One such proposed revision was sent to the 1979 session of the Connecticut General Assembly.

54. New Jersey Division of State and Regional Planning, *State Development Guide Plan* (Trenton, N.J., DSRP, 1977). The court decisions were made by the Superior Court of New Jersey, Hunterdon Co., in *Round Valley, Inc.* v. *Clinton Township* (1978) and *Glenview Development Co.* v. *Franklin Township* (1978). They are subject to appeal to higher courts. The court's authority to overturn local zoning rested on a finding that it was exclusionary, a power claimed in the New Jersey Supreme Court's 1975 *Mount Laurel* decision.

55. State of Hawaii, Department of Planning and Economic Development, *The Hawaii State Plan* (Honolulu, State of Hawaii, 1978).

56. Honolulu *Star-Bulletin,* June 5, 1978, reproduced in ibid.

57. Oregon, Senate Bill 487 (1973); and Colorado, Senate Bill 35 (1972).

58. California, Assembly Bill 1301 (1971).

59. California Government Code, §§ 65560(d), 65561(d), 65563, 65566, 65567, 65860(a), and 65910.

60. See Jens Sorensen, *State–Local Collaborative Planning: A Growing Trend in Land Use Management* (Berkeley, University of California Institute of Urban and Regional Development, forthcoming, 1979).

61. For an account of the law's passage, see Charles E. Little, *The New Oregon Trail* (Washington, D.C., Conservation Foundation, 1974). Current information on implementation may be found in Oregon Land Conservation and Development Commission, *Oregon Lands* (monthly) and *1000 Friends of Oregon Newsletter* (monthly); H. Jeffrey Leonard and Cynthia Whitehead compare the use of urban limit lines in Oregon and Bavaria in "Comparative Federalism: A Case Study of Land Use Policies in West Germany and the United States," unpublished paper prepared for the Conservation Foundation (February 1979).

62. State of Colorado, House Bill 1041 (1974). As had been the case in Oregon, the legislation originally proposed (and defeated in 1973) called for direct state regulation of critical areas, key facilities, and large private developments. For an account of the demise of this earlier legislation, see *Land Use at the State Level— the Growing Edge* (Washington, D.C., League of Women Voters Education Fund, 1973).

63. Budget information from *Land Use Planning Reports,* Sept. 19, 1977, p. 301. Other information in letter from Ted Rodenbeck, principal planner for the commission, Jan. 2, 1979.

64. William G. Flynn, state secretary for communities and development, quoted in James C. Breagy, "Housing Appeals Statute Provides Powers," p. 548.

65. Eighteen states require that some or all projects involving agencies or state funds be evaluated through preparation of an environmental impact statement. See Stuart L. Hart and Gordon A. Enk, *Green Goals and Greenbacks: A Comparative Study of State-Level Environmental Impact Statement Programs and Their Associated Costs* (Rensselaerville, N.Y., Institute on Man and Science, 1978).

66. *The California Tomorrow Plan,* pp. 43–45.

67. "Proposition 13 Triggers Varied Land Use Shifts," *Conservation Foundation Letter* (April 1979).

68. The latter have been proposed in Florida (1974) and California (Quimby Act, 1965; Senate Bill 1118, 1972; Assembly Bill 1144, 1974; Assembly Bill 2090, 1974).

69. U.S. Department of Agriculture, Economic Research Service, *Our Land and Water Resources,* Miscellaneous Publication 1290 (Washington, D.C., GPO, 1974) pp. 12–22. These figures exclude the rather considerable land area recently acquired from the federal government by the state of Alaska.

70. Between 1962 and 1970, acreage in state parks increased by about 350,000 acres yearly. National Recreation and Parks Association, *State Parks Statistics, 1970* and *Parks and Recreation, August 1971,* cited in *Statistical Abstract of the United States* (Washington, D.C., GPO, 1974) p. 206.

71. Recent bond issues for state acquisitions of parkland or environmentally valuable areas have included $240 million in Florida (1972); $175 million in New York (1972); and $100 million in California (1974). In 1978, the year of Proposition 13, King County, Washington, voters voted 58.8 percent in favor of a $35 million bond issue to buy farmland development rights around Seattle. Because bond issues require the support of three-fifths of voters, the issue will be reconsidered.

72. California Legislature, Joint Committee on Open Space Lands, *State Open Space and Resource Conservation Program for California,* 1972, p. 46 (errata sheet).

73. Telephone interview with Paul Massicot, Maryland Department of Natural Resources, April 6, 1979. Another Maryland official observed that utilities may continue to search for their own sites, using the state program as a long-term alternative in the event that their own choices are not acceptable to state or local governments. Telephone interview with Lee Zeni, Maryland Department of Natural Resources, July 29, 1974.

74. For a survey of such programs, see note 13 above. See also U.S. Department of Agriculture, Economic Research Service, *State Programs for the Differential Assessment of Farm and Open Space Land,* Agricultural Economic Report No. 256 (Washington, D.C., GPO, 1974); or International Association of Assessing Officers, *Use Value Farmland Assessments: Theory, Practice and Impacts* (Chicago, IAAO, 1974). Preferential assessment programs have not been very successful in preventing the urbanization of farmland on the urban fringe, mainly because the amount of subsidy they offer is trivial compared with the potential profits of development.

75. See Mendes Hershman, "What Went Wrong with UDC?" *Urban Land* vol. 36, no. 4 (April 1977) pp. 3–6; and "New Direction for the U.D.C.," *The New York Times,* Feb. 25, 1979.

76. See Natural Resources Defense Council, *Land Use Controls in the United States* (New York, Dial Press, 1977) chap. 3–10.

77. Interview with Francis Parker, Department of City and Regional Planning, University of North Carolina, Chapel Hill, Jan. 30, 1974.

78. Hinkley, "Land Use Planning in North Carolina: A Current Picture," address to Regional Environmental Workshops, September 1973.

79. The Urban Institute's National Wetlands Study examined the stringency of wetlands laws in many states, and compared the effectiveness of the enforcement efforts in four of them, including North Carolina. See Nelson Rosenbaum, "Enforcing Wetlands Regulations." Speech presented to the National Wetlands Symposium, Lake Buena Vista, Fla., Nov. 7, 1978; and National Wetlands Study, "Preliminary Report: North Carolina Case Study" (Washington, D.C., Urban Institute, October 1978).

80. Interview with David R. Godschalk, chairman of the Department of City and Regional Planning, University of North Carolina, Chapel Hill, Oct. 3, 1978.

81. Steven French, "Land Classification in North Carolina Coastal Planning" (University of North Carolina at Chapel Hill, Center for Urban and Regional Studies, 1977).

82. Interviews with Milton S. Heath, Jr., Institute of Government, University of North Carolina, Chapel Hill, Oct. 2, 1978; and with Arthur W. Cooper, School of Forest Resources, North Carolina State University, Raleigh, Oct. 3, 1978.

83. Godschalk, interview.

84. Land Policy Council, "A Land Resources Program for North Carolina" (Raleigh, 1976).

85. David R. Godschalk, "A Rejoinder: Questions on North Carolina Land Policy," *Carolina Planning* vol. 2, no. 1 (Winter 1976) pp. 23–25.

86. Interview with Mark B. Sullivan, Division of Land Resources, Department of Natural Resources and Community Development, Raleigh, Oct. 2, 1978. The governor endorsed some such legislation in his 1979 State of the State address, reported in a letter from Sullivan, Jan. 26, 1979.

Issues in Implementing State Land Use Controls

LAND IS IMPORTANT to people. It is a source of livelihood for those who farm it, trade in it, erect structures on it, or simply own it.[1] It is a very visible part of everyone's daily environment. Changes in its use tend to be long lasting, sometimes irreversible. Land arouses feelings of personal and community identity. Anyone who has attended a zoning hearing, talked to a farmer, or invested his life savings in a house can attest to this.

When government tries to increase its control over an area that has so many meanings for people, the issues that its efforts stir tend to be important ones. Sometimes these issues appear dramatically, as when angry property owners denounce controls at public hearings. Sometimes the issues are subtle and long term, and pass by decision makers unremarked, only to reappear as the problems of the future.

In this chapter we will consider three kinds of issues that inevitably arise in any effort to implement land use controls—issues of political power, economic issues, and social issues. (Obviously, there is considerable overlap among broad categories such as these.) We will look at them from the perspective of the states, but most will arise in the implementation of a serious program of land regulation by any unit of government.

Political Power

"Local Control"

Because land is important to people, control over its use is a sought-after source of political power. Nowhere is this more apparent than in the debate over "local control." Local control means at least three things, which vary in relative importance from state to state and from community to community. First, it might mean no control at all, with full rights to use property reposing with the individual landowner. Second, it can mean control by and for the local community, with community interests given precedence over those of the wider society. Finally, it can mean continued control by local decision makers, regardless of whether their decisions emphasize the rights of property owners, the rights of the community, or the rights of society as a whole.

The most articulate advocates of local control as no control see interference with property rights as an erosion of human rights. Idaho Congressman Steve Symms has argued, "The most basic of [private property] rights is the right to use and enjoy. [Under state land controls] this right will now be regulated in the interests of society as a whole. The right to exchange will be destroyed as the right to use and enjoy is circumscribed. . . . The duke and baron of old will be replaced by the State, supposedly acting in the name of 'the people.' Today's independent landowner will become the serf of tomorrow's New Feudalism."[2] This attitude is found especially often in rural areas, where there is no tradition of local zoning and where property is the chief form of private wealth. Sometimes even the mildest kinds of state controls are seen as literally "taking away" the land for state use.[3]

In the second interpretation, local control is seen as control by the local community. Local land use control offers one of the few ways the political system can determine the economic and social nature of the community. Here the controls on individual landowners may be quite strict, but they are directed at achieving community goals, rather than statewide ones. This feeling is often found in localities containing critical areas or other amenity resources. Here local officials fear that the statewide interest in preservation will stifle their economic growth and their chances to capitalize on industrial or tourist-oriented development. A planning board member from a county on North Carolina's Outer Banks argued, "We don't want our destiny controlled by the governor. We want to control it ourselves."[4] Similar fears are voiced in the impoverished communities of northeastern Vermont, the Adirondacks, and rural Colorado.

Another sector that often takes this view of local control is the sophisticated, planning-conscious local government on the metropolitan fringe. Here state-administered controls may actually be seen as interfering with the local planning process. Said a Montgomery County, Maryland, supervisor, in opposing state land control, "We . . . recognize that

193 elected officials [in the Washington, D.C., area] from 15 major jurisdictions in two states and the Federal District cannot act completely independently to solve these problems. On the other hand, we do not believe it necessary to create a new supergovernment to deal with these problems. We believe that local officials acting together with a sense of the metropolitan consequences of our actions can help us make better decisions."[5]

Finally, local control involves the political power of individuals. Deciding permitted land uses is one of the major discretionary powers of local government. It can be used to reward political friends, penalize enemies, or simply to put into practice a local official's ideal vision of his community. In a more sinister sense, such power can be a marketable commodity. One state legislator, a supporter of a state land use bill, said of the local officials who opposed it, "These guys want to keep this their own ball game. There are a lot of political contributions available from people in the development business. The local officials don't want it all going to [the governor]."[6]

The latter two views of local control do not necessarily imply a passive role for the state, for states have several avenues for actually *increasing* the effectiveness of community control over land. State enabling legislation, the ultimate source for local planning and zoning power, can be strengthened. State agencies can and do fund local planning, provide communities with data on soil types and limitations to development, formulate model standards, and inform localities about the long-term capital programs of the state. If communities wish to pursue growth management policies, the state can help, with legislative authorization, funding, and legal and planning advice.

The degree to which a local government encourages these kinds of noncoercive state initiatives is perhaps a good indicator of what that community really means when it cries for local control.

Since the heady days of the "quiet revolution," many advocates of better land use have come to appreciate the political resources and potential implementation advantages that local governments have to offer. Hence the current popularity of collaborative planning, characterized by one researcher as "a mid-point compromise between a centralized, top-down and a decentralized approach . . . designed to involve cities and counties significantly without relying on them so heavily that important regional and statewide goals are compromised."[7] California's experience with the collaborative approach in its coastal program will provide a crucial test of how smoothly such a process may work and of how well nonlocal interests are actually protected. Land use control advocates, by now keenly aware of the general public's mistrust of centralized regulation, are likely to warmly embrace the collaborative approach if it is implemented successfully in California.

Citizen Participation

Another crucial political issue in state land use control is the form and extent of citizen involvement. There has, of course, been a general movement toward greater public participation in administrative decisions, but demands for such involvement in state land use programs have been especially widespread. One study attributes this to two reasons: the "immediate and pervasive impact" of land use decisions on people's lives and the "distance and unfamiliarity of state government" from ordinary people.[8] Certainly the encouragement of citizen involvement has been a near-universal feature of state land use programs. But the methods used and the seriousness of the bureaucratic commitment to public participation have varied widely from state to state.

Former Vermont governor, Thomas Salmon, claimed that "Vermont's land management and development regulation mechanisms are unique and have won public acceptance largely, in my view, because they are decentralized and citizen administered. . . . In contrast to the approach taken by other states and by the American Law Institute in its Model Land Development Code, Vermont relies most heavily not upon professional input and administration but upon its tradition of citizen-centered government."[9]

This is true in two respects. First, the district commissions, which make the overwhelming majority of permit decisions, are composed of private citizens, although this feature is certainly not unique to Vermont. Second, Act 250 and the subsequent plans have received extensive publicity within the state, in part because of a $120,000 public education program funded by the Ford Foundation. There have been television presentations, a widely circulated slide show, a mass mailing, and dozens of frequently stormy hearings attended by several thousand Vermonters. It is said, in fact, that the relative neglect of public participation at the time of the 1974 land use plan was an important factor in its defeat.

On the other hand, Act 250 limits parties by right at permit application hearings to specified state and local officials and *abutting* property owners. We have mentioned earlier that these standards often have been relaxed in practice, but there has been at least one case in which the state environmental board did not allow a group of property owners to protest a condominium because their property did not abut that of the developer.[10] Similarly, Florida's law makes no provision at all for citizens to become parties to development of regional impact proceedings, although anyone is free to testify at the hearings that are held.

These limits on citizen standing contrast sharply with those under California's coastal program, where citizen involvement was literally built into its most central decision-making processes.[11] California's 1976 Coastal Act continues the practice begun under Proposition 20 of allowing any "aggrieved person" to participate in hearings and, more important, to appeal a regional commission's decision to the state commission or to the courts. In its regulations, the state commission has interpreted "aggrieved person" to encompass anyone who made an appearance or even filed a letter at the time of the regional hearing.[12] In California it is a proud boast of environmentalists—and a bitter complaint of developers—that a citizen can appeal "for the price of a postage stamp." Over the years, literally hundreds of appeals have been carried to the state commission by individual citizens, by neighborhood associations, by general purpose environmental groups such as the Sierra Club, and by groups formed especially for that purpose, such as the Coastwatch chapters in some coastal cities. Although there are currently some signs that citizen interest may be waning in California, the agenda of one recent state commission meeting found ten permits appealed by individuals, as well as appeals by PACE, the Sierra Club, and the neighborhood-based Ocean Beach Planning Board.[13]

The level of expertise marshaled by California citizen groups has been surprisingly high. Often they come to hearings armed with maps, charts, and scientific testimony as well as the usual petitions and letters of protest. Most appellants are quite well informed about the Coastal Act's policies and can quote chapter and verse from the law, the interpretive guidelines, or past permit cases to buttress their objections. During hearings on the coastal plan, one southern California group illustrated its concerns by showing the regional commission a well-made movie on the effects of development on its neighborhood.

Public participation has also been a hallmark of Oregon's land use program, although citizens must show they are "substantially affected" by local land use plans in order to appeal them to LCDC. Involvement through public workshops and hearings has been emphasized, although there is also an official state Citizen Involvement Advisory Committee. Oregon's state land use agency claims that by the time the original fourteen statewide land use goals were adopted in late 1974, it "had involved over 10,000 Oregonians directly in their development," and "in excess of 100,000 viewed television programs about the Oregon Land Use Program and its development."[14] One significant aid to public participation has been the work of a conservation organization called "1,000 Friends of Oregon," which sponsors educational seminars on land use issues and, since 1975, has published a monthly newsletter devoted primarily to tracking and commenting on actions of the state land use commission.

A broad array of new techniques has become available to facilitate citizen participation in land use regulation, including use of sophisticated audiovisual aids for public education, increased reliance on professional citizen advocates, use of formal and informal advisory committees, and various kinds of administrative decentralization.[15] Nearly all of them have been used in one or more state programs. Yet there is evidence that more traditional methods may be the most effective. Rosenbaum surveyed citizen participants in state land use programs in California, Hawaii, North Carolina, and Oregon. He found that formal public hearings, informal workshops, and sending letters and documents to the public agency were the methods most often used by participants and (along with direct personal contacts with officials) were those they judged most effective.[16]

Even among those states using innovative methods for encouraging participation one finds heavy reliance on that workhorse of local planning administration, the public hearing. In virtually every state which has enacted some form of control, hearings are required when regulations are adopted, when plans are considered, and when permits are decided upon. In most places, hearings are waived for routine permit applications, but are almost always held if there is an objection by a commissioner or a citizen. Used as a means of securing public input, the public hearing has been frequently attacked as inefficient at best and perfunctory at worst, yet it seems to have found a secure place in the administration of land use regulations by the state as well as by the municipality.

Public participation in planning sounds like a concept all reasonable people should embrace. Clearly, many of its aspects are unassailable: open availability of draft planning documents; workshops to explain technical issues; the opportunity for everyone to express an opinion and present new information; public decisions publicly arrived at. Yet more active forms of public participation involve serious questions of philosophy as well as implementation. At the most abstract level, they raise "the central question of how far it is possible (or desirable) to move from the present system of representative democracy to a system of participatory democracy."[17] One of the major objections to regulatory centralization has been that it has generally resulted in decisions made by appointed rather than elected officials. Giving self-selected citizens real power in a land use process would even further weaken the concept that ultimate political authority rests with the electorate. More concrete is the question of which members of the "public" are likely to participate.

On one hand, developers and landowners are understandably indignant when private individuals claim to represent the public interest in testifying against or in appealing projects, without having to prove that they have no personal conflict of interest. Although we know of no specific cases in which this has been alleged, it is easy to envision a situation in which a member of the public could use a land use process to prevent commercial competition (say, a rival hotel) or to increase the value of his already developed property.

On the other hand, the public involvement process might be quietly taken over by development interests. Landowners are likely to maintain their participation through months of tedious hearings and reviews of bulky draft plans—they have large amounts of their own money involved. But individual citizens, who have much less of a personal stake, will be tempted to drop out. In one suburban Maryland jurisdiction, for example, a citizen advisory committee that advocated rezoning a large tract of land to much more intensive use was found to be packed with affected landowners.[18] In California, the coastal commission has pointed proudly to one city's use of a citizen committee to help draw up its local coastal program. But a planner from a nearby city terms it as being "loaded with special interests." She adds that "If we had a committee like that, every developer in town would be on it, pressuring us to do what they wanted us to do. After a while the people who do not have strong coastal interests, such as representatives of minority groups, tend to drop out." Public subsidies have been advocated to encourage citizen participants, if only to reimburse them for travel and research costs. Yet who will decide how such funds will be distributed? The balance among public participation, political re-

sponsiveness and responsibility, and bureaucratic professionalism will
continue to be a hard one to find.

What the Public Thinks

Even under ideal conditions, only a small minority of the public will
be interested enough to actually participate in the planning or regulatory process. What of the rest of the citizenry—how do they feel and
what do they want?

Rarely has the land control issue been a deciding or even a major
factor in statewide political contests. Oregon's former governor, Tom
McCall, and Delaware's Russell Peterson won wide popular acclaim for
their outspoken support of state land use controls in the early years
of this decade, as did Colorado's Richard Lamm and Florida's Reubin
Askew.[19] But since about 1974, most gubernatorial candidates have
shied away from taking highly visible positions, pro or con, on the
potentially explosive issue of land use. Perhaps the best indication of
an adroit political strategy was that taken by California's Jerry Brown
in 1976. During most of the nine-month debate over the Coastal Act,
Brown virtually ignored the issue, merely calling generally for "reasonable rules" for coastal protection. But at the last moment, Brown
brokered the compromise between environmentalists and developers,
earning plaudits from both camps. After the act passed, a Sacramento
newspaper published a cartoon of Brown, dressed as a lifeguard, and
carrying a mermaid labeled "Coastal Bill" out of the ocean surf.

On the relatively few occasions when state land use laws (or closely
related bond issues) have been submitted directly to the voters, they
have generally fared well. Successes have included Proposition 20;
the 1972 Colorado initiative barring state funds for the Winter Olym-
pics; Oregon's defeat of antiregulation initiatives in 1976 and 1978;
Florida's 1972 bond issue, which activated the critical areas program;
and California's 1976 bond issue for beaches and for the coastal
conservancy.

In the column of electoral failure must be placed the repeal of Utah's
land use law by a 3–2 margin in a 1974 referendum vote before it
could even be implemented. Apart from these few cases, land use is
now rather quiet as a statewide electoral issue. After the 1978 general
elections, one land-planning newsletter reported that "Environmental
and land use issues did not play a major role in most statewide races,
and few major policy shifts are anticipated as a result of last week's

voting. States which have taken a strong role in land use planning will continue to do so, while others will probably be reluctant to adopt new planning programs."[20]

Other evidence of how the public feels is more ephemeral. We can observe that public hearings are often dominated by those who oppose controls. One writer speculates that this is due to an asymmetry in the distribution of costs and benefits: "Unlike the case with food stamps or school buses where public expenditure produces immediate tangible and very obvious outputs, returns to comprehensive planning are difficult to pinpoint. The benefits usually are reduced future costs. . . . The costs of a particular plan or implementing law, on the other hand, may be vivid to those affected. The frequent result is that political support for specific control proposals is more illusive than the objections."[21] Typical of those opposing controls are owners of affected properties, persons philosophically opposed to government intervention of any sort, developers (who often maintain that they accept the "spirit" of controls, but not their implementation), and various groups such as real estate brokers and construction tradesmen, who are dependent on the general level of building activity.

A political scientist has noted that the main proponents of state land use laws, among them planners, environmentalists, citizen activists, and land use lawyers, typically lack statewide political strength and permanent organization. They also lack economic influence compared with the development and business interests which oppose such laws. Many of the latter are well organized to lobby state legislatures and to make campaign contributions and have the resources to bring this influence to bear year after year.[22]

Public opinion surveys can run counter to the impression gained at hearings. We have already mentioned that polls in Vermont, and a straw vote in Collier County, Florida, indicated that there was far more support for state land regulation than was apparent from the stormy public hearings held at about the same time.

One of the most comprehensive surveys of public attitudes toward land use controls was that taken (statewide) in Vermont in 1972.[23] On a list of local and state problems of all kinds considered "very serious" by those polled, most land use issues ranked rather far down the list. These included land speculation (31 percent considered it "very serious"), housing developments (13 percent), and scenic pollution (39 percent). Moreover, only 12 percent of those polled said they were willing to spend $100 or more to reduce pollution of all forms. But, when asked their opinion on specific land use controls, surprisingly high proportions approved of state intervention.

Fifty-eight percent approved a law requiring a state permit for developments larger than 1 acre if these were outside a town with permanent zoning. Forty-nine percent wanted to require a state permit for projects larger than 10 acres, even within areas with local zoning. And 84 percent supported strict control of mobile home developments.

We cannot, of course, generalize from a survey of a single state at a single point in time. Land use control is a complex and sometimes technical issue. Public opinion in such cases undoubtedly depends as much on how the issue is presented as on the substance of the conflict. A popular governor or legislative leader may build wide support for state planning as a comprehensive answer to the public's often demonstrated fear of "growth" and its consequences.[24] On the other hand, opponents of control may find ready support for the position that land use planning is merely another extension of government control over individual freedom. Much depends on how and by whom the issue is presented.

So far, we have discussed the political issues in land use control in terms of the electorate and the state and local officials it chooses to represent it. Now we should consider another source of power, indirect but occasionally formidable. This is the set of state laws and institutions that are already in place.

Land Use and Bureaucratic Power

One of the strongest arguments for comprehensive state land use planning and regulation is that it can coordinate the mass of piecemeal and sometimes conflicting policies that already exists. Frequently overlooked is the fact that those who presently administer these policies are not waiting eagerly to be coordinated. Some of this is purely a question of personal power—a concern that lawmakers ignore at their peril, but one that we might pass over here as something inherent in personalities rather than in the system itself. One thing that *is* inherent in the system, however, is that scores of state agencies are already pursuing narrow, land use-related goals. In many cases they are doing a good job of it, but even that creates problems.

Consider, for example, the existing state agencies that control pollution. Pursuing their mandate to improve water quality, they approve sewage treatment plants that open up new lands to urbanization. State land planners, taking a more comprehensive view, will sometimes oppose these same projects. Sometimes the problem is just lack of communication between agencies, but frequently real conflicts of objectives are also involved. It is easy to envision a situation, for example, in which a land use agency tries to increase a project's off-street parking while an air pollution agency, seeking to reduce emissions associated with automobile use, tries to decrease it. Similarly, water pollution agencies that have limited hookups to overloaded sewage plants have encouraged new growth to sprawl onto rural lands where septic tanks could be used.

Conflicts can also arise between land planners and those charged with building highways, universities, and irrigation projects. Interagency relations are not helped when the participants not only have different missions, but come from different professional backgrounds as well.

Some classic interagency conflicts have occurred in California, where the coastal commissions were superimposed on a governmental structure already deeply involved in environmental control. We have mentioned earlier that one commission tried to make new sewage plants meet water quality standards higher than those required by state pollution laws. The state's Water Resources Control Board, feeling both that its power was being usurped and that the higher standards were not cost-effective, for a long time would not agree to release federal and state funds to construct facilities meeting the coastal commission's requirements. And when the 1976 Coastal Act was passed, it included a provision explicitly preventing the coastal commissions from imposing regulatory controls or standards replacing those established by state agencies, such as those concerned with air, water, forest practices, and fisheries.[25]

In another California case, the South Coast Regional Coastal Commission proposed in a draft of the energy element of its plan that existing oil refineries and fossil-fueled power plants be removed from the 5-mile-wide coastal planning zone. The staff report argued that air pollution in the coastal zone was already "sufficiently severe to damage life and threaten coastal resources."[26] Spokesmen for the air pollution control districts in Los Angeles and Orange counties objected, questioning the logic of forcing pollution sources inland, where the smog is even thicker than along the coast. The proposal was quickly shelved by the commission.

Other disagreements between planners and mission-oriented agencies have arisen with regard to the type of vapor emission controls that should be required in gas stations along the California coast,[27] and in the debate over whether to locate a second campus of the University of Hawaii on Oahu, or on one of the outer islands.

John Banta has pointed out five distinct spheres in which a new state land use agency can interact—and conflict with—the state's existing functional bureaucracy.[28] First, the land use agency can interfere with other agencies' budgets by modifying or delaying their development projects. This can be particularly irksome for the agencies if delays cost them federal grants. Second, the land use body can accept or challenge other agencies' roles as traditional providers of expertise in their area of specialization. Third, it can modify other agencies' regulatory decisions, mostly through the multiple-veto route. Fourth, the land use agency can cooperate or fail to cooperate with other agencies in monitoring and enforcement. Fifth, policies promulgated by the land use agency can affect other agencies' long-range plans and policies.

Interbureaucratic conflicts are particularly unfortunate, since the mission-oriented agencies are undoubtedly the land use planners' best source of technical information, both about the current impacts of development and the long-run growth plans of the state. Expertise in such specialized areas as emission control or marine biology is not usually available on the staff of the land regulatory agency, but can be easily obtained from elsewhere in state government. Vermont has been particularly eager to use the expertise of other state agencies, circulating Act 250 project applications to them and holding meetings to hear agency comments. California and Florida have been less prone to involve other agencies, although the latter is showing increasing reliance on the large professional staffs of the state's water management districts for assessment of the environmental impacts of major projects. Federal agencies, principally the U.S. Fish and Wildlife Service, have also provided technical assistance in more than one state.

Mission-oriented agencies and land use agencies can also be a great help to one another in enforcement. The land use agency, which often stands at the end of a multiple-veto process, can serve as an administrative checkpoint, making sure that other required permits have been secured. The mission-oriented agencies, for their part, are more likely to have the manpower and technical monitoring capability needed to see that those who receive permits from the land use agency actually comply with conditions.

Despite bureaucratic reluctance, some states have made progress in coordinating their agencies' diverse activities. Efforts range from simply requiring agencies to notify one another that a development application has been made, through formal or informal consultation among agencies (as in Vermont), to provisions for multiagency hearings and decisions.[29] Perhaps the most ambitious such effort is Washington State's Environmental Coordination Procedures Act (1973). It provides for coordinated applications, hearings, and review of nearly all permits issued by state government. If a developer chooses to use this law— not all do—a central department provides him with all necessary forms and arranges for a common hearing involving the relevant state agencies. Each agency continues to judge the application according to its own statutory criteria, but there is a common hearing record and a single administrative appeal. Other states, including Georgia and California, have attempted to coordinate and, therefore, speed up state agency decisions involving industrial siting.

Economic Issues

The economic effects of state land use controls are difficult to assess, for analysis has been hampered by both methodological and practical problems. For one thing, many state programs regulate a variety of types of projects and types of land, with decisions made case-by-case. If one wanted to analyze Florida's DRI program, for example, he would have to consider subdivisions and shopping centers, oil refineries and jai alai stadiums, many subject to widely varying terms and conditions. A separate economic analysis would have to be done for each individual case. The types of effects that are of interest are also varied: impacts on jobs, on land prices, on tax rates, on housing prices, and on the distribution of wealth. Moreover, readily available data rarely allow one to differentiate a regulated zone (say a 1,000-yard coastal strip) from one that is nonregulated. Finally, it is often not possible to separate the impact of land use controls from the simultaneous operation of other variables, including housing demand, interest rate changes, and the effect of other environmental legislation.

And this list merely addresses the economic costs of controls—the benefits which are supposed to justify them are even harder to quantify, much less to express in dollar terms. How much, for example, is habitat for an endangered species worth to society? Or how shall one value a shoreline view?

In the absence of solid analysis, public debate over the economic effects of land use controls has often been characterized by exaggerated statements. A few days after the passage of California's Proposition 20, the *Los Angeles Times* reported that, "The controversial proposition to freeze most coastline development until 1976 was sending shivers through the real estate industry even before the voters approved it." In fact, fears in California and elsewhere that state land controls would bring bankruptcy to developers, unemployment to construction workers, and ruin to local economies have not been borne out. Nevertheless, the potential economic effects of such programs are considerable. They can affect what is built both within the regulated area and outside of it; can create windfall profits and unexpected losses; can change the cost and availability of housing; and can affect the tax bills of individuals and the tax bases of communities.

Impact on the Overall Economy

Rigorous evaluation of the economic effects of controls was beyond the scope of this study,[30] but in the course of collecting information on the implementation of controls in several states, we found little evidence that state land controls have had an unfavorable impact on any state's overall economy. For example, the population of Hawaii, which has the oldest (1961) law of all, grew by 22 percent over the succeeding decade.[31] Only eight other states grew faster. Within a year of its implementation, California's coastal law permitted more than $4 billion in coastal construction, and a building boom in the noncoastal area took up any slack.

The specter of economic decline is almost certain to be raised in any public discussion of a significant new land law. During the debate over North Carolina's Coastal Area Management Act in 1974, the president of the state's fourth largest bank talked intensely about his fears that state planning along the coast could seriously wound eastern North Carolina's chances for economic prosperity. "We're spending tens of millions of dollars on technical schools in North Carolina to teach people to participate in a modern society," he said, "If we were to be so foolish to adopt this no-growth legislation, it would be the cruelest sort of action. These people would be all ready to get out of school with no place to go.[32]

He is echoed by a banker in fast-growing Arizona, who notes that he "fail[s] to see that slow growth or no growth has done much for places like New York or Cleveland."[33]

At a public hearing in Vermont, a man who made his living as a bulldozer driver testified that before his state's second-home boom he had been happy to find work at eighty cents an hour. When construction prospered, he began to earn ten times that, clearing land for ski slopes and condominiums. He complained bitterly that a state land use plan could choke off his new prosperity.

Particularly prone to such fears are depressed rural communities, which view any sort of new development as their only salvation from economic decline. It is easy for residents of such places to feel that new laws are a means of preserving them in picturesque poverty for the holiday pleasure of city dwellers. Predictions of doom are also likely to come from places with a recent history of rapid growth, for these tend to have an unusually large part of their economy dependent on the level of new construction. Such places may forge unusual coalitions of business and labor interests, who oppose strict controls in the name of "environmental balance" or "balanced growth." Apprehension about the effects of controls on the overall economy is understandable, but it is probably shortsighted.

There are three principal reasons for thinking so. First, state land use laws rarely regulate more than a small fraction of a state's land area or a small fraction of total construction. This is implicit in the theoretical rationale for state involvement developed in chapter 1 and has also been true in practice. Hawaii's law, for example, does not control development in and around existing cities. Florida's law regulates "areas of critical state concern" but limits these to a maximum of 5 percent of the state. Delaware and New Jersey legislation is limited to wetlands and to the coastal zone.

Because of this differential coverage, development not allowed at one site is usually able to shift to another site, either an area within the regulated zone more acceptable to the decision-making agency (say, from in front of a coastal dune to a location behind the dune) or to a location not subject to the regulation. In the long run, the total volume of construction will fall only if the original location was the only one acceptable to consumers. That situation is possible in the case of second homes and specialized industrial facilities, but highly improbable in the case of ordinary residences. And even if consumers do decide to buy fewer dwellings, the money they would have spent will probably be recycled elsewhere in the state's economy.

Second, the state land use laws enacted to date have been oriented much more toward raising the quality of growth than toward reducing its quantity. Programs relying on permit processes have had extremely high rates of permit approval, and conditions, rather than outright denial, have been the principal tool of land protection. Programs relying on land use mapping (such as Hawaii's and the Adirondack Park's) have designated for development an amount of land equal to many years' worth of housing demand.

Third, we can speculate that states with reputations for stiff land use and other environmental controls may find that this enhances their desirability as destinations for tourists, retirees, and other migrants.[34] Moreover, if the laws really do improve environmental quality, they add to the state's potential for certain types of growth. A state that imposes restrictions on the kinds of industry that it will accept may even find that the restrictions themselves make it more attractive to "acceptable" high-technology, amenity-oriented firms.

Impact on Land Uses and Prices

It is at the level of individual parcels of land that the economic effects of controls become most significant, and the redistributive effects most worrisome. Suppose, for example, that a state regulates the dredging and filling of its wetlands, which are under pressure for recreational development. This reduces the potential supply of recreational land in the state and should, if the reduction is substantial, increase the pressure to develop on the high ground bordering the wetlands, along the beaches, perhaps even in the mountains. Building on lots in existing subdivisions on already filled land should increase, and the value of these lots should rise. Owners of wetlands will find the value of their property diminished, and owners of unregulated lands will obtain a windfall gain. A windfall will also accrue to owners of existing buildings in the regulated zone, as their properties (beach houses for example) gain a new scarcity value.

Empirical studies of such price shifts are just beginning to be conducted.[35] But there is at least anecdotal evidence of their existence. In California, the coastal law is widely believed to have raised the price of coastal parcels that were either already built upon or which could easily obtain development permission.[36] As the Los Angeles County assessor put it, "People have realized that developable land along the coastline and in other open areas is a diminishing quantity, and they are buying [it] up like crazy."[37]

Sales of large unsubdivided coastal properties (whose future development prospects were uncertain) virtually ceased. Assessors guessed that their value had dropped, giving them discounts in assessed valuation ranging from 15 to 50 percent.

In Delaware, announcement of the possible construction of a coastal oil refinery caused the value of nearby marshlands to rise from $40 to $100 an acre to $1,000. The state law prohibiting such construction removed much, but not all, of this speculative value. A nature conservation trust later bought one such parcel, originally offered at $1,000 per acre, for $140 per acre.[38]

Hawaii has had the longest experience with state controls. Its system is also one of the simplest possible—some land may be urbanized, some may not. There is considerable suspicion in the state that this restriction on the urban land supply has raised prices. University of Hawaii economist Richard Pollock believes that "by bleeding out the agriculture land to urban use at such small increments, over time, the demand pressure has kept the price of urban land well in excess of any market equilibrium level."[39] Moreover, the supply restriction, he claims, has encouraged land speculators to withhold urban-zoned land from the market in anticipation of even greater price increases.

While at first glance the owners of land in the agricultural zone may seem to have been hurt by the law, they may in fact be its chief beneficiaries. Much of the agricultural land in Hawaii is owned by a handful of corporations, many of whom are phasing out their farming operations there. The state's zoning law encourages them to place land on the market slowly, as the amount zoned as urban land is periodically increased. The price is thus maintained at a higher level than it would have been if thousands of acres of pineapple and sugarcane fields were suddenly dumped on the residential land market.

There are, of course, many different kinds of controls. The property owner whose land is regulated may find himself limited in the *kind* of use to which he can put his land, the *density* of development permitted, or the *quality* of his development. A law regulating the type of use would be one prohibiting mining or certain types of heavy industry or one which limited lands to agriculture or to forestry. For some parcels, the difference between a piece of land's value as farmland and its value for suburban homes is 500 percent or more. The chance, however remote, of such gains explains the reluctance of farmers to place their lands in permanent agricultural zones, even when they have no current plan but to continue farming.

Laws regulating density (usually expressed in terms of residential units per acre) may indicate allowable density on a zoning map, as in New York's Adirondack Park, or may impose density cuts when a state board reviews a particular project, as has been frequently done in Vermont and California. At times, these reductions can be substantial, as in the case of the California man who had initially planned a ten-story, thirty-unit condominium on his bluff-top parcel, but wound up with three stories and twenty-one units.

It is generally true that the higher the density allowed, the higher will be the developer's profit per acre. It is not true, however, that a 50 percent cut in density will necessarily cut profits in half. With fewer units, individual lots will be larger and more desirable and units will command higher prices. The developer usually endeavors to keep a constant ratio between the cost of the structure and the cost of the lot, and will probably build larger, more expensive units on the larger, more expensive lots.[40] In many cases the developer is allowed to cluster his units on a small section of the total acreage, reserving the rest for community open space. This can result in considerable savings in the costs of roads and utilities. In addition the developer will usually build on those portions of the acreage that require the least site preparation, which simultaneously protects such ecologically vulnerable areas as floodplains and marshy soils and reduces the per unit cost of preparing the site. In apartment buildings, as in developments of single-family homes, cuts in density often mean units of larger floor area, greater "luxury," and higher rent.

By far the most common type of state land use controls are those that regulate what we might call the "quality" of development. For example, under its Beach Preservation Act (1972), Delaware requires that buildings on oceanfront lots must be placed on that part of the lot that lies behind the first line of sand dunes. In other states, permit boards have required developers to install central sewage treatment systems where the soil is unsuitable for septic tanks or to install catch-basins to reduce erosion during construction. These conditions are typical, for example, of those attached to permits by Vermont's district environmental commissions and by the Adirondack Park Agency. The cumulative effect of such quality-raising regulations on the costs of construction is often substantial. In Vermont, for example, which has some of the most stringent environmental standards on new construction in the nation, new vacation homes are quite comparable in both quality and cost to permanent residences in other parts of the country.

Quality restrictions can affect both type of land use and density as the developer tries to maximize his profits within the limits of what the law permits him to build. For example, if the law prohibits septic tanks on small lots, he may decide to build town houses, connecting his units to a package sewage treatment plant. If he is required to provide two parking spaces for each apartment unit, as is commonly required by California's coastal commissions, he may build larger, more luxurious units, catering to families that have two or more cars to park. The side effects of a given quality regulation may be quite subtle and hard to predict: some will simply result in the developer assuming the costs of whatever environmental improvement is required; others will cause drastic adjustments or even abandonment of the project.

Despite his efforts to minimize them, the developer (or more accurately the landowner, if they are not one and the same) is usually confronted with at least a portion of the costs of controls. His ability to pass part of the cost on to the final consumer depends, of course, on the elasticity of demand for his product and on his own elasticity of supply. In general, if there are many good substitutes—for example, units in other states or units on land with naturally good drainage—the developer absorbs most of the costs. If substitutes are few, the purchaser of the final product, whether it is a suburban home, a steel mill, or an ocean-front condominium, must bear most of the burden.

The fact that controls often raise the costs of finished units does not mean that they are uneconomic. A law that raises private costs (for a sewer hookup) may lower social costs (water pollution) even more. A provision that the developer build roads or donate a school site will save money for the general taxpayer, even as it burdens the home buyer. Sometimes controls protect the purchaser from his own folly, such as those that restrict building in floodplains. Moreover, the fact that the landowner's neighbors must also build to higher-quality standards tends to raise the value of his property.

Procedural Costs

In addition to the cost of actually meeting standards imposed by state land use laws, developers face considerable delays and expenses in going through the various application processes. One Vermont developer estimated that it cost at least $100,000 to do the groundwork needed to present his large recreational–residential complex to an Act 250 permit hearing. The developer of Florida's Three Rivers spent more than $200,000 on planning before his application was denied. Drawings, soil studies, drainage plans, wildlife surveys, economic impact studies, and the services of attorneys and planners are far from inexpensive.

Most of this planning adds to the value of the final project; much would have to be done in any case. However, by requiring a large investment even before the developer knows whether he will be allowed to build, the permit process adds to the developer's risk and to the minimum profit he expects. These costs may, in the long run, favor large developers over small ones, since the former can afford to spread the risk of refusal over several unrelated projects. Says a Florida developer, "The little guy can no longer be in the development business." He estimates that his company spent $500,000 on planning its large residential community before even breaking ground.

We must also consider the costs of delay. Although it might allow more time for better design, delay adds nothing in itself to the final quality of the project. While awaiting approval, the prospective developer must often carry substantial interest costs and property taxes. Such costs can be particularly troublesome in a business where even successful firms are thinly capitalized (that is to say, highly leveraged).

Costs of delay are significant, but are easy to exaggerate. For example, interest charges accrue at rates as high as 1 percent per month, but the developer need pay interest only on what he has invested in the project to date, not on total project cost. In some cases the developer merely holds an option on the land and thus has no out-of-pocket carrying cost until after the project is approved.[41] Similarly, much has been made of the steady escalation of construction costs during the time that a given project is delayed. Yet while this item may be a real loss to the project's developer, it is not a loss to society as a whole, for the capital not invested in the delayed project will undoubtedly be invested profitably elsewhere in the economy.

Delay costs vary widely from project to project, but a reasonable estimate of costs borne by the developer probably falls in the range of 0.3 to 0.6 percent of total project costs for each month that the project is delayed. The real resource costs to society are probably closer to 0.1 to 0.2 percent per month.[42]

Perhaps the most serious aspect of delay is the uncertainty it adds to business investment. According to a utility company executive, "In the 1950s it took about three to five years to build a major power plant. We used to study one [site] and make a proposal. Now we must work on three sites and see if one will work."[43]

Most state permit systems attempt to speed up the process by setting maximum time limits for each stage of the process.[44] These are effective only if the time limits allow the permit body enough time to evaluate the application—to send its staff to inspect the site and verify the developer's contentions, to have confusing or incomplete claims amplified, and, in some cases, to work with the developer in redesigning the project. Legislatively specified time limits offer the developer little protection from a permit board bent on securing more time. The board need only threaten to reject the application because of "unresolved problems," and the developer will almost always grant an extension of time.

Tax Issues

Land use controls are inextricably linked to the property tax. Among the possible tax consequences are changes in the affected owner's tax burden, changes in the local revenue base, and shifts of the tax burden to owners of nonregulated properties.

Almost any measure that changes the permitted uses of land will bring calls for a revision of assessments.[45] If a state zoning map classifies a parcel of developable land for agricultural or conservation use, it is only fair that its tax burden should drop accordingly. If the new restrictions on the parcel are reflected in an immediate drop in its value, the usual system of assessment at a percentage of market value will produce a corresponding reduction in tax burden—at least when the land is next assessed.

On the other hand, landowners may believe that classifications can be changed if there is sufficient pressure to develop, much as in the case of current municipal zoning. Then market value would continue to be above agricultural or timber value and taxes would be higher than if the land were taxed on the basis of its permitted use.

This presents a dilemma for tax assessors. They can continue to assess at market value, besieged by complaints from property owners that the assessments are based on uses that are clearly prohibited to them. Or, assessors can use the value of the land in its highest permitted use, even though the market value remains considerably higher. This would give a tax subsidy to any landowner whose land was likely to be reclassified.

State land use laws usually make no explicit reference to the tax consequences of controls (although state assessment laws often list "zoning" as one of the factors an assessor must consider). An exception is Vermont's land use law, which requires that land be assessed on "the use of the land consistent with this act."[46] This provision currently has little effect on assessments, since Act 250 controls now affect only those lands for which an actual project is proposed. It would be much more significant if the land use plan, specifying permitted densities for much of the state, were to be enacted.

When assessments are reduced, local governments have to make up the lost revenue elsewhere. In the long run, one might argue, the increased value of properties where development is permitted should be enough to offset the loss in value for properties where it is restricted. Moreover, the public service burden should be correspondingly less in communities where the amount of development is lower. But despite such possible offsets, loss of tax base is a real worry for local governments, particularly for jurisdictions having large proportions of their total area subject to strict density limits.

As a result, states imposing land use controls may come under pressure to compensate localities for any net loss of tax base. California, New York, and Vermont already have provided for state payments to local governments to make up at least part of the local tax revenues lost under state programs lowering assessments on farms and open-space lands. New York's Adirondack Park Agency Act (1973) contained a requirement that the state's Board of Equalization and Assessment study property tax impacts, but the study, released five years later, proved inconclusive and no compensation program has yet been enacted.[47]

Social Issues

We have seen that land use controls redistribute political power and that they create economic burdens and benefits. The following section deals with the more subjective aspects of these shifts—the equity questions, the effects on different social classes, and the impact on the aspirations of cultural and other minorities.

Limits to Regulation—Law and Fairness

In chapter 1 we discussed land use in terms of conflicts over property rights. On one side of the issue is "society," demanding protection from the negative spillovers that changing land uses might cause and oftentimes staking an additional claim to the positive spillovers that the undeveloped land had long produced. Here "society" might mean an adjoining farmer, concerned with the effects of a development on his activities; a special interest group, such as wildlife fanciers; or a large and representative part of the general public. On the other side we find the landowner, rarely malicious, but determined to claim the "reasonable" uses that ownership has historically conferred on him. Governments, as arbiters of these disputes, are limited in their actions by their constitutional powers and by basic concepts of fairness.

The legal limits of how stringently a city or state can regulate the use of land without paying compensation to the owner are currently in flux. At issue is just how broad an interpretation one should give to the constitutional Fifth Amendment guarantee known as the "taking clause": ". . . nor shall private property be taken for public use without just compensation." Some would argue that the clause goes no farther than to prohibit physical seizure or outright use of property by the government; others claim that it makes a wide range of regulations subject to compensation. Courts in various states have handed down widely varying rulings. The Supreme Court has been of little help in stemming the confusion.[48] A full discussion of the constitutional limits of land use regulation is best left to others.[49] But we might note that the United States has a long tradition of regulating problems that spill over property lines, stretching back to Colonial times and deriving from the practices of Tudor–Stuart England. Nearly all of this regulation is noncompensable, even when it causes considerable loss of land value. In 1915, for example, the U.S. Supreme Court sustained a Los Angeles ordinance that forced the closure of a brick factory whose emissions were causing sickness to occupants of the surrounding residential area. The court was unimpressed by the factory owner's claim that this regulation reduced the value of his land from $800,000 to $60,000.[50]

More recent cases have included several in which courts have recognized that harmful effects may be transmitted through the environment in complex ways. In a Wisconsin case, for example, a landowner was not allowed to fill in his swamp, on the grounds that the swamp served a vital function in the natural environment. The court said that "An owner of land has no absolute and unlimited right to change the essential natural character of his land so as to use it for a purpose for which it was unsuited in its natural state and which injures the rights of others."[51]

During the early 1970s, two influential books suggested that land use regulators may be unduly fearful that their efforts will be invalidated as unconstitutional "takings." Bosselman, Callies, and Banta argued that "Our strongest impression [from a survey of land use problems around the country] is that the fear of the taking issue is stronger than the taking clause itself. It is an American fable or myth that a man can use his land any way he pleases regardless of his neighbors."[52] Similarly, the Rockefeller Brothers Fund's Task Force on Land Use and Urban

Growth maintained that "Ignorance of what higher courts have actually been willing to sustain has created an exaggerated fear that restrictive actions will be declared unconstitutional. Such uncertainty has forestalled countless regulatory actions and induced numerous bad compromises. The popular impression of the takings clause may be even more out of date than some court opinions."[53]

In the presence of so much diversity of opinion in the courts, the idea of legal limits on the state's powers to regulate land use gives us only limited guidance as to how to proceed. We do know that courts look with disfavor on regulations that lack a clear public purpose— they should have some basis in promoting the public's health, safety, or welfare. Moreover, the Fourteenth Amendment requires the "equal protection of law." Farmer Jones should not be allowed to build apartments while Farmer Smith's identical property is designated as open space. Both the Fifth and the Fourteenth amendments require "due process," guaranteeing procedural standards that have been given considerable amplification by the courts, and protecting the landowner from "arbitrary" or "capricious" behavior by regulating authorities. Finally, the government may neither appropriate private land for its own use without full compensation nor regulate so strictly that the owner is left with no reasonable use of his property. But beyond these precepts, and until the courts say differently, we might well rely on our own standards of what is reasonable and fair.

Reasonable observers have come to strikingly different conclusions, depending on the balance they wish to strike between the rights of landowners and the rights of "society." The aforementioned task force argued that, because modern society is so vulnerable to the adverse and unforeseen consequences of development, "It is time that the U.S. Supreme Court . . . declare that when the protection of natural, cultural, or aesthetic resources or the assurance of orderly development are involved, a mere loss in land value will never be justification for invalidating the regulation of land use."[54] Arguing that the impact on the landowner should be emphasized, the minority report of the House Interior Committee on the 1974 Federal Land Use Planning Act claimed, it is not fair "that the burden for providing the presumed welfare of others should be borne by the owners of only those properties used for public purposes. The accident of ownership and location would select those persons in society to carry the burden of paying for benefits that will accrue to others. It amounts to a rather crude way of redistributing wealth on a most unfair and irrational basis."[55]

Others have suggested that there may be some reasonable middle ground, taking the position that when regulation in the public interest reduces the potential value of private property, the landowner be given partial compensation, even though a judicial "taking" did not occur. Costonis, for example, has argued for a concept of "fair compensation" that would "serve as an intermediary between the police power's absence of compensation and the eminent domain power's requirement of 'just compensation'."[56] Similarly, Hagman and Misczynski note that government actions create land values (by transportation improvements for example) as well as reduce them. They suggest that these "windfalls" be partially taxed away and the revenue used to partially compensate those unfavorably affected by land use controls or other government actions.[57]

One way of making our own value judgment is to consider the kinds of spillovers that various land uses produce. We might envision a continuum of spillovers or externalities that are created when the use of a piece of land is changed. Toward one side of this continuum, we find the direct negative spillovers—the nuisances. Few would argue that one should have the right to introduce a pig farm or a machine shop into a quiet residential neighborhood.[58] Far to the other, or positive side, would be the confiscation or takeover of private land for public use. Much as society could benefit from using land owned by its individual members, there is general agreement that the needed land should be purchased rather than confiscated.

Away from these extremes, cases become more arguable. Negative effects may be indirect and difficult to assign to a parcel of land. Development of stream valleys, for example, tends to increase downstream flood dangers. But it is virtually impossible to measure the marginal increase in flooding attributable to a single upstream development, even if the development is large. Efforts to regulate such indirect effects can easily become discriminatory. For example, every time a piece of land is urbanized, a little more wildlife habitat is lost. Should we penalize the landowner for imposing this cost on society? Should we differentiate between urbanizing one acre and urbanizing one hundred? Should we distinguish between owners of land that harbors only mice and squirrels and those whose land happens to be the haunt of the whooping crane or the Florida panther?

Some spillovers are visual rather than physical. Erecting a billboard might be offensive to society; so might be building an "ugly" house or painting a store an eccentric color. We can regard these as negative spillovers but should note that the courts have usually been less sympathetic to efforts to regulate them than they have to claims of physical invasion or damage. "Most courts," writes L. L. Leighty, "have been very reluctant to impose restraints on property interests merely on the basis of aesthetic considerations. This reluctance is based on a strong policy in favor of allowing the fullest possible beneficial use and enjoyment of real property and upon the belief . . . that beauty is a matter of individual taste."[59]

Continuing toward the positive end of the continuum, consider the case of a landowner who wishes to erect homes on a piece of land long considered part of a community's open space. (As we have seen, this has been a recurring situation along the California coast.) Assuming that only visual quality is at issue, the local population might feel that the new homes were not themselves unesthetic, but that they were nevertheless much less desirable than the open fields that were there before. Should we conclude that, by keeping his land undeveloped for so long, the owner had given the community a permanent right to this positive spillover? And would it matter if the land's original beauty was due to its natural state or to its use in farming or managed forestry?

Another kind of positive spillover is that afforded by structures of architectural or historic significance. A number of these have been lost forever. Others are under intense economic pressure. The roster of those destroyed already includes distinguished individual structures such as New York's Pennsylvania Station and Chicago's Old Stock Exchange, and the many less celebrated blocks and neighborhoods that have lent character and distinctiveness to our older cities. Many would consider it unfair to require the owner to continue to provide this amenity to the public if it becomes unprofitable to do so. (Some might argue, though, that many landmark buildings are not *un*profitable, but merely *less* profitable than alternative uses of the land.[60]) The question is complicated by the presence of discrimination: why should the owner of a distinguished building be prevented from maximizing his profits while the owner of a more ordinary structure is not? Over the long run, such discrimination might even discourage the construction of distinguished buildings, for owners would feel that they would never be allowed to alter or demolish them.

Finally, we find cases in which society requires the landowner to provide some *new* positive spillover. A state might, for example, decide that owners of beaches or timberlands should provide access for public recreation.[61] Setback requirements and esthetic standards might be included here, as well, although these frequently are complicated by an implicit compensatory mechanism (I'll put a tile roof on my house if you, my neighbor, do the same).

We might wish to use this continuum to differentiate cases where regulation alone is "fair" from those in which government should be expected to pay compensation.[62] One might say simply that a landowner should be required to get society's permission to impose a negative spillover, but may terminate a positive one at his discretion. Alternatively, we might allow existing negative spillovers, but not new ones. This is the rationale behind the "preexisting use" provision of most zoning codes, which allows existing nonconforming uses to continue but not to expand.[63]

This simple positive–negative distinction leaves the landowner with considerable discretion, including the power to do great environmental damage, so long as its effects are confined to his own land. It is also difficult to draw a distinct line between the positive and the negative. Is the owner of a Florida wetland, for example, creating a negative spillover when he fills it, or terminating a positive one? A solution might be to consider natural systems as a permanent part of the public domain with the private landowner as caretaker and the government as trustee. Any positive spillover that these natural systems create would have to be maintained, except in cases in which society decided otherwise. Manmade spillovers, such as those afforded by the architectural landmark, would be considered private property—those generated by natural systems would not.

We might posit a concept of public trust similar to that expressed in the constitutions of several states having "environmental bills of rights." As Pennsylvania's constitution, for example, declares: "The people have a right to clean air, pure water, and to the preservation of the natural, scenic, historic and esthetic values of the environment. Pennsylvania's public natural resources are the common property of all the people including generations yet to come. As a trustee of these resources, the Commonwealth shall conserve and maintain them for the benefit of all the people."[64] In Massachusetts, the constitution states that "The people shall have the right to clean air and water, freedom from excessive and unnecessary noise, and the natural, scenic, historic, and esthetic qualities of their environment; and the protection of the people in their right to the conservation, development and utilization of the agricultural, mineral, forest, water, air and other natural resources is hereby declared to be a public purpose."[65]

As private individuals come increasingly to stake claims to these resources, governments may be expected to assert the prior claim of society as a whole. Our own value judgment about the ownership of these rights will depend on several considerations. Do individual owners of scarce environmental resources have a duty to preserve them unchanged for future generations? Does the fact that a landowner thinks he has paid for these rights mean that he is entitled to them? Does the fact that he has paid taxes on the land's development value make a difference? In the end, law and economics can only structure the argument, they cannot decide it. Analysis such as we have presented above cannot tell us "what is fair." It can only help us to apply our own values in an internally consistent way.

Elitism and Discrimination

In addition to affecting landowners, land use controls produce costs and benefits for other subgroups. A recurrent charge is that controls are elitist, ensuring a quality environment for those who can afford it and denying opportunities to those who cannot.[66] We have seen that controls—whether by restricting where development can locate, reducing its density, or mandating minimum standards of quality—quite frequently result in costs that are passed on to the consumer.

One argument is that controls limit housing opportunities, particularly for the poor. Recent increases in housing prices have pointed up the difficulty that many Americans have in achieving their personal housing goals, whether it is the middle-class desire for a single-family house in a pleasant neighborhood or the welfare family's simple aspiration to decent shelter.

Cost increases caused by land use controls have their most direct impact on consumers of so-called threshold housing, the cheapest new housing available without government subsidy. Purchased by those earning perhaps $12,000 to $20,000 a year, these units are usually built on cheap land at the very edge of the urban area or at higher than average density, or both. Buffeted by soaring construction costs, high interest rates, and speculative increases in land prices, this large group of consumers is likely to resent being asked to absorb the additional costs of environmental improvement.

It is not unlikely that many in the threshold group will see land planning as something imposed on them by a high-income, conservation-minded elite. As a popular magazine put it, conservationists "are not steelworkers or assemblyline workers or small farmers or hotel clerks.

They are Wall Street lawyers and junior faculty and editors and writers and corporate vice-presidents. . . . Searching for their hundred-fifty-year-old Vermont farmhouses, conservationists wonder how people can actually want to live in a new $25,000 split-level in the suburbs, apparently never thinking that for most people the alternative is a three-room walk-up in the downtown smog."[67]

Consider, for example, the case of a Miami policeman, who lives with his wife and children in a "double-wide" housetrailer on one of the upper Florida Keys. The trailer park where he lives is unsightly when viewed from the adjoining highway; the artificial waterways that criss-cross it are polluted; the policeman's long commute to work is wasteful of energy. It was consideration of what this very kind of development was doing to the unique environment of the keys that caused that chain of tropical islands to be nominated as an area of critical state concern.

The policeman is aware of this argument, but has an additional perception of his surroundings—as a place where he can find housing at moderate cost; as an environment with clean air and a nearby ocean; as a safe place to raise his family. Clearly there is a social gain that balances some of the environmental damage, although perhaps not enough to offset it. Given a choice between additional trailer parks and public open space, we might choose the latter. Too often, however, the alternative is a more expensive, no less intense, kind of development, producing fewer environmental problems, but catering to a much narrower segment of society.

The case of the poor is somewhat more complex. They are unable to purchase new housing on the private market, whether the minimum price is $25,000 or $40,000. A few of the poor, in fact, may benefit from land use controls that place artificial limits on the supply of new housing, for this could lead to nonmarket allocation of new housing sites. Indeed, communities such as Ramapo, New York, and Fairfax County, Virginia, have coupled their growth controls with measures to increase the local supply of subsidized housing. But the rest of the poor probably are left worse off than before, as reductions in the production of new housing interfere with the filtering process, by which lower-income groups inherit units formerly occupied by those higher up on the income ladder.

Land use controls with a strong antihousing bias are unlikely to survive in a society in which such a large proportion of the population is at or below the "threshold housing" level. Controls seem by their very nature to raise private housing costs—if they did otherwise, they would have been adopted by profit-seeking developers without the need for legislation. But, as we will detail in chapter 8, pro-housing features can be included at the same time that environmental restrictions are imposed. There are so many opportunities for improving the operation of an imperfectly functioning land market that pro-housing policies should easily be able to offset the costs of stiff environmental controls—provided that we have the foresight to include them.

A virtually unrecognized area of potential intergroup conflict is the effect of land use controls on the distribution of recreational opportunities. The proposition that everyone is entitled to "a cottage at the lake" (or its equivalent) is, of course, far less defensible than the basic right to decent housing. A federal court has already drawn this distinction, allowing a New Hampshire town to slash the density of a second-home project by imposing minimum lot sizes of 3 to 6 acres. The court claimed that previous cases in which suburbs were not permitted to require such large lots were irrelevant to a project "which does not seek to satisfy an already existing demand for suburban expansion, but rather seeks to create a demand . . . on behalf of wealthy residents of Megalopolis. . . ."[68]

But it is not difficult to imagine a time when recreational activities formerly considered luxuries will become the reasonable expectation of large portions of the population. A good example of this kind of progression is the history of the paid vacation, a luxury early in this century but now an accepted part of nearly all labor contracts. As social chronicler Stephen Birmingham puts it, "I think it started when Frank, the fresh-faced young man who delivers milk to our house on alternate days (I have never, alas, troubled to learn Frank's last name) announced that we would be having a substitute milkman for the next three weeks. He was taking his family on a skiing holiday to Val d'Isere. 'Oh,' I said. 'That sounds very nice.' I had never been to Val d'Isere."[69] More and more Americans are looking forward to—and learning to expect— weekends at a beach house, excursions on the family boat, a vacation at a golf or a tennis resort, a "wilderness experience," and eventual retirement to a warm and pleasant place.

Many of these activities require very scarce amenity resources. While we have enough suitable land to accommodate almost any conceivable level of housing demand, the supply of many recreation amenities is rather small. Oceanfront homesites, for example, are already under pressure, with prices rising out of reach of all but the rich. Places with highly desired combinations of amenities, such as Martha's Vineyard,

Massachusetts; the Florida Keys; and Aspen, Colorado, have experienced both steeply rising land prices and movements to limit new growth.

It is well known that overuse tends to destroy amenity resources, that various forms of recreation conflict with one another, and that many activities do grave damage to natural systems. But if state land use policies are introduced to prevent these excesses, how is use of the amenity to be rationed? In the absence of policies to prevent it, it is likely that the resources will become the property of those who happened to get there first, and of the affluent few who can afford to buy in at the new, higher price. The practice of renting second homes to other users, if widespread, would allow more people to use amenity resources, but this alternative is still limited to the relatively affluent. Undoubtedly, far fewer persons can be so accommodated compared with a situation in which commercial development of the resource was allowed.

No state policy can completely counter such maldistribution. Indeed, our society may not want to, for it has historically tolerated a fairly high degree of inequality in both income and wealth. But land planners might at least encourage a more equal distribution of amenity resources by implementing a few broad policies, which will be discussed further in chapter 8.

We have mentioned earlier in this chapter that land use controls can affect the economic prospects of different social subgroups. Intergroup conflict may arise between those whose livelihood depends on local growth and those who are indifferent to growth or actually harmed by it. Land developers and construction workers are not the only local people with a vested interest in growth. Operators of service establishments, shopkeepers, newspaper publishers, bankers, and insurance salesmen are only a few of those who might capitalize on the opportunities that new population brings. Opposed to them might be retirees and others on fixed incomes, who see growth in terms of higher taxes and higher prices rather than economic opportunities.[70] They might be joined by farmers, who fear higher property taxes and restrictions on their production methods, and by teachers and other professionals who are insulated from the vagaries of the local economy.

Sometimes, even the direct benefits of growth are not so great as they first appear. Construction jobs, although high paying, are seasonal and cyclical, and often go not to local workers but to workers from outside the area. Jobs generated by resorts or by second-home developments are low wage and seasonal and offer little opportunity for advancement.

An important task for future research in land planning is to determine just who does gain by growth, and how.

A particularly difficult intergroup conflict is that arising between the long-time resident and the newcomer. The latter may be of a different age group or a different social and cultural background and have different values and aspirations. Resentment of such "outsiders" is particularly noticeable in Maine, Vermont, and rural Oregon and Colorado—places with a strong indigenous culture that have experienced rapid growth through in-migration or tourism.

The desire to keep things as they are is understandable, but it conflicts with the equally understandable desire of others for social and geographic mobility.

As Boyd Gibbons put it, in describing a classic land use conflict on Maryland's Eastern Shore,

> The line between insiders and outsiders, between the excluders and the excluded, is a fluid one at best. And the rules by which people should be permitted to close off their communities to others are yet to be decided. Pitted in opposition are two fundamental prerogatives that Americans rightly cherish: to keep one's neighborhood familiar and unchanging, and to improve one's life by moving on. The resolution of these conflicts, therefore, is less a matter of determining natural and physical limits of the environment than it is a balancing of human aspirations and values.[71]

Unfortunately, even the most astute and sensitive planning will not be able to make *everyone* at least as well off as before. Some will gain and others lose, whether by unchecked development or by carefully conceived land policies.

Notes

1. The value of all land in the United States has been estimated (1975) at $1,285 billion, or 23 percent of the country's total tangible assets. Of this, $336 billion is privately owned farmland; $706 billion is private nonfarm land; and $243 billion is public land. The estimated value of structures is an additional $2,555 billion, or 46 percent of assets. John W. Kendrick, with Kyu Sik Lee and Jean Lomask, *The National Wealth of the United States, by Major Sector and Industry*. Table reproduced in *Statistical Abstract of the United States* (Washington, D.C., GPO, 1976) p. 428. An anthropological analysis of people's complex feelings about land may be found in Constance Perin, *Everything in its Place: Social Order and Land Use in America* (Princeton, N.J., Princeton University Press, 1977).

2. Minority view, U.S. Congress, House Committee on Interior and Insular Affairs, *Land Use Planning Act of 1974*, H. Rep. 10294, 93 Cong. 2 sess. (1974) p. 104.

3. In describing the somewhat weakened version of the coastal area management bill passed by the 1974 North Carolina legislature, one coastal legislator claimed,

"This is a terrible bill. People tell me . . . that when the people come *to take their land away* you can call the undertaker because they're going to leave them right there in the field." Raleigh (N.C.) *News and Observer,* April 9, 1974.

4. Raleigh (N.C.) *News and Observer,* Feb. 1, 1974.

5. Testimony of Idamae Garrott, chairman, Metropolitan Washington Council of Governments Land Use Policy Committee before the Maryland legislature, March 1974.

6. Washington *Post,* Mar. 21, 1973.

7. Jens Sorensen, *State-Local Collaborative Planning: A Growing Trend in Coastal Zone Management* (Washington, D.C., U.S. Office of Coastal Zone Management, pre-publication draft, 1978) pp. 2–7.

8. Nelson Rosenbaum, *Citizen Participation in Environmental Planning: The Quest for Community Consensus* (Washington, D.C., Urban Institute, forthcoming 1979).

9. Thomas Salmon, "Vermont: Public Support for Land Use Controls," *State Government* (Summer 1973), p. 197.

10. Rutland (Vt.) *Daily Herald,* July 26, 1973.

11. William J. Duddleson, "How California Citizens Secured Their Coastal Management Program," in Robert G. Healy, ed., *Protecting the Golden Shore* (Washington, D.C., Conservation Foundation, 1978) pp. 3–64.

12. In one suit brought under the California law, a twenty-five-year-old pottery instructor and ardent surfer—whose personal assets totaled $2,500—got the courts to halt construction on a $5 million oceanfront condominium. Resolution of his suit was expected to take one to three months, during which time no construction could take place. *Los Angeles Times,* June 12, 1973.

13. California Coastal Commission, agenda for meeting of November 28–29, 1978. An additional fifteen permits were appealed by applicants dissatisfied with regional denials or stringent conditions.

14. Oregon Land Conservation and Development Commission, *LCDC Facts,* pamphlet, n.d., p. 7.

15. Nelson Rosenbaum, *Citizen Involvement in Land Use Governance: Issues and Methods* (Washington, D.C., Urban Institute, 1976).

16. Rosenbaum, *Citizen Participation in Environmental Planning.* Overall, three of the four programs studied seemed to satisfy the majority of those who participated. Asked, "Were affected citizens provided with enough opportunities to express their preferences to the decision makers?" 61 percent of respondents in Oregon, 60 percent in California, 56 percent in Hawaii, and 44 percent in North Carolina replied affirmatively.

17. W. R. Derrick Sewell and J. T. Coppock, eds., *Public Participation in Planning* (London and New York, Wiley, 1977) p. 9.

18. Washington *Post.*

19. One of Peterson's favorite political slogans was, "To hell with Shell," referring to a proposed coastal oil refinery. His electoral defeat in 1972 is commonly attributed to factors other than his stand on environmental protection.

20. *Land Use Planning Reports,* Nov. 13, 1978. One small piece of evidence that state land use policy retains political support in places where it has been already adopted comes from Florida. In late 1978, when the Florida Supreme Court struck down the state's critical area designations, nearly every large newspaper in the state called editorially for a special legislative session to protect the critical areas. See Orlando *Sentinel–Star,* Nov. 26, 1978; Tampa *Tribune,* Nov. 28, 1978; Miami *Herald* and Saint Petersburg *Times,* Nov. 30, 1978.

21. Lawrence W. Libby, "Comprehensive Land Use Planning and Other Myths," *Journal of Soil and Water Conservation* vol. 29, no. 3 (1974), p. 106.

22. Frank Popper, in "The Politics of Land Use Reform," draft manuscript prepared with the support of the Twentieth Century Fund, ch. 5.

23. Vermont Natural Resources Council, Environmental Planning Information Center, "Vermonters on Vermont" (Montpelier, VNRC, 1972).

24. Traditional local planning and zoning, with its visible failures and frequent hints of corruption, seems to be in some disrepute among the public. A nationwide Gallup poll taken in 1973 found that 55 percent of those polled believed their community was doing only a fair or a poor job of planning for future growth. Washington *Post*, Sept. 17, 1973.

25. California Coastal Act, sect. 30401.

26. *Los Angeles Times*, April 16, 1974.

27. California Coastal Zone Conservation Commission, Appeal 49–74, June 5, 1974.

28. John S. Banta, "The Coastal Commissions and State Agencies: Conflict and Cooperation," in Healy, ed., *Protecting the Golden Shore*, pp. 97–131.

29. See Fred Bosselman, Duane Feurer, and Charles Siemon, *The Permit Explosion: Coordination of the Proliferation* (Washington, D.C., Urban Land Institute, 1976); Robert G. Healy, "Coordination: The Next Phase in Land Use Planning," *Journal of Soil and Water Conservation* vol. 31, no. 4 (July–August 1976); John H. Noble, John S. Banta, and John S. Rosenberg, *Groping Through the Maze: Foreign Experience Applied to the U.S. Problem of Coordinating Development Controls* (Washington, D.C., Conservation Foundation, 1977).

30. Only recently have economists been turning serious attention to actually measuring the impacts of controls. To date, one must choose between rather descriptive studies of broad impacts and more rigorous studies of narrow ones (for example, costs of compliance or delay). For examples of the former see Robert G. Healy, "An Economic Interpretation of the California Coastal Commissions," in *Protecting the Golden Shore*, pp. 133–175; and Urban Land Institute, *The Economic Benefits of Coastal Zone Management* (Washington, D.C., Urban Land Institute, 1976). For an example of the latter, see Dan K. Richardson, *The Cost of Environmental Protection: Regulating Housing Development in the Coastal Zone* (New Brunswick, N.J., Center for Urban Policy Research, 1976). The best survey of current literature is Robert Kneisel, *Economic Impacts of Land Use Control: The California Coastal Zone Conservation Commission* (Davis, Calif., University of California Institute of Governmental Affairs, 1979).

31. So rapid has been Hawaii's growth that its current governor has made controlling population growth his top priority. In order to keep the state's population at about one million, he has suggested laws favoring long-time residents in public and private jobs and a higher tax structure for recent immigrants. Economic growth has also been vigorous, with gross state product up fivefold between 1959 and 1978. *The New York Times*, Dec. 3, 1978, and Jan. 21, 1979.

32. Lewis F. Holding, quoted in Raleigh (N.C.) *News and Observer*, March 12, 1974.

33. J. Paul Jones, senior vice-president of Valley National Bank of Arizona, quoted in the *Wall Street Journal*, Dec. 28, 1977.

34. In fact, the publicity which has often attended the attempts of states and cities to limit their growth may generate even more growth, as people try to be the "last one in before the door closes." In the year following Boca Raton, Florida's "growth cap," which would limit the eventual size of the city to about 100,000, the city's population surged from 32,000 to 45,000. Said a local builder, "It's a sellers' market in this city, not a buyer's market—a guy selling chicken coops can make a killing." Saint Petersburg (Fla.) *Times*, Nov. 11, 1973.

35. We do have some evidence from studies of the price effects of local zoning laws. A survey found that in six studies of that relationship there was "a weak to moderate, but uniformly positive, relationship between single family housing costs and zoning controls in metropolitan areas." Edward Bergman et al. *External Validity of Policy Related Research on Development Controls and Housing Costs* (Chapel Hill, University of North Carolina Center for Urban and Regional Studies, 1974) p. 196. A study of land values in Fairfax County, Virginia, found land prices "highly sensitive" to zoning classification. At close-in locations, the study found, lots zoned for ten units per acre sold at prices almost seven times as great as similar lots zoned for one unit per acre. George E. Peterson, "Land Prices and Factor Substitu-

tion in the Metropolitan Housing Market" (Washington, D.C., Urban Institute, 1974), Working Paper 0875-02-01.

36. See for example the results of a 1975 survey of assessors in fourteen of California's fifteen coastal counties, which is summarized in Healy, "An Economic Interpretation," in *Protecting the Golden Shore,* pp. 164–167.

Frech and Lafferty, however, using data for the coastal city of Oxnard, California, found that between 1971–75 prices of developed residential sites in the coastal permit zone rose *less* rapidly than did developed sites inland. H. E. Frech, III and Ronald Lafferty, "The Economic Impact of the California Coastal Plan: Land Use and Land Values," in *The California Coastal Plan: A Critique* (San Francisco, Institute for Contemporary Studies, 1976). Robert Kneisel of the University of California, Riverside, is currently studying appreciation rates for a much larger sample of single-family homes in the coastal region of Los Angeles County. Robert Anderson of the Environmental Law Institute is studying rates of land price change in the Adirondacks before and after implementation of the Adirondack Park Agency Act.

37. Philip Watson, quoted in *Coastline Letter,* no. 14 (Sept. 1973).

38. Interview with Edmund Harvey, Delaware Wild Lands, Wilmington, February 1974. The continued presence of some speculative value may reflect not only unrealistic expectations, but the possibility that some future legislature may modify the law.

39. Letter of Richard Pollock to Phyllis Myers, July 15, 1974.

40. See Bergman, *External Validity,* pp. 60–63. This upgrading of the entire package can go on only if there is a market for higher-priced units. There is evidence that builders may be overestimating the capacity of this segment of the market to absorb their products. We should also note that, over a long time period, builders have reacted to the steady relative increase in raw land prices by allowing the ratio of land value to package price to rise.

41. The landowner does temporarily lose the use of his equity in the land, although that is not an out-of-pocket expense.

42. See Healy, "An Economic Interpretation," pp. 171–173. A somewhat lower estimate may be found in Franklin James and Thomas Muller, "Environmental Impact Evaluation, Land Use Planning and the Housing Consumer," *Journal of the American Real Estate and Urban Economics Association,* vol. 3, no. 5 (Fall 1977).

43. Nolan Daines, vice-president of Pacific Gas and Electric, quoted in the San Diego *Union,* Jan. 14, 1979.

44. California's A.B. 884 (1978) is a unique attempt to both coordinate and expedite state permit issuance. It provides that *all* state permit requirements may not delay a project more than eighteen months.

45. For example, four years after New Jersey passed its wetlands protection act, the *Wall Street Journal* editorialized, ". . . owners of some 320,000 acres of wetlands are asking for big cuts in their taxes on grounds that it is almost impossible to get state permits to use the land for any purpose at all . . . the message is clear: However desirable the objectives, land use regulation can never be as simple as it might seem at first. Any resulting diminution of real value will have to be borne by the owner at first, perhaps, but eventually the public will most likely pay as well." *Wall Street Journal,* Sept. 18, 1974. Similarly, when Collier County, Florida, reclassified thousands of acres of wetlands as a low-density "special treatment zone" the county assessor cut their value for tax purposes from $20,000 an acre to $1,500, reducing the county's tax base by more than $15 million. Telephone conversation with Neno Spagna, county planner, July 25, 1975.

46. Vermont Land Capability and Development Plan (1973), § 7(a)(14).

47. See Ann Purdue, "The APA Act: Land Use Regulations and the Real Property Tax," *Albany Law Review* vol. 42, no. 4 (Summer 1978).

48. In June 1978, the Supreme Court ruled that New York City's restrictions limiting redevelopment of historic Grand Central Terminal did not amount to a taking. *Penn Central Transportation Company* v. *City of New York,* 46 U.S.L.W. 4856, 30 Z.D. 434. Land use attorneys disagree over the implications of the case,

some calling it a landmark taking issue decision, others maintaining that it circumvented important issues. See discussion in *Land Use Law and Zoning Digest* vol. 30, no. 9 (1978).

49. The interested reader will find excellent discussions of this issue in Jon Kusler, "Open Space Zoning: Valid Regulation or Invalid Taking," *Minnesota Law Review* vol. 57, no. 1 (November 1972), pp. 1–82; in Fred Bosselman, David Callies, and John Banta, *The Taking Issue* (Washington, D.C., GPO, 1973); and in "Developments in the Law—Zoning," *Harvard Law Review* vol. 91, no. 7 (May 1978) pp. 1427–1708.

50. *Hadacheck v. Sebastian* 239 U.S. 394 (1915).

51. *Just v. Marinette Co.* 201 N.W. 2d 761 (1972).

52. Bosselman, Callies, and Banta, *The Taking Issue,* pp. 318–319.

53. Task Force on Land Use and Urban Growth, *The Use of Land* (New York, Crowell, 1973), pp. 147–148.

54. Ibid.

55. U.S. Congress, House Committee on Interior and Insular Affairs, *Land Use Planning Act of 1974,* p. 76.

56. John J. Costonis, "Fair Compensation and the Accommodation Power: Antidotes for the Taking Impasse in Land Use Controversies," *Columbia Law Review* vol. 75, no. 6 (Oct. 1975) pp. 1021–1082.

57. Donald Hagman and Dean Misczynski, *Windfalls for Wipeouts* (Chicago, American Society of Planning Officials, 1977).

58. Rather than banning the use outright, however, we might allow the intruder to strike a deal with the neighbors to compensate them for their loss of amenity. See Ronald Coase, "The Problem of Social Cost," *Journal of Law and Economics* vol. 3 (October 1960).

59. Leighty, "Aesthetics as a Legal Basis for Environmental Control," *Wayne Law Review* vol. 17 (1971) p. 1347.

60. The economics of reusing old buildings is discussed in John J. Costonis, *Space Adrift* (Urbana, University of Illinois Press, 1974). In the Grand Central case (see note 48 above), the Supreme Court noted that the company owning the historic terminal could still obtain a "reasonable return" on its investment.

61. We should distinguish this case from those in which, as with Oregon's beaches, the state intervenes to ensure the continued enjoyment of a "customary" right long exercised by its citizens.

62. Such compensation need not be a cash payment. Payment "in kind" may be arranged through the ingenious device of transferrable development rights, discussed in chapter 8.

63. An interesting problem here is how to treat activities that are "nuisances" simply because over time they have been surrounded by more recent developments. This has long been a problem for airports, gravel pits, and fringe-area farmers, who begin to face controls on noise and dust as residential growth spreads toward them. In these cases, courts have tended to consider the nature of the spillover as well as the question of precedence in time.

64. Art. I, § 27 of Pennsylvania's constitution; cited in Richard J. Tobin, "Some Observations on the Use of State Constitutions to Protect the Environment," *Environmental Affairs* vol. 3, no. 3 (1974).

65. Article 97 of Amendments to the Massachusetts constitution. Cited in Tobin, "Some Observations."

66. General accusations that environmental restrictions hurt the disadvantaged may be found in Richard Neuhaus, *In Defense of People* (New York, Macmillan, 1971); and in Peter Passell and Leonard Ross, *The Retreat from Riches* (New York, Viking Press, 1973). They make little mention of land controls per se, probably because the cost impact of such controls is not yet so well recognized as are those of other environmental laws. For specific indictments of land use controls, see Richard Babcock and David Callies, "Ecology and Housing: Virtues in Conflict," in Marion Clawson, ed. *Modernizing Urban Land Policy* (Baltimore, Md., Johns Hop-

kins University Press for Resources for the Future, 1973); and Bernard J. Frieden, *The Environmental Protection Hustle* (Cambridge, Mass., MIT Press, 1978).

67. Jon Margolis, "Land of Ecology," *Esquire* (March 1970), quoted in Babcock and Callies, "Ecology and Housing," p. 215.

68. *Steel Hill Development, Inc. v. Town of Sanbornton,* 469 F.2d 956 (1972).

69. Birmingham, *The Right Places (for the Right People)* (Boston, Little, Brown, 1973), p. 3.

70. Already, in some small Florida counties, retirees are so numerous that they have caused county governments that would otherwise have welcomed growth to adopt an antigrowth posture. Interview with Dr. John DeGrove, FAU–FIU Joint Center for Urban and Environmental Studies, Fort Lauderdale, June 1974.

71. Boyd Gibbons, *Wye Island: Outsiders, Insiders, and Resistance to Change* (Baltimore, Johns Hopkins University Press for Resources for the Future, 1977) p. 227.

CHAPTER EIGHT

Toward New Policies for the States

LAND USE PLANNING is not a new idea. If one looks at discussions of the land use issues of ten, twenty, or even thirty years ago, one is struck by the similarity of both problems and solutions to those of the present day. But two very basic things have changed. First, actual implementation of land use controls is for the first time moving from its traditional place in local government into the purview of regional and state bodies. Second, planning practice is catching up to planning theory. Imaginative types of controls, discussed by planners for decades, are actually being put into effect by governments. Planners, long accustomed to preparing policy documents that they knew would never be implemented, are being taken seriously by decision makers. It is a sobering experience.

This country's experience with state land use policies is still quite brief. We have pointed out the strengths and weaknesses of the approaches that have been tried (or given consideration) by one or more states and have discussed some major issues that have arisen in their implementation. To date, no single state has enacted a truly comprehensive system of controls. Indeed, the legislative climate in most states appears more favorable to incrementalism in planning than it is to sweeping, uniform solutions.

Therefore, looking to the future of land use and the states, we should consider a far wider range of policies than any individual state has yet adopted. In this final chapter we will set tentative criteria for judging new policies by adding to some widely accepted political and social concepts the knowledge we have gained from preparing the case studies and interviewing the regulators and the regulated. Then we will describe our own vision of what a comprehensive land policy might include.

Criteria for Better Land Policies

Power over land use should be lodged with the level of government appropriate to the problem. This is a seeming truism, but failure to put it into practice has been one of the principal reasons for our dissatisfaction with the results of fifty years of local land use planning and control. As we pointed out in chapter 1, there is a surprisingly large number of cases in which even the most honest, competent, and well-intended local land use program can produce unsatisfactory results. These include cases where development has interjurisdictional spillovers; cases in which local and regional interests diverge; and cases in which the principal policy levers are simply beyond the grasp of the local authorities.

Unfortunately, the often dismal record of local government in doing even what it *could* be expected to do has obscured its inherent strengths and its inherent weaknesses.[1] This record has caused some to believe that local governments in their states are so unresponsive to environmental problems that direct state control is the only answer. This is a short-sighted position. Large centralized agencies, which may indeed begin with brave purposes and enthusiastic staffs, can easily fall into a complacent middle age. The record of state and federal regulatory agencies and licensing boards outside the land use field offers many examples too familiar to repeat. While local officials may be removed in a single electoral sweep, centralized, nonelective agencies are effectively insulated against the demands of the citizens. Tempting as it might be to replace all of those "good ol' boys" down at the county courthouse with a bright and professional state agency, one should pause to consider the situation five or ten years hence.

Let us review the strengths and weaknesses of three alternative levels of government, local (city and county), regional (substate), and state, disregarding the quality of those currently holding power in each.

Local government is the most accessible, at least in the physical sense. It is far easier for a citizen to attend a weekly meeting of a board of supervisors or a planning commission in his home town than to go to Sacramento or Albany to present his position. Developers, on the other hand, can afford to hire lawyers and planners to argue for them, regardless of where the decision is made. Local government has easy access to information on local problems and local attitudes. As one writer puts it, "The [local] planner or planning commissioner riding around in a station wagon can quickly become the world's expert on what is happening to [critical areas] in his community. He knows the social forces by name and what is happening to them from season to season. He has an experiential expertise and an administrative closeness that is impossible to duplicate at other levels of government."[2] Finally, local officials are exposed to local election campaigns, where volunteer labor and community opinion count more than the size of a campaign war chest.

On the negative side, local governments are often too small to afford the professional talent needed to do a good job of planning. Moreover, as we have shown again and again, they have little incentive to pursue other than local goals. Too frequently, they monopolize the benefits of development, while sharing the costs with the rest of society.

Regional control is a tempting alternative, but currently the institutions through which to exercise it do not exist. Florida's experience with the review of developments of regional impact has shown the weakness of regional bodies that have no independent political base. With few exceptions, the regional institutions that now exist in this country are "councils of governments," made up of local government officials who show an understandable tendency to be most responsive to their individual local constituencies. There is little likelihood that these councils would be more effective in protecting regionwide interests in land use than they have been in ensuring regional investment coordination through their existing A-95 review power. Elected, multipurpose regional government, on the other hand, would be ideal for implementing land use policy, but it exists in only a handful of places and shows few signs of rapid spread.

There is much to be said, however, for using county governments as a means of unifying the land use activities of city and township units. A step toward this is North Carolina's 1974 Coastal Area Management Act, which puts considerable plan-making power in the hands of county, rather than city officials, if the city involved had previously failed to enforce zoning and subdivision controls. Similarly, Florida's 1975 Local Government Comprehensive Planning Act provides an opportunity for counties to comment on city comprehensive plans. Much of our discussion of the split of power between state and local governments can easily be applied to a similar division between county and town or city authorities, at least in those states in which counties are viable units of government.

State government can take a comprehensive view of land uses, balancing the need of one subregion for jobs with the need of another subregion for recreation. It can back up its plans with formidable dollar investments in highways, schools, and irrigation facilities and can coordinate land use with social and economic policies. States can afford to hire large and capable planning staffs. The major actions of state government are usually well publicized and under the scrutiny of organized citizens' groups and of the press.

Among the disadvantages of state control are its physical distance from the citizenry, its difficulty in gathering and assessing data on local problems, its tendency to bureaucracy, and the large amounts of money needed to wage statewide election campaigns.

On balance, there are strong arguments for local governments to continue to make the vast majority of land use decisions.[3] Indeed, state government should strengthen local effectiveness by financial support, by sharing its technical expertise, and by publishing long-range plans for state investment. But we strongly believe—and the experience of several states has confirmed—that there are a number of major decisions in which the state must intervene to protect nonlocal interests.

The state should regulate the following types of uses and types of land:

1. *Areas of critical state concern*—places that have scenic, historic, or environmental value of more than local concern
2. *Developments of regional impact*—developments that because of their size or location produce spillovers affecting more than one locality
3. *Developments of regional benefit*—projects, including power plants, landfills, and low-income housing, that are shunned by localities but produce significant benefits for larger areas
4. *Unregulated areas*—places where local government has not yet instituted planning, zoning, and subdivision controls. Here state intervention should be only temporary, pending local adoption of such controls
5. *Developments affecting or affected by major state investments*—here the state should use its power to further the aims of local government, except when there are spillovers to other jurisdictions or to the investment itself.

State intervention should be limited to the minimum needed to protect nonlocal interests. In many cases the state need only impose standards and criteria for local control, for example, beach setbacks or erosion control standards. In other, more complex cases, the state should provide for a regional or state appeal of local decisions, reserving initial consideration of the application to local authorities. This will assure that local interests have a fair hearing, the decision process is accessible to the citizenry, and local officials become educated as to the nonlocal interests that their decisions affect.

The state decision process should be open and "political." Land use policies must balance the desires of all classes of land users, including those of future generations. Only rarely will there be situations in which some gain but no one loses. It is tempting to believe that these tradeoffs can be made "scientifically," with impartial professionals wielding such modern tools as cost–benefit analysis and carrying-capacity studies. But useful as these tools are, most land use decisions hinge on value judgments.

As unsatisfactory as the political process sometimes seems, it is the institution best suited for making such decisions. Thus elected public officials should be accountable for land use decisions, even if they do not make the actual decisions by themselves. The method of accountability may vary from state to state. In some it may be desirable to make any state land use board of appeal an independently elected body. There are advantages, however, to lodging political accountability with general purpose government, responsible to the electorate for social and economic policy as well as land policy. One method would be to allow each incoming governor to appoint a majority of the appeal board, making the governor implicitly responsible for the board's decisions. Similarly, staff responsibility for land use planning and its coordination with state investment policy should be placed directly in the office of the governor.

A "political" land policy will be successful only if the political system is open to public scrutiny and public participation. At minimum, all deliberations of land use decision makers, whether local officials, state planning staff, or members of a state appeals board, should be open to public view and all relevant documents open to public inspection. Florida's 1970 "government in the sunshine" law is a good model for such a requirement. Legal "standing" to speak against proposed projects or to bring appeals to the state should be liberally interpreted. And finally, campaign finance reforms and tough conflict-of-interest laws must be instituted to ensure that money is not given undue weight in the political process.

Effective controls require a clear definition of goals; a knowledge of how the land resource relates to those goals; and an understanding of how landowners and others adapt their behavior in response. A lack of understanding of this principle has been particularly evident in attempts to preserve open space. Confusion about just what characteristics of land we wish to preserve—and why—has permeated our open-space policies. In many cases small parcels of land have been purchased outright when the public's desires would have been better served by the purchase (for the same dollar amount) of scenic easements over far larger tracts. Some preferential assessment laws, intended to preserve agricultural lands on the fringes of expanding cities, have given substantial tax subsidies to large corporate farms in areas where development would not occur in any case. Other programs have exempted agricultural activities from land use controls despite evidence that farming can do significant damage to natural systems.[4] Local "agriculture" or "conservation" zoning classifications have allowed development at densities as high as one unit per acre.

Perhaps the problem is not just with the regulatory tools but in an imperfect understanding of the goals we wish to attain. We might ask ourselves the following questions: What do we mean when we say we want to leave land "open?" What characteristics of the land must be preserved in each open-space use? How do we preserve these characteristics most efficiently?

Some land should remain open because it has an ecological function for which there is no good substitute. Wetlands, for example, absorb flood runoff, purify water, shelter waterfowl, and act as breeding grounds for marine life. Other open lands help disperse air pollution and counteract the climatological effects otherwise associated with large cities.

Another function of open land is to create pleasure in human beings, either for those who use the land for active recreation or those who simply look upon it. Its naturalness provides a kind of psychic anchor in a society in which the landscape is changing at a rapid rate.

Open spaces have a planning function. By physically separating neighborhoods and cities from each other they help to create a sense of community identity. Large open tracts provide space for the orderly expansion of cities, avoiding the interim half-urban, half-rural condition that characterizes the fringes of most of our metropolitan areas. Finally, open space may be lands used for farming or forestry, activities that are considered inherently attractive and, in a kind of throwback to an earlier rural ethic, socially desirable.

These distinct functions make very different demands on the land. They have little in common but the requirement that the land not be built upon. In many instances, one desirable use conflicts with another. Farmlands, for example, do not preserve the ecological systems that we find in wildlands—indeed, farming often contributes directly to flooding, siltation, and air pollution. Open lands may do a good job of defining the boundaries of cities but have little esthetic appeal. The supposedly desirable activity "agriculture" may cover anything from a family-owned orchard to an unsightly commercial feedlot.

If we have a good idea of the relative importance of our goals, we can also rank the qualities or characteristics that we most desire from our open space. How important, for example, is public access? Is there anything to be gained by delaying a parcel's development for ten or twenty years or must the land be open permanently? Are there any economic activities that can use the land while maintaining its ecological functions?

After we have identified the characteristics that contribute most to open-space values, we can decide how best to preserve them. The surest, but most expensive, method is outright purchase. Alternatively, we may fully secure our goal by acquiring only a partial ownership interest, such as a scenic easement. We may wish to encourage certain specific uses by incentive, say, by making a cash payment to encourage small farming on the urban fringe. Finally, we may wish to use regulation—zoning land exclusively for agricultural or forest use; setting minimum lot sizes so high that urbanization is not economically feasible; or prohibiting subdivision into smaller parcels.

Having decided on an effective policy, we must predict how landowners and developers will respond. For example, exclusive agricultural zoning will not preserve farming if the changing economics of farm production has rendered the activity unprofitable. And purchase of easements will not be effective if only a minority of owners elects to sell them. We should also consider the side effects that will occur when a particular policy is implemented. Some policies will significantly reduce the local tax base; others will not. Some policies will stimulate the local construction industry; others will injure it. Some policies will reduce opportunities for the poor to enjoy good housing or environmental amenities; others will broaden those opportunities.

This discussion illustrates the three steps involved in formulating effective policy, whether for open space or for other land-related problems. First, we must carefully define program goals. Second, we must identify the land characteristics necessary to achieve those goals. And third, we must take the minimum amount of government action needed to protect these land characteristics, remaining always mindful of the side effects that can occur when landowners and users adjust their behavior in response to the public action.

Land use controls need not—and probably should not—await the adoption of comprehensive plans. A comprehensive statewide development plan should eventually be part of every state's land control program. But effective regulation need not wait until such a plan is prepared.

During the "quiet revolution" days, a major justification for such a view was the breakneck pace of development. If Vermont, California, Florida, and other states had waited until plans had been completed before implementing regulations, much of what they wished to preserve would have been irretrievably lost. Moreover, in the absence of interim regulations, prospective developers would have anticipated the contents of the comprehensive plan, qualifying tens of thousands of future units for a vested rights exemption.

Today's somewhat slower rate of development reduces—but by no means eliminates—the urgency of interim regulation. But two other reasons remain to regulate first and plan later. First, there are lessons to be learned from the regulatory process itself. Debate over the proper regulation of a scenic area or whether an airport or a ski resort should be granted a development permit identifies the public's goals and crystallizes planning issues in a way that abstract discussion can never do.

Second, the knowledge that the plan will affect an ongoing regulatory process makes the participants take the plan seriously. Planning is hard, time-consuming work, the result of intergroup competition, of argument, and compromise. It is often said that the planning process is at least as important as the plan document that is eventually produced. But only if planning is intimately related to regulation or other specific action will either plan or process galvanize the participants. As the former executive director of the California Coastal Commission put it, in justifying the commission's regulate-first approach, "There's just no way that you could [better] dramatize and make clear the issues than the sort of adversary, controversial, attention-getting thing that a permit hearing is. I think it's very hard for a planning staff to really grab people's attention with the [same] effectiveness of a real case with real lawyers and real landowners and real feeling."[5]

Comprehensive plans are still needed—if only to secure consistency among goals and help prevent arbitrary treatment of individual pieces of property. But we believe that states which have already followed the "regulate first–plan later" path, are far better prepared to do such substantive planning than are those states which have never allowed specific land use conflicts to be debated at the state level.

Land policies should promote desirable forms of development as alternatives to those which do environmental or social damage. Virtually all of the state land use control programs that we have examined have been regulatory in their approach. Their aim is to prevent undesirable kinds of development or to mitigate its effects.[6] Because planning has limited itself to this regulatory function, it has earned itself a reputation as a luxury, something that is certainly desirable when the economy is strong but which should be given lower priority when industry is depressed and unemployment high. We can speculate that the quiet revolution in land use control would have had a much more difficult time in state legislatures had it begun in less prosperous times.

This image is an unfortunate one. Although land use decisions can impose heavy costs on some individuals, mainly landowners, there is no reason why a well-conceived land use program need have negative impacts on jobs, on the availability of housing, or even on the profits of the development and construction industries.[7] To do this, however, means that land planning must move beyond its regulatory focus to include positive programs for regional development and public investment.

First, land policies should encourage economic growth, including new construction and the creation of new sources of employment, in those areas of the state where growth would not injure the environment, overload public facilities, or destroy the character of a community. We have seen from the case studies that growth presents many difficulties. There will be a number of locations in which it should be stopped or its nature severely modified. Nevertheless, land policy makers will improve their credibility with a job-hungry public if they encourage an equal amount of growth in those places where it can be accommodated, keying new development to local resources and to the job needs of the resident population. The state's capital budget can be a powerful tool in modifying the location of job growth. To a lesser extent, so can the industrial incentive programs that many states already administer. Particular attention might be paid to more intensive use of areas that are already urbanized and where public facilities are already in place, including land within the older urban centers.

Second, state land policy should be actively pro-housing, encouraging the renovation of old units and the construction of new ones in suitable locations. There are several measures that the state might take. Policies which limit suburban sprawl can reduce the costs of extending public utilities, resulting in lower property tax bills.[8] Local ordinances requiring inordinately large lot sizes can be overridden by state plans that call for a mixture of densities and housing types.[9] The state's power of eminent domain can be used to assemble sites for new towns or planned residential developments, greatly reducing the average cost per acre.

A little-appreciated fact is that "developers" are a diverse group. Some, more concerned with land speculation than with actual building, thrive on uncertainty and inflated expectations. But many, including homebuilders, the real estate industry, the construction trades, utilities, and companies seeking industrial sites, are concerned less with windfall land profits than with building, marketing, and operating structures. As these diverse members of the development industry become more sophisticated about their economic self-interest in various forms of land control, we can expect a greater range of political positions to emerge among them.

Finally, the control process should avoid unnecessary delays, which add little to the quality of decisions and impose substantial costs on prospective developers. In this sense, Florida's development of regional impact process, which integrates regional and local project evaluation, is preferable to the procedure followed by California's coastal commissions, which tend to ignore what happens in the local approval process. There is a real need to rationalize forms, impact statements, and hearing schedules, not just among various land-planning bodies but with environmental and licensing agencies as well.

Some developers have suggested a kind of "one-stop shopping." A single agency would pass on a major project's compliance with air and water quality standards, health requirements, land controls, and so forth. Such a body would be able to speed up the decision process, make it more visible to the public, and make tradeoffs among conflicting social goals. There is merit in this idea, although the standards that are enforced would have to be much more exactly specified in law than they are at present and care taken to avoid a capture of the agency by the industry which it regulates.

The desire to minimize delay might even turn some developers into supporters of comprehensive state land planning. A frank statement of which areas the state wished to see developed and which it wished preserved might eventually be a welcome sight to developers tired of *ad hoc* project reviews. If such a plan were integrated with local and state capital investment programs, developers could look forward to an ample supply of preserviced lots; adequate transportation, schools, and sewer facilities;

as well as easily secured approvals from all levels of government. The accompanying reduction in uncertainty might even add a welcome stability to the development industry.

If assuaged of their fears that land use planning is synonymous with a no-growth philosophy, many in the development industry may even become advocates of planning and controls.

Policies should consider the interests and aspirations of all classes of users. Our society is made up of individuals with a wide range of tastes, incomes, and aspirations. Increasingly, they will be competing with one another for the use of scarce land and amenity resources. If state government is to take a greater role in allocating these resources, it must make sure that it does not unduly favor certain income groups or certain types of use.

Raising the standards that new development must meet and restricting the number of locations that can be developed will probably further increase the already high prices of amenity-rich lands, such as mountain and coastal properties. To offset the distributional effects of these policies, the states should aggressively purchase land in the areas of greatest excess demand, providing public use in ways that emphasize the land itself, rather than capital-intensive forms of development. We already have considerable experience with this through our systems of state and national parks. These programs include not only the maintenance of natural areas but the active provision of campsites, lodges, and some environmentally compatible forms of recreation.

Land policies might also encourage commercial uses that allow a wide cross section of the public to enjoy the resource. Thus, developers could be permitted to build hotels in a scenic area, but not second homes; commercial marinas but not private boat clubs. California's coastal commissions have, as we noted, shown an inclination toward such policies in their permit decisions.

Policies should also recognize that those who choose to drive a snowmobile or to vacation in a house trailer have no less right to recreation than does the naturalist or the hiker. We have enough land to accommodate all of these uses, if only we plan its use effectively. The key to such planning is to discourage recreational uses from utilizing scarce amenity resources, when the amenity is not vital to the use. Thus, water skiing might be encouraged in reservoirs but prohibited in high mountain lakes. Commercial amusements might be outlawed in areas of scenic or historic value,[10] but permitted elsewhere.

This policy can be strengthened by state provision of alternate facilities for recreational activities that make heavy demands on the environment—snowmobiling, off-road vehicles, trailer camping. Accommodation of these activities may go against the grain of some planners and environmentalists, who find them inherently objectionable. This kind of attitude, with its overtones of class prejudice, will not endear land planning to the majority of the American public.

Elements of a State Land Use Policy

No two states need have exactly the same land use decision process, much less the same substantive policies. States differ in size, in extent of growth pressure, in environmental sensitivity, in social values, and in existing environmental regulations. Particularly important is the wide variation from state to state in the size, power, and competence of local government. Moreover, our experience to date has shown that variety can produce valuable innovations. Keeping this in mind, let us sketch the broad elements of a possible state policy. Administrative details and substantive policy decisions might vary widely from state to state, but this overall framework should serve well almost everywhere.

In a sense, these policies are conservative ones. They contain little that has not been tested, at least piecemeal, in one or more states. They envision only minor changes in governmental structure—although a considerable shift in power is involved. They take account of the interests of such important constituencies as farmers, local officials, and the construction industry. They are compatible with the criteria we have set out earlier in this chapter, and they would go far toward easing the variety of discontents that we discussed in chapter 2.

Pillars of the New State Policy

Two elements are central to any effective state land use policy. The first is mandatory local planning and land regulation. The second is state review of certain local land use decisions. Together, they force local governments to make careful decisions in matters of purely local interest, while making it possible for the state to intervene if nonlocal interests are injured or ignored.

Almost everywhere, local governments have long been authorized by their states to prepare master plans, to regulate the subdivision of land,

and to use zoning to limit the type and density of development on specific parcels. But they have not been required to do so. Moreover, even when communities do have planning and zoning, there has been no guarantee that the zoning map would bear any strong resemblance to the plan. Thus, the first component of an effective state land policy is a legislative requirement that local governments produce a land use plan and zone all the lands within their boundaries to correspond to the plan.[11] This zoning need not be nearly so detailed as traditional zoning, which can be quite specific as to the exact land uses and densities that will be permitted. For example, Fairfax County's (Virginia) zoning ordinance contains thirty-two distinct use and density categories; that of the city of Los Angeles, thirty-nine. Indeed, we will argue later that communities should be encouraged to zone their vacant land only in broad categories, perhaps simply distinguishing land where development will be permitted in the near future from land where development will be long deferred, or prohibited entirely.

Local planning is already mandatory for all cities and counties in California. Plans must include several specific elements, including a housing element, a land use element, and an open-space element. Zoning ordinances must be consistent with the community's general plan.[12] Amendments to the plan (and hence to the zoning map) may be made only twice yearly, avoiding the piecemeal zoning changes and variances that have made zoning a mockery in so many localities. Each local government is also required to have a subdivision ordinance and can disapprove a proposed subdivision if not in accordance with the general plan.

We have already described the mandatory local planning requirements of Oregon's state land use law (1973) and Florida's Local Government Comprehensive Planning Act (1975). The Florida law specifies the elements the local plan must contain, provides for state and regional comments, and requires consistency between adopted plans and land use regulations. The Oregon law goes further, for it provides that local plans be consistent with state goals and guidelines and allows the state to reject plans not found to be in compliance. Perhaps the most important features of the Oregon approach are the requirement that local governments designate twenty-year urban growth boundaries and the protection given agricultural land lying outside those locally designated limits.

The Oregon approach has much to recommend it, but given the level of local control sentiment in most state legislatures, it may not be a politically realistic alternative at this time. Our own proposal therefore would go no further than either the California or the Florida law, except that (as in Oregon) local governments would have to specifically designate where they wished their future growth to occur.[13] Under our proposal, the initial land classification would be done by local, not state, authorities. It would require no new institutions, except in those cities and counties that had failed to form local planning and zoning commissions under earlier, nonmandatory state enabling laws.

This proposal raises the question of whether the state should have the power to review and modify the local plans. There are advantages to state review and comment, which could improve the technical quality of plans and bring issues to the public's attention. It is probably unwise, however, to allow the state to force modifications to the plans, except in those cases in which nonlocal interests are involved.[14] In all other cases, local governments should be allowed to make their own decisions, and if necessary, their own mistakes, provided only that these decisions are taken openly and after full discussion.

The second vitally necessary element of state land use policy is provision for state review of those land use decisions significantly affecting more than one locality. The review would be limited to those categories listed on page 251. Initially, this would be done by the state's "land use board of appeal," which would promulgate rules for permit hearings before local governments, then hear any appeal that may be brought after the local decision. After local governments have prepared their mandatory plans, the state appeal board would approve those portions involving nonlocal interests. From that time on the state board would merely rule on whether an appealed development was consistent with the approved local plan. Similarly, the board (or its designate) would review all development in jurisdictions having no land use regulations, pending adoption of local planning and zoning.

Any citizen or group that appeared before local government in a permit proceeding should have the right to appeal the project.[15] In order to prevent frivolous appeals, the board might adopt a screening procedure to quickly reject those appeals that were clearly without merit.[16] Appeal hearings should be held *de novo,* rather than on the record of the local hearing. Without this requirement, local hearings would quickly become both overly legalistic and burdensomely expensive for local governments and the participants.

The appeals board should be well staffed, including a permanent group of field investigators who could monitor compliance with permit conditions. In the larger states, it may be desirable to make board members full-time state employees, with compensation appropriate to the responsibility. Alternatively, the state board could delegate some of its review authority to regional boards, composed of residents of the region, but directly responsible to the state board.

Members of the appeal board(s) might be required to have expertise in particular subject areas, including ecology, agriculture, planning, and land development. They would, however, be emphatically "political," responsible to the governor who appointed them and through the governor to the electorate. In their decisions, they would be bound by the policies contained in approved local land use plans and by plans and policy statements passed by the legislature.

State Policies and Standards

Once permit processing got underway and local governments began to draw up their mandatory plans, the state board could turn to broad policy questions. It would work closely with a state planning office (a staff function lodged in the governor's office, also charged with preparing the state's capital budget). Jointly, the board and the planning office would recommend for legislative consideration the documents discussed below.

STATE ENVIRONMENTAL STANDARDS. These broad policies would guide the board in its permit decisions and in its evaluation of local plans. They would put the state on record as requiring that new developments and subdivisions be built with minimal damage to the natural environment and to valued man-made environments. The ten criteria listed in Vermont's Act 250 show that this is not only a feasible undertaking, but one that is useful in guiding those who make permit decisions.[17]

STATE HOUSING POLICY. This broad statement of housing goals would commit the state to give full consideration in its land use decisions to the promotion of decent housing and pleasant neighborhoods for persons of all income classes. The policy might include a statement to the effect that "It is the opinion of the legislature that our commitment to this housing goal involves no necessary conflict with our goal of preserving and enhancing the natural environment. Indeed, a healthy natural environment is a vital part of the human environment."

The policy statement might more specifically provide that (1) local plans make adequate provision for land for housing; (2) decisions of the state appeals board give due consideration to impacts on housing costs; (3) decision processes at all levels of government avoid unnecessary, cost-increasing delay. We have already suggested that the state take direct control of the location of publicly financed low-income housing developments, under the rubric "development of regional benefit." The state housing policy might set forth guidelines for the amount of such development that any single community would be expected to accept as its "fair share" of the burden. Massachusetts' 1969 "Anti-Snob Zoning Law," for example, finds that a locality is automatically in compliance if 10 percent or more of its housing stock is subsidized low- and moderate-income units. In states in which local growth management efforts are significantly reducing the supply of new housing, the state might also assign each community a fair share of the unsubsidized units. Alternatively, the state could project regional housing requirements, then allow regional councils of governments to determine each community's share.

STATE AGRICULTURAL POLICY. A great number of states are deeply concerned about the urbanization of their agricultural land. The problem as we see it is not so much in the loss of the farmlands that are actually put to urban use—a relatively small acreage—but in the land that is idled as a consequence of *nearby* urbanization. Farmers in these transitional zones, not urban yet no longer completely rural, find their taxes increased to pay for urban services. They find their agricultural practices, such as crop-dusting, curtailed. And they find that even the remote chance that their land will be bid for by a developer makes it unwise for them to make long-term capital investments in their farming operations.[18] Planners often refer to this group of impacts as the "impermanence syndrome."

Land use specialists are currently in the midst of a vigorous debate over whether current rates of land conversion pose a real threat to the nation's cropland base.[19] The existing land supply seems more than ample to meet current or even projected demand, but among the unknown factors are future supplies of energy-related inputs, a possibly slowing rate of technological change, uncertain output prospects of less-developed countries, and long-term negative impacts of soil erosion on land productivity.

We face a choice between unpleasant alternatives. To err on the side of underprotecting farmland could be disastrous. Yet being overly restrictive of farmland conversions could exacerbate an already serious problem of high housing costs. While awaiting further research on this difficult issue, we believe that a prudent state agricultural policy should not attempt to outlaw farmland conversion, but should instead concentrate on reducing the amount of land affected by the impermanence syndrome.

A promising approach, used since 1971 in the state of New York, is the creation of "agricultural districts." These zones, created by petition of groups of landowners and approved by state and county governments, are places where first priority is given to agricultural use. Within them local governments may not regulate farm practices beyond the requirements of health and safety. The power of special districts to levy fees for urban improvements is limited. And government agencies are discouraged from using eminent domain to acquire lands within them for new highways or other public facilities.

According to one study, "Provisions of law encourage farming and discourage other uses within the districts but do not involve direct control of land use through the police power. The goal sought is to keep good farmland in farming until it really is needed for other purposes; in other words, to block the destructive impact of speculation on farming, but not to make permanent city parks out of farmland."[20] By 1979 over 5 million acres of New York farmland—more than half the state's total farm acreage—had been placed in 389 agricultural districts.[21] Other states, including Virginia, Oregon, and Illinois, are also studying this approach.

Our own proposed agricultural policy would go no further than to promote the creation of similar districts, where agriculture could be protected from the spillovers of nearby urbanization. Many will consider our suggestion incomplete, for it does not solve farmers' tax problems, nor preserve farmland as open space, nor attack the "shortage" of prime farmland. We believe that these issues are best dealt with more directly. The tax problems of farmers can be best addressed by a use value tax policy applied not just to farmland but to all land where development is restricted.[22] We will outline such a policy later in this chapter. The problem of farmland as open space should be the subject of open-space policy, not farm policy. And the loss of that small portion of farmland that is actually converted to productive urban use is not a problem but a natural consequence of a free market. If a farmland shortage appears, farmers will soon begin to outbid the developers and the process will reverse itself.

A State Development Plan

We have emphasized that setting up a regulatory framework and formulating specific policies are the first order of business in state land use planning. Only when they are well underway should the state begin writing its comprehensive plan. Such plans are useful documents, but because of their very comprehensiveness they should not be produced without considerable debate over their contents. State permit processing, critical areas designation, the beginnings of local planning, and legislative debate over environmental standards and other specific policies will contribute much to later comprehensive planning.

In the past, comprehensive plans have been produced before there was an effective demand for them. We suggest that such plans will never be taken seriously until decision makers, public and private, actively demand them for guidance. As the state moves against specific land use problems, a demand for coordination and for guidance will spontaneously arise, both among the regulators and the regulated. Only then will the time be ripe for a state plan.

We prefer to call such a plan a "state development plan." It would embrace not only land use and environmental goals, but social and economic ones as well. The plan would specify not just desired end products, but the process by which they would be secured. It would be a long-term blueprint for the state budget and for the whole range of state economic policy. In drawing up their yearly budgets, both operating and capital, heads of functional agencies would be required to provide written justification for any deviations from the plan.

Its individual elements might include the following:

1. A state capital facilities element, covering future public investments in highways, airports, canals, harbors, and water resources
2. An energy facilities element, including plans for power plant siting, mining, petroleum extraction and processing. It would include applicable state policies on environmental safeguards, leasing of public lands, and energy conservation
3. A recreation and conservation element. It would forecast future demands for recreation of all types, list priority areas for state acquisition, and set up a program of purchase, easement, and subsidy for scenic areas, including desirable forests and agricultural lands. It would provide a means of systematically reviewing the state's designation of critical areas

4. A pollution control element, including federally mandated land use plans for air quality, water quality, and solid waste. For example, this element would include the mapping of areas in which future industrial growth must be limited in order to prevent the deterioration of air quality, a requirement imposed on the states by 1977 amendments to the federal Clean Air Act

5. An economic development element. This element would contain state policies for attracting industry and other economic activities to certain parts of the state, while restricting or excluding them from others. These policies would be explicitly coordinated with the state's energy and pollution control policies and with transportation investments. This element would also contain state policy on new towns, on the future growth of rural areas and the expansion of urban areas. It would explicitly recognize the importance of the future location of jobs to the location of people, and would use the former as a major policy lever in influencing the latter.

Each element would be based on a uniform set of projections of population, economic activity, and local and state tax revenues, updated yearly.[23] No longer would a state find that its department of natural resources is planning a water supply for an additional 2 million people while the department of education plans schools for a far smaller number.

Other elements might be added by states having special interests or special problems. Coastal states may wish to include a specific coastal zone element. States experiencing especially rapid growth may want to frame a policy on future population growth, to be implemented through the economic development element.[24]

The state plan, like the state environmental standards, would be prepared by the state planning office, with the consultation of the land use board of appeal. It would require the approval of the legislature and of the governor. It would undoubtedly be the major action of one or more entire legislative sessions. Upon approval of the plan, no state investment could be made that was not consistent with the plan.[25]

Our proposal does not call for a specific land use element. We believe that if adequate provision is made for the various land-using activities, including new industry and open space, and for protecting critical areas, a state land use map is redundant. The state plan, the state standards, and the specific state housing and agricultural policies will fully protect statewide interests. All other detailed regulation should properly be left to local governments. The "land use element" will then consist of the approved local plans prepared by each locality.

Improving Local Regulation

In doing this detailed regulation, local governments should be encouraged to use the most modern available tools for land planning and control. State enabling legislation should be passed to permit localities to institute a new type of zoning and a new method of property taxation and to experiment with long-term capital budgeting, land banking, and transferable development rights.

ZONING. Traditionally, zoning has meant the assignment of specific parcels of land to narrowly defined use categories.[26] Once a parcel is assigned to a category, its owner is permitted certain uses by right. Subsequently, he usually requires only perfunctory approvals to proceed with his project. Local governments have always found it difficult to foresee the future demand within their boundaries for each kind of land use and have reacted in three rather different ways. Some have "over-zoned," allowing uses and densities far in excess of any realistic demand. This has encouraged speculation and has meant that the future expansion of the area could take any number of forms, controlled more by the market than by the plan. Other areas have zoned a realistic amount of land for each use. They have found themselves locked into a rigid pattern, unable to react to the demands of new industry and commerce, and have conferred virtual monopoly rights on those few landowners fortunate enough to have their land assigned to particular high-intensity uses.

Still other cities have zoned most of their land to low-intensity uses, such as agriculture and single-family residential, then changed the zoning to suit the demands of the developers. The combination of paying lip service to zoning categories, while changing them parcel by parcel, has done much to cause widespread cynicism about zoning. In many places, localities are not allowed to impose conditions on the parcel in exchange for rezoning. Some do anyway, but in an underhanded (and sometimes discriminatory) way. For instance, a developer who is allowed to build town houses rather than single-family dwellings may "voluntarily" donate a school site to the city.

Our proposal is to replace local zoning (except within already built-up areas) with a local "development permit" system. A landowner would be allowed by right only the very lowest intensity uses, usually agriculture.

If he desired to put the land to some other use, he would petition the local government for "development permission."[27] This permission would be granted only to those developments which were consistent with the community's approved local plan. Conditions could be imposed solely to further the objectives of the local plan. Communities might also charge a "development fee," imposed according to a schedule specified in local law.

This system would give local government considerable leverage over not only the location, but the environmental, fiscal, and public service impacts of new developments. Abuses of local discretion could be controlled by forcing communities to adhere to their own local plan, by the landowner's traditional right of appeal to the courts, and by requiring that communities accept their fair share of growth, as specified in the state's housing and economic development plans.

Under this system, there would be a residual form of zoning. Each community would be required to assign all lands within its boundaries to broad classes, depending on the *time* at which future development would be encouraged. It would probably be sufficient to distinguish those lands where development would be expected within, say, five years, from those lands where development would be long deferred or prohibited entirely. This rudimentary zoning would be a guide to developers (although the local plan would be a much more specific guide) but would have its main use in the assessment of property taxes.

TAXES. Farmers, forest operators, and others holding land in lower-intensity uses have long complained that the current system of taxing property on the basis of its market value is unfair, and sometimes ruinous. They argue that they cannot be expected to refrain from developing their land unless they receive some form of tax relief. There is much truth to this argument. It is very difficult, however, to design a system that will help those who wish to continue desirable low-intensity uses, without at the same time subsidizing those who simply hold land for speculation.

We propose that after the completion of approved local plans and the classification of lands into broad zoning categories, all land would be assessed at two values. The first is current market value, which would depend on both current zoned use and on the future uses permitted in the approved local plan. The second is the land's value in the highest use permitted in its current broad zoning category.[28] In any given year, owners of vacant land not zoned for immediate development would have the option of being taxed either at market value or at "highest permitted use" value. If they chose the latter, the tax saving would become a permanent lien on the land, recorded by the county assessor on the deed. This deferred tax would become due (with interest) in two circumstances. First, it would become due in full upon the grant of a landowner's petition for development permission. Second, it would become due within three years after the land was reclassified by local government into the "immediate development" zoning category.

This tax system would have a number of advantages. It would enable farmers, at their own option, to pay taxes on the basis of agricultural value only and to continue to do so for an indefinite period of time. It would recoup the full value of deferred taxes from speculators (or farmers turned developers) at the moment at which they realize their capital gain. It would force development of vacant land within existing urban areas, which would have to bear a proportionately larger share of the tax burden. And it is likely to lower the price of land for housing and other urban uses, by forcing those whose land was reclassified to develop quickly in order to meet their tax bills.[29]

The system is no more complicated than that set up by most states' agricultural assessment laws, which require assessment at both use value and market value. It would be a boon to those who genuinely wished to keep land in farm or open-space uses, but would give almost no benefit to those whose minds are set on eventual development.

Another useful change in the tax system concerns the property tax itself. This tax raises several points of controversy, some of them involving land use. First, its current administration presents local governments with almost irresistable temptations to choose new developments on the basis of fiscal rather than planning criteria. Second, under the present system of local assessment, developers of tax-generating projects can play one community off against another, avoiding part of the tax burden that they would otherwise have to bear. Finally, municipal competition for tax revenues has led to zoning practices that have contributed greatly to the exclusion of low- and moderate-income families from suburban areas.[30]

A number of observers have proposed sweeping changes in the way in which property taxes are levied, ranging from uniform statewide rates to outright abolition of the tax. There is a major difficulty with each of these suggestions, for reasons that have little to do with their impacts on land use. A uniform tax would limit the ability of each community to choose a level of public services higher or lower than that provided by other communities. This would place yet another restraint on the individual citizen's freedom of choice. Abolition of the property tax, on the other hand, would end that tax's useful role as both a fee for public services rendered to real property and as one of the few taxes that society levies on wealth rather than income or expenditure.

We will simply propose here that the state move toward property tax reform by making assessment, the setting of assessment ratios, and the actual collection of the tax a state, rather than a local, function. Local governments and special districts would still be free to determine the rate at which that assessed value will be taxed in their jurisdiction. This state administration would bring increased professionalism to tax assessment and would eliminate some of the worst aspects of municipal competition for rateables through assessment concessions. It should be merely the first step in a long process of defining the future role of the property tax, a role that depends on our value judgments as to how much public service levels should be allowed to vary among municipalities and how much of the tax burden should be borne by wealth holders and how much by income earners.

LONG-TERM CAPITAL BUDGETING.   Local governments should be encouraged to control their future growth by preparing and making public a long-term capital budget.[31] This would be a major means of implementing the approved local plan. As a town or city expands, local governments would simultaneously move large tracts of land into the "immediate development" zoning category and supply these tracts with the necessary public services. Changes in state enabling laws may be necessary to permit this practice.

LAND BANKING.   Some localities may wish to take a more direct role in planning their expansion. States should authorize cities and towns to purchase, hold, lease, and resell land, not only for future sites of public facilities but for general development purposes. Such land banking is now virtually unknown in this country, but it was a common practice in the growth of many American cities in the eighteenth and nineteenth centuries.[32] It is currently in use in Sweden, Norway, and Finland, Puerto Rico, the Prairie Provinces of Canada, and elsewhere.[33] At the state level, a form of land banking is practiced by the California Coastal Conservancy.

Most communities will probably find the combination of planning and control, which we have already suggested, adequate to their needs and will not choose to attempt land banking, particularly because of the large amounts of capital it requires. It may have appeal, however, to selected communities, which wish to combine good land use practice with an aggressive push for economic growth.[34]

TRANSFERABLE DEVELOPMENT RIGHTS. As we have noted earlier, a recurring issue in land use control, whether state or local, is whether the newly restricted landowner should be compensated for his loss of potential development value. In chapter 7, we showed that compensability is a complex question both in law and in ethics, and one over which reasonable people may differ sharply. If we decide that some cases do require compensation, however, we face an additional problem. At present there is no proved method of compensable land regulation that is within the financial reach of any level of government. The amount of "hope value" that would be affected by any effective land use control program is immense. We can only afford to compensate the losers if we simultaneously manage to penalize the winners.

A promising, but still unproved, way of doing this is through "transferable development rights" (TDRs).[35] Each parcel of land within a jurisdiction would be assigned a certain number of development rights, probably in proportion to its current market value. The land would then be regulated, with some owners allowed to develop and others restricted. Under TDRs, those who were granted development permission would be required to buy a certain number of rights from those in the restricted class. In fast-growing areas a market in such rights would quickly arise and transactions costs would be low. There is much interest in this idea, which seems particularly effective in preserving historic buildings in urban areas, or in developing large tracts of open land with fragmented ownership. As yet, actual experimentation is rare.[36] But it is an idea that local governments should be authorized, and perhaps actively encouraged, to try.

The Question of a Federal Land Use Law

In 1971, amid the first stirrings of the "quiet revolution," staff members of the federal Council on Environmental Quality (CEQ) drafted a federal land use bill.[37] Based on the ALI Model Land Development Code, it provided generous grants ($800 million over eight years in one version) to state governments which would take responsibility for controlling critical areas, developments of regional impact, key facilities, and developments of regional benefit. Versions of the bill twice passed the Senate (in 1972 and 1973) but the House Rules Committee prevented the legislation from reaching the floor of the House of Representatives. As time went on, the bill was progressively weakened, so that the version finally reaching the House floor in June 1974 lacked both substantive policies binding the states and any sanction, other than loss of the planning funds provided, for nonparticipation. Even so, the bill was rejected by the House, with 204 members in favor and 211 opposed. That vote marked the end of the federal land use bill, for the Ford and Carter administrations did not attempt to revive it.

Past congressional debate over the federal land use bills was marked by a great deal of confusion. Proponents sometimes hoped, unrealistically, that land use was a panacea for all the environmental problems not already addressed by the National Environmental Policy Act (NEPA) and by the EPA's regulatory programs. Opponents sometimes asserted, incorrectly, that the bill would mean direct federal control of how land was used.

Now that some of the emotion has subsided, what might we reasonably expect from a federal land use law? First, such a law should require the federal government to coordinate its own myriad programs directly or indirectly affecting land. Each federal agency should know what the others are planning and should know how its projects relate to state goals and policies. Where feasible, federal agencies should be bound by adopted state plans—an incentive for states to adopt them.

Second, a federal law should help those states that are already serious about land use policy, rather than either blindly dispensing money to all or imposing sanctions on states that do not wish to participate. The availability of planning money is simply not enough of an incentive to induce a state that is otherwise unwilling to implement effective land use controls. The most pressing need for federal funding, we believe, is not to finance the creation of state programs but to support the local portion of collaborative planning efforts.[38]

Third, a federal land use law should allow a great deal of flexibility among state programs. Some states will be most interested in farmland, others in wetlands, still others in reducing housing costs or rationalizing industrial plant siting. Although we continue to believe that comprehensive approaches are more efficient—particularly from the standpoint of coordination—than incremental ones, the sentiment in state legislatures now seems to strongly favor the latter.

A Chain of Decisions

The history of direct state involvement in land use control is a short one. With scattered exceptions, it was not until the early 1970s that states began to reclaim powers long delegated to local governments. There has been some federal encouragement of this movement, but in the main it has originated spontaneously, state by state. As it has spread, there has been considerable borrowing of ideas, with newcomers learning from the experience of those states that were pioneers.

At first the movement was aptly called a quiet revolution. More recently its progress has been more difficult, as public opinion gave way not to indifference, but to increased appreciation that land use control is more than just another kind of environmental protection. Its goals are too diffuse for that, and the social and economic interests that it affects are too important.

Over time, the movement toward greater state involvement in land use matters has had two persistent themes. First, it has increased the general level of consciousness of the environmental and other impacts of land development and has shown that stringent controls can indeed make a difference. In many cases, local governments and developers have responded, improving their own land use practices. Thus, this role for state government has been an important, but probably temporary one. Second, the experience of the states has shown that there are indeed nonlocal interests in how land is used. Such interests arise in only a small proportion of all land use decisions, yet their protection must be a permanent responsibility of higher levels of government.

Land use is not a single problem, to be solved by a single decision or a single piece of legislation. It is a developing chain of decisions, involving the conscious design of the future human environment. They are decisions that cannot be made by any single level of government, but must involve all the actors in the land development process—landowners, developers, consumers, and all levels of government. The states, which bear the responsibility of protecting statewide interests in this process, had traditionally failed to do so. Now a number of states have made a bold break with past practice. One hopes that others will follow, not dominating the process but asserting interests that have been long neglected.

Notes

1. These are currently being exposed in those places where local planning is most effective, such as the many cities whose "growth controls" address local environmental concerns at the expense of the interests of the region or state.

2. Charles Thurow, "Local Control over Critical Areas," Urban Land Institute *Environmental Comment* vol. 12 (August 1974) p. 8.

3. It is frequently said that some 90 percent of all land use decisions are of purely local interest. See, for example, testimony of Richard Babcock in *National Land Use Policy,* Hearings before the Senate Committee on Interior and Insular Affairs, 92 Cong. 1 sess. (June 23, 1971) p. 392. The figure is not unreasonable, but it is only a guess.

4. For example, agriculture is specifically exempted from Florida's critical area regulations, despite the fact that it can interfere with natural systems by draining wetlands or by destroying the natural ground cover. The potential of agriculture to damage the environment is described in a Pulitzer Prize-winning series of articles by *Des Moines Register* writer James Risser, reprinted in *Conservation Foundation Letter,* December 1978.

5. Joseph Bodovitz, interview, San Francisco, Calif., January 1976.

6. There is an interesting split between the two major groups of intellectuals who have concerned themselves with spatial patterns of development in this country. One is the regional economists and geographers, who tend to look at growth as an economic process and cluster their policy recommendations around some kind of "national urban growth policy" based on locational incentives to people and industries—new towns, migration subsidies, "growth poles," and federal procurement policy. The other consists of city planners, lawyers, and environmentalists, who seek to solve many of the same problems through regulatory policies that come under the general rubric of "land use control." There has been little communication between these groups, not because they disagree but because one emphasizes understanding the growth process, while the other concentrates on the effects of growth.

7. See Robert G. Healy, *Environmentalists and Developers—Can They Agree on Anything?* (Washington, D.C., Conservation Foundation, 1977).

8. For studies relating public service costs to development density, see U.S. Council on Environmental Quality, *The Costs of Sprawl* (Washington, D.C., GPO, 1974); Marion Clawson, *Suburban Land Conversion in the United States* (Baltimore, Md., Johns Hopkins University Press for Resources for the Future, 1971) pp. 152–162; and R. W. Archer, "Land Speculation and Scattered Development," *Urban Studies* vol. 10 (1973) pp. 367–372.

9. It has been estimated that 50 percent of the vacant land zoned as residential within a 50-mile radius of Times Square is limited by local regulation to minimum lot sizes of 1 acre or more. See "Large Lot Zoning," *Yale Law Journal* vol. 78 (1969) p. 1418.

10. This simple principle has been grossly violated in the past, as witnessed by the gambling casinos on Lake Tahoe's Nevada shore, the large amusement park proposed near Virginia's Bull Run battlefield, and the tawdry commercial areas of Lake George Village in the Adirondacks and of Myrtle Beach in South Carolina.

11. One analyst argues that "States should offer incentives, rather than penalties, to communities that see no reason to plan at present." See Lawrence Susskind, "Should State Government Mandate Local Planning? . . . No," *Planning* vol. 44, no. 6 (July 1978) pp. 17–20. We agree that incentives are preferable to coercion— but we suspect that sticks as well as carrots will be needed to get results. Going through the exercise of planning, however unwillingly, will force communities to gather information on their land use problems and will give local citizens a forum to air their concerns.

12. California Government Code, §§ 65560(d), 65561(d), 65563, 65566, 65567, 65860(a), 65910.

13. Such a law should also require that local plans be updated at regular intervals.

14. North Carolina's 1974 Coastal Area Management Act is a good example of a system in which a state commission, in this case dominated by regional interests, reviews mandatory plans prepared by cities and counties. The commission can impose plan modifications when nonlocal interests are involved. When the development is small or is not in an "area of environmental concern," the commission may only "transmit recommendations for modification to the adopting local government." See § 113A-111.

15. This broad grant of "standing" is identical to that allowed under California's Coastal Zone Conservation Act.

16. The California coastal commissions briefly considered charging appellants a small fee. This has proved to be unnecessary, and frivolous appeals have been infrequent and disposed of quickly.

17. Other useful environmental criteria are found in California's state subdivision law; the "California standards" in California Tomorrow, *The California Tomorrow Plan* (San Francisco, Calif., California Tomorrow, 1972); and the "Florida standards" proposed by Luther Carter in *The Florida Experience: Land and Water Policy in a Growth State* (Baltimore, Md., Johns Hopkins University Press for Resources for the Future, 1975).

18. New York State Commission on the Preservation of Agricultural Land, *Preserving Agricultural Land in New York State* (Albany, Executive office, State of New York, 1968) pp. 7–8.

19. This statement reflects views expressed by several authors in unpublished papers prepared for a forthcoming book on agricultural land retention, to be published by the Soil Conservation Society of America.

20. H. E. Conklin and W. R. Bryant, "Agricultural Districts: A Compromise Approach to Agricultural Preservation," *American Journal of Agricultural Economics* vol. 56, no. 3 (1974) pp. 607–613.

21. *The New York Times*, Feb. 18, 1979.

22. The New York law provides for a more generous use-value assessment treatment for land within an agricultural district than is available for farmland outside a district. Such a concession may be needed to ensure farmer participation.

23. This function, which involves prediction rather than policy making, might appropriately be conducted at the state university rather than by the planners.

24. At least two states have permanent commissions on their future population growth. See Hawaii Commission on Population Affairs (1972) and Colorado Population Advisory Council (1972).

25. Cf. the similar provisions of the California Tomorrow plan and the 1974 Vermont land use plan.

26. The ideas expressed here, although by no means identical, owe a considerable debt to the Task Force on Land Use and Urban Growth, *The Use of Land* (New York, Crowell, 1973) ch. V.

27. This would be much like the practice followed in Great Britain since 1947. As Clawson and Hall describe it: ". . . A central feature of the [British] system is that the owner no longer has an automatic right to do what he likes with his land. If he wishes to carry out any operation on it that constitutes a development in law, he cannot do so without first obtaining planning permission—a phrase that has now become part of everyday language and experience in Britain." See Marion Clawson and Peter Hall, *Planning and Urban Growth—An Anglo–American Comparison* (Baltimore, Md., Johns Hopkins University Press for Resources for the Future, 1973) p. 161.

28. This is not necessarily identical to value in current use. If farmland were held idle, the land would still be assessed at its value in the most productive agricultural use. This is the current practice under the agricultural assessment laws of ten states. See International Association of Assessing Officers, *Use Value Farmland Assessments: Theory, Practice and Impacts* (Chicago, Ill., IAAO, 1974) p. 18.

29. Theoretically, a tax which became due upon rezoning would be "neutral" in its effects on land use, for it would not change the marginal return to holding a

piece of land relative to selling it or developing it. See Louis Rose, "The Development Value Tax," *Urban Studies* vol. 10, no. 2 (June 1973) pp. 271–275. Such an analysis abstracts from the very real liquidity problems that a landowner, newly liable for a large tax, would face. Just as in the case of an heir facing high death duties on an estate, such a landowner would be likely to liquidate all or part of his holdings. Moreover, once rezoned, land would be subject to yearly property tax levies. These *would* change the marginal costs of holding land and should be capitalized (negatively) into its value.

30. This issue was central in two important New Jersey cases, in which the state supreme court strongly condemned the practice of zoning out low-income people for fiscal reasons. *South Burlington County N.A.A.C.P.* v. *Mount Laurel Township,* 67 N.J. 151 (1975) and *Oakwood* v. *Madison Township,* 72 N.J. 481 (1977).

31. Use of a long-term capital budget as a means of staging growth is often called a "Ramapo ordinance" after Ramapo, New York, which instituted the practice in 1970.

32. John Reps, "Public Land, Urban Development Policy, and the American Planning Tradition," in Marion Clawson, ed., *Modernizing Urban Land Policy* (Baltimore, Md., Johns Hopkins University Press for Resources for the Future, 1973).

33. See Kermit Parsons, et al., *Public Land Acquisition for New Communities and the Control of Urban Growth: Alternative Strategies* (Ithaca, N.Y., Cornell Center for Urban Development Research, 1973).

34. A good discussion of the virtues and shortcomings of land banking, with emphasis on Swedish experience may be found in Sylvan Kamm, "Land Banking: Public Policy Alternatives and Dilemmas" (Washington, D.C., The Urban Institute, 1970) U.I. Paper 112–28. A more recent account of international experience is Neal Roberts, ed., *The Government Land Developers* (Lexington, Mass., Lexington Books, 1976).

35. The best discussions of TDRs to date are John J. Costonis, *Space Adrift* (Urbana, University of Illinois Press, 1974); and Frank Schnidman, "Transferable Development Rights," in Donald Hagman and Dean Misczynski, *Windfalls for Wipeouts* (Chicago, Ill., American Society of Planning Officials, 1978) pp. 532–552. The Hagman and Misczynski book also has extensive discussions of other compensable development techniques.

36. Among the very few places to have adopted some variant of the TDR idea are New York City; Buckingham Township, Pennsylvania; Saint George, Vermont; and Collier County, Florida. Serious proposals for using TDRs have been made in Puerto Rico (environmental lands), New Jersey (farmlands), and Chicago (historic buildings).

37. A year earlier, Sen. Henry Jackson (D–Wash.) had introduced a national land use bill (S. 3354) based on comprehensive state master plans. By 1972 Jackson had embraced the CEQ/ALI "big cases" approach, and pushed for it, even after the Nixon administration had cooled to the idea. See John C. Whitaker, *Striking a Balance* (Washington, D.C., American Enterprise Institute, 1976) pp. 155–166.

38. An alternative source of funding for collaborative planning would be redirection of existing federal programs that aid local planning, such as HUD's 701 program.

Additional Reading

THE FOLLOWING selections offer a wealth of additional material on land use problems, issues and policies.

American Institute of Planners. *Survey of State Land Use Activity* (Washington, D.C., U.S. Department of Housing and Urban Development, 1976).

Bosselman, Fred, and David Callies. *The Quiet Revolution in Land Use Control* (Washington, D.C., GPO, 1972). Good coverage of early years of programs in Hawaii, Vermont, San Francisco Bay, Massachusetts, Maine, and Wisconsin.

————, ————, and John Banta. *The Taking Issue* (Washington, D.C., GPO, 1973).

Carter, Luther J. *The Florida Experience: Land and Water Policy in a Growth State* (Baltimore, Md., Johns Hopkins University Press for Resources for the Future, 1975).

Clark, John. *Coastal Ecosystems: Ecological Considerations for Management of the Coastal Zone* (Washington, D.C., Conservation Foundation, 1974).

Clawson, Marion. *Suburban Land Conversion in the United States* (Baltimore, Md., Johns Hopkins University Press for Resources for the Future, 1971). Background material on the land development process.

Creighton, Thomas. *The Lands of Hawaii: Their Use and Misuse* (Honolulu, University of Hawaii Press, 1978).

Devanney, J. W. III, G. Ashe, and B. Parkhurst. *Parable Beach: A Primer in Coastal Zone Economics* (Cambridge, Mass., MIT Press, 1976).

Fishman, Richard P., ed. *Housing for All Under Law: New Directions in Housing, Land Use and Planning Law* (Cambridge, Mass., Ballinger, 1978).

Gibbons, Boyd. *Wye Island: Outsiders, Insiders, and Resistance to Change* (Baltimore, Md., Johns Hopkins University Press for Resources for the Future, 1977). Readable account of the social conflicts engendered by a proposed rural development.

Hagman, Donald, and Dean Misczynski. *Windfalls for Wipeouts* (Chicago, Ill., American Society of Planning Officials, 1978). An exhaustive study of proposed methods of compensable regulation and windfall recapture.

Healy, Robert G., John S. Banta, John R. Clark, and William J. Duddleson. *Protecting the Golden Shore: Lessons from the California Coastal Commissions* (Washington, D.C., Conservation Foundation, 1978). Essays on public participation, economic issues, permit administration, relations with state agencies, and the role of scientists.

Hershman, Marc J., and James H. Feldman. *Coastal Management: Readings and Notes* (Seattle, University of Washington Institute of Marine Studies, 1979).

Robert Kneisel. *Economic Impacts of Land Use Control: The California Coastal Zone Conservation Commission* (Davis, Calif., University of California Institute of Governmental Affairs, 1979).

Lyday, Noreen. *The Law of the Land: Debating National Land Use Legislation, 1970–75* (Washington, D.C., Urban Institute, 1976).

Mandelker, Daniel. *Environmental and Land Controls Legislation* (New York, Bobbs-Merrill, 1976). Legal analysis of federal and state controls, ALI code, Vermont and Hawaii laws.

Myers, Phyllis. *Zoning Hawaii* (Washington, D.C., Conservation Foundation, 1976).

Natural Resources Defense Council. *Land Use Controls in the United States: A Handbook on the Legal Rights of Citizens* (New York, Dial Press/James Wade, 1977). Good section on federal laws currently impacting land use.

Odell, Rice. *The Saving of San Francisco Bay* (Washington, D.C., Conservation Foundation, 1974).

Real Estate Research Corporation. *The Costs of Sprawl* (Washington, D.C., GPO, 1974).

Reilly, William K., ed. *The Use of Land: A Citizens' Policy Guide to Urban Growth* (New York, Thomas Y. Crowell, 1973).

Rosenbaum, Nelson. *Citizen Involvement in Land Use Governance: Issues and Methods* (Washington, D.C., Urban Institute, 1976).

————. *Land Use and the Legislatures* (Washington, D.C., Urban Institute, 1976). Discusses diffusion of state land use laws and characteristics of states adopting them.

Schnidman, Frank, Jane A. Silverman, Rufus C. Young, Jr. *Management and Control of Growth:* Vol. IV, *Techniques in Application* (Washington, D.C., Urban Land Institute, 1978).

Soil Conservation Society of America. *Land Use: Tough Choices in Today's World* (Ankeny, Iowa, SCSA, 1977).

Index

Adirondack Mountains, N.Y., 1, 15
Adirondack Park Agency, 187, 193, 228
Adirondack Park Agency Act (1973), 232
Adirondack Park Plan, 10, 11, 178, 181, 185–187, 203, 208, 227
Agricultural land, 2, 8, 13, 43, 61, 109, 185, 194, 200; "districts," 264; price of, 25; protection of, 68, 92, 98, 110, 112, 119, 179, 253; urbanization of, 4, 18–19, 92, 99, 186, 227, 263; zoning, 99, 253–254
Alabama, 33
Amenities, 5, 9, 10, 17, 29–31, 87, 202, 240, 254; man-made, 130, 236; visual, 23–24, 101
American Law Institute (ALI), Model Land Development Code, 133–135, 161–162, 167, 169, 177, 201, 214, 271
Amusement parks, 26, 39, 95
Aquifers, 22, 59, 131, 135, 137, 153; Floridan, 129, 139
Arizona, 11, 18, 26; growth rate, 18
Arkansas, 30
Army Corps of Engineers, 130
Askew, Reubin, 133, 141, 218
Atomic Energy Commission (AEC), 102

Beaches, 5, 9; development of, 81, 82; public access to, 39, 83, 87, 88, 93–98, 115, 117; state acquisition of, 81
Big Cypress, Fla., 136–138, 182
Boca Raton, Fla., 15, 132, 244
Bodovitz, Joseph, 28, 89, 95, 97, 107
Bond issues, 13, 21, 218; land acquisition, 81, 134, 137, 198
Bosselman, Fred, 133
Broward County, Fla., 26, 158
Brown, Jerry, 218
Bureaucracy, 6, 14, 220, 222, 251. See also Government; Jurisdictional considerations.
Burlington, Vt., 55

California, 1, 2, 6, 8–9, 10, 11, 12, 14, 21, 41, 80, 193; agricultural land, 87, 98, 99, 109, 110, 112; ballot initiative, 80, 85, 87, 119; beach crises, 82; Coastal Commission, 86, 89, 91–93, 100, 110, 257; coastal land use plan, 106, 114, 198; critical areas, 82; density standards, 97, 116; local government, 84, 97, 108; local coastal programs (LCPs), 114–115, 117, 118; power plants, 83, 101, 102–104; property taxes, 110, 115; state land acquisition, 81. See also specific cities.
California Coastal Alliance, 85
California Coastal Commission, 28, 36, 113, 215
California Coastal Zone Conservation Act (1972), 3, 28, 36, 221; development permits, 197
California Proposition 13, 21, 115, 198
California Proposition 20, 85–90, 92, 93, 111, 215, 218, 223
California Supreme Court, 90
California Tomorrow Plan (1972), 182, 197
California Water Project, 12
Clean Air Act (1970), 201
Cluster development, 17, 62
Coastal Zone Management Act (1972), 178, 179
Collier County, Fla., 137–139, 219
Colorado, 16, 24, 193; Land Use Commission, 195
Commercial development, 10, 12, 17, 23, 32, 44, 54, 140
Condominiums, 5, 24, 26, 31, 41, 50, 81, 95, 128
Conference on State–Local Intergovernmental Relations, 65
Conflict-of-interest laws, 6, 87, 252
Connecticut, 199; Plan of Conservation and Development, 192
Cost–benefit impact, 10, 20, 28

Council on Environmental Quality, 271
Critical areas, 126, 134–137, 139, 141, 169, 195, 196, 204, 225, 251

Davis, Deane C., 58, 64
Delaware, 1, 33, 181, 185, 188; Beach Preservation Act (1972), 228; proposed oil refinery, 188
Depressed areas, 10, 225
Developments of Regional Impact (DRI), 126, 134, 144–150, 154, 155, 158, 162–165, 169, 173
Disney World, Fla., 27, 39, 127, 139, 156
Disneyland, Calif., 39
Doral Park, Fla., 153
Douglas, Peter, 82–83
Dow Chemical Company, 27

Easements, 117, 198–199, 254
Economic considerations, 4, 5, 7, 8, 9, 10, 12, 19–22, 63, 88, 199, 223–229. *See also* Taxation.
Ecosystems. *See* Natural systems.
Energy crisis, 2, 27, 30
Energy production, 2; power plants, 13, 27, 32, 33, 181, 199, 221, 251
English Town and Country Planning Act (1971), 167, 275
Environmental considerations, 2, 3, 4–5, 8, 9, 12, 14, 15, 17, 18, 19, 22, 48, 83, 100, 102, 126, 131, 140, 183, 187, 237
Environmental Protection Agency (EPA), 39, 201, 272
Equity, 35, 232
Erosion, 19, 22, 42, 45, 263
Esthetic standards, 5–6, 17, 23, 36, 45, 49, 50, 100, 191
Everglades jetport, 132, 135
Exurbs, 17, 30

Fairfax County, Va., 15, 37, 260
Federal land use law, 1, 2, 234, 271–273; funds, 13, 24; current programs, 23, 38, 201
Fertilizers and pesticides, 5, 19
Fifth Amendment, 233
Flagler County, Fla., 11, 128
Floodplains, 23, 38, 182
Florida, 1, 2, 11, 22, 23, 26, 30, 41, 126; Administration Commission, 136; Cabinet, 134, 191, 201; development permits, 147, 151; Division of State Planning, 141, 147, 152, 156, 160; Electrical Power Plant Siting Act (1973), 166, 172; Environmental Land Management Study (ELMS) Committee, 165; Land and Water

Florida *(continued)*
Adjudicatory Commission, 144, 147, 149, 161; local government, 136, 139, 140, 142, 144, 153, 156, 161, 168; New Communities Act, 167; regional planning councils, 158–159, 161. *See also specific cities.*
Florida Environmental Land and Water Management Act (1972), 3, 36, 126, 134, 164, 169
Florida Keys, 10, 139–142, 239
Florida State Comprehensive Plan, 168
Florida Supreme Court, 141
Fourteenth Amendment, 234

Gettysburg, Pa., 10, 15
Government, county, 7, 11, 133, 158
Government, local, 1, 2, 4, 5–7, 11, 12, 13, 14, 15, 17, 24, 126, 185, 189, 213, 249. *See also* California; Florida; Vermont
Government, state, 1, 2, 4, 7, 12, 132, 250
Graham, Robert, 141
"Grandfather" clause, 187
Great Lakes, 1
Green Swamp, Fla., 139
Growth, 8–9, 13, 15, 18, 20, 24, 28, 33, 56, 127, 241; amenities, impact on, 202; control, 9, 13, 27, 60, 61, 132, 261, 271; effect of state facilities on, 12–13, 182; future growth areas, 192; growth policy statement, 166; no growth or slow growth, 88, 98, 160, 224, 258; patterns, 12, 16–17, 25, 30, 39, 182; planning, 131, 168, 225; population ceilings, 132; public services, impact on, 20–22, 55–56, 60, 129, 160. *See also* Land use.

Hackensack Meadowlands Development District, N.J., 184
Hawaii, 2, 14; growth, 224; state land law, 181, 203; State Land Use Commission, 185; State Plan, 192; state zoning, 185
Hazard areas, 23, 38
Highways, 12, 15, 17, 21, 27, 30, 41, 44, 45, 49, 106, 132
Historic American Building Survey (1933), 24
Historic structures, 24, 98; preservation, 142
Housing, 2, 5, 17, 24, 25, 29–30, 35, 82; low-cost and subsidized, 10, 21, 24–25, 95, 109, 158, 167, 183, 200, 239, 251, 263; shortage, 24, 29, 31–32, 238; threshold, 238–239

Housing Act (1949), 35
Housing developments, 24, 26–27, 32; planned communities, 11, 26, 32, 82, 150. *See also* Second homes.

Industrial developments, 13, 15, 16, 26, 32
Infrastructure, 15, 20, 30, 32, 52, 119, 145, 167, 182, 183, 197, 198. *See also* Public services.
ITT developments, 11, 128, 156

Jackson, Schuyler, 44
Job growth, 13, 41, 200, 241, 256
Jurisdictional considerations, 7–9, 18, 19, 28

Kaiparowits power plant, 27

Lake County, Fla., 150
Lake Ola, Fla., 153–154
Lake Tahoe, Nev., 178, 205
Lamm, Richard, 218
Land: accessibility, 12; classification, 179, 185, 203; long-term demand for, 33; prices, 24, 25, 38, 41, 127, 199, 227, 258; value, 226–229
Land banking, 270
Land sales disclosure laws, 13
Land use: changes, 2–3, 9, 27–28, 43, 52, 84, 191, 198; conflicts, 23, 28–29; controls, economic effects of, 223; density regulations, 227–228; "double-veto" system, 189–190; planning, 1, 2, 3, 7, 10, 11, 14, 35–36; quality regulations, 179, 228; variety, 192. *See also* Public interest; Zoning.
Local Government Comprehensive Planning Act, 165, 166, 168, 193, 250, 260
Long-term capital budgeting, 270
Los Angeles, Calif., 24, 88, 90, 260

McCall, Tom, 194, 218
Machiasport, Me., 7
Maine, 1, 15, 16; Land Use Regulation Commission, 180, 188; state zoning, 185
Maine Site Location of Development Act (1970), 7, 184, 204
Martha's Vineyard, Mass., 24, 240
Maryland, 8, 179, 191; Department of Natural Resources, 199
Massachusetts Housing Appeals Law (1969), 183, 195, 263
May, James W., 165
Mendocino, Calif., 98, 116
Michigan, 10
Montana, 15

National Association of Home Builders, 24
National Environmental Policy Act (NEPA), 196, 272
Natural systems, 4, 22, 129, 131, 135, 167, 237, 241, 253
Nevada, 11
New communities, 11, 26, 32, 62, 128, 135, 152, 169
New Jersey, 21, 199
New Mexico, 26
New Orleans, La., 24
New York, 1, 10, 11, 14; State Environmental Plan, 192; Urban Development Corporation (UDC), 183, 200
North Carolina, 10, 15, 30, 202; Coastal Area Management Act, 202, 224, 250, 275; Land Policy Act, 203; land policy council, 202, 204
Nuclear power plants, 101, 132, 182

Office of Management and Budget (OMB), 15
Oil refineries, 7, 154, 158, 188
Open space, 18, 19, 97, 99, 164, 184, 192, 199, 236, 252–254
Oregon, 1, 2, 14, 72, 193; Citizen Involvement Advisory Committee, 216; Land Conservation and Development Commission (LCDC), 180, 194–195, 215; state land use law, 260
Orlando, Fla., 27, 127, 156
Outer Banks, N.C., 10

Parklands, state, 81
Pennsylvania, 10
Petaluma, Calif., 15, 100
Peterson, Russell, 218
Pine Barrens, N.J., 178
Planned-unit developments (PUDs), 32, 91, 128, 153, 154
Political issues, 4, 8, 211–214; local control, 211–212
Pollution, 22; air pollution, 22, 37–38, 45, 55, 129, 221, 253; controls, 201; indirect sources, 129; interagency conflicts, 221; standards, 33; water pollution, 22, 37, 45, 201
Prescriptive rights, 34, 39
Property rights, 5, 35, 39, 41, 81, 167, 212
Public interest, 3, 5, 6, 9, 14, 20, 40; conflicts, 6, 8–10, 184
Public opinion polls, 219–220
Public services, 11–13, 14, 17, 18, 20, 21, 25, 41, 42, 45, 55, 84, 146, 154, 232; investments, 11–13, 30, 182, 197

"Quiet revolution," 1, 26, 255–256, 271, 273

Ramapo, N.Y., 15, 100
Recreation, 34, 35, 95, 236
Recreational developments, 5, 10–12, 15, 57, 94
Redondo Beach, Calif., 97, 106
Regional planning agencies, 126
Retiree market, 30, 127
Return to the soil movement, 17, 41
Runoff, 4, 8, 53, 55, 130, 151, 201, 253

Salmon, Thomas, 62, 65, 214
San Andreas fault, 23
San Diego County, Calif., 88, 98
San Francisco, Calif., 24
San Francisco Bay Conservation and Development Commission (BCDC), 85–87, 90, 107, 111
San Onofre power plant, Calif., 102–104
Santa Clara Valley, Calif., 8
Santa Monica, Calif., 8, 116
Second homes, 10, 15, 20, 27, 30, 31, 41, 42, 49, 62, 65, 81, 128, 186, 202, 224, 240, 241
Seminole County, Fla., 151
Senecal, Kenneth, 48
Septic tanks, 13, 42, 100, 130, 152, 228
Sewer facilities, 12, 98; drainage, 49; outfall, 98, 100
Snelling, Richard A., 65
Social issues, 2, 4, 19, 232–242. *See also* Equity.
Speculation, 25–26, 38, 40, 67, 71, 264
Spillovers, 7–9, 11, 19, 58, 153, 158, 172, 232, 235–237, 251
Stowe, Vt., 49
Strip development, 9, 18, 54
Strip mining, 22, 26, 142
Subdivisions, 1, 2, 6, 11, 16, 17, 21, 36, 38, 43, 48, 69, 169, 260; leap-frog, 99; map laws, 193

"Taking" clause, 233, 235
Task Force on Land Use and Urban Growth, 12, 233
Taxation, 2, 5, 9, 10, 18, 20, 21, 26, 42; assessments, 43, 200; capital gains tax, 40, 69, 198; deferred, 269; land use change tax, 68, 78; preferential, 66, 179, 199, 253; property taxes, 6, 8, 13, 39, 66, 68, 154, 171, 198, 230–232, 256, 268–270; relief, 268; state allocation, 13; tax incentives, 13, 68
Three Rivers, Fla., 150–152, 158, 164, 229

Traffic, 4, 18, 20, 37, 42, 45, 49, 55, 94, 158, 168
Transferable development rights (TDRs), 271

U.S. Congress, 1, 103, 234, 272
U.S. Department of Agriculture, 18
U.S. Fish and Wildlife Service, 222
U.S. National Park Service, 10
Urbanization, 16, 38, 139, 194; urban sprawl, 3, 17–18, 22, 202
Utility lines, underground, 23

Vermont, 1, 2, 11, 14, 40; agriculture, 46, 67; capital gains tax, 40, 67, 69–71; development permits, 40, 44, 45, 72, 197, 228; district commissions, 44, 46, 48, 55; environmental board, 44, 46, 48, 59, 161; growth patterns, 41; land use plan, 40, 61, 197; local government, 43, 58, 62, 64; property taxes, 41, 42, 61, 66, 67. *See also specific cities.*
Vermont Environmental Control Act (Act 250), 3, 36, 40, 43, 46, 65, 110, 189, 214; avoidance tactics, 50, 58; criteria, 45, 59, 75, 196, 262; effect, 46, 49, 53, 54, 57; exemptions, 51; Interagency Review Committee, 58; Interim Land Capability Plan, 59; Land Capability and Development Plan, 59; Land Use Plan, 61
Vested rights, 156, 241, 255

Washington, D.C., 8, 37
Washington Environmental Coordination Procedures Act (1973), 223
Washington Shoreline Management Act (1971), 206
Water Pollution Control Act Amendments (1972), 201. *See also* Pollution, water.
Water supply, 18, 22, 45, 142, 150
Wetlands, 22, 35, 100, 117, 129, 130, 135, 139, 145, 171, 184, 225, 253; draining, 22; dredging and filling, 165
Wilderness legislation, 9
Wilmington, Vt., 41–42, 51
Wisconsin Farmland Preservation Act (1977), 180
World food crisis, 19, 31

Zoning, 2, 5–7, 10, 11, 14, 19, 24–26, 38, 133, 157, 260, 267; local, 43, 58, 61, 62, 84, 132, 166, 173, 187, 212; state, 28, 67

Library of Congress Cataloging in Publication Data

Healy, Robert G
   Land use and the States.

   Includes index.
   1. Land use—Planning—United States—States.
I. Rosenberg, John S., joint author.   II. Resources
for the Future.   III. Title.
HD205 1979.H4   333.7′0973   79-4864
ISBN 0-8018-2284-X
ISBN 0-8018-2285-8 pbk.

Emory & Henry College Kelly Library